Racisms in a
Multicultural Canada

Racisms in a Multicultural Canada
Paradoxes, Politics, and Resistance

Augie Fleras

WILFRID LAURIER
UNIVERSITY PRESS

Wilfrid Laurier University Press acknowledges the financial support of the Government of Canada through the Canada Book Fund for our publishing activities.

Library and Archives Canada Cataloguing in Publication

Fleras, Augie, 1947–, author
    Racisms in a multicultural Canada : paradoxes, politics, and resistance / Augie Fleras.

Includes bibliographical references and index.
Issued in print and electronic formats.
ISBN 978-1-55458-953-1 (pbk.).—ISBN 978-1-55458-954-8 (pdf).—
ISBN 978-1-55458-955-5 (epub)

    1. Racism—Canada. 2. Canada—Race relations. I. Title.

FC104.F545 2014   305.800971   C2013-905983-0
                                            C2013-905984-9

Cover design by Angela Booth Malleau. Front-cover image: *Untitled (Diamond)* (1968; acrylic on canvas, 61 x 40¼ inches), by Takao Tanabe, courtesy the Mira Godard Gallery. Text design by Angela Booth Malleau.

© 2014 Wilfrid Laurier University Press
Waterloo, Ontario, Canada
www.wlupress.wlu.ca

This book is printed on FSC recycled paper and is certified Ecologo. It is made from 100% post-consumer fibre, processed chlorine free, and manufactured using biogas energy.

Printed in Canada

Every reasonable effort has been made to acquire permission for copyright material used in this text, and to acknowledge all such indebtedness accurately. Any errors and omissions called to the publisher's attention will be corrected in future printings.

No part of this publication may be reproduced, stored in a retrieval system, or transmitted, in any form or by any means, without the prior written consent of the publisher or a licence from the Canadian Copyright Licensing Agency (Access Copyright). For an Access Copyright licence, visit http://www.accesscopyright.ca or call toll free to 1-800-893-5777.

CONTENTS

Preface vii

Section 1 **Reappraising Racism** 1
Chapter 1 The Politics of Racism: Evolving Realities, Shifting Discourses 3
Chapter 2 Reconceptualizing Racism: From Racism 1.0 to Racisms 2.0 27
Chapter 3 The Riddles of Race 55
Chapter 4 Deconstructing Racism: Prejudice, Discrimination, Power 97

Section 2 **How Racisms Work: Sectors and Expressions** 123
Chapter 5 Interpersonal Racisms 127
Chapter 6 Institutional Racisms 145
Chapter 7 Ideological Racisms 159
Chapter 8 Infrastructural Racisms 171
Chapter 9 Ivory Tower Racisms: An Intersectoral Analysis 181

Section 3 **Explaining Racisms, Erasing Racisms** 201
Chapter 10 Contesting Racisms: Causes, Continuities, Costs, and Consequences 205
Chapter 11 Rooting Out Racisms: Anti-racism Interventions 223
Chapter 12 Official Multiculturalism: Anti-racism or Another Racism? 243
Chapter 13 Summary and Conclusion: Inconvenient Truths/Comforting Fictions 263

References 269
Index 319

PREFACE

Not long ago, everyone knew what racism meant. Racism consisted of loutish individuals with twisted attitudes who had it in for those less fortunate "coloured" folk. Or, to put a finer academic spin on it, racism was about mistreating minorities because their membership in a devalued race condemned them to a life of punishment, pity, or exclusion. Race-based typologies evolved to justify this racist line of thinking. Prevailing race doctrines partitioned the world into a fixed number of races arranged in a hierarchy along ascending/descending lines of superiority/inferiority. Each race was thought to possess a distinctive assemblage of physical, cultural, moral, and psychological attributes whose combined impact shaped thought and behaviour. The potency and reach of race in constructing a "white" Canada cannot be underestimated. The evaluative, explanatory, and predictive powers of race for determining the worth of those on the wrong side of the racial divide reinforced its status as a powerful ideology of exclusion and division.

Few dispute that racism played a formidable role in shaping public attitudes, government policies, and institutional arrangements (Satzewich 1998, 2011). But what about the present day? Like other Western societies, Canada increasingly embraces a commitment to the principles of a post-racial and colour-blind society, one in which Canadians try to look past skin colour, abolish racial discrimination as a basis for entitlement, and endorse multiracial tolerance on the grounds that everyone is equal and deserves an equal break. Canada also commits to the principle of an inclusive multiculturalism, namely, that no one should be excluded from equality or participation for reasons of race or ethnicity. A combination of factors—from human rights legislation to shifting ideologies—has transformed racism into a social no-no on par with other unsavoury stigmas such as scab labour or fascism. Politicians and the general public prefer to distance themselves from any reference to racism, even if many of the major twenty-first-century issues (from terrorism to migration to global warming) are inextricably race-infused (Dwyer & Bressey, 2008). Few Canadians are foolhardy enough to *explicitly* endorse those racist doctrines that elevate whites to the top of the pinnacle, with minorities ranked accordingly in descending order. Nobody in this age of political correctness wants to be accused of racism, nor do they want to be scorned or shunned for endorsing antiquated race dogmas (Doane, 2006).

Yet racism perseveres in spite of seemingly insurmountable odds. Consider the contradictions: Racism is neither legal nor socially acceptable, yet its tenacity attests to the staying power of latent appeal, social inertia, or public indifference (Kawakami et al., 2009). Hardly anyone admits to being a racist or believing in race, yet Canada stands accused of being a racist country. The vast majority of Canadians do not see themselves as racists, as might be expected in a multicultural society that ostensibly abides by the post-racial and colour-blind principles of multiculturalism. They may even concede the impact of societal structures and prevalence of racialized attitudes that deny or exclude. Yet many continue to accuse minorities of inflicting discrimination on themselves through (in)actions or cultural differences (McCreary, 2009; also D'Souza, 1995). To be sure, improvements at the level of racial tolerance are unmistakable. But eradicating racism and discriminatory barriers is proving a formidable challenge because of broader social processes and racialized institutional arrangements (McCreary, 2009). These massive inconsistencies point to an incontestable conclusion: Contemporary debates over the nature and magnitude of racisms in Canada tend to be splintered and splayed in ways more evocative of politics than of prejudice (see Hier & Walby, 2006). (In this book, I use "racisms" when referring to its plural existence in Canada, and "racism" when referring to it as a concept or abstraction.)

In light of such confusion and contradiction, racism is seldom defined with any precision or consistency, much less with any appreciation of its complex logic and contested dynamics (Kundnani, 2007a). Consider the different ways of framing racisms: As a disease, human nature, a bad habit, a conspiratorial plot, a cultural blind spot, a structural flaw, arrogance or ignorance, political correctness, or a relic from the past? To amplify the complexities, racisms are reconfiguring in ways that elude both consensus and conceptualization, while generating controversy and contestation (Galabuzi, 2004). The irony is inescapable because of this transformational flux. The fact that racism can mean whatever people want it to mean invites uncertainty and confusion, no more so than when references to racism neither mean what they say nor say what they really mean, in the process negating the possibility of a singular meaning (or consensus). The implications of such contestation are far-reaching. As overt racisms disappear and blatant forms of racial discrimination drift into oblivion, new and covert expressions materialize that are often more daunting and durable than ever in defining the concept or rebuking its existence.

The concept of racism is experiencing the metaphorical equivalent of an identity crisis of confidence (see also Lee & Lutz, 2005). Nobody can agree on what it means or refers to, while disagreement continues to mount over "what it's doing, to whom, why, and how." What prevails instead of a consensus is a contested domain of multi-racisms that span the spectrum from (1) the interpersonal and infrastructural to the institutional and ideological; (2) acts of commission ("doing something") to the neglect of omission ("doing nothing"); (3) the overt to the covert; (4) the deliberate to the inadvertent; (5) its status as a thing (noun) to that of a process or activity (verb); and (6) from a singular dimension to a plural multi-dimensionality. The persistence and proliferation of these "neo-racisms" as concept and reality point to two key conclusions:

- First, theorizing the persistence of racisms is proving trickier than many thought. More than simply individual prejudice because of ignorance and fear, racisms are increasingly implicated aross a broad range of unequal power relations and within the wider institutional frameworks of a racialized ("racially infused") social system (Bonilla-Silva, 1997; Feagin, 2006). The concept of racisms has shifted accordingly. The idea of racism as a monolithic "entity" is superseded by reference to a burgeoning range of racisms, from the outspoken and aggressive (for example, genocide or expulsion) to the tacit and institutionalized (systemic discrimination) (Lentin, 2008). But such expansiveness comes with costs: Without a clear frame of reference to anchor or guide, racism has "morphed" into a "floating signifier" that can mean everything yet nothing, depending on the context, criterion, or consequences (Anthias, 2007). The challenge is further complicated by the fact that racisms (1) are differently experienced by racialized minorities; (2) cannot be understood without acknowledging the intersectional dynamics of gender, ethnicity, sexuality, age, and class; and (3) are evolving over time and varying across space. Finally, moves to eradicate racisms are compromised by fluctuating frames of reference that make it difficult to pin down or put away. Racism is no longer about hierarchy of races; rather, it connotes the oftens subtle ways in which people of colour are marginalized or excluded (Stanley, 2012) because of mainstream resentment of minority demands, ingratitude, and differences. Complexities of such magnitude render it more difficult than ever to devise anti-racism strategies that counter its slippery and elusive nature (Conference Notes, 2006). The consequences of such disarray go beyond the academic; after all, for a problem to be solved, it must be appropriately framed to secure a sustainable outcome consistent with a problem-solution nexus (Fleras, 2005; Bhavnani et al., 2005).

- Second, consider the paradox of racisms in a multicultural Canada that abides by the principles of multiculturalism yet commits to a colour-blind ("post-racial") society (see also Henry & Tator, 2010). Canada claims to be a race-neutral and colour-blind society, thanks to its impressive array of formal equality statutes, human rights legislation, employment equity initiatives, and anti-racism programs, including Canada's five-year, $56 million Action Plan Against Racism (2005–10). Of particular salience is Canada's embrace of an inclusive multiculturalism anchored in the principle of ensuring no one is excluded from equality or involvement for reasons largely beyond his or her control. To the extent it exists, racism is brushed off as a relic from the past, relatively muted and randomly expressed, isolated to a few lunatic fringes or articulated by the sadly misinformed, and banned from public domains. In a comparative sense, this assessment may be true. Compared to its past and in comparison to other countries, Canada sparkles as a paragon of progress. But in contrast to Canada's constitutional values and multicultural principles, a worrying gap prevails when aligning societal ideals with racialized realities. Racism is not an aberration in Canada, neither now nor in the past, as Wallis, Sunseri, and Galabuzi (2010, p. 8) argue. It's a constitutive component of Canadian society that conflates racialized hierarchies with differentials of power, privilege, and property (income and wealth). Not only do racisms proliferate in varying ways as more actions (and inactions) are defined as racist. Ideas and ideals about race are so deeply ingrained within Canada's foundational framework (from constitutional design to institutional structures to core values) that notions of what are normal and acceptable continue to be locked into racial(ized) frames (see also Goldberg, 1993). In short, no matter how defined or perceived, the politics of racisms continue to inform a multicultural yet racialized Canada, albeit more discreetly and systemically than in the past, but whose consequences remain as punitive as ever.

Clearly, then, reference to racisms requires a conceptual reappraisal (see also Hier & Walby, 2006). A more politicized and theoretically grounded approach to racism is proposed in lieu of a descriptive or quantitative format, one whose lens focus on its persistence, pervasiveness, and multi-dimensionality (including historical, sectoral, and geographical specific forms) in a diverse and changing Canada. The politics of racism must be reconceptualized as a moving target or scavenger ideology that bends, shifts, bobs, and evades, only to resurface from the dead—zombie-like—into perversely new forms (or greater awareness of existing forms). The British academic Dr. A. Sivanandan (2002) puts it cogently: "Racism never stands still. It changes shape, size, contours, purpose, function, with changes in the economy, the social structure, the system, and, above all, the challenges, the resistances, to the system."

Failure to appreciate the politics and multi-dimensionality of racisms detracts from the goal of co-operative coexistence. The impact of such conceptual murkiness further erodes the identities, experiences, and opportunities of the historically disadvantaged in a Canada that nominally commits to the principles of multiculturalism. This seeming contradiction—proliferating racisms in a multicultural Canada—makes it doubly important to deconstruct the politics of what is going on, why, and how. A commitment to deconstructing Canadian racisms goes beyond the theoretical or abstractions. Rather, it embraces a quintessential twenty-first-century challenge: How to live together with differences without the differences precluding a living together. Or, as Michael Ignatieff (once a professor, then Liberal Party leader in Canada, then again a professor) pointed out in his book *The Rights Revolution* (2000), neither the environment nor the economy constitute the primary challenges of the twenty-first century. However important these issues, the key to any functioning future depends on constructive and co-operative engagement. Put bluntly, without the social trust for getting along and co-operating, nothing can get done. Yet debates over racisms continue to miss the mark, despite their centrality in forging a living together, in the process generating more heat than light. In hopes of casting light on a topic that many think is best left in the dark—namely, how racisms work in contemporary society—this book utilizes a sociological perspective to address the dynamics and paradoxes of *racisms in a multicultural Canada* with respect to *theory, practices, politics*, and *resistance*.

- The *theory* component conceptualizes the domain of racisms in terms of origins and persistence, magnitude and scope, manifestation at different levels, and continued reinvention in light of evolving realities and shifting discourses. It explores the different dimensions and definitions of racisms (racism as race, as ideology, as culture, as structure, as power); examines the four major sectors of racisms in Canada (interpersonal, institutional, ideological, and infrastructural); analyzes the constituents of racism (prejudice, discrimination, and institutional power); discusses its diverse expression and impact on Aboriginal peoples and racialized minorities such as Asian Canadians, Muslim Canadians, and African Canadians; and explains how and why racisms continue to flourish despite widespread opprobrium. The plurality of neo-racisms is problematized as well in shifting the discourse of blame from individuals and attitudes to society and structures. The theory component also examines the complex and often contested domains of race, racialization, and racisms against the backdrop of an official multiculturalism (Fleras, 2004). In doing so, we are reminded that racisms do not stand alone as privatized pathologies. More accurately, they are integral to the functioning of a racialized society, even one claiming to abide by multiculturalism principles (Lentin, 2008; Giroux, 2004).

- The *practices* component builds on the theoretical by exploring the expression of racisms in Canada both historically and at present. This theme of manifestations is predicated on a simply stated premise: Racism may not be as pervasive in Canada as critics suggest. Nevertheless, it is certainly more prevalent than those who would whitewash Canada as a colour-blind society whose racism has lapsed into irrelevance (see also Satzewich, 2011). Gay McDougall, the UN independent expert on minority issues, captured a sense of this contradiction in her 2009 preliminary report. Canada was commended for its enlightened intentions, yet soundly criticized for its discriminatory mistreatment of Aboriginal peoples and racialized minorities (cited in Cross & Wallace, 2009). Acknowledging the centrality of racism as practices draws attention to different dimensions at varying levels of intent, awareness, magnitude and scope, styles of expression, depth of intensity, and consequences. Racisms in Canada are inextricably linked to capitalism, class, sexism, and state laws that disempower some while privileging others in a country that claims to be inclusive and multicultural (Wilmot, 2005; Thobani, 2007; Giroux, 2004). Finally, the "quiet" racism of white Eurocentricity, unlike those involving open discrimination and blatant demonization, may well constitute the pivotal twenty-first-century challenge (Kobayashi, 2009). Particular attention is subsequently devoted to the politics of "whiteness" as a racialized entitlement involving multiple acts of exclusion at the level of (1) ideology, (2) mindsets and discourses that legitimize dominance, and (3) institutional structures and everyday practices that systemically bolster "pale male" privilege (Giroux, 2004).
- The *politics* dimension addresses controversies over the politicization of racisms in a diverse and changing Canada. A sense of perspective is critical in sorting out the politics of racisms. To say that all differences and disparities between the mainstream and racialized minorities can be attributed to to racism is surely an exaggeration (McGibbon & Etowa, 2009). But no less mistaken is any tendency to underestimate racism as a pivotal factor in deciding who gets what and why. Some see racism as a fundamental organizing principle of society; others perceive it as more situational, subtle, and muted; still others acknowledged the design of society along racialized lines, but not necessarily an equivalent to racism; and yet others believe emphasizing racism as an explanatory variable does an injustice to class or gender as identity markers (Satzewich, 1998). Debates over the magnitude and scope of racisms are critical in unraveling this paradox, as are discussions over impacts, effects, and implications. Analyzing the politics of "ivory tower racisms" provides a deeper insight into the dynamics of racisms within a mainstream institution in denial. Additional topics for debunking and debate include the following points of discussion: the politics of police racial profiling; the "racial rashomon" underpinning Canada's racial divide; the justification for black-focus ("Africentric"') schools; debates over the term "visible minority" as implicitly racist;

deconstructing the concept of Canada as a racist society; the digitalization of racisms by white supremacists; and the politics of "playing the racism card" to secure advantage or to advance agendas.
- Reference to *resistance* is twofold. One dimension examines the context of those policies and programs (both explicit and implied) that sought to unsettle Canada's self-proclaimed status as a white man's society. The second dimension looks at those formal initiatives collectively known as anti-racism that challenge Canada's racialized narratives. The conflict of interest is palpable: The moral impropriety of racism in civilized circles is widely acknowledged, yet there is far less agreement for its removal (Pitcher, 2009). Unmasking the multi-dimensionality of racism is pivotal in establishing a broad array of anti-racism initiatives around the individual, institutional, infrastructural, and inclusive. Furthermore, proposing an inclusive anti-racism framework embraces the principle of intersectionality: Attention is aimed at how racism intersects with gender and class (in addition to sexuality, ability, age, and religion) to amplify overlapping patterns of exclusion and disempowerment (Dei, 2005). Finally, the awkward status of Canada's official multiculturalism is put to the test. That is, can any multiculturalism ever prove to be an anti-racist solution? Or is it more accurate to frame Canadian Multiculturalism as racist and a form of racism in its own right? (In this book, Multiculturalism, when capitalized, refers to Canada's official policy; multiculturalism, when lower case, refers to its generic use.)

Every age has its hierarchy of crimes. This era is no exception, with racisms near the pinnacle of infractions against humanity (Benoist, 1999). Admittedly, racisms are neither a uniform concept with a singular frame of reference nor an isolated phenomena outside an ideological context and structural framework. Multi-dimensionality prevails with respect to dynamics and logic, as well as types and targets. Paradoxes are no less prevalent: To one side is a growing commitment to egalitarian norms, alongside a corresponding decline in the social acceptability of racisms. To the other side is a worrying persistence of bias, prejudicial discrimination, and racial violence (see Dovidio, 2009). Racism may be coming out of the closet, so to speak, because of global migration, minority assertiveness, and deteriorating economic conditions (United Nations, 2006). But racism as a dynamic and a discourse may also be burrowing underground at both individual and institutional levels, making it difficult to conceptualize or challenge. But it's precisely the interplay of complexity, multiplicity, and contextuality that must be addressed in advancing a racism-free Canada. Instead of reducing racisms to a privatized domain that erases any sense of history, structure, or society, analysis and activism must focus on broader context, including the politics of power through which racialized politics are organized and played out (Giroux, 2004).

Racisms in a Multicultural Canada is built around three core themes: (1) the persistence and proliferation of racisms; (2) the dynamics of contemporary racisms ("doing racism" or "how racisms work"); and (3) and the emergence of new discursive frameworks to account for "neo-racisms." More specifically, this book is concerned with how racisms work in Canada at present, despite ongoing initiatives and commitment to reduce and remove them. It attempts to explain the seemingly counterintuitive, namely, the expansion and continuities of racisms in a Canada organized around the principles of multiculturalism and a commitment to a colour-blind society. The book also analyzes the emergence of new ways of thinking and talking (discourses) about racism as principle, politics, and practices. This seemingly counterintuitive notion of multi-racisms in a seemingly racism-aversive Canada yields two important objectives: *First*, by combining practice and politics with theory and practice, *Racisms in Multicultural Canada* instills students with insights into racism at a time when many think it shouldn't or couldn't. The book doesn't necessarily instruct readers what to think; more accurately, the focus is on what to think about with respect to what racisms are; how they are manifest; their origins, perseverance, and complexities; impact and effects; and proposed remediation (see also Hier & Bolaria, 2007). Nor does the book trot out a raft of politically correct bromides as simplistic solutions to complex issues. Rather, the focus is on how to *think critically about* racisms in a multicultural Canada by challenging conventional wisdom, debunking half-truths and comforting fictions, and confronting those contradictions and conundra Canadians seem reluctant to ask, including:

- Is Canada a racist society? Or is it more accurately a racialized society?
- What is the relation of racialization and race to racism in a racialized Canada?
- How does Canada's "success" in combatting more egregious forms of racism contribute to public perception of yet more racisms?
- Why do racisms persist in a Canada that claims to be both multicultural (culture-sensitive) and post-racial (colour-blind)?
- Is there a proliferation of new racisms, or is it more accurate to acknowledge an enhanced public awareness of actions and situations that formerly were ignored or dismissed, but are now perceived as racist because of changing notions related to inclusion, equality, and difference?
- How do neo-racisms work in a Canada that, arguably, reflects the principles of a white superiority society?
- Is there a distinct Canadian racism that differs in kind from its counterpart in the United States or Europe?
- Is racism about churlish attitudes or about the founding assumptions, institutional structures, and foundational principles of Canada's constitutional order?

- Are race-based solutions appropriate for solving the problem of racisms?
- Is race objectively real or socially constructed as a lived reality?
- How is Canada's official multiculturalism both anti-racist (solution) in advancing a more inclusive society, yet more racist (a problem) by virtue of masking its ideological basis under the pretense of political neutrality?

Racisms in Multicultural Canada does not pretend to have all the answers as to why racisms continue to persevere, proliferate, and provoke. The issues are much too complex and contested to suggest otherwise, although there is much of value in asserting that true knowledge arises from asking the right questions. Worse still, the unwelcome status of racism in Canada complicates the process of speaking out against it, in part because racism talk violates cherished Canadian principles, in part because racisms are perceived as an embarrassing relic from a racist Canada (see also Lentin & Lentin, 2006). But neither denial nor rhetoric can mask the obvious. It's time to awaken from the historical amnesia (Henry & Tator, 2010) that blankets the contradictions of a settler society: On one side of the contradictory divide is a Canada committed to liberal ideals, democracy, and equality; on the other side, it continues to be imbued with patterns of colonialism, racism, and exclusions that prevailed in the past and persist at present. Racisms may reign, in other words, but they need to be reined in by deconstructing and contesting the politics of racisms in a multicultural Canada that remains racialized in design, racist in practice, and racism by consequences.

Second, this book embraces Marx's prescient notion that it's not enough to understand the world. Acquired knowledge must be actively utilized to progressively transform it. Capitalizing on an expanded knowledge base enables readers of *Racisms in Multicultural Canada* to transform theory into practice, abstraction into lived experience, awareness into transformation, and the personal into the political (see also Henry & Tator, 2010). Two priorities prevail: First, to encourage those marked by race privilege to critically reflect upon their largely unearned (based on accident of birth) yet privileged entitlements in perpetuating patterns of structural racism and cultural superiority (see Green, 2004). Second, to instill in every reader a commitment to anti-racism action rather than simply compartmentalizing racisms as abstractions for analysis. People must learn to "walk the talk" instead of just "talking the walk" by "painting themselves as active participants into the anti racism picture" (James, 2003). The prospects for living together with differences, in dignity and equitably, is compromised by anything less than a critically reflexive commitment to doing what is workable, necessary, and just in transforming a racialized Canada into a multiculturally inclusive society.

SECTION 1

REAPPRAISING RACISM

References to reconceptualizing reality are proving both popular and pervasive. What most of these references endorse is a commitment to problematize ("to deconstruct") those processes and conditions often perceived as unproblematic—that is, as natural, normal, and necessary yet socially constructed and ideologically loaded (Spencer et al., 2007). A reconceptualizing commitment goes beyond official pronouncements or commonly assumed explanations of what happens, why, and how. There is a tacit assumption that appearances can prove deceiving when deconstructing what is really going on. Proposed instead is the need to be counterintuitive by going against the grain while reading between the lines. A commitment to reconceptualizing reality also entails the formulation of logically related propositions that link and explain otherwise seemingly unrelated and often unstated aspects of social reality.

A reappraisal of racism is subject to similar challenges and contradictions. Things are not always what they seem when it comes to racism, given the paradoxical interplay of (1) doing something, (2) doing nothing, (3) doing the right thing for the wrong reason, (4) doing the wrong thing for the right reason. But there are additional complexities that complicate the reappraisal process. Appraisal of racism must incorporate interconnected references to transnational economic and political forces, while demonstrating how racism is mutually constituted in and through the interplay of race, whiteness, capitalism, modernity, and colonialism (Dua et al., 2005; Giroux, 2004). Any reappraisal must address a range of spiralling racisms; their manifestations in individual behaviours, institutional norms and practices, cultural values, and constitutional priorities; and expression at varying levels from the interpersonal and ideological to the institutional and infrastructural. An intersectional focus prevails as well. In theory, racisms may be analyzed independently of other factors; in reality, however, they routinely intersect with often devalued identity markers such as class, gender, and ethnicity to amplify the exclusions of inequality.

In short, reassessing racism is proving more elusive than many anticipated (Satzewich, 2011; Burnett, 2013a). In this postmodern world we live in, words can mean whatever people want them to mean, with the result that they can mean everything or nothing. Moreover, as postmodernists like to remind us, there is no such thing as truth, reality, or objectivity in a mind-dependent world. Only discourses about truth, reality, or objectivity exist that are anchored in contexts of power and inequality. References to racism are no exception to the politics of obfuscation (Lentin, 2008). Now is the time for debunking the many myth conceptions that have infiltrated the conceptual domain to the detriment of living together. Section 1 rises to the challenge by exploring the politically charged and sociologically contested site of racisms as concept and reality. A commitment to reappraising racism draws attention to its analytic features without sacrificing insights into its contested nature.

Chapter 1 begins by looking at the politics of racisms in Canada. The chapter "surveys the damage" by demonstrating the pervasiveness of racism in the past, its proliferation at present, and its persistence into the foreseeable future, not necessarily because of more racists or more racism, but possibly because of changing public perceptions and social changes.

Chapter 2 reveals how perceptions, theories, and definitions of racism have shifted because of evolving debates that arguably yield more heat than light. References to racism as bad attitudes have given way to new discursive frames that acknowledge its structural centrality to society in advancing elite priorities and class domination (Zuberi & Bonilla-Silva, 2008). Of particular note is growing awareness of racisms as multi-dimensional phenomena, with a corresponding need to customize discourses along neo-racism lines if there is any hope of understanding and solutions.

Chapter 3 acknowledges a fundamental contradiction in Canada. Institutional reform and legislative protection deny the legitimacy of race as grounds for differential treatment, or at least in theory (de jure) if not always in practice (de facto). Nevertheless, the politics of race remains pivotal in racializing the organization of a so-called post-racial and colour-blind society (Li, 2003). The chapter on the riddles of race explores the relation between race and racism by capitalizing on the centrality of racialization in mediating this relationship. Particular attention is paid to the politics of whiteness as racialized privilege within the framework of a white superiority Canada.

Chapter 4 examines racism by deconstructing its constituent components with respect to prejudice, discrimination, and institutional power. The interconnectedness of these constituents demonstrates how racism is a lot more complex, contested, and contradictory than many had predicted or anticipated, in effect making it much more difficult to pin down as a concept or to put down as a practice.

CHAPTER 1

THE POLITICS OF RACISM
EVOLVING REALITIES, SHIFTING DISCOURSES

Introduction: Surveying the Damage

> *There is a strange kind of enigma associated with the problem of racism. No one, or almost no one, wishes to see themselves as racist; still racism persists, real and tenacious.*
> —Albert Memmi, *Racism*

To say we live in interesting times may be clichéd, yet strangely apropos when applied to the politics of racism. Instead of atrophying into irrelevance as many had expected or hoped, the spectre of racism continues to haunt and hurt in ways that catch many off guard. The pre-conference notes preceding the Durban Review Conference in Geneva, April 20–24, 2009, captured the magnitude of the problem when it conceded the global scope of racial discrimination, xenophobia, and related intolerance. Racism was accused of hampering the progress of millions of lives despite moves to eradicate it (Human Rights First, 2009), in the process impeding economic opportunities, thwarting basic human rights of equality, or fuelling hatreds by way of ethnic cleansing, expulsion, or genocide. Worse still, concluded the pre-conference notes, the future is hardly promising, especially as societies increasingly diversify due to international migration; as competition stiffens over valued yet dwindling resources; and as racialized identity politics proliferate in advancing claims for recognition and rewards.

However gloomy this global assessment, Canada is widely commended as bucking this unflattering prognosis. Racism may loom as the single most explosive and divisive force in other countries, including the United States, but presumably not in Canada, where racism is publicly scorned and officially repudiated (Fleras, 2012). Laws are in place that criminalize racism; brazen racists and white supremacists are routinely charged for disseminating hate propaganda; race riots are virtually unheard of except in history books; and blatant forms of racial discrimination are illegal and socially unacceptable. Canada is much more favourably disposed toward immigrants of colour than it once was, while Canadians are more accepting of differences because of tolerant mindsets and multicultural commitments (Lupul, 2005; Kymlicka, 2008b). The demographic revolution that has transformed Anglocentric enclaves such as Vancouver and Toronto into vibrant and cosmopolitan dynamos must surely attest to Canada's pluck in managing the art of living together with differences. Finally, reference to a colour-blind Canada prompts many Canadians to say they don't see any color or race—just people—so that references to racism and racial discrimination are dismissed as passé in shaping outcomes (see also Bonilla-Silva, 2003). To the extent that racisms linger in a supposedly post-racial Canada, they are thought to be relatively muted, isolated to fringe circles, a survival from the past, or hyped as a smokescreen.

But in assessing the paradox of *"racisms without racists,"* appearances have proven deceiving. Contrary to national myths or global reputation, Canada is neither the paragon of racial tranquility nor the racist-free haven that many admire or aspire to. A sense of contradiction is conveyed by Dua et al. (2005), who conclude that:

> Canada is located in a peripheral location within Western hegemony and is characterized in national mythology as a nation innocent of racism. In the postwar period, state policies of multiculturalism have represented Canada as a welcoming haven for immigrants and refugees, while in reality these policies worked to create structures that kept new Canadians of color in a marginal social, political, cultural, and economic relationship to Canada. Internationally, Canada is often constructed as a "peacekeeping nation" that is outside larger imperialist agendas. Such national mythologies erase the history of colonization, slavery, and discriminatory immigrant legislation.

The past speaks for itself: Racism was deeply ingrained in Canada's history, culture, law, and institutions, resulting in imbricated patterns of racialized inequality that persist into the present (see Satzewich, 1998; Walker, 1998; Backhouse, 1999; Hier & Bolaria, 2007; Das Gupta et al., 2007; Wallis & Fleras, 2008; Wallis, Sunseri, & Galabuzi, 2010; Henry & Tator, 2010; Razack, Smith, & Thobani, 2010; Satzewich, 2011; Satzewich & Liodakis, 2013). Racism proved the ideological life support for capitalism at large and Canada-building in two ways: first, through the exploitation of racialized and immigrant minorities (Bolaria & Li, 1988; Bishop, 2005; also Feagin,

2006); second, by colonizing its Indigenous peoples through the appropriation of their land and theft of their resources (Alfred, 2005; Belanger, 2008; Cannon & Sunseri, 2011). Hate and fear compelled authorities to intern thousands of racialized and ethnic minorities during World Wars I and II at great personal cost to themselves due to family separations, property loss, and destruction of community (Fukawa, 2009). Minorities such as Jews and African Canadians were routinely denied access to public and private institutions. Even institutes of higher learning proved anything but enlightened, with strict quotas that regulated the enrolment of Jews, Ukrainians, Poles, and other racialized groups, regardless of grades or qualifications (Levine, 2009). Canada was not even exempt from those much reviled symbols of white supremacist America. Contrary to national myths, the Ku Klux Klan flourished during the 1920s and 1930s in central and western Canada (called the "Kanadian Klan"), with much of its racist bile directed at blacks and Catholics, French Canadians, and Asians. Slavery existed as well, with Aboriginal peoples and blacks as the main victims (Wigmore, 2013).

As recently as sixty years ago, racism was rife in securing a "white" Canada. Racist ideals and practices so permeated the entirety of Canadian society that minorities perceived as unassimilable paid a steep price for admission. Disparaged as stubborn, ostracized as backward, punished as suspicious, and penalized as inferior (Backhouse, 1999), new Canadians confronted a host of demeaning slights and ethnoracial slurs as the cost of entry into Canada. Immigration restrictions were racialized in favour of northern Europeans in hopes of preserving a white Canada, although the circle of acceptance expanded throughout the 1950s with the collapse of conventional sources. Both immigrant and racialized minorities were victimized by sometimes blatant expressions of discrimination. For example, consider how patterns of segregation involving black separate schools remained on the books in southwestern Ontario and Halifax well into the 1960s. In other cases, racial discrimination tended to be more muted, albeit no less exclusionary in denying access to services or accommodation. To be sure, the situation improved with passage of the federal Bill of Rights in 1960 and Ontario's Fair Accommodation Practices Act in 1954, which superseded the Racial Discrimination Act of 1944. In most cases, however, racism simply changed tack by going underground and away from government scrutiny, media spotlight, and public discourse.

Contrary to popular belief and government publicity, the present may be equally racist, albeit more discreetly and by consequence rather than intentionally or consciously. Modern racism is more complex and contradictory since the combination of anti-racism and multiculturalism propels it to go underground or to reform into something ostensibly more indirect and subtle. The overt racism of the past with its roots in theories of racial superiority is now reformulated along more covert lines that often go undetected by conventional measures (Fleras, 2004; Zong, 2007; Henry & Tator, 2009; Berg & Wendt, 2011). For example, the banning of baggy pants, baseball caps, dreadlocks or corn rows, and athletic wear by bars and clubs may serve as a twenty-first-century (dress) code for no "coloureds" allowed (Kareem, 2009b). Racialized minorities continue to be politely denied equitable access to housing, employment, media, education, policing, and social services (Henry & Tator, 2010). As a group, they not only earn less, they experience higher levels of poverty and unemployment (Block & Galabuzi, 2011). They are also precluded from management, making up only 13 percent of leadership positions in a Toronto where over 40 percent of the population is racialized (Lewington, 2009). New Canadians are finding it easier to fall into poverty, but harder to get jobs or earn incomes commensurate with their educational credentials and overseas experience (Reitz & Bannerji, 2007). Even the world's oldest hatred, anti-Semitism, is seemingly on the rise, owing in part to the backlash against globalization and conspiracy theories over shaky economics and lost jobs. Anti-Semitic hostility is also fuelled by those who accuse Israel of colonialism, apartheid, and human rights violations in its treatment of Palestinians both within and outside Israeli borders (Strauss, 2003).

To be sure, uncritically employing racism to explain all racialized disparities is rashly inappropriate (see also Richeson, 2008). Racialized inequities in society reflect a raft of factors ranging from cultural values and personal dispositions to structural barriers and institutional routines. For example, disparities in income and employment are not necessarily the fault of racism. Market dynamics, labour availability, and personal choices may also be contributing factors. Blaming racism for every socio-economic gap may generate inferences unwarranted from the data, such as shifting responsibility for personal failure (Satzewich, 2011). Playing the "race card" by inserting racism into the equation to confuse or accuse reinforces an unhealthy and excessive reliance on victimization, as actor and activist Bill Cosby contends:

> Racism is pervasive, but it's no excuse to fail or stop striving, not through protests but cleansing their culture, embracing personal responsibility, strong families and communities, and reclaiming the traditions that once fortified them.

Not surprisingly, debates over the politics of racisms in Canada elicit a mix of reactions. The framing of racism at present increasingly reflects minority definitions of racism by signifying it as widespread, institutionalized, and systemic, as well as more nuanced, unconscious, and inadvertent. Compare this with traditional mainstream definitions of racism that relegated it to the individual, attitudinal, and random. Not surprisingly, now that whites no longer have the exclusive authority to decide what is racism and who is a racist (Lippard, 2011), people are confused about whether it exists or how racism works (Dodd, 2013) (for example, Americans cannot fathom the rationale behind those who still see racism in a post-racial America of Tiger, Oprah, and Obama). Reactions in Canada are equally ambivalent: For some, Canada is less racist than in the past, if evaluated by legislative activity, opinion polls, and socio-economic indicators as a barometer of the progress (see Hier & Walby, 2006). For others, racism is alive and well, perhaps even more entrenched than a generation ago, when anti-racism resources were more plentiful. A surge in mixed marriages, celebration of diversities, anti-racist initiatives, and varied inclusiveness gestures cannot conceal the obvious. Racisms persist and proliferate, albeit less bluntly than before but continue to thrive in private conversations, avoidance patterns, and subtle discriminatory put-downs (see also Parrillo, 2011). In their report on the root cause of youth violence in Ontario, Curling and McMurtry (2008) convey a sense of dismay: "We were taken aback by the extent to which racism is alive and well and wreaking its harmful effects on Ontarions and the very fabric of this province."

References to the magnitude of racism are no less varied. Critics argue that racism and discrimination have become more overt and acceptable as public discourses since 9/11 and the "war against terrorism" (Dua et al., 2005). Others disagree with this assessment. But rather than ameliorating, as might be expected in the light of social engineering moves, many fear the situation is deteriorating, with the worst effects tempered by a Teflon veneer of tolerance and politeness (Curling & McMurtry, 2008). Even Canada's much-lauded commitment to an official multiculturalism may be dismissed as racism in disguise, little more than a calculated ploy that simultaneously conceals yet consolidates patterns of power and privilege (Thobani, 2007; Bannerji, 2000). Or as Sherrow Pinder (2010) concludes (admittedly in the American context), an inclusive multiculturalism cannot realistically take root or do meaningful work in a monocultural state. Criticized as well is a glaring contradiction between multicultural ideals and exclusionary realities that may yield the possibility of a distinctly Canadian racism (Henry & Tator, 2010).

So what is going on? The very notion of racisms in Canada and Canadians as racists may strike many as counter-logical or unnecessarily polemical (McParland, 2012). How could such an accusation hold up to scrutiny in a country widely commended as a beacon of enlightenment in the artful management of progressive intergroup relations? Yes, it may have once been normal and acceptable—even obligatory—to be a racist in a white Canada. Yet how to explain its persistence in a multicultural Canada where accusations of racism constitute a slur (or stain) on people's character while exposing their moral bankruptcy (Pitcher, 2009)? No one wants to be accused of racism for fear of being lumped together with the ignorant or the extreme, the backward and unwashed, and the socially pathological (Titley & Lentin, 2012). Small wonder, then, that politicians and pundits on all sides of the political spectrum use and abuse the term "racism" to tar their opponents (Ford, 2009). But however much the concept it maligned as a cynical ploy, the evidence for racism is irrefutable. The Ontario Human Rights Commission (2005b, p. 1) pulls no punches in pointing out the reality of racisms in the midst of denial:

> Racialized persons experience disproportionate poverty, over-representation in the prison population, underrepresentation in the middle and upper layers of political, administrative, economic, and media institutions, and barriers to accessing employment, housing, and health care to name just a few. Courts have recognized that racism exists in Canada. It's all too easy for those who do not experience it to deny the reality of racism. This is counterproductive and damaging to our social fabric. Racial discrimination and racism must be acknowledged as a pervasive and continuing reality as a starting point....

The shifting terrain of race and racism reinforces the importance of paying attention to (1) the workings of racism along both structural yet subliminal lines; (2) the relationship of socially constructed notions of race ("racialization") to other ascriptive categories (such as gender or class); (3) the proliferation of new strands of racial antipathy, along with new discourses; and (4) the privileging of whiteness, white actors, and white indifference/apathy in advancing the white superiority complex of a white supremacist society (Winant, 2004). But moves to alert Canadians to the presence and pervasiveness of racisms are proving a formidable challenge. Many Canadians appear to have internalized the values of tolerance, equality, and justice, at least at the cognitive level. But ambiguities in their actions continue to betray a disconnect between ideals and reality, between professed beliefs and unconscious (subliminal) attitudes, between thoughts and actions, between comforting fictions and inconvenient truths (Henry & Tator, 2010). In short, racism and racial prejudice persist invisibly at subconscious levels.

Contradictions are rife. Institutions may have abolished the most egregious patterns of racial discrimination. Nonetheless, they continue to deny and exclude because of rules and protocols hard-wired into the organizational system, with the result that many individuals unknowingly act without deliberate intent to systemically discriminate. At yet another level are macro-racisms. Racism is so normalized and naturalized in history and society that the combination of historical amnesia and collective denial glosses over the harsh realities of a racialized society divided by colour and ethnicity (Thobani, 2007). Racisms are persistent, pervasive, and pivotal in defining who gets what, yet virus-like by mutating into new forms difficult to recognize or combat (Mistry & Latoo, 2009, p. 20). Their centrality in securing a racialized and white "superiority" society deserves serious consideration. This excerpt by Feagin (2006, p. 47) nails the pervasiveness of racism in (American) society:

> Today we still live in a substantially racist society. Much of the social terrain of this society is significantly racialized. Most institutional and geographical spaces, acceptable social norms, acceptable societal roles, privileged language forms, preferred sociopolitical thinking, and favoured understanding of history are white-generated, white-shaped, white-imposed, and/or white-authenticated. All people, whether they are defined socially as white or non white, live largely within a substantially white-determined environment. Those who are not white, whether recent immigrants or long term residents, are under great pressure ... "to assimilate" to the white-determined folkways. The word "assimilate," however, does not capture the everyday reality of pressure-cooker demands on individuals to conform to that white environment and white folkways. There is often no choice for those who are not white but to more or less accept, mostly emulate, and even parrot the prevailing white folkways, including white-generated negative images of racial outgroups, usually including one's own group. People of color constantly resist these pressures for conformity, but most have to accept and adapt to some extent just to survive in a white-controlled society.

There is much to commend in a Canada that remains largely free of race riots, racialized ghettoes, and cross burnings. However commendable such accolades, this fortuitous state of affairs may reflect exceptional good fortune, together with a powerful myth-making machine, rather than enlightened policies, political will, or public embrace.

Which picture is more accurate? Is Canada essentially an open and tolerant society, with only isolated and random incidences of racism ("a few bad apples")? Or is it as racist to the structural core as critics say ("a rotten institutional barrel")? Is Canada a society where individuals are rewarded on the basis of merit, where no group is singled out for negative treatment because of the irrelevance of race in determining a person's status? Or does Canada prefer to mask this racism behind a mythology of racelessness by concealing it under a blanket of whiteness (Backhouse, 1999; Razack, 2002; Kobayashi, 2003; Das Gupta et al., 2009)? To what extent are debates about racism driven by politically expedient claims that blame it for all racialized disparities in Canada? Or is it safer to say that racism and racial discrimination are but one of many factors (variables) that generate exclusions (Hier, 2007; Hum & Simpson, 2007). Perhaps it's more accurate to say any assessment of racisms in Canada falls somewhere between the poles of naive optimism and cynical pessimism. Canada is home to a baffling blend of hard-core racists and resolute anti-racists, with most individuals aligned somewhere along this continuum of extremes. In other words, exaggerating the magnitude of racism as its harshest critics might makes no more sense than to underestimate its impact and scope as those in denial might (see also Satzewich, 2011). Competing points of debate, questions, and contention complicate any tendency toward glib assessment, as demonstrated in the Question Box.

> **? QUESTION BOX**
>
> The following questions reflect many of the debates over the politics of racisms in Canada, namely: Why are racisms proliferating? How do they work? Where and when can they be recognized? Who is framing the discourses? That these points of contention have yet to be answered in a definitive way or with any degree of consensus speaks volumes of the complexities involved.
>
> - Can racisms be conceptualized in singular and static terms? Or do the politics of racisms reinforce their multiplicity, complexity, malleability, and contradictory nature?
> - Are racisms proliferating or is it more accurate to say that (in)actions once ignored or deemed to be acceptable are now defined (or labelled) as racist or racialized because of the void created by the demise of "big" racism? If racisms are socially constructed conventions, who or what accounts for this claims-making activity, i.e., how and why do certain conditions come to be labelled as problematic?
> - Is it possible for individuals to be colour-blind yet stand accused of racism? For some, taking differences seriously is critical in challenging racism. For others, the idea of taking differences into account is fundamentally racist. A conundrum prevails: Exaggerating people's difference when irrelevant may be racist, yet ignoring their differences when necessary may prove equally racist.
> - Is racism about doing something to someone (action), or about not doing something (inaction) when something needs doing? Inaction or passivity in the face of racism may encourage it (Trepagnier, 2010; Alvarez & Juang, 2010). For example, a report by the Native Women's Association of Canada concluded that since 1970, nearly six hundred Aboriginal women and girls have been murdered (67 percent) or gone missing (24 percent). Where is the outrage? Where are the actions? In that inactions speak louder than platitudes, the spectre of racism is unavoidable.

- Is racism about intent on the part of institutional actors or, alternatively, about the effect of such actions regardless of intent? Even well-intentioned actions may be perceived as racist if their consequences prove disempowering or are perceived as disadvantaging (Paradies, 2005). Neither individuals nor institutions need be openly racist to inadvertently promote racially discriminatory outcomes.

- Who decides what constitutes racism and what racism constitutes? Increased emphasis on the primacy of consequences and context demonstrates the centrality of racially marginalized groups as arbiters of racism. Shifting the focus of racism from sender-oriented to receiver-dependent legitimizes minority views of racism as institutionalized and systemic, as well as subtle and subliminal, while displacing white sources of authority in defining racism (i.e., as individual, attitudinal, random).

- Are incidents of racism increasing across Canada? Or are Canadians increasingly repulsed by public displays of racism, with a growing willingness to report violations to proper authorities? Are Canadians less racist than in the past, or are they simply more fearful of causing an affront by breaching Canada's multicultural consensus?

- Is racism an aberration (random, isolated, individualized)? Or is a constitutive feature of Canada and Canada-building by which racial classifications are transformed into values, structures, and outcomes that influence access to power, privilege, and property (Wallis, Sunseri, & Galabuzi, 2010)?

- To what extent is racism a case of individual ignorance or fear? Or should racism be interpreted as a complex array of practices and discourses that are historically defined, embedded within institutional structures, reflective of patterns of power, woven into an ideological fabric, and normalized in everyday practices? If racism is the metaphorical equivalent of an iceberg, the core of any analysis must address the massively submerged section.

- In what way is racism an objective "thing" out there (i.e., racism as a noun)? Or should it be defined as a process involving an attribute applied to an action after the fact, depending on the context, criteria, or consequence (i.e., racism as a process, a verb)? Are some ideas or actions inherently racist regardless of motives or situation, or should priority be assigned to consequences and context? Is racism as a dislike or fear of outgroups natural to the human species?

- Is there a danger of overusing the word "racism"? To what degree is racism a catch-all that soaks up (explains or excuses) all disparities (Lippard, 2011)? Blaming racism for every socio-economic problem when race is irrelevant may be racist in its own right, in part because attention is deflected away from the root causes of minority problems. Constant repetition of the "r" word can also have the unfortunate effect of trivializing its impact for those who routinely suffer from its consequences.

- Is any criticism directed at racialized minorities a sign of racism? Or is a reluctance to criticize minorities a kind of racism in its own right by implying minority actions are beyond reproach or immune to criticism? How racist is it to question the existence and pervasiveness of racism, regardless of intent or context (Satzewich, 2010)? Is there a tendency to play the "racism card" by using racism as a scapegoat for personal failures or, alternatively, as a smokescreen to foreclose debate or divert unwelcome attention (Wallis & Fleras, 2008)? How often is racism wielded as a hammer to intimidate by stigmatizing the accused with a stain that is difficult to remove (Murray, 2008)?

- Covert or overt? Overt racisms assume blatant and insidious forms, whereas the more subtly subversive covert racisms tend to reflect coded terms that duck behind the facade of politeness, political correctness, or colour-blindness (Coates, 2008). For example, many Arab Canadians find themselves victimized by a racism that does "its dirty work" by invoking the pretext of security or safety to deny or demonize them.

- Is the logic behind racism rational or irrational? Many regard racism as essentially irrational in negativizing others on the basis of physical or cultural characteristics. Others see racism as a "rational" strategy employed by vested interests for advancing their interests (Bonilla-Silva, 1997).

- Is racism about bigotry involving negative racial images and attitudes in white minds (for a psychological/psychoanalytic approach to racism, see Rasmussen, 2013)? Or is it about the institutionalization of power that sustains supremacist patterns of white privilege despite an ongoing struggle between those seeking to preserve unjustly derived power and privilege, versus those seeking a fundamental redistribution of valued resources (Bolton & Feagin, 2004; Kundnani, 2007b).

- Do all minorities experience racism in the same way, or is racism differently encountered by, say, Aboriginal peoples, Asian Canadians, Muslim Canadians, or African Canadians? Do whites who rarely experience racism see it differently than racialized minorities (Trepagnier, 2010), thereby establishing a perceptual divide (a "Rashomon effect") that complicates any analysis or assessment?

- Can racism be isolated and analyzed independently? Or must it be seen as constitutive of other indicators of exclusion related to class, gender, ethnicity, or sexual preference in ways that intersect and amplify (Lee & Lutz, 2005)?

- Cause or effect? Is racism the cause of racialized inequality? That is, does racism arise because it's embedded in (1) the legal and social structure of society, (2) a system of ideas and ideals, and (3) the rationale behind policy and law (Bonilla-Silva, 1997)? Or should racism as symptomatic of racialized inequalities be construed accordingly in light of deeply embedded disparities related to history, politics, economics, and culture (Kundnani, 2007a)?

- Is there a distinctive Canadian form of racism reflecting Canada's status as a multicultural society that claims to abide by the principles of multiculturalism and a colour-blind society? Or, should racism be framed along universalistic grounds that apply to all times and all places?
- Is racism about social and economic exclusion based on race (Gilman, 2006)? Or is it about the privileging of whiteness as normal, desirable, and superior? Are whites by definition racist since no one (including those in positions of dominance) is immune to those prevailing ideas on race and racism that permeate the culture and society (Trepagnier, 2010; Wise, 2009a? Can minorities be racist toward other minorities? Can minorities display racism toward their own group (Moore, 2012)?

The fact that responses to these questions and conundra rarely yield anything even remotely consensual is telling in its own right. Its status as a conceptual paradox and series of puzzling riddles ensures that debates over the nature and scope of racism will remain at the forefront of Canadian controversies.

The Paradoxes of Racisms: Puzzles as Riddles Inside an Enigma[1]

A twenty-first-century Canada must confront an inescapable paradox. Canadians openly reject racialized notions of biological inferiority as wrong and unacceptable. Yet many continue to rely on racially based prejudices at subconscious levels to organize, define, and assess (Caines, 2004). Institutions may endorse a commitment to equality and inclusivity, even as they inadvertently discriminate against minorities because of seemingly neutral rules that exert a systemically exclusionary effect when evenly and equally applied to unequal contexts. On one side, Canada remains at the forefront in fighting racism at individual, institutional, infrastructural, and ideological levels. Inclusiveness, equity, and fairness measures are introduced to compensate for the historical and social disadvantages that blocked racialized minorities from otherwise competing on a level playing field. On the other side, awareness is mounting that (1) racism is an everyday reality for many Canadians of colour; (2) racist practices impact on individuals in subtle yet real ways; and (3) racism is not some anachronism from the past, but both dynamically invasive and socially toxic. On yet another side, there is a growing awareness of the changing face of racism in response to a diverse and changing society. Rather than a vanishing act or staying pat, the politics of racisms are proving a moving target both elusive yet enigmatic (Frederickson, 2002). A comparison of racism to parasites is cleverly insightful:

> Parasites mutate and evolve to mimic the functioning of the host in order to fool the host into thinking that the parasite is a good and

healthy part of itself. This results in the parasite dropping "below the radar" of the defence systems of the host in order to sneak into its body. Once ensconsed, the parasite leeches on the resources of the host, depleting and weakening it.... In some cases, like that of the cuckoo, the host is sufficiently fooled into *actively* feeding and nourishing the parasite to the detriment of itself. (Dalal, 2011, p. 20)

Acknowledging the existence of many racisms instead of only one poses the question of what is going on and why. How to explain the seeming paradox? For some, things are not getting any better; for others, they appear to be improving; for yet others, the situation is either better or worse depending on criteria; and for still others, the good coexists with the bad and the indifferent. Granted, Canada is not nearly as openly racist as it was in its defiantly supremacist past. Canadians no longer tolerate open expressions of racism in the public domain, although this rejection may not reflect the outrage of injustice, but a fear of causing an affront to others in a society that disowns the legitimacy of racism, with sanctions ranging from social ostracism to legal penalties. A sense of perspective is critical. In societies where hatred toward others is the norm, even the most egregious forms of racial violence or discrimination often go unnoticed or unpunished. But the smallest misdemeanour in a so-called society of multicultural saints gets blown out of proportion (Levitt, 1997). In a society like Canada, where racism and racial intolerance are socially unacceptable and against the law, the slightest provocation elicits public debate or vigorous rebuke. It is precisely this juxtaposition of optimistic standards with questionable practices that generates a pessimism that not only intensifies people's perceptions of the problem. More important, additional problems are uncovered that few acknowledged in the past as once unproblematic actions are now problematized (labelled as racist) by the removal of blatant racism. Three paradoxes in problematizing racisms can be discerned: progress, proliferation, and proportion (see Best, 2001; see also Hier & Bolaria, 2007).

The Paradox of Progress
The search for *perfectionism in an imperfect world*—an ideological commitment to societal perfection and progress—is a surefire way of setting up people for failure. Notwithstanding numerous improvements in the quantity and quality of human existence in general (from life expectancy to standard of living), there remains a tendency among both academics and the general public to fixate on the negative and the divisive. The public's pessimism is derived from a widespread belief in the attainment of a perfect society, clearly an unrealistic situation despite its ascendancy as an ideal. The end result is a recipe for disappointment. A society defined by rising expectations invites the disappointment of relative deprivation, which, in turn, creates failures where none existed before (Chandra, 2002). Or as Joel Best (2001,

p. 3) explains with respect to the paradox of perfectionism, "optimistic beliefs in social perfectibility tends to accentuate failures; after all, real world initiatives invariably fall short of these high standards, thus promoting and justifying yet more disappointment and pessimism." Furthermore, both sociologists and activists are reluctant to acknowledge equality progress on the social inequality front for fear of encouraging public complacency or backlash.

The politics of racisms demonstrates how the paradox—the more things improve, the worst the world seems—is played out. Racisms continue to be seen as a growing problem even though evidence would suggest appreciable improvements for racialized minorities in terms of equity, access, and representation. For example, a half century ago, blacks in the United States were routinely perceived as inferior or irrelevant; as a result, the likelihood of blacks occupying important political offices was unthinkable. No one took them seriously except as entertainers and athletes. Even the prospect of mixed marriages and interracial relationships was illegal in nearly half of the United States when a white mother and a black father gave birth to the current president of the United States. But blacks in general have benefited from desegregation and formal equality through removal of explicit discriminatory barriers in the political, economic, and cultural domain. Yet improvements in these domains are offset by perceptions that reality is moving too slowly in matching ideals, resulting in a sense of relative deprivation. As Orlando Patterson (1995) writes in his article "Paradoxes of Integration," the greater the equality experienced by minorities, the greater their outrage at previous discriminatory treatment, their disenchantment with current gaps, their dismay at the distance yet to be travelled, and their despair over the prospect of real change.

The Paradox of Proportion

A second paradox is that of *proportion*. The paradox of *proportion* argues that the profile of smaller problems is magnified by the reduction or elimination of bigger problems. The end result is that racist slights, once ignored in the past, are now blown into and out of proportion. The reduction or elimination of big problems through public policies encourages a surge in the visibility of formerly unrecognized problems that now loom larger than they once did because of the resulting void. Racialized minorities once confronted life-threatening situations from lynching to Jim Crow colour bars that curbed life chances. These overtly racist contexts no longer prevail. What prevails instead are those subtle and covert racisms not noticeable to everyone except to those who experience them. In other words, more insidious forms of racial discrimination now circulate beneath the radar of a commitment to a post-racial and colour-blind society, occupying the space once reserved for now discredited forms of overt racism (Winant, 2004).

For example, *The Princess and the Frog* may have been Disney's first film to feature an African American princess, which was a significant move in its own right, but not enough to deter critics from picking it apart for everything from stereotyping to an unsympathetic portrayal of voodoo (Kareem, 2009d). Or consider how the decision of Vancouver's BC Transit to curtail late-night public transport was criticized as racist because it imposed a disproportionate impact on those racialized workers without private vehicles and/or who work late-night jobs. Presumably no one set out to discriminate against minorities; nevertheless, discrimination arises from the consequence of applying policies equally and evenly in unequal contexts. Just think: Sixty years ago, minorities may have experienced difficulty in getting a seat at the front of a bus. Today, they are mobilizing in the hopes of contesting bus schedules and routes that compromise minority realities and experience.

The Paradox of Proliferation

A similar line of reasoning applies to the *proliferation* paradox. Put bluntly, a commitment to social progress and attainment of the perfect society encourages a perception of proliferating problems. That is, as once egregious problems are brought under control, a multiplier effect kicks in. Newer and seemingly smaller problems begin to multiply at the level of people's awareness, in time overtaking former racism problems in magnitude and scope. Actions or inactions that once were deemed inoffensive are now defined as racism as notions of exclusion expand to reflect the gap between the ideals of multiculturalism and inclusion versus the reality of relative deprivation. Similarly, racism was once defined as deliberately doing something to somebody, resulting in denial, exclusion, or harm. But this bald-faced form of racism is socially unacceptable and legally inadmissible in societies that claim to be multicultural and/or post-racial. Instead, racism is increasingly expressed by not doing something when something needs to be done to foster inclusion or equity. Racism usually meant treating someone differently because of race; at present, however, racism may be directed at those who insist in treating everyone the same regardless of their difference, despite the fact their lived experiences and needs-based differences must be taken into account in levelling the playing field.

Accounting for the Paradoxes

Repeated and expanded reference to racism ensures its status as a victim of its own success. Canadians have become so attuned to the evils of racism that references to racism are routinely applied to patterns of (in)activity that in the past would have been tolerated as acceptable or normal. Charges of racism are levelled at any criticism directed at Aboriginal peoples or racialized minorities, in addition to government policies ranging from multiculturalism to immigration to employment equity. Or the racism label may be pinned on any pattern of mainstream inactivity (from indifference and arrogance to passivity or cowardice) that implicitly condones the prevailing and unequal status quo. Racism is invoked as an explanatory framework to account for minority failures in society, disparities in power and privilege, and the domination of pale male privilege. On many occasion, racism is the catch-all term when it might be more accurate to employ the concepts of prejudice or discrimination. Still, the danger of such excessive usage by playing the "racism card" should not be lightly dismissed: If racism is used to mean everything, it could well end up meaning nothing, with the result that genuine victims may be doubly victimized.

What drives the anomaly of multiplying racisms in a multicultural Canada? The concept of a media-driven politics of fear plays into the paradoxes of progress, disproportion, and proliferation. Fear is fostered by news media that specialize in hyping discourses related to risk and danger, including crime and terrorism (Altheide, 2002, 2003). But consequences follow from the news media's preoccupation with framing negativity as newsworthy or newsworthiness as negative. A steady diet of "everything is out of control" generates such high negativity levels that reference to fear is routinely implied when not openly articulated (for example, reference to Toronto's Jane and Finch neighbourhood as synonymous with guns, drugs, and gangs). Similarly, a mood of fear is elicited by the news media's framing of racialized and immigrant minorities as "troublesome constituents." This demographic is routinely portrayed as "problem people" who are problems (undocumented migrants who pose a terrorist threat or challenge the integrity of a sovereign Canada), or who create problems (too many who arrive from the wrong part of the world), or who are associated with negative contexts such as crime or poverty. The end result of this combination of government policies and public ignorance with negative media framing of issues? A culture of fear that tills fertile grounds for perceptions of problems to multiply.

To be sure, no one is accusing the media of fear-mongering. But exclusive references to minorities as troublesome constituents create coverage that is systemically biasing by virtue of this onesidedness (Fleras, 2011c; see also Chapter 6, "Institutional Racism," in this book). In addition to the media, there are other factors driving the paradoxes. Any criticism of minorities may be interpreted as racism in this era of political correctness, with the result that mainstream racism is routinely blamed for any minority failures or disparities in power, privilege, or property (Steyn, 2009). For example, journalists who ignore or deny contexts of racism in their coverage may be accused of racism when resisting the notion that racism is systemic and inherently embedded in a society's values and institutions (see Miller, 2005). Playing this "racism card" not only raises the bar in assessing the volume of racism. People increasingly fear being labelled or stigmatized as racist if they say anything negative about minorities; if they are critical of policies involving diversities and difference (from immigration to multiculturalism); and if they do not act proactively to accommodate minority sensibilities. The following questions arise from jumping too quickly to conclusions from playing the "racism card":

- Is it racist to criticize multiculturalism for going too far in accommodating diversities, thereby compromising national security and undermining mainstream values? Is it racist to be critical of multiculturalism for failing to accommodate minorities and de-normalize whiteness as privilege (see also Pinder, 2010)?
- Is racism involved when criticizing Canada's immigration program for its stand on "who," "why," "how many," and "what for"?
- Is it racist to insist that new Canadians must live by mainstream rules/identity even though no one is quite sure what these are since they are evolving and contested (Hamilton, 2007)?
- Is it racism to insist that Canada possesses the right and duty to draw the line over what is acceptable with respect to what differences count and what count as differences (Johnston, 1994)?
- Is it racist to argue that in a world of human agency, minorities must take responsibility for their actions or inactions, albeit within a broader political or economic context beyond their control?
- Is it racist to argue that no one should be assigned privileges because of their race? Or is such a seemingly egalitarian stance a case of camouflaging racist attitudes behind a principled platform?
- Is it racist to deny the existence of race and racism in a society that claims to be colour-blind, yet is racialized as a site of racisms?

Responses to these questions are varied, often contextual rather than categorical, and reflect a more nuanced position than a simple yes or no. Questions of this nature also point to another reason for the proliferation of racism: expanding parameters. Racism was once assumed to consist of individual acts that someone openly did something to somebody. The inception of an official multiculturalism in 1971 gradually delegitimized these racialized slurs or discriminatory actions. Canada evolved into a seemingly open, tolerant, and inclusive society, with full participation and equal opportunity regardless of race or ethnicity. And yet racisms prevail in a multicultural Canada that promotes the principles of multiculturalism, in part because (1) the underlying logic/foundational principles behind a state multiculturalism are racialized in favour of the status quo; (2) multiculturalism is incapable of addressing broader questions of structural racism and social inequality (Dei, 2011; Pinder, 2010); and (3) multiculturalism in a racialized Canada (despite claims to be a post-racial society) invites new forms of racism across a variety of situations (see also Lentin, 2012).

A different dynamic prevails at present: Blatant forms of hate racism are generally discredited within polite company; accordingly, people are activating more subtle forms of racisms as proxies. In a politically correct world, where open criticism or dislike is frowned upon as un-Canadian, toxic attitudes toward the other must be hidden behind euphemistic and politically neutral language that serves as a proxy to disguise racism. In other words, it is not a case of more racisms in society, despite the illusion that the situation is deteriorating. More to the point, it is about greater awareness of those racisms that historically always existed, but were either ignored or normalized in upholding a perception of white supremacist Canada. This, in turn, raises an interesting question: If old-fashioned racism consolidated a colour-conscious Canada, does the emergence of a colour-blind ideology elicit new kinds of postmodern racisms that function in fundamentally different ways? The case study on "Halloweenism" provides an answer.

"We're a Culture, Not a Costume." "Halloweenism": Inappropriate Costume Appropriation as Racism 2.0

Not too long ago Halloween costumes were inspired by hell motifs (zombies, devils, ghosts). Few paid much attention to the impact or implication of hell-inspired costumes or the occasional blatant stereotypes associated with turbaned maharajas or Mexicans in sombreros. More recently, however, themes from popular culture have replaced the underworld as the most popular choice, with people increasingly dressing in costumes that capitalize on images from other races, ethnicities, nationalities, or lifestyles (Nittle, 2013). The most popular costumes include choices from geisha girls and sumo wrestlers to Native warriors and blackface, with hillbillies/white trash, gangsta rappers, and suicide bombers thrown in for good measure (Grinberg, 2012). But many of these costumes have come under criticism as offensive, insensitive, or racist in ways that may startle and surprise.

So what is going on? Where do we draw the line between playful and distasteful? Offensive and cool? Why is it okay for men to dress as gladiators, ER doctors, priests, or convicts, but not as imams or "Indian" chiefs? Is it ever permissible to dress up as a Hitler look-alike or to wear Nazi paraphernalia? Remember the controversy that erupted in 2005 when Prince Harry was caught wearing a swastika armband to a friend's themed party of "colonials and natives" (BBC, 2005). Why is okay for women to dress up as nuns, hotties, nurses, or French maids, but not as Pocohantas or fully veiled Muslim women? In brief, why are some outfits framed as racist and culturally inappropriate? Who decides, and on what grounds? The ground rules are shifty and shifting. For example, Nadra Kareem Nittle, in her online posts <about .com> considers it okay to dress as Michael Jackson or Kobe Bryant (specific people), but minus the blackface or Afro wig, but it is fine to wear dreadlocks if impersonating Bob Marley (Nittle, 2013).

Supporters argue that the issue of inappropriate Halloween costumes is little more than a "tempest in a teapot" blown out of proportion by a politically correct crowd. After all, they might point out, it is doubtful if people would go out of their way to make costume choices with malicious intent to stereotype, mock, or spoof. It is about fun, laughs, and having a good time. In fact, if imitation constitutes the sincerest form of flattery, why not choose a costume accordingly? For example, Tyler Bozak of the Toronto Maple Leafs, who wore blackface as part of his Michael Jackson outfit, tweeted the following response to criticism over his choice of a Halloween party costume: "This is a tribute to one of my favorite artists! For anyone to call it racist is crazy! (Canadian Press, 2012). Or consider Johnny Depp's excuse in justifying his physically outlandish portrayal (KISS meets Jack Sparrow) of Tonto in the film *The Lone Ranger*. His claim to be part Aboriginal (no proof) sought to remove the taint of cultural appropriation ("red face") since it is no longer acceptable for whites to play another race, even if the role playing secures a positive role model for Aboriginal youth.

Critics counter by arguing that neither intent nor awareness is the real issue. Dressing inappropriately may not be as innocent a gesture as many believe. Rather, it may reflect some deeply seated (subliminal) biases that can be legitimately projected within the ambiguities of a Halloween context. An inappropriate costume impersonates, perpetuates, and exaggerates a negative and derogatory stereotype that misrepresents an often marginalized culture by stigmatizing or racializing it, while reinforcing white racial dominance in contemporary society (Din, 2012). Dressing up in another culture is an act of privilege in which someone who does not experience that oppression is able to temporarily play an exotic other without experiencing any of the attendant discrimination or stigma (Johnson, 2011). Or, as students from Ohio State's STARS (Students Teaching About Racism in Society) group put it: "You wear the costume for one day. I wear the stigma for life." In an open letter to someone who wants to dress up as "Indian" for Halloween, the author named Adrienne K. (2011) provides a poignant reminder that there is nothing funny about being Native (indigenous) in North America:

> I already know how our conversation will go. I'll ask you to please not dress up as a bastardized version of my culture for Halloween, and you'll reply that it's "just for fun" and I "should get over it." You'll tell me that you "weren't doing it to be offensive" and that "everyone knows real Native Americans don't dress like this." You'll say that you [have] a "right" to dress up as "whatever you damn well please." You'll remind me about how you're Irish and the "Irish were oppressed to." Or you'll say you're German, and you "don't get offended by people in lederhosen."
>
> But you don't understand what it feels like to be like me. I am a Native Person. You are (most likely) a white person. You walk through life everyday never having to fear of someone mis-representing your people or your culture. You don't have to worry about the vast majority of your people living in poverty, struggling with alcoholism, domestic violence, hunger, and unemployment caused by 500+ years of colonialism and federal policies aimed at erasing your existence. You don't have to walk through life everyday feeling invisible because the only images the public sees of you are fictionalized

stereotypes who don't represent who you are at all....

You are in a position of power. You might not know it, but you are. Simply because of the color of your skin, you have been afforded opportunities and privilege, because our country was built on the foundation of white supremacy....

I am not in a position of power. Native people are not in a position of power. By dressing up as a fake Indian, you are asserting your power over us, and continuing to oppress us. That should worry you.

What lessons can we glean from this insight into Halloweenism and costume appropriation?

First, the point of this consciousness-raising exercise is not to take the fun out of dressing up for Halloween. University students love Halloween parties, if only to blow off some mid-term steam. But partying is no longer a cultural time out as was once the case. A precondition of living smartly in an "always on" society is the need to anticipate the feelings of others by taking responsibility for messages sent, however inadvertently and innocently. Perhaps the best advice is to think ahead (Segers, 2012). How awkward and embarrassing to imagine yourself dressing up as a "sexy squaw" at a Halloween party, only to meet an Aboriginal woman who may have experienced sexual violence (Johnson, 2011).

Second, it is clear that racisms are proliferating and assuming a more proportional profile, not because of new racist actions but because once uncontroversial behaviours are now defined as racist or discriminatory. For example, people have been doing blackface (or face paint for Aboriginal peoples) for a century without much reaction or criticism. Now, however, it's deemed to be racist and offensive (Din, 2012). Clearly, this cultural shift in drawing the line over what is appropriate and what is appropriation should not be underestimated. Rather, the new racisms reflect the paradoxes of proliferation and proportion in a progress-oriented Canada.

A third lesson provides insight into how racism works at present. Most individual racism is rarely intentional or conscious. Rather, it consists of actions that may be interpreted by others as racist depending on the situation. In other words, it's the consequences and context that count in defining contemporary racism. Defining racism as receiver-dependent rather than sender-oriented puts racialized minorities in charge of determining what is or is not racism.

A final lesson points to the possibility that Halloween as an institution may be systemically racist. The very act of act dressing up under the banner of Halloween exerts a systemically biasing effect in a racialized and unequal society, given the unintended consequences of stereotyping, mocking, or spoofing some demographic. Perhaps it is time to mothball Halloween as a twenty-first-century anomaly, not unlike other previously popular but now deviant pastimes such as smoking in public.

Sources: Adrienne K., *Open Letter to the PocaHotties and Indian Warriors This Halloween: Native Appropriation*, October 26, 2011, retrieved from http://nativeappropriations.com; BBC News, *Harry Says Sorry for Nazi Costume*, January 13, 2005; Canadian Press, *Bozak Defends MJ Costume, Says It's Not Racist*, October 31, 2012; M. Din, [No title], retrieved from www.sociologyinfocus.com; E. Grinberg, *In Debate Over Offensive Halloween Costumes, Where's the Line?* CNN, October 30, 2012; K. Johnson, *Don't Mess Up When You Dress Up: Cultural Appropriations and Costumes*, Social Commentary for Bitchmedia, October 25, 2011, retrieved from http://bitchmagazine.org; N. K. Nittle, *Dressing Up as Someone from a Different Race for Halloween*, retrieved from http://racerelations.about.com; M. Segers, *Is Your Halloween Costume Racist?* October 30, 2012, retrieved from www.marketplace.org.

Contextualizing Racism: Canada's Official Multiculturalism

The politics of multi- or ethnocultural diversities represents a core twenty-first-century dynamic and challenge (UNESCO World Report, 2009). Then as now, multicultural societies must construct a balancing act that respects cultural diversities while promoting national unity, universally shared values, and creative encounters among groups as grounds for governance (Fleras, 2009). The challenge of preserving multicultural identities while managing social justice by promoting intercultural dialogue assumes a new prominence within the context of globalization, international migrations, and mounting urbanization.

Yet reactions are varied and shifting in assessing the costs/benefits of multicultural diversity. Many believe multicultural diversities are inherently positive in consolidating a co-operative and connected coexistence (Adams, 2007). For example, Canadian multiculturalism emerged as part of a broader civil rights movement for shoring up individual minority rights by abolishing (1) inherited forms of inequality because of prejudicial discrimination, (2) the tyranny of French-English nationalism, and (3) capricious patterns of exclusion consistent with Canada's long-standing self-image as a "white man's country" (Kymlicka, 2008a, 2008b). Others contend these diversities create conflicts by contributing to the erosion of common humanity and shared commonalities at the heart of any living together (Mansur, 2011; Pacquet, 2008). Worse still, critics argue, multiculturalism resembles an opiate for the masses that distracts and deadens by fostering the illusion of inclusion (Dua et al., 2005; Chazan et al., 2011). Still others point to the combination of globalized communications and increased intercultural contacts for creating a major challenge. In a transnational and transmigrant world, where notions of belonging and identity are increasingly de-territorialized (Fleras, 2011a), how does one go about constructing a place-based governance model for (1) engaging (governing or managing) the dynamic nature of these diversities; (2) addressing the challenges of identity within the framework of ethnocultural change; and (3) coping with a global network of diasporas and transmigrants (Walton-Roberts, 2011; Carruthers, 2013; Fleras, 2011b)? Yet others still raise a troubling question: Is Canada's multicultural response to managing this diversity an exercise in anti-racism or, alternatively, a racist instrument that glosses over issues of racism and inequality beneath a veneer of managed conviviality (Chazan et al., 2011)? Does any state multiculturalism run the risk of silencing debate over power and race, in effect generating new forms of racism ("neo-racism") in the process?

Canada represents one of a few liberal democratic societies that embraces multicultural principles as a principled basis for living together differently (Kymlicka, 2007c; Reitz, 2009). Official multiculturalism originated as political calculation aimed at addressing the national unity crisis by offering symbolic recognition and some financial assistance (Jaworsky, 1979; Plamondon, 2013). It arose as an afterthought (or expediency) for neutralizing (appeasing) established European ethnic opposition to federal moves over accommodating (defusing) Québécois nationalism and Aboriginal assertiveness over hidden government agendas (Omar, 2012; Haque, 2012). Only later did multiculturalism evolve into a "master narrative" about Canadian diversity (Chazan et al., 2011, p. 2). That it has managed to pull off the seemingly impossible by doing the wildly implausible in achieving the nearly improbable is quite astonishing: namely, to forge a working unity from its disparate parts, including a more inclusive pattern of integration, without compromising integrity, identity, and unity in the process (see Saul, 2008). In hopes of harmonizing competing ethnicities without losing control of the overall agenda, Canada's multiculturalism persists for similar reasons—that is, the pursuit of political, ideological, and economic considerations involving state functions, private interests, policy trade-offs, and electoral survival.

Multiculturalism Policy: Doing What Is Workable, Necessary, and Politically Expedient

Canada is universally regarded as a multicultural society that endorses the principles of multiculturalism. References to a multicultural society may be differently interpreted depending on the proposed level of meaning, including: Multiculturalism as *fact* (the reality of diversity in Canada); as *ideology* (beliefs, values, and norms that support the principles of living together with difference); as *policy* (official programs and formal initiatives for accommodating diversities and difference without sacrificing equality or unity); as *practice* (application of multicultural principles for practical reasons and political goals); and as social movement (the use of multiculturalism as a platform to challenge, resist, and transform) (Fleras, 2009). The descriptive or prescriptive sense of the term is downplayed in deference to Multiculturalism as official policy (hence the use of the upper-case *M*).

Official multiculturalism constitutes a complex and contested governance policy that has evolved over time in response to historical changes and socio-political contingencies (Walcott, 2011; Galabuzi, 2011). Multiculturalism originated in Canada's quest for society-building by establishing an inclusionary framework for managing diversity through removal of prejudicial attitudes and discriminatory barriers to full and equal participation (Fleras, 2012; Kunz & Sykes, 2007). It continues to persist for precisely the same reasons, namely, to make Canada safe from/for diversities by depoliticizing diversities and difference as grounds for living together differently. The goal of multiculturalism as governance has never wavered from its foundational logic: *the possibility of living together with differences without differences getting in the way of "peace, order, and good government."* Or, to put it slightly differently, to create an inclusive Canada without disrupting the status quo. Only the rules of engagement for achieving minority inclusion have changed because of demographic upheavals and political developments. Ethnicity-based solutions have given way to equity-grounded and anti-racism reforms, followed by the promotion of civic belonging and active participation, and, most recently, an integrative focus through shared values, social cohesion, and common citizenship. Table 1.1 compares each of these stages—*ethnicity, equity, civic, and integration*—on the basis of criteria in the left-hand column. Keep in mind the inevitability of (over)simplification when comparing ideal-typical categories across time and space in a world that is contextual rather than categorical (Fleras, 2012).

Analyzing the evolving stages yields several themes that draw attention to the racialized (and potentially racist) logic behind Canada's official multiculturalism (discussed in more depth in the last chapter), including:

TABLE 1.1 Program Shifts in Canada's Official Multiculturalism: From 1971 to Present

Ethnicity Multiculturalism (1970s)	Equity Multiculturalism (1980–early 1990s)	Civic Multiculturalism (1995–2005)	Integrative Multiculturalism (2006–present)
Dimension			
Cultural	Structural	Social	Societal
Focus			
Respecting differences	Fostering equality	Living together	Integration
Mandate			
Ethnicity	Race relations	Citizenship	Social cohesion
Magnitude			
Individual adjustment	Institutional accommodation	Full engagement	National Safety/security
Problem			
Prejudice	Racism/discrimination	Exclusion	Segregation/extremism
Solution			
Cultural sensitivity	Remove barriers	Inclusion	Values
Outcomes			
Cultural capital	Human capital	Social capital	National (comm)unity
Key Metaphor			
Mosaic	Level playing field	Belonging	Living together cohesively

- *Multiculturalism as Political Act:* Canada's official multiculturalism is first and foremost a political act to achieve political goals in a politically acceptable manner. It originated to address political problems and continues to flourish for precisely the same reasons, namely, an exercise in impression/conflict management that improves Canada's prospects for living together *despite* diversities and difference. In keeping with its status as a political act to advance national and vested interests, official multiculturalism dispenses with the notion of challenge and change in favour of a commitment to consensus, containment, and control.
- *Multiculturalism as Governance:* Multiculturalism in Canada goes beyond an add-on status or default option. It has evolved into a governance framework for organizing and managing the relations between dominant sector and racialized minorities (Galabuzi, 2011, p. 59). Governance can be defined as a framework of rules for governing by establishing a principled relationship and decision-making processes between ruler and ruled, with a corresponding exchange of rights and obligations in addition to principles and norms to prevent conflict and promote cohesion (Turton et al., 2007). A multicultural governance for living together differently exemplifies the politics and policies employed by central authorities (or government as a shorthand) for constructing a Canada that is safe from diversities, yet safe for diversities.
- *Multiculturalism as Canada-Building:* Building a Canada along inclusive lines is the primary objective of an official multiculturalism. The challenge is fairly straightforward: Canada must somehow transform approximately 250,000 newcomers each year into a community of citizens with a shared sense of commitment, conviction, and consensus. Multiculturalism aspires to create a social climate in which this transformation transpires. Conversely, multiculturalism focuses on creating a climate of inclusiveness that improve the terms of immigrant integration in ways that are workable, necessary, and fair.
- *Multiculturalism = Depoliticizing Differences:* Official multiculturalism is not about promoting ethnicities, celebrating diversities, tolerating an "anything goes" mentality, or establishing ethnic communities with separate power bases and group-specific rights. It is not about creating a governance that endorses collective rights over the rights of individuals. More accurately, multiculturalism is about depoliticizing (neutralizing) differences to ensure that they don't get in the way of living together. This depoliticizing rejects deep differences as inimical to a functioning Canada but tolerates differences of a relatively superficial nature, preferably within the private or personal domains. The *"pretend pluralism"* of such a liberal multiculturalism ensures the right of each person to identify with the ethnocultural tradition of his or her choice provided, of course, that cultural practices do not break the law, violate individual rights, and contravene core constitutional values (e.g., gender equity).

- *Multiculturalism as Culture-Blind Ideology of Liberal Universalism:* Multiculturalism in Canada is predicated on the principles of a liberal multicultural model. According to a liberal multiculturalism, a society of many cultures is plausible and beneficial as long as certain governance rules are in place for managing differences. This ideology claims people's commonalities as freewheeling and rights-bearing individuals take precedence over group-based differences in defining recognition or rewards. People can be culturally different (within limits) under an official multiculturalism, yet individuals should be neither penalized *nor rewarded* because of who they are or where they come from. Under the principles of a colour-blind multiculturalism, cultural differences should never be taken seriously as a matter of course (because all Canadians are equal before the law, they must be treated *equally*). Not surprisingly, Canada's official multiculturalism commits to the principle of equal opportunity for all individuals regardless of race, nationality, or ethnicity (Ghosh, 2011). Nevertheless, difference-based needs may be taken into account when necessary to foster a truly level playing field in which all Canadians are treated *as equals* (differently).

Canada's official multiculturalism as a work in progress creates a framework for innovative possibilities (Ghosh, 2011), not all of which are consistent with each other. A social climate is created in advancing (1) a respect for diversities, (2) a commitment to equality, (3) an adherence to the principles of inclusion, and (4) facilitating the integration of newcomers into Canada (Fleras, 2012). Emphasis is focused on Canada-building by constructing an inclusive Canadian governance of many (multi) depoliticized cultures through removal of discriminatory/prejudicial barriers to ensure full and equal participation for all Canadians. The doctrine of liberal universalism plays a key role in depoliticizing diversities for purposes of entitlements or recognition. The salience of differences is dismissed as little more than a superficiality or a residue—a kind of pretend pluralism—in which differences are perceived as skin-deep and irrelevant for purposes of respect or reward. In short, the inclusiveness commitments that inform an official multiculturalism are arguably anti-racist. No one, regardless of race or ethnicity, should be excluded from democratic citizenship and equal involvement in advancing the principles of an anti-racist and culture-blind governance. But an official multiculturalism that eschews transformative change in a racialized Canada leaves itself open to charges of racism as discussed in more depth in the last chapter.

Note

1 In 1939, Winston Churchill referred to Russia as a riddle wrapped in a mystery inside an enigma.

CHAPTER 2

RECONCEPTUALIZING RACISM
FROM RACISM 1.0 TO RACISMS 2.0

Introduction: Rethinking How Racisms Work

> *Nowadays we seem to have a lot of racism but very few racists. How do you explain this paradox?*
> —James M. Blaut, "The Theory of Cultural Racism"

How did racism work in the past? There once was a time when a racist could be spotted from a mile away because everyone knew what racism was and who racists were (Anderson, 2010). Racism 1.0 consisted of words, actions, and beliefs that (1) espoused the extreme right (from the Ku Klux Klan to neo-Nazi thugs); (2) endorsed Jim Crow laws segregating whites from racialized minorities; and (3) entailed ideologies that hoisted whites to the top of the evolutionary heap, thanks to their so-called superiority in mind, body, and morality. Minorities were automatically assumed to be racially inferior, although salvageable with a dollop of indoctrination, with the result that they deserved what (little) they got. Doctrines that linked race to inferiority were (1) often coded into law; (2) institutionalized in organizational practices and government programs; (3) framed as a minority problem; and (4) conveyed through policies and programs that bolstered the privileges of a white society. Racists were no less offensive in spouting racist dogmas. Loud and proud and prone toward racial slurs and derogatory slings, they stood out because of their antediluvian attitudes and loutish behaviour. More genteel racists tended to tone it down a bit by politely expressing their superiority in more condescending (patronizing) ways. These patronizing put-downs were socially acceptable in polite circles, although more extreme diatribes by the dimwitted were dismissed as a blot on an otherwise normal functioning society. The net result was largely the same: A racial caste system was constructed that bolstered the workings of a white supremacist society (West, 2012).

In short, modern racism 1.0[1] could be described as overt, blunt, direct, and deliberate. Racism 1.0 draws its inspiration from the earliest definitions of racism, which were based on the dogma that race is real and determines the appearance, thought, and behaviour of racial group members. And unless an incident was as aberrant as the Holocaust, apartheid, or segregation, it was not deemed to be racism (see Law, Phillips, & Turney, 2004). But contemporary (postmodern) racisms 2.0 differs from its modern counterpart in ways innovative yet infuriating. Hardly surprising since younger Canadians differ from their parents. Having grown up surrounded by minorities and immersed in diversity, they are less likely to panic over push-button issues related to race-based identity politics, overt prejudice, and stereotypes of racial inferiority (Byrd, 2011). In other words, both racists and racism have morphed into something different (see also Satzewich, 2004) now that old-fashioned racism is no longer socially acceptable in many social arenas (Dovidio et al., 2010b; Gilman, 2006; Pearson et al., 2009). The overtly racist activities, mindsets, and policies of the past have yielded ground to racially coded actions and coded subtexts that operate through "inaction, silence, neglect and indifference" (Battiste, 2009), yet are no less controlling or exclusionary (Alexander, 2012). The end result of this "tabooification" (Gilman, 2006) of active and open racism is twofold: First, many believe that racism is no longer a problem in a post-racial society; second, others believe we live in an era of racism without either race or racists in contrast to the open racial thinking and brazen racism of the past. More specific trends include the following themes, which expose the workings of a postmodern racisms 2.0:

- There is little consensus around the concept of racism. Its meanings, dynamics, and impacts are constantly undergoing change as the world changes (Satzewich, 2011; Titley & Lentin, 2012). For some, racism covers a multitude of actions and inactions that exclude, demean, and marginalize. For others, racism is a catch-all sin covering any injustice or criticism directed at racialized others (Lippard, 2011). For others still, racism works through active malice (bigotry) instead of structurally linked exclusions and passive indifference (Gilman, 2006). For still yet others, it is nothing less than a scavenger ideology that inhales everything in sight and spits it out in hydra-headed (multiple-headed snake) ways (Seymour, 2010). Not surprisingly, such a (dis)array of definitions leads to confusion and controversy over the amount and nature of racism in contemporary Canada.

- The fundamental divide in debates over racism is simple enough: those who see it as essentially a question of individual psychology (an ideology) versus those who frame it as a social (structural) phenomenon (Gilman, 2006; Bonilla-Silva, 1997). Privileging the notion of racism as something in the minds of racists (i.e., active malice) rather than a social condition runs a major risk, as Nils Gilman points out. It fails to address how racism and racial discrimination reflect deeply ingrained social practices and institutional habits that infiltrate people's minds and interactions between individuals.
- The application of racism labels must cover an expanding array of actions and mindsets. Instead of singular agreed-upon phenomena for analysis and measurement, many different racisms in terms of dynamics, targets, and contexts are now part of the discursive framework (Weiner, 2012). Whereas old-fashioned racism proved to be colour-conscious, neo-racisms may (1) reflect colour-blindness; (2) involve doing nothing instead of doing something when something needs improving; and (3) entail the primacy of consequences over intent as a definitive feature. There is also increased awareness that racism entails the accumulation, incorporation, and convergence of long-standing racialized practices into a society's structures, institutions, and values (Grassroots Policy Project, n.d.; Gilman, 2006). In short, racism is not necessarily the property of the morally depraved and the culturally unwashed. It is structurally central to a racialized democratic society, with a corresponding white power hierarchy (Coates, 2013).
- How do neo-racisms work in shifting from noun to verb? Racisms 2.0 are no longer framed as a relatively static thing "out there" (a noun) readily recognized and isolated. Instead of something inherent in an act, racism is increasingly conceptualized in dynamic terms (a verb) involving a process by which its status (or the label) is applied after the (f)act, depending on the context, criteria, or consequences. The focus on racism as a social construct puts the spotlight on claims-making activities that call attention to how and why troublesome issues become problematized as racism (see Best & Harris, 2013).
- Who decides what is racism? Those racialized minorities who once experienced racism were excluded from the right to define it on their terms. But there is currently an ongoing struggle over who has the power to define racism (Titley & Lentin, 2012; Pilkington, 2012). An earlier emphasis on racism as a sender-oriented phenomena (whites defined racism as something inflicted on someone else) has shifted to focus on racism as receiver-dependent process (i.e., defined by those experiencing it). Participants in A Race, Violence, and Health Project Study (2002) confirmed this by acknowledging how racism is complex, ongoing, interrelated with other incidents, and all consuming:

> There is no way to unravel a person's experiences of racism, because there is no beginning or end to these experiences in

education, employment, interactions with police and the justice system, and within their lives—these threads are interwoven with each other and throughout a person's life. Because racism is "everywhere, everyday, all the time" research participants told us that it forms a "filter" or it becomes a "smog" through which they view the world. Some said it was like water for fish: simply the element in which life is lived.... It is this continuing Canadian reality—a nightmare for some—that our project set out to explore. (Benjamin et al., 2010, p. 2)

- Racism is much more subtle in how it works. Racisms 2.0 are increasingly framed at the level of unconsciousness and consequences, supplanting an earlier emphasis on intent and awareness. These deeply wired racisms are discursively located at the institutional and cultural level instead of individual bias, with special emphasis on their systemic embeddedness in the founding assumptions and foundational principles of a society's constitutional order.
- Explicit expressions of racism (from jokes to stereotypes) are no longer tolerated in the public domain (but see Health Council of Canada, 2012). Predictably, most people go out of their way to appear non-racist to others and even to themselves (Henkel, Dovidio, & Gaertner, 2006), in the process making racism even more insidious by virtue of being normalized, resistant to change, invisible, and more difficult to detect (Anderson, 2010; Byrd, 2011). They may speak in codes by producing proxy statements to disguise their bigotry from others (polite) and from themselves (subliminal), especially in ambiguous situations when an individual can hide behind a principled excuse to justify criticism or exclusion without being labelled as a racist (Anderson, 2010).
- Expressions of prejudice and racism may have decreased in volume and popularity. Nonetheless, people appear reluctant to give up their racialized privilege (see also Norton & Sommers, 2011). Yes, Canadians may be more tolerant and accommodative, although many appear unwilling to make any concessions that entail cost or inconvenience (Anderson, 2010). There is growing support for equality in principle but not necessarily in practice, especially if loss of status is involved. Antipathy toward the "other" is expressed by a white superiority complex and a defensive white nationalism increasingly more resentful of minority demands and perceived gains (Anderson, 2010; Seymour, 2010).
- Notions of biological inferiority are increasingly passé. What prevails instead is a belief in certain cultural practices as incompatible with the mainstream, unacceptable in society, and barriers to integration. Byrd (2011, p. 1006) writes accordingly: "What is particularly distinct about the modern form of racial prejudice is the defense of traditional values (such as belief in meritocracy ... that allow victim blaming to occur ...), exaggeration of cultural differences instead of claiming outright genetic inferiority and difference...." Yet the culturalization of racism is

no less exclusionary in its effects, especially when cultural differences are so essentialized that they become naturalized and as inherent to a group as biology (Seymour, 2010; Fleras, 2004).
- There is a tendency to delegitimize race and racism as determinants in defining who gets what. Individuals are increasingly in denial about the existence of racism in those race-blind jurisdictions where race is deemed to be irrelevant, thanks to the inception of an official multiculturalism, human rights legislations, and an ideology of inclusion. A commitment to racial color-blindness reflects a belief that ignoring differences promotes intergroup harmony by virtue of denying the salience of race in allocating valued resources (Williams, 2011; Southern Poverty Law Center, 2009). In reality, a belief in a colourblind, post-racial society allows white privileged folk to ignore the disadvantaged experiences of others, hence proving a form of racism in its own right by virtue of transforming disadvantaged groups into perpetrators of their own exclusion.
- Awareness is growing that race as racism does not work in isolation. Instead of disappearing, becoming less of a problem, or losing its sting, race as racialized category intersects with other negative identity markers (or axes of power and difference), such as gender or class, to amplify the exclusion or exploitation (Das Gupta, 2009; Douglas, 2008).
- Is racism normal or an aberration? Although routinely practised by many, racism was framed as a departure from the normal functioning of society. By contrast, racism is increasingly framed as a normal part of the human experience, albeit with negative effects. For example, consider how racial stereotypes reflect a universal tendency to simplify by classifying experience into meaningful categories (Cohen, 2011; Dovidio, Hewson, Glick, & Esses, 2010). But the normalization of universal human experience raises an awkward question: Should racism as cognition be tolerated as another point of view?

In sum, racisms at present no longer work the way they did in the past. Older theories tended to link racism with a specific set of beliefs and actions, with clearly defined victims and victimizers. This racism-as-a-thing approach is increasingly out of scholarly vogue, having been replaced by a focus that acknowledges the complexity of racisms 2.0 as a contested and contingent dynamic (racisms-as-process). Discourses have shifted as well: References to institutional and systemic racism are challenging those individualistic models that tended to blame the victim or victimizer. Finally, singular references to racism are increasingly displaced by frames to *acknowledge a plurality of forms, impacts, and solutions.* The politics of racisms are shown to exist at different levels; are expressed in a variety of ways; and impact differently on racialized minorities. Table 2.1 compares modern racism 1.0 with the postmodern racisms 2.0.

Table 2.1　Shifting Discourses: How Racisms Work

Racism 1.0	Racisms 2.0
Aberrant individual/institutional behaviour	Normal individual/institutional behaviour (stereotyping)
Contrary to Canadian values	Constitutive feature of Canada-building and Canadian society
Deliberate Intended Conscious Overt	Inadvertent Unintended Unconscious (subliminal) Covert
Doing something	Doing nothing
Focusing on differences	Discounting differences when necessary
Minority problem (inferior)	Majority problem + white superiority complex
Attitude (prejudice) driven + Individual	Systemic and institutionalized + Societal
Singular frame of reference	Multiple expressions
Racism alone	Intersecting inequalities (race, gender, class, etc.)
Racism as thing (noun)	Racism as process (verb)
Easily defined as a thing out there	Constructed and contested • contextual/situational • multi-perspectival

CASE STUDY

The Dynamics of Anti-Chinese/Asian Racisms: From "Yellow Peril" and White Xenophobia to Model Minority Racism

The evolution of anti-Asian (especially anti-Chinese) racism in Canada captures the transformational shift in how racisms worked in the past, in contrast to how they work at present (Abrams & Moio, 2009). Historically, few groups endured more racism and discrimination than the Chinese (Wong, 2007). Canada's reaction to early Chinese immigration reveals an embarrassing legacy that many Canadians would prefer to ignore or forget (Baureiss, 1985; Li, 1988). Canadians may be upset to learn that racism in the past was openly and ruthlessly directed at non-whites. Both the courts and the legal system were profoundly and institutionally implicated in Canada's racist treatment of Asian/Chinese immigrants prior to entry and upon settlement (see Walker, 1998; Backhouse, 1999). Even more dismaying is an awareness of how Canada-building was built upon and inseparable from institutionalized racism. In that anti-Asian/anti-Chinese racism persists into the present, albeit in a more subtle manner, the adage of "continuity in change" is confirmed.

The earliest Chinese migrants came to Canada in 1858 to take advantage of the gold rush. The second cohort arrived as virtually indentured labour for building the Canadian Pacific Railway, with nearly 17,000 arrivals from mainland China between 1882 and 1885 (the total population in British Columbia was 53,000 in 1891) (Xiao-Feng & Norcliffe, 1996). Chinese migrants were seen as cheap and exploitable workhorses for the most hazardous sections of the railway, but expendable once the task was completed. A split labour market quickly prevailed: Chinese workers earned $1 a day (only 80 cents if they did not buy provisions from the company store), compared to $2 a day for Canadian workers or $3.50 for American workers (Baureiss, 1985).

From the time of their arrival in Canada, Chinese immigrants were subjected to legislation that sought to destroy the community, restrict political activity, and inhibit healthy social growth (Wong, 2007). According to Liu Xiao-Feng and Glen Norcliffe (1996), virtually every industry in British Columbia relied on Chinese labour. Nevertheless, the Chinese were targets of prejudice and discrimination, exploited as cheap labour, and manipulated as strike-breakers in defiance of labour union relations. They were denied the right to vote, prohibited from working on government projects or in coal mines, excluded from holding hand-loggers' licences, prevented from settling on Crown land, barred from the professions of law or pharmacology, and banned from hiring white women to work in restaurants or laundries. Numerous tactics were deployed for restricting their entry in Canada; nonetheless, these stalling tactics proved ineffective because of the demand for cheap labour during the railway construction period (Bolaria & Li, 1988; Satzewich, 2000).

Public antipathy was openly palpable. Federal plans to import an additional five thousand Chinese for the construction of the Grand Trunk Railway elicited a sharp editorial rebuke from the September 1906 issue of *Saturday Night*:

> We don't want Chinamen in Canada. This is a white man's country and white men will keep it so. The slant-eyed Asiatic with his yellow skin, his unmanly humility, his cheap wants, would destroy the whole equilibrium of industry…. We cannot assimilate them. They are an honest, industrious, but hopelessly inferior race. (cited in Fraser, 1988, p. 12)

Upon completion of the railway, many returned to China with their savings. Others were stranded in Canada because of insufficient funds, with few options except unskilled employment in laundries and gardens. Those who stayed behind were subject to caricature and abusive treatment by the general public and provincial politicians. In the same year the railway was completed, the British Columbia government passed the 1884 Chinese Regulation Act, arguing that Chinese "were not disposed to be governed by our laws; are useless in instances of emergency; and desecrate graveyards." The demonization of the Chinese knew no limits. They were frequently subjected to racial invectives by organized labour, who demonized them as strike-breaking "scabs." In Vancouver's first race riot in 1887, three hundred white workers, fearful of losing their jobs to inexpensive foreign labour hired by local contractors, destroyed a Chinese labour camp and expelled hundreds of workers out of town (Donaldson, 2013). Others vilified them as a kind of "yellow peril" that would undermine the purity and integrity of a "white man's province" (Roy, 1989).

CS The exploitation of the Chinese as a political football or as electoral scapegoats played into white xenophobia. Even the withdrawal of Chinese into their own communities for protection had the perverse effect of inflaming public hostility by reinforcing suspicion. For example, Vancouver's best-known race riot in 1907 laid waste to much of Chinatown (Donaldson, 2013; Crompton, 2012).

The lack of political voice or representation rendered the Chinese vulnerable to exclusion and exploitation (Roy, 1989). This is not to say that they all passively accepted these injustices. Protests, strikes, and lawsuits were employed in reaction to negative government legislation and discriminatory practices (see Ip, 1990). But resistance proved somewhat futile. Under public pressure, successive governments imposed financial disincentives to deter entry. The first federal Chinese Exclusion Act in 1885 imposed a head tax of $50 on Chinese immigrants. This amount was increased by increments until it reached a total of $500 in 1903—a sum equivalent to two years' wages or the cost of a new home in Vancouver. An additional $200 was required in 1910 as landing tax for all Asian immigrants. Between 1886 and 1923, more than $22 million was collected in head-tax payments. Admittedly, the first Immigration Act of 1869 had imposed a head tax of $1.50 per person on everyone, while a 1914 landing fee of $250 was universally applied, but only the Chinese were singled out for special taxation.

The head tax interrupted the flow of Chinese migrants, but did not curb it (Xiao-Feng & Norcliffe, 1996). The federal government curtailed Chinese immigration in 1923 following passage of the Chinese Immigration Act, making the Chinese the only racialized group to be specifically prohibited from entry to Canada because of race. This exclusionary injunction also forced the separation of Chinese men from their wives and partners, in effect aborting any Chinese population growth in Canada. Only forty-four Chinese were granted permission to enter Canada between 1923 and 1946 (Xiao-Feng & Norcliffe, 1996). This racist ban was lifted in 1947 with the repeal of the Chinese Immigration Act and passage of Canada's first Citizenship Act, yet only spouses and unmarried children of Chinese in Canada were allowed admission until 1962, unlike the relatively unrestricted immigration from Europe and the United States. The introduction of the point system in 1967 facilitated ease of entry for Chinese immigrants from Hong Kong or Taiwan, but none from the Communist mainland.

The status of Chinese Canadians has improved in recent years. Successive generations of Chinese have moved from relative social isolation to active involvement in claiming their rightful status as Canadian citizens. Chinese Canadians are increasingly seen as model minorities because of their working habits and family values. Nevertheless, they remain ensnared in a paradox of simultaneous acceptance yet rejection. They are wanted for their labour, capital, and expertise, but dismissed when they assert their rights to be an integral part of the Canadian community (Gilmour et al., 2012). This double standard ("damned if they do, damned if they don't") reflects a distinction between "good" Asians and "bad" Asians. Chinese and Asian Canadians are acceptable when they embrace capitalist and liberal values by exerting themselves and constructing success stories that legitimize the principles and myths of meritocracy. Bad Asians, on the other hand, exploit the generosity of the nation, excel to the point of embarrassing Canadians, create social divisions through their loyalty to their homeland and ethnic culture, and retreat to their ethnic enclaves. The dialectics/paradox of being "too Asian" is unmistakable.

> Asians are admired for their perceived economic efficiency and intelligence and fear for their frugality and cunning; revered for their exceptional work ethic and vilified as unknowable due to their inhuman inability to withstand hardship; respected for their family values and perpetually suspect due to their fierce loyalty to home, ethnic community, and foreign nation. Rather than being perceived in an either/or linear dichotomy, Asians can be both good and bad as they bolster national mythologies while simultaneously endangering the status quo. (Park, 2011, p. 646)

Their current status has proven equally contradictory and double-edged: The stereotyping of Chinese/Asian Canadians as model minorities has seen to that. But unlike a stereotype threat, which can depress performance, reference to stereotype promise involves framing through the lens of a positive type cast, with the result that the success frame is validated and imposed in ways that define Asians as smart, industrious, and high achievers (Lee, 2012). The end result of this stereotype promise is undue pressure on model minorities to excel, their sense of failure if they are unable to fit into a narrowly defined success frame, and the possibility of an emerging Asian tax in the United States, where Asian students need nearly perfect SAT scores (1,550) for acceptance into elite universities, compared to test scores among both whites (1,410) and blacks (1,100) (Espenshade & Radford, 2009; Lee, 2012).

In short, prejudicial attitudes and racist attacks persist (Li, 1988). Canada has become friendlier, Donald T. Wong concedes (cited in Donaldson, 2013), yet Chinese contribution to Canada-building continues to be downplayed. Instead of being labelled inferior or unassimilable, Chinese Canadians are criticized for cultural practices denounced as disruptive to Canada's natural harmony. Asian Canadians are taken to task for establishing ethnic enclaves in the Greater Toronto Area, such as Markham, or scapegoated for driving up real estate prices in Vancouver (Crompton, 2012). They are also chided for creating a host of social problems, from monopolizing medical and postsecondary schools (for example, the 1979 current affairs show *W5* scapegoated Chinese students for stealing spaces from white students [Heer, 2012]), to transforming certain universities such as UBC or Waterloo into largely "Asian spaces." The November 2010 issue of *Maclean's* magazine published an article entitled "Too Asian?" which approvingly quoted students who criticized universities with too many "Asians" for increasing the competition for entry and grades, while imposing a dampening effect on the party scene. In doing so, the article reinforced the same tired stereotypes of the dreaded "yellow peril" that have circulated for the past 150 years (Gilmour et al., 2012). These attacks are less direct than in the past. Nevertheless, the undercurrent of thinly veiled dislike is no less disconcerting in reinforcing the obvious. Racism in racialized societies never disappears; it reappears in a variety of different disguises as demonstrated in the Insight box that follows.

INSIGHT

Too Asian: Plus ça change, plus c'est la même chose

The politics of "Too Asian" came to the fore yet again in mid-2012. The currency designers for Canada's $100 bill had purged the ethnicity of a woman from an early draft of the banknote, following focus groups' complaints that the woman was "too Asian" to represent country and currency. According to material acquired by the Canadian Press under the Access to Information Act, focus groups' participants in Fredericton and Montreal objected to a contentious image on the back of a bill that featured a photograph of a "South Asian"-looking woman[1] peering into a microscope. (Interestingly, the focus group on Toronto approved of the image on the grounds that it represented Canada's multicultural diversity.) Their objections were fourfold:

- This image did not represent Canada
- It was unfair to depict one ethnicity without including other minorities
- Images invoked stereotypes of "Asians" as scientists or excelling in technology
- The yellow-brown colour of the bill reinforces the racialization of "Asians"

In a move consistent with the Bank of Canada's policy of not highlighting specific ethnicities (i.e., ethnic neutrality),[2] the bank ordered a redrawn image of a woman based on a supposedly neutral (fabricated) ethnicity, who looks lighter and more Caucasian.

Reaction to this about-face was swift. The bank's attempt to neutralize (sanitize) the woman's ethnicity came under criticism for caving into racist rant. Spokespersons for the Chinese Canadian National Council called the reversal "racist" for "ethnically cleansing" racialized minorities from Canada's public domain (see also Decoste, 2013). Critics also argued that the Caucasian-looking woman is not ethnically neutral. More accurately, she reflects the racialized ethnicity/whiteness of the dominant group in Canada. Besides, others pointed out, what generic features would qualify as Canadian enough to meet people's expectations? In hopes of damage control, the Bank of Canada governor issued an apology for those "offended" and criticized his bank's handling of the situation as below "standards Canadians justifiably expect." But the apology did little to mollify the anger of those who acknowledged the unattractive truths of polite racism brought to the surface by the Mint Switch controversy,[3] including the following unspoken truths:

1) What is not said or done in racialized contexts may be more important than what is when the politics of political correctness are involved.

2) Subliminal racism? Were the focus groups concealing a latent dislike of racialized minorities by hiding behind the smokescreen of principled objections to the image?

3) Whiteness continues to be perceived as neutral, i.e., neither an ethnicity nor a race, but the norm/default option, a standard by which others are judged and evaluated.

4) What does it mean to be a Canadian in our collective imaginary? Why can't people of colour represent a multicultural Canada that claims to abide by the principles of multiculturalism?

5) Media articles repeatedly used the word "Asians" rather than "Asian-Canadians," thus reinforcing an "us" versus "them" mentality in a Canada that strives for inclusion.

Was this a tempest in the proverbial teapot? The evolving face of racism in a white Canada? Admittedly, controversy over "the colour of money" appears petty in a world convulsed by hatred of others (from the protracted civil war in Syria to gang warfare in Mexico). However miniscule the incident, it reinforces the following insight: Once the big problems of racism are addressed (our parents' racism, for example, from racist slurs to open discrimination), many existing smaller problems now loom larger because of greater awareness and shifting intellectual tides, resulting in inevitable disappointment and dismay for racialized minorities. Regardless of the assessment, the conclusion seems clear. Contemporary racisms in Canada are not always what they appear to be or what we thought they look like. They assume a variety of discourses and different forms because of varying contexts, criteria, and consequences. The new Canada just got a bit more interesting and unsettled.

1 The focus groups commented on the woman as Asian (normally from China or thereabouts), whereas the Bank of Canada referred to a retouched photograph of a South Asian woman (i.e., from India or Pakistan or regions nearby).
2 Only images of the Queen or Canadian prime ministers as actual people are permitted to appear on banknotes. This policy may explain why Frederick Banting did not appear on a banknote (the theme of medical innovations was originally slated for the five-dollar bill), although a bottle of insulin was prominently featured at the forefront.
3 It is interesting to note that recently the Bank of Canada dropped the idea of celebrating gay marriages, black hockey players, and turban-wearing RCMP officers on its new plastic bank notes in favour of more conventional images (a train, a ship, a monument), despite widespread support among focus groups for themes of diversity, inclusiveness, and multiculturalism (Beeby, 2013).

Sources: G. Robertson, Woman's Ethnicity Edited Out of Redesigned $100 Bill, *Globe and Mail*, August 18, 2012; M. Mahtani, Don't Bank on Inclusivity, *Globe and Mail*, August 21, 2012; L. Kane, Carney Sorry for Design Debacle, *Toronto Star*, August 21, 2012; D. Beeby, Image of Asian-Looking Woman Removed from New $100 Bills, *Canadian Press*, reprinted in the *Waterloo Region Record*, August, 18, 2012; D. Beeby, Canada $100 Bill Controversy: Mark Carney, Bank of Canada Governor, Issues Apology, *Huffington Post Business Canada*, August 20, 2012; R. Ruparelia, The Currency of Racism in Canada, *Toronto Star*, August 22, 2012; P. Banwatt, Cut the Bank of Canada Some Slack, *Huffington Post Business Canada*, August 21, 2012; D. Beeby, Gays, Blacks, Nixed as Images for Bank Notes, *Canadian Press*, reprinted in the *Waterloo Region Record*, February 11, 2013.

Deconstructing the Problem of Racism

Racism has proven one of those "snarl" words that manages to provoke even as it perplexes. Yet perplexities over racism have not prompted a call for greater clarification. Nor has public debate yielded much consensus over its magnitude (how much) or scope (what kind). The prospect of conceptualizing racism under a singular frame of reference now appears remote to nonexistent, judging by proliferating terms of references:

> Politically correct racism (Chesler, 2013); entitlement racism (Essed, 2013); closet racism (Gorski, 2004); casual racism (Athwal, 2013) homey racism (Sharma, 2011); benevolent/altruistic racism (Weiner, 2012; Prashad, 2000); medical racism (Hoberman, 2012); incidental racism (Gallagher, 2003); globalized racism (Fekete, 2009); two-faced racism (Picca & Feagin, 2007), laissez-faire racism (Bobo, 2004); silent racism (Trepagnier, 2010); environmental racism (Pulido, 2000); inferential racism (Hall, 2000); "soft" racism (Hundal, 2006); new age racism (Brown, 2003); civic racism (Soutphommasanes, 2013); aversive racism (Dovidio, Gaertner, & Kawakami, 2010); transit racism (Mann, 2007); transportation racism (Bullard et al., 2004); neo-racism/racism without race (Balibar & Wallerstein, 1991); neo-liberal and colour-blind racism (Giroux, 2004); experiential racism (Bolton & Feagin, 2004); integrative racism (Dei, 2000); masked racism (Davis, 1998); intellectual racism (Huston, 1995); closet racism (Gorski, 2004); racism 1.0/2.0 (Wise, 2009a); reverse racism (Wise, 2002); enlightened racism (Jhally & Lewis, 1992); double-blind racism/dog-whistle racism/image-borne racism (Galabuzi, 2010); differentialist racism (Taguieff, 2009); religious racism (Blaut, 1992); cultural racism, modern racism (Barker, 1981); anti-racism racism (Jeanpierre, 1965); quiet racism (D'Angelo, 2013); genteel racism (Coates, 2008); masked racism (Davis, 1998); multicultural racism (Fleras, 2004); democratic racism (Henry & Tator, 2010); discursive racism (Henry & Tator, 2002); two-faced racism (Picca & Feagin, 2007); acute racism (E. Anderson in Adkins, 2013); colonial racism (Patton Jr., 1996); paternalistic racism (Meyers, 2004); Eurocentric racism (Asante, 2011); new racism (Sivanandan, 2009); elite racism (Finnegan & Johnson, 2011); table-side racism (Rusche & Brewster, 2008); anti-Muslim racism (Moor, 2010); anti-immigrant/anti-asylum racism (Bhavnani et al., 2005); elite racism (Finnegan & Johnson, 2011); subjective/objective racism (Mayer & Michelot, 2001); nice racism (Goldberg, 2006); white racism, anti-white racism, hegemonic racism (Winant, 2004); internalized racism (Jones, 2000); epistemological racism (Scheurich & Young, 1997; Kuokkanen, 2009); civilizational racism (Scheurich & Young, 2002); intellectual racism (James & Shadd, 2001); pre-reflective/post-reflective gut racism (Halstead, 1988); global racism, state racism (Hesse, 2004); infrastructural racism (Sammel, 2009); xeno-racism (Fekete, 2009); internalized racism (Grassroots Policy Project, n.d.); elite/situated racism (Bhavnani, Mirza, & Meeto, 2005); neo-racism (Cassin et al., 2007); muted racism (Davis, 2007). And last, but hardly least, the possibility of a Canadian racism (CRRF, 2008).

Clearly, then, references to racism can span a spectrum of bewildering possibilities in terms of what they look like, how they work, and why they multiply (Fekete, 2013a). On one side are the overtly personal and the openly defamatory expressions whose intent is to harm or exclude; on the other are those subtle and subconscious forms that generally escape detection except to victims; on yet another side are institutional patterns that deliberately or inadvertently confer advantage to some but not others; and on still yet another side are those systemic racisms embedded in the founding assumptions and foundational principles (*infrastructures*) of society's constitutional order (Bonilla-Silva, 1997). Racism may be spontaneously and sporadically expressed in isolated acts at irregular intervals because of individual impulse or insensitivity. Or it may be institutionalized and routinized through discriminatory patterns that inadvertently exclude or exploit without public awareness of either process or impact. Certain actions are unmistakably racist, others are labelled racist to foreclose debate, and still others come to be defined as racist because of context or consequence. Some see racism as something that individuals do (i.e., inflict on others), while others claim racism involves what people don't do when something needs doing. Finally, racism is increasingly conceptualized as a multifaceted process (verb) rather than a singular thing (noun) out there as was the case in the past. Such a raft of questions complicates the process of defining racism, since meanings and forms are complex and contingent on different historical circumstances and specific situational contexts (Gopalkrishnan & Babacan, 2007).

Victims often experience racism differently depending on race, ethnicity, gender, class, age, sexuality, and other markers of identity. Aboriginal peoples endure racism from a continuing legacy of (neo)colonialism, resulting in inferiorizing of aboriginality as hopelessly naive, pathologically dependent, or dangerously menacing. Blacks are exposed to anti-black racism that reflects an ideology of diminished and racialized expectations associated with the legacy of institutionalized slavery and Jim Crow laws (West, 2012), as well as media-driven stereotypes of black males as violent, dangerous, and prone to criminality (ACLC, 2009). As Stephen Lewis wrote in his 1992 report to the premier of Ontario:

> First, what we are dealing with, at root, and fundamentally, is anti-Black racism.... It is Blacks who are being shot [by police], it is Black youth that is unemployed in excessive numbers, it is Black students who are being inappropriatedly streamed in schools, it is Black kids who are disproportionately dropping out, it is housing communities with large concentrations of Black residents where the sense of vulnerability and disadvantage is most acute, it is Black employees, professionals, and non-professional, on whom the doors of upward equity slam shut. Just as the soothing balm of multiculturalism cannot mask racism, so racism cannot mask its primary target. (cited in ACLC, 2009)

As well, Canadians with Middle Eastern backgrounds are victimized by racisms involving a deep antipathy to Islam compounded by the post-9/11 war on terrorism. The term "Islamophobia" (literally a fear of Islam) refers to hostility toward Muslims and Middle Eastern peoples that tends to dehumanize an entire faith as fundamentally alien, its followers as irrational and violent, and its underlying message as one of global domination (Rendall & Macdonald, 2008). In short, the concept of racism does not reflect a one-size-fits-all dynamic, as Stuart Hall (1978) famously notes, particularly in relationship to other social relations:

> There have been many different racisms—each historically specific and articulated in a different way within the societies in which they appear. Racism is always historically specific in this way, whatever common features it may appear to share with other similar social phenomenon. Though it may draw on the cultural and ideological traces which are deposited in society by previous historical phases, it always assumes specific forms which arise out of the present—not the past—conditions and organizations of society.

Such diverse specificities pose a conceptual challenge. Efforts to conceptualize racisms can prove tricky insofar as references to racism can mean everything, yet nothing—a kind of floating signifier ostensibly full of sound and sizzle signifying everything yet nothing (Walcott, 2012). Any consensus in rethinking racisms collapses because debates are splintered over (1) definitions; (2) nature and magnitude; (3) causes, consequences, and persistence; and (4) proposed solutions. Consider the challenges: First, racism refuses to go away even though many would like it to. Instead of atrophying out of existence as many had predicted, racism has proven notoriously resistant and adaptive—intellectually dead, but never quite interred—with the potential to provoke during times of stress or anxiety. For example, a new brand of a white superiority complex flourishes under the guise of a commitment to a colour-blind, post-racial society (Alexander, 2012; Williams, 2011). Second, racism is proving to be a "scavenger" ideology that parasitically pounces on the most unlikely of sources, bobbing and bending to escape detection, and losing its precision when loosely used or analyzed too closely (Frederickson, 2002). Third, racism can mean whatever people want it to mean, with the result that it can mean everything yet nothing. Not surprisingly, unpacking (deconstructing) its "what," "why," "where," and "when" has proven more elusive than many imagined. Fourth, racism has become so expansive in scope and application, with such an array of meanings from context to context, that it no longer conveys an air of menace.

INSIGHT

The Banality of Racism: Normalizing Toxicity

In 1963, Hannah Arendt published a book entitled *Eichmann in Jerusalem: A Report on the Banality of Evil*. Arendt argued that the greatest evils in history generally, and the Holocaust in particular, were rarely the result of fanatics or sociopaths. On the contrary, unspeakable crimes against humanity were perpetrated by ordinary people who, uncritically, went about their everyday business with a view that their actions were normal and consistent with societal premises and state priorities (see also Edward Herman's *The Triumph of the Market*). In the case of Eichmann, a key functionary in the Nazi death camp machinery, his complicity in the mass annihilation of millions of Jews and other undesirables reflected a failure to critically imagine reality from another person's point of view. In other words, concluded Arendt, evil was banal because it was "thought-defying," namely, uncritical, mechanical, routine, and egocentric.

Reference to Arendt's expression "the banality of evil" spawned a host of experimental studies from Stanley Milgram's obedience experiment to Zimbardo's work on staged role playing among prison inmates and prison guards to Jane Eliott's much-celebrated blue eye/brown eye experiments. The expression also triggered philosophical debates over the nature of human nature. That is, to what extent is there a "little Eichmann" in all of us, so that everybody is capable of deplorable acts in situational circumstances? Consider only the normalized patterns of torture and abuse demonstrated most recently in Iraq's Abu Ghraib prison by none other than fighting-for-freedom American soldiers.

A parallel line of reasoning can be applied to racism. For many, racism is perceived as a deviant and/or irrational act by the deficient or the defiant, with an intention to hurt, exploit, or deny. Paradoxically, racism was not always perceived as an aberration. Until the early 1950s, racism (as we now know it in the sense of inferiority and hierarchy) was so ingrained in the normal functioning of society that just drawing attention to it (let alone doing something about it) took volumes of incidents, protests, and traumas to overturn people's deeply embedded biases (Herman, 1995). For example, intellectuals prior to the 1860s defended slavery on grounds of its moral superiority as a service to slaves, with a corresponding burden imposed on whites. Stephen Jay Gould, in his *Mismeasure of Man*, has also demonstrated how science was manipulated by way of IQ testing (scientific racism) as proof of black inferiority. Finally, the word "racism" did not even enter the English language until the mid-1930s. As a result, dislike or mistreatment of the "other" was deemed acceptable or unavoidable, and justified in the grounds of Divine Will, laws of nature, or the relentless march of Progress.

Now, of course, people know better. Or perhaps it is more accurate to say people know better than to spout racist drivel without inviting scorn or risking reprisals. Racism works in a different way. Emphasis has shifted away from overt and direct acts of racism and racial discrimination to incorporate more covert and indirect forms embedded and normalized at individual (subliminal) and institutional (systemic) levels. Overwhelmingly, racisms are expressed by people who go about their daily lives without much awareness of how their whiteness privileges them but disprivileges others. Or racism is perpetuated within institutions and by institutional practices without much thought to the systemic bias implicit in a "business as usual" mindset. As well, a commitment to "treating everyone the same around here" may sound progressive in theory. In practice, however, it can exert unintended yet negative racist consequences since a one-size-fits-all mentality can prove discriminatory when differences need to be taken into account to reverse the legacy of past discrimination. In short, racism has become "*boring*." A focus on consequences (not intent), the systemic (not conscious), and the unintended (not deliberate) reinforces its status as banal rather than egregious, predictable rather than exceptional, mundane rather than extraordinary, implicit rather than explicit, and fundamental rather than incidental (Gopalkrishnan & Habacan, 2007). Even perpetrators of racial violence may be ordinary people who offend as they go about their daily lives, given the presence of everyday sentiments of prejudice woven into a society's social fabric (Iganski, 2010). The expression "the banality of racism" captures the routinization of racism within the very functioning and foundations of society. Or, as pointed out by Gershevitch, Lamoin, and Dawes (2010, p. 230), when applied to the Australian context:

> Racism today involves, generally, a more slippery and subtle process. It can be supremely nuanced ... most Australians behave in racist ways unconsciously and surreptitiously....

Exclusion may occur with purportedly good excuses such as refusal to employ somebody because of poor English language competency even when good skills in this area are not a job requirement. But the most common form of racism ... a kind of racism toward otherness, toward the different outsider who is not seen to belong or could be a potential threat. Racism in the twenty-first[-century] Australia, like racism in many parts of the world, has therefore morphed into a complex pattern of dislike based on a range of qualifications around difference.

To be sure, no one is suggesting that racism is a trivial problem. On the contrary, its "banalization" has rendered it even more problematic in terms of recognition or responses. The silences of a banal racism intensify its potency precisely because it is perceived as harmless (Trepagnier, 2010). Nor is there any intent under the banner of normalcy to justify or minimize its destructive impact on racialized minorities. Rather, references to the banality of racism reflects its mundane status as thought-defying, even as people begin to celebrate the emergence of a so-called post-racial society that, paradoxically, remains as racialized and Eurocentric as ever in terms of what is normal, acceptable, and desirable. Its ordinariness is a reminder that, no matter what people say, racism is integral to the functioning of a racialized society (Chandra & Airhihenbuwa, 2010).

Theorizing Racisms: Ideological Versus Structural Paradigms

Any theorizing of racism must address its ontological status—that is, the nature of its existence. To date, the theorizing of racism proposes two ideal typical camps: ideological and structural (Bonilla-Silva, 1997). Each of these paradigms differs discursively in defining the relationship of racism to society with respect to origins, characteristics, and impact. Both paradigmatic models also provide a framework for exposing how racisms work differently, although any distinctions should be construed as categorical rather than contextual, analytical rather than empirical.

Ideological Racisms

Most theorizing tends to frame racisms within an ideological frame of reference (Hier & Bolaria, 2007, p. 31). Both micro and macro variations prevail. With micro-level theories, racism is framed at the level of social psychology, with individuals and their attitudes as a primary focus. Variations in ideological theories of racisms notwithstanding, a pattern can be discerned involving widespread applicability. First, racism is defined as a set of ideas (beliefs) and ideals (norms or values). Second, these beliefs induce individuals to formulate negative attitudes (prejudice). Third, these prejudicial attitudes generate the discriminatory actions that exclude and exploit. Fourth, changing people's attitudes provides the key to eradicating racism.

Racisms at the macro-ideological level are conceptualized at collective levels. Racially formed categories secure an organizing principle of social organization that shapes both individual identities and societal dynamics. Take Marxist or socialist theories of racism (Pitcher, 2012; West, 2009; Bolaria & Li, 1988). Racisms are critical in securing a modern capitalist economy. They are generated by the material conditions of life involving the means of production that divide the society into owners and workers, with racism as a hegemonic device dividing the working class while enhancing profit margins. Those theories that posit class as a central explanatory framework tend to reduce racism to the level of a legitimating ideology, concocted by the rich to divide or distract the working classes. Racism reflects a combination of prejudice and power that allows dominant sectors to impose their dominance at all institutional levels of society (Carmichael & Hamilton, 1967). Equating racism with false consciousness situates it within an ideological framework of explanation.

However popular, ideological theories are no analytical match for theorizing the complexity of racism. As Joe Feagin explains, racism is neither a surface-level feature nor is it reducible to an epiphenomenal by-product of more fundamental forces. Racism must be seen instead within the broader context of society, with many interrelated features (systemic) that pervade and interconnect major social groups, networks, asymmetrical power relations, and institutions. Moreover, critics of ideological theories argue that racism within the workplace (split labour markets) and xenophobic attitudes cannot be reduced entirely to the level of epiphenomena. On the contrary, racism constitutes an organizational system in its own right that acknowledges its mutually constitutive relations to culture, language, and ideologies of white superiority (Bonilla-Silva, 1997; also West, 2009).

Structural Racisms

Structural theories of racism do not reject the importance of ideological theories. On the contrary, racism is theorized as the controlling ideology of a racialized society (i.e., a society structured along race lines) (Bonilla-Silva, 1997). Racism is thus the *source* of much ideology rather than the result of it since societies are inherently (structurally) racialized. First, racialized societies are structured along the lines of founding (white) assumptions and foundational (Eurocentric) principles. The constitutional order of society (from values to agendas) is racialized to reflect, reinforce, and advance whitestream realities, priorities, and interests. Second, racism is also structured around the placement of racialized actors into preconceived categories for purposes of exclusion, control, or exploitation. References to these racial ideologies not only explain the status of racialized minorities, they also account for the allocation of valued resources along socially constructed racial(ized) lines. The totality of these racialized social relations and racialized practices constitutes the racialized structure of society, alongside a racialized hierarchy that benefits some and disadvantages others. The principles of critical race theory capture the theorizing of racism along structural lines.

Several characteristics inform a structurally based theorizing of racism:

- The enduring and systemic character of racism must be situated within the bigger picture, namely, the reality that society is *founded on* the principle of advancing a racialized and Eurocentric society; *grounded in* the exploitation and oppression of Aboriginal peoples and racialized minorities; and *bounded by* the need to preserve the prevailing and racialized distribution of power and privilege (Feagin, 2006, p. 47). According to critical race theory, society and its constituent components are neither value-free nor neutral. More to the point, all societies are racialized because, as social constructions, they reflect, reinforce, and advance the privileged subjectivity of those in power. Appeals to neutrality or objectivity are neither realistic nor unattainable; after all, both the substance and process of law (other institutions too) are structured in patterns of dominance. A commitment to Eurocentricity permeates national narratives and institutional discourses, in the process creating duplicitous fictions in promulgating the primacy of white superiority (Valdes et al., 2002). Preserving the interests of power rather than the pursuit of justice also constitutes the guiding force behind legal judgments and institutional processes (Aylward, 1999).
- For ideological theories, racisms are normally framed as individual prejudice, expressed in hostile words or discriminatory deeds toward others who are racially or ethnically different (Law et al., 2004). But racism is not just about individual attitudes and personal acts. Society as a whole and the relations between different strata or groups are involved as well, including patterns of exclusion and power involving

FYI: What Is Critical Race Theory?

A critical race theory employs a critically informed analytical lens to study the structure of race relations, power, and inequality in society (Rollack & Gilborn, 2011; Chandra & Airhihenbuwa, 2010; Abrams & Moio, 2009; Thobani, Smith, & Razack, 2010). The race concept is refracted through the prism of racialization and racism, as the following attributes of critical race theory demonstrate:

- Race is not a biological reality but a socially constructed convention resulting in a lived reality that reflects and reinforces the interests of those who constructed or control it.

- Neither society nor its institutions are ideologically neutral or colour-blind but are ideological loaded to reflect its socially constructed status as a white supremacist regime. Race and racism are thus inextricably linked to historical, political, and economic moments (Davis, 2007).

- Institutional racism is pervasive and ingrained in the fabric of society (Bell, 2008; UCLA School of Public Affairs/Critical Race Studies, n.d.). Law and justice play a key role in maintaining ingrained white power, privilege, and supremacy.

- Critical race theory rejects a race-neutral approach to law and justice (Odartey-Wellington, 2011). Race is shown to be significant in constructing law and the role of law in constructing and maintaining social domination (Aylward, 1999; Bell, 2008). It is a reaction to the race-blind approach of Martin Luther King Jr. and the civil rights movement (Hylton, 2008).

- The centrality of race is muted by the gloss (or comforting fictions) of multiculturalism discourses (Davis, 2007; Odartey-Wellington, 2011). The ordinariness and embeddedness of race and racism render its reality invisible to those who enjoy racialized privilege (Abrams & Moio, 2009).

- Instead of something aberrant or random, racism is an everyday occurrence for racialized minorities, given its entrenchment in the social fabric of society (Rollack & Gillborn, 2011; Abrams & Moio, 2009). Its ingrained and business-as-usual features mean that racist practices look natural and normal rather than aberrant and painful to dominant members, thus making it difficult to eradicate with conventional measures.

- Intersectionality points to the multi-dimensional nature of oppressions. Colonization (including racism, sexism, and classism) remains an ongoing project, according to critical race feminism, sustained by interlocking systems of oppression (Razack, Smith, & Thobani, 2010).

- It is committed to actively pursuing social justice by interrogating questions about race and gender through a critical and emancipatory prism (lens) (Razack, Smith, & Thobani, 2010).

benefits for some at the expense of the subordinated others. A structural (or infrastructural) view of racism draws attention to the paramountcy of laws, conventions, practices, historical dimensions, group experiences, and interlinkages to other forms of oppression like gender or sexuality.
- Racism is inextricably linked to the politics of racialization. The centrality of the race concept in structuring intergroup relations reinforces its status as foundational to the functioning of society (Omi & Winant, 1994). Once society is racialized through the construction of racialized categories, racism as exclusion and exploitation assumes an ideological life of its own that cannot be reduced to other forms of oppression such as gender or class. Both class and gender may at times prove a more relevant formal category of analysis, but the utility of race as a social organizing principle for analyzing oppression cannot be framed as a by-product (epiphenomena) (Dei, 2007). Phrased differently, racism constitutes a complex system of structural relations that stand in oppositional and asymmetrical relationship, enriching and empowering some, disempowering and impoverishing others.
- Racism is not some irrational activity or deviant departure from the normal functioning of society. Quite the opposite: Racism constitutes a "normal" outcome implicit in the racialized structures of society and those social, cultural, economic, and political institutions embedded that exclude or deny in the competition for valued resources (Rollack & Gillborn, 2011).
- A structural theory of racism incorporates an infrastructural dimension. With an infrastructural racism, values, beliefs, and norms pertaining to race and racism are so deeply embedded in the founding assumptions and foundational principles of a society's constitutional order that what is defined as societally normal, desirable, and superior is tacitly assumed and unquestionably accepted.

To sum up, a theorizing of racism reveals a concept that is profoundly more complex than many would have imagined, incorporating a broad range of ideas and activities, perceptions and reactions. At one end are those ideological theories that theorize racism as predominantly an individual and collective pathology for eradication through education or economic uplift. Or racism is equated with a kind of false consciousness that perpetuates injustices without individual awareness of the perpetuation. At the other end are those theorizings that reject the notion of racism as a personal aberration or collective mystification. Racism as structural is theorized as foundational to a society's constitutional order—that is, the bedrock upon which it is founded, constructed, and defended. In contrast to conventional approaches, a structural understanding conceives of racism as: (1) a societal outcome; (2) a dynamic force acknowledged more for its effects instead of intent; (3) involving both overt and covert expressions; and (4) a historical phenomena reflecting conditions and institutions established in the past rather than just an anomaly in the present (Bonilla-Silva, 1997). Reference to structural racism may explain why racisms continue to persist despite a raft of initiatives to remove and destroy them. Its removal involves nothing less than the radical transformation of societal priorities, institutions, and values that unsettle power differentials by advantaging subordinate racialized groups while disadvantaging dominant racialized groups (Paradies, 2005).

Framing Definitions, Defining Racism

Despite its central to debates, racism is rarely defined with any degree of precision or accuracy, and seldom conceptualized in a way that would demonstrate its contestation, multidimensionality and complexity (Kundnani, 2007). Definitions of racism have multiplied over time and across place resulting in numerous definitions (see Fleras, 2012). Reviewing even a small portion would be exhausting and tedious, with most definitions of racism aligned along an ideological versus structural split. Definitions fall into one of five ideal-typical categories, namely, racism as race, ideology, culture, structure, and power. Phrased differently, definitions of racism historically have revolved around five major frames: (1) dislike of others because of who they are (racism as biology); (2) disdain for others because of a particular world view (as ideology); (3) distrust of people for what they do, how they live, or what they value (as culture); (4) marginalization of others that is institutionalized (as structure); and (5) domination over others (as power). To be sure, many definitions of racism incorporate several of these dimensions, a not surprising admission since attempts to classify reality should be seen as contextual rather than categorical. Nevertheless, these distinctions may be analytically separated for conceptual purposes; after all, failure to acknowledge a multiplicity of definition could easily culminate in miscommunication when the same word (racism) expresses fundamentally different dimensions, perspectives, or applications (Chait, 2009). In short, references to racism are multi-dimensional rather than singular or monolithic (Winant, 1998), and this multi-dimensionality is captured by exploring the range of definitional options.

Framing Racism as Race

Many definitions of racism are anchored in the root, "race," with its attendant notion that biology is destiny. References to *racism as biology* entail a belief in innate differences as socially significant in two ways. First, racism is defined as any belief that links thought and behaviour with biology (biological determinism). Qualities such as intelligence or morality are thought to be determined by genes or biology, according to this line of thinking, with the result that these hard-wired racial differences are perceived as fixed and unalterable. Racist stereotypes proliferate: Germans are typed as industrious; Muslims as "bombers, billionaires, or bellydancers" (Shaheen, 2001); Aboriginal peoples are either warriors or on welfare; Blacks are natural-born athletes or criminals; and the Japanese are naturally gifted whizzes but emotionally bankrupt. The conflating of biology (race) with personality is thought to justify discriminatory treatment of others by judging them on the basis of their racial identity rather than on individual merit. The consequences of such racial determinism are hardly inconsequential, as a noted French expert Pierre-André Taguieff (2009) explains:

> Racist thinking is built on the premise of the fixedness of the "essence" or "nature" that every human being possesses because of his "birth" or because he belongs to an origin asserted as a prime or determining origin. The unity of humanity has broken down and fragmented into "essential categories" between which there are, as a rule, neither doors, windows, or bridges. Racism works as a method of separation. It separates and differentiates before classifying into a hierarchical order.

Second, racism in the biological sense can be defined as any treatment—either negative or positive—directed at others, solely because of race (or skin colour). To deny or exclude others because of race is normally defined as racism. But to provide preferential assistance to others because of race is no less racist. In both cases, individuals are singled out for different treatment on the basis of who they are rather than what they need or are entitled to. For example, a professor who conferred preferential treatment on racialized students (such as higher marks for mediocre work because of diminished expectations) would be regarded just as racist as one who deliberately punished students of colour by assigning lower marks for work of equal value.

Framing Racism as Ideology

Strictly speaking, the concept of race is concerned with perceived differences. Racism as racialism transforms these differences into a relatively coherent cognitive framework (or ideology) that extols the superiority of one group over another. Or, as Lynnette Steenveld writes, racism as an ideology or discourse makes references about people on the presumed notion of a hierarchy of races for maintaining unequal power relations. Defining racism as ideology reflects a partitioning of the human world into a set of fixed, distinct, and discrete categories of population known as race. Each of these racial categories embraced an immutable and inherited assemblage of physical, cultural, and psychological characteristics arranged in ascending or descending order of acceptance or desirability; assigned an intellectual or moral superiority; believed that human abilities are determined by race, and that the superior races have a right to rule inferior races (Vickers, 2002). The end result? A hierarchy of superior and inferior races that unjustly diminished others and justified this discrimination by reference to race. Ideologies in themselves are not necessarily evil or destructive. Nevertheless, when wedded to institutionalized power relations and xenophobic nationalisms, they can inflict injury in legitimizing unequal relations and justifying socio-economic inequality, including the purging of 6 million "undesirables" under a Nazi Germany (see also Taguieff, 2009).

Framing Racism as Culture
In recent years, the definitional focus of racism has shifted: References to cultural incompatibility and/or inferiority are replacing a preoccupation with pigment-focused inferiority (race or biology) as a basis for denial or exclusion (Barker, 1981; Sharma, 2011). Racism is no longer defined as a universal discourse of dominance over racial inferiors as was historically the case. The objective then was to destroy the other as an impediment, to exploit them for gain, or to absorb them in the name of progress. Racism in a post-racial era is increasingly articulated through reference to culture (Lentin & Titley, 2011), although it works the same as old-fashioned racism since culture is naturalized and people are defined solely in those terms.

The language of cultural racism speaks of a new exclusionary rhetoric. This language is anchored in the discourses of social cohesion and national unity, respect for the integrity and culture of the national community, and a linkage between culture and national identity. The issue is no longer about biological dominance or racially endowed differences, although culture and biology may be fused in ways difficult to disentangle. It is about the danger that foreign cultural practices pose to national unity, identity, and citizenship (Fleras, 2004). For example, while Islamophobia (fear of Islam) is widely acknowledged and pervasive, a racism of fear toward Muslims does not necessarily imply racial inferiority. Rather, religion and culture are racialized as an integration problem, an attack on Western values, an assault on human rights, or a terrorist threat (Dunn, Kockler, & Salabay, 2007). Accordingly, the new *colour*-blind but *culture*-conscious racism (racism without race) can be defined as the dislike of the other not because of who they are, but in perceptions of what they do or how they think.

A rhetoric of exclusion draws on the perceived incommensurability of cultural differences as blueprint for living co-operatively. The cultural "other" is perceived as posing a danger or threat to the mainstream, in part because of incompatible cultural differences that preclude belonging and acceptance, in part because of their refusal to integrate or participate (Kundnani, 2007b). Dominant sectors are not defined as racially superior but as culturally normal and preferred, while subdominant groups are dismissed as a culturally threatening to a secular and liberal society rather than innately inferior. To be sure, culture and race (biology) are not mutually opposed. Culturalist discourses are introduced that combine race (biology) with culture to diminish the "other" on the grounds that immutable cultural differences are no less innate as racial divides (Vasta & Castles, 1996). Just as references to race and racial doctrines are culturally prescribed social constructions, so too are dialogues about cultural exclusion underpinned by race and racist imagery. Cultural differences are racialized by drawing on racial metaphors; conversely, racial differences are culturalized as socially anomalous and societally inappropriate. The conflation of culture and race should come as no surprise: As noted by Joel Kahn in a 1989 issue of *Dialectical Anthropology*, both race and culture as totalizing systems of exclusion share much in common. Each constitutes explanatory frameworks for defining and classifying that are deterministic, reductionist, essentialist, and monocausal. Put bluntly, recourse to culturalist definitions of racism has proven as exclusionary as those that reduced race to biology (see Fleras, 2004).

Framing Racism as Structure

Another set of definitions focuses on racism as structure (further clarification in this chapter). This broader definition goes beyond racism as a set of ideas or individuals on the margins of society, despite the tendency for many to equate racism with extreme acts that incite prejudice, hatred, or violence. Such acts are common enough, but equally prevalent are those structural biases embedded within the broader context of social processes and institutional practices. Reference to racism as structure emphasizes the racialized arrangement of practices and beliefs that privileges one group to the perpetual disadvantage of another. Instead of something random and individualized, Peter Li explains (cited in Eisenkraft, 2010), structural racism is regularized by virtue of being embedded in the normative fabric of society, systemically embedded in institutions, practised unobtrusively through communication, and experienced as part of the informal culture and ordinary interaction. This embedded bias and attendant exclusion becomes so normalized that people tend to think of it as natural or inevitable (Kobayashi, 2001; Cassin et al., 2007). A post-racial, colour-blind society is articulated instead, conveniently ignoring the racialization of its constitutional order, from founding assumptions to foundational principles. In turn, institutions are so racialized in power and privilege that inequities are transmitted from one generation to the next without much disruption to the status quo. Not surprisingly, the system is designed and organized to ensure that even successful racialized minorities confront enormous pressures to conform or excel. The end result is a system both self-perpetuating and resistant to change, and more potent than ever, as Angela Davis points out: "We now have structural entrenchment of racism that makes it in some ways worse than it was in the days when people were involved in the struggle for civil rights" (cited in Ward, 2013).

Framing Racism as Power

Definitions of racism increasingly attend to the centrality of power. Relations of power are implicated as drivers of racism, insofar as racism is the state-sanctioned enactment of power disparities in contexts of inequality (Kundnani, 2007a). Racism as power consists of virtually any type of exploitation or exclusion by which the dominant group institutionalizes its privilege at the expense of others (Al-Krenawi & Graham, 2003). Power is monopolized by one group of individuals or, more accurately, the *abuse* of power in claiming special privileges (Mistry & Latoo, 2009), resulting in a system of subordination, dominance, and control by a powerful group over another group through a system of ideas, laws, and practices that regulates the aspirations, actions, and livelihood of racialized minorities (Brown, 2005). The power in racism can also reflect its capacity to mobilize symbolic resources to promote or restrain social change in a favourable direction (Omi & Winant, 1994). For example, the power differential inherent within an old white boys' network effectively screens out minorities through hiring and promoting practices that may unintentionally deny or exclude. Or, as deftly phrased by Christine Silverberg (2004), former chief of the Calgary Police Services, "Racism is not just an overt act of discrimination, or even a series of such incidents, but rather the use of institutional power to deny or grant whole groups of people rights, respect, and representation based on their skin colour."

To be sure, power can be framed in systemic terms instead of focusing on individuals (agency) or institutions (structure) that manipulate power as an instrument of coercion or sovereign acts of domination (Gaventa, 2003). Defining racism as systemic power acknowledges that it is not necessarily something possessed by sovereigns or located in law. Rather, it constitutes a set of capacities or network of relationships that are pervasive and dispersed throughout society (Dhamoon, 2009). For Foucault (1991, 1998), for example, power is everywhere insofar as it is diffused (rather than concentrated), discursive (rather than coercive), and entrenched (rather than possessed) in discourses (accepted forms of knowledge and ways of knowing) and representations, arrangements, and allocations. Instead of wielding power in the conventional sense of control or domination, people discipline others (and themselves) without any wilful coercion from others because of embedded values, beliefs, and norms both pervasive yet beyond awareness.

Put bluntly, racism is about power, not pigmentation (Zachariah, 2004; Khayatt, 1994). Racism goes beyond individual prejudice or belief in the superiority of some races. A racialized system of disadvantage prevails instead that manipulates power to differentiate, categorize, and exclude. It entails an interrelated system of political, economic, and ideological practices that entitles a dominant group to exercise hegemony over subordinate groups (Hall, 1980). Racism is not about differences per se but about how those in positions of power can racialize differences to protect ruling-class privilege. Racism is not about treating others differently because they are different, but about their differential treatment within contexts of power that limit or oppress (Blauner, 1972). Finally, racism is not about manipulating people's attitudes. It is about the power to establish agendas regarding what is normal, necessary, desirable, or acceptable, thus reinforcing the superiority of one group over another. bell hooks (1995, pp. 154–55) puts it into perspective by linking racism with power: "Why is it so difficult for many white folks to understand that racism is oppressive not because white folks have prejudicial feelings about black people ... but because it is a system that promotes domination and subjugation."

The next Insight box provides a look at the interplay between a culture of power and the power of culture within contexts of inequality.

INSIGHT
The Power of Culture, the Culture of Power

Consider the following not-so-hypothetical situations of power. People experience a culture of power that is not their own if they are immigrants who have "walked" into a new country; or racialized minority people who have walked into a predominantly white organization; or Muslims who have walked into a Christian space; or women who have walked into a men's meeting (taken from Kivel, 1996/2002). Treading carefully in these contexts is important because they are feeling culturally unsafe, insecure, disrespected, or marginalized. This awkwardness is not surprising: When one group accumulates more power than other groups, the more powerful group constructs an environment that privileges its members at the expense of others. This privileged positioning within a culture of power makes it difficult for those in positions of power to see or to acknowledge the benefits they receive because their status is the norm.

For example, white males often don't notice that women or racialized minorities are treated differently. This differential treatment exists because, as men, they are inside a pale male culture of power that is largely invisible to them (at least until pointed out to them by someone outside that culture of power). They expect to be treated with respect, to be listened to, to have their opinions valued, to be welcomed, to see people like them in positions of authority, and to experience a world organized to address their needs and aspirations. Conversely, white men don't notice that (1) racialized women and men are treated less respectfully, ignored, or silenced; (2) they rarely appear in positions of power and authority; and (3) they are not always welcomed into certain spaces but made to feel culturally unsafe. By disadvantaging or marginalizing those who are judged and evaluated by whites on white terms, this pale male culture of power reflects and reinforces the institutionalized power that bolsters a Eurocentric constitutional order.

Toward a Working Definition

This overview of definitions makes it abundantly clear: Defining racism is a formidable challenge as it changes forms and meanings in specific historical periods and different situational contexts (Gopalkrishnan & Babacan, 2007). Its expressions are multiple, often contested, and sometimes contradictory, gendered, and classed, and interconnected with religious identities and nationalist ideologies in complex ways. Any comprehensive definition must go beyond an individual frame or set of attitudes. Racism is more than an expression of collective prejudices; it also incorporates a complex system of exclusionary dynamics involving an interplay of ideologies, discourses, discursive practices, institutions, and values within a specific social, cultural, and historical context (Goldberg, 2002; Macedo & Gounari, 2006). Emphasis draws attention to a system of disadvantage founded on institutional power, anchored in racialized values and beliefs, and predicated on a supremacist mindset. Keeping these conditions in mind, racism can be defined as

> those ideas and ideals (ideology) embedded within individual attitudes, cultural values, institutional practices, and those (infra) structures of society that assert or imply the normalcy, acceptability and superiority of one racialized group over another, together with the institutional power to put these perceptions into practice in ways that exclude or exploit those defined as culturally different or racially inferior either through consequence or by intent. (Fleras, 2012, 76)

This definition draws attention to key attributes of racism—namely, its status as an ideology either articulated or implied; those pervasive assumptions about the inherent superiority or inferiority of groups based on perceived physical and cultural differences; its entrenchment in the foundational principles of a society's constitutional order; a corresponding set of practices that involves deliberate intent or reflects inadvertent consequences; and an impact that encompasses both personal and institutional dimensions. Three interrelated dimensions are also implied: (1) an "us" versus "them" dichotomy; (2) processes that racialized, inferiorize, and dehumanize; and (3) the centrality of power in inducing negative consequences (Hervik, 2013). In that racism is about power, and because those with power rarely want to share it with those perceived as inferior, any unmasking of racism is unlikely without a protracted struggle.

Note

1. The celebrated American anti-racist Tim Wise used the expression "Racism 2.0" in his book *Between Barack and a Hard Place*.

CHAPTER 3

THE RIDDLES OF RACE

Introduction: Racializing Race, Racialization as Racism

The past is never dead. In fact, it isn't even past.
—William Faulkner, "Requiem for a Nun"

Race remains a factor in society.
—President Barack Obama, July 24, 2009, responding to the high-profile police takedown of a prominent black academic

Few will dispute the significance of race in shaping intergroup dynamics (Goodman, Moses, & Jones, 2012; Tattersall & DeSalle, 2011; Comack, 2011; Brace, 2005). References to race historically permeated Euro-American society in its encounters with the largely non-Christian "other." Nineteenth-century Europeans justified colonization by conferring a pseudo-scientific legitimacy on an ideology that pigeonholed people into stratified categories. The classification of colonized peoples into racialized "others" secured a simple yet self-serving explanation (McCalla & Satzewich, 2002). Race "mattered" for various reasons, but primarily in conjunction with religion and class as (1) a tool for justifying domination, control, and inequality; (2) an excuse for doing the inexcusable such as enslaving people; (3) a framework for explaining human differences; and (4) a rationalization for salving/absolving guilty consciences over mistreatment of the cultural other. Over time, perceptions of race became embedded in dominant forms of representation across society, while assuming increased significance in shaping social patterns, societal organization, government policy, and state functions (Goldberg, 2002).

That race "mattered" in the historical past is beyond doubt (Wallis & Fleras, 2008; Fleras, 2012). The term was applied originally to the breeding of domestic animals and plants. From the 1500s to 1800s, however, it began to denote cultural distinctions such as lineage or religion. References eventually shifted focus to biologically grounded classification systems based on the paired criteria of locality and physicality (Durodoye, 2003). Both the United States and Canada openly endorsed an essentialized vision of race as real: that is, as natural and static, universal and immutable (Dalmage, 2004). Over time, the ontological status of race shifted from objective to constructed, from real to fiction. But while the race concept may have been little more than a socially constructed fabrication in defense of white domination, its capacity to inflict injury was anything but fictional. Odious practices from the transatlantic slave trade to the colonization of indigenous peoples around the world attest to that.

Many are dismayed that race continues to matter at a time when people should know better (Goodman, Moses, & Jones, 2012; Fredericko & Luks, 2005). Perceptions and social patterns associated with race remain one of the most powerful signifiers for engaging with the world "out there" (Brown, 2009). The race concept constitutes a negative lived experience for many, with the result that a person's racial(ized) location in society will influence opportunities and outcomes (Dei, 2005a, 2005b; Free & Ruesink, 2012). Furthermore, neither race nor racism can be theorized in isolation from gender and class; after all, systems of domination, power, and control tend to be mutually constitutive in reinforcing each other (Joseph et al., 2012). Finally, race exerts a pervasive influence at varying levels of expression and organization, from where people live, to who they hire, to what they can expect from life. It can do so not because race is ontologically real—because it isn't—but because people *believe it is real* and (re)act accordingly, often with discriminatory consequences (also Tattersall & DeSalle, 2011).

Race as social construction has also proven socially controlling (Alexander, 2012). As an instrument of social control, race restricts and regulates the behaviour of specified racialized groups, sometimes deliberately, often unconsciously. The fact that race continues to "matter" for precisely the same reasons as in the past—namely, to explain or rationalize for purposes of control or exploitation—provides a sobering reality check. Race and inequality are no less linked. Racialized minorities continue to bear the brunt of negative treatment, ranging from polite snubs and blatant barbs to both overt and covert discrimination. Patterns of social exclusion are preserved in the process, as are stark socio-economic disparities involving barriers to participation and access to power (Coates, 2008; Dei, 2007; Galabuzi, 2006; Hier & Bolaria, 2007; see also King, 2011; Hunt & Wilson, 2011; Evans & Feagin, 2012). Social rewards remain divvied up on the basis of perceived racial affiliation, while public participation and political decision making reflect prevailing stereotypes and racial prejudices (Fernando, 2006). Moreover, as long as racism and racialized inequality persist in societies that claim to be colour-blind in dispensing rewards, the conclusion appears inescapable: Whether people like it or not, approve or disapprove, race will continue to matter in privileging some while disempowering others (Cose, 1997; Morris & Cowlishaw, 1997; Galabuzi, 2004).

The situation in the United States is instructive. Moves to disprove notions of hierarchy and remove social, political, and economic barriers have not dislodged the legacy and reality of race in organizing society and for shaping people's lives and life chances (Goodman, Moses, & Jones, 2012). Many had hoped the election of Barack Obama would usher in a post-racial era of equality and inclusiveness (Roberts, 2011). Obama himself was viewed as the poster "boy" for a post-racial America because of his ability to transcend race, with a content and style unlikely to rock the boat or provoke a backlash. The emergence of a post-racial America meant that race no longer mattered in defining who gets what; as a result, whites no longer were responsible for black inequality in a colour-blind society (Hunt & Wilson, 2011; Evans & Feagin, 2011; Bonilla-Silva & Dietrich, 2011). Hard work, persistence, and education were key, in effect, in supporting Martin Luther King's vision of a society in which people would be judged by the content of their character rather than the colour of their skin (Newman, 2012). In short, the success of Obama and other racialized high-flying successes (from Oprah to Tiger) make it abundantly clear. The salience of race as a marker of exclusion had little credibility in a post-racial society except, perhaps, in the shadowy region of innuendos and code phrases (King, 2011).

However aspirational, the ideology of a colour-blind society did not match reality. More accurately, it legitimized a racialized social order with its perpetuation of deeply embedded racial inequalities (Bonilla-Silva & Dietrich, 2011). The election of a black president appears to have had little positive effect on the socio-economic status of blacks, especially if those in prison are included in equality surveys (Harris, 2012). Poverty in the twenty-first-century United States continues to be coloured-coded along racialized lines (Lin & Harris, 2009).

Attitudes are no less stagnant. A University of Michigan (University of Michigan News Service, 2012) study (see also Ward, 2012) indicated that 48 percent of Americans in an online questionnaire in 2008 expressed anti-black attitudes. By 2012, the figure had increased to 51 percent. Admittedly, others see improvement in white racial attitudes (Welch & Sigelman, 2011; Tuch & Hughes, 2011), despite a growing number of hate groups, from 602 in 2000 to 1,018 in 2011 (*New York Times*, 2012). As well, the politics of race continue to spark controversy as demonstrated by the recent debate over the blackness of Afro-Latina actress Zoe Saldana. Was she was "black" enough to play the very black-skinned singer and activist Nina Simone in a forthcoming biopic film? For critics (see Nittle, 2012; Vega, 2012), Saldana's selection not only whitewashed black stories, it also misrepresented the robust activism that informed Simone's politics. If nothing else from this representational controversy, people were reminded of how quickly the insertion of race into any encounter can transform the dynamic because, as Rex Murphy (2009) writes, the politics of a racial(ized) melodrama drowns out all other considerations. Or consider this response in reaction to the fallout over the Zimmerman-Martin trial in which George Zimmerman was acquitted by a jury of six white females in the shooting death of an unarmed black youth, Trayvon Martin, allegedly in self-defence: "A generation after the triumph of the civil rights movement, the prism of race still dominates the discourse about politics, crime, class, and justice in America. It is the ancient wound that never heals. And everyone likes to pick the scabs" (Wente, 2013).

In other words, the legitimacy of race as a "theoretical lens" (Tyson, 1998, p. 22) has not been delegitimized as basis for debate or denunciation, as demonstrated by reference to the so-called Obama effect:

INSIGHT

The Obama Effect: The More Things Change, the More Racism Changes

What does the (re)election of Obama as president say about the state of race, race relations, and racism in America? An African American man occupies the world's most powerful office—one of those rare instances in human history when a member of a previously disenfranchised racial group is elected chief executive by a majority of the electorate (Craemer et al., 2013)—yet more blacks languish under correctional control at present (jail, probation, parole) than the number of slaves in 1850, ten years before the Civil War (Alexander, 2012). A black president may have been voted into office on the strength of a massive black voter turnout that surpassed a white voter turnout for the first time in American history, yet there is not a single elected black senator and only one black governor out of fifty states (Editorial, Globe and Mail, August 31, 2013). The contradiction is stunning. For a country built on the foundation of slavery, segregation, and white domination, the election of Obama is not without import and impact on race relations. His appeal tended to transcend race, while his efforts to defuse racialized rhetoric exemplified his ability to be trusted with the presidency.

But is it possible to overplay the "Obama card"? The ongoing salience of racism in influencing people's lives and life chances has not been eradicated or even substantially diminished despite President Obama's individual success and predictions of a post-racial era—that is, race will no longer play a role in defining who gets what while confirming the end of racism and irrelevance of anti-racist programs (Kitossa, 2011; Pew Research Center, 2013). Blacks and racialized minorities continue to confront unequal opportunities and patterns of systemic discrimination that exclude or exploit (Wise, 2009a). Racialized wealth gaps and differentials in household wealth are deeply entrenched, with white families worth twenty times more than black families, owing in part to slavery, Jim Crow laws, and discrimination that severely limited black access to housing equities (National Urban League, 2009). The Great Recession, which ended in 2009, saw black median household wealth drop by 66 percent and 53 percent for Latino/a largely because of plummeting house values. By contrast, white households experienced only a 16 percent decline (Kochhar, Fry, & Taylor, 2011).

Paradoxically, the election of Obama has launched a new kind of racism that Wise (2008) calls racism 2.0 (in contrast to Racism 1.0 or old-fashioned bigotry). His win may perversely legitimize a new model of blackness acceptable to whites, not unlike that associated with the popular 1980s sitcom *The Cosby Show*. The success of both Cosby and now Obama, like that of Tiger or Oprah, is highlighted to "prove" (1) the potential for black success; (2) the viability of the merit principle; and (3) the irrelevance and racism of race-based affirmative action programs. The fact that race no longer mattered in defining life chances, blacks had only themselves to blame for failure (Jhally & Lewis, 1992). But the few successful exceptions are precisely that: exceptions to the rule since many blacks continue to live on the margins. Rather than ending racism, the Obama effect has merely glossed over its scope and impact without disrupting the racialized status quo, so that reference to a post-racial era functions as a new system of social control under the principle of a colour-blind America (West, 2012).

A "racism without race" reveals the workings of racism in the post-racial era. Each generation creates and employs new tactics for achieving the same goals of exclusion and discrimination without appearing to do so (Alexander, 2012). The (infra)structure of society doesn't change, only the language to justify it, since it is no longer acceptable to use race explicitly as justification for racialized inequality. For instance, Alexander (2012) points how the criminal justice relabels blacks as criminals to justify discriminatory practices and social control practices, not unlike those convict leasing programs that prevailed during the Jim Crow era (see the PBS documentary *Slavery by Another Name*). The achievements of successful minorities are celebrated since these individuals are seen as more appealing. They know their place; they neither rock the boat nor make whites feel guilty or uncomfortable; and, best of all, they play the game according to white rules. Needless to say, minorities perceived to be uppity by playing outside white-sanctioned norms are dismissed as dysfunctional, pathological, or criminal. That they continue to be distrusted, feared, and ostracized goes without saying.

The conclusion should come as no surprise. Electing a black president does not mean that historical injustices will disappear because race will no longer matter—at least no more so than, say, the election of Benazir Bhutto as Pakistan's first female Muslim prime minister improved the collective lot of Pakistani women. Paradoxically perhaps, Obama's victory may have raised the bar for achieving black success, while creating added psychological barriers for the vast majority of blacks. On the bright side, however, it is no less valid to assume an optimism

> mixed with caution over the impact and implications of this profound cultural shift, as did one of the contributors to ENAR's Report on Racism, Aryeh Neier (2013, p. 131), who writes:
>
> > The election of President Obama was not nirvana. It was not the end of racism in the United States by any means. But it was an immensely significant step in reducing the ongoing and damaging practices of racism. I attach immense importance to maintaining and building the moral character of the struggle against racism, helping people to aspire to the idea that they should live in a non-racist society and helping them to see themselves as not racist. The next step then is to transform those perceptions into actual practice.
>
> In short, the Obama effect did not eradicate the inequalities of racism and racial discrimination. Nor has it eliminated the salience of race as symbols of identity and experiences. The symbolic level of political surfaces exposes yet conceals the actual substance of black and minority communities devastated by mass unemployment, social neglect, economic abandonment, mass incarceration, and intense police surveillance (West, 2012). What prevails instead under the banner of colour-blindness is largely ideological in advancing the belief that race and racism no longer matter as barriers in analyzing post-racial, colour-blind society or defining people's life chances (Hunt & Wilson, 2011; Titley & Lentin, 2012). That this aspiration doesn't come close to matching reality is a paradox pursued more closely in Chapter 5, "Racialized Inequality."

Canadians are no less deeply conflicted over the concept of race (Fleras, 2012). References to race in a supposedly merit-based and achievement-oriented society are thought to be awkward or offensive, especially when conflating the value of a person with a stigma beyond his or her control. In a Canada that aspires to colour-blind status, the race concept represents a deeply discredited and tainted status. A preoccupation with race is thought to contradict the colour-blind principles of neo-liberal universalism, including the assertion that our commonalities as rights-bearing and morally autonomous individuals are more important—at least for purposes of recognition or reward—than what partitions people into racially distinct groups. Admittedly, a general aversion to race as description and explanatory framework has not insulated minority women and men from marginalization and discrimination. Nor has Canada's claim to race-aversiveness resulted in any major realignment in the distribution of valued resources (Kunz et al., 2001; Galabuzi, 2006). Nevertheless, a reliance on culture rather than race to explain, justify, and entitle has consolidated Canada's reputation as a model multicultural society.

Recourse to race as discourse and practices no longer possesses the discursive legitimacy it once flexed in Canada, but the riddles of race are all too real as the following contradictions demonstrate (Wallis & Fleras, 2008). Canada claims race to be meaningless yet is deeply divided by race (Diangelo,

2012). Race remains a pivotal part of the social landscape, although almost no one admits to believing in the race concept. Race may conjure up a singular frame of reference, yet it is conflicted in meanings and contradicted by the demands of logic or proof (Pascale, 2007, p. 23). Race may reflect an accident of birth, but it is a lifelong reality that profoundly shapes a person's life chances. Race is not based on phenotype, yet the resulting socially constructed representations are attached to physical differences (Daynes & Lee, 2008). Race may be skin-deep, but many believe it provides a quick indicator of a person's worth and predictor of success. Race should never justify differential treatment, either positive or negative, yet it is increasingly assigned a role in reversing discrimination (for example, Canada's Employment Equity Act). Finally, reference to race is explicitly rejected in evaluating people's capacities and talents, yet Canadians implicitly condone a racialized status quo, with its corresponding distortion in the distribution of power and privilege.

The centrality of race to society raises a provocative yet perplexing question: Why has a biological concept of minimal scientific worth continue to exert such a punishing impact in shaping history or intergroup relations? Why, indeed, does a largely discredited concept enjoy such enduring power in a multicultural Canada that aspires to the post-racial principles of colour-blindness? However profound the import of such questions, there remains a reluctance to debate race as concept or catalyst. George Sefa Dei (2005a) nails it succinctly when alluding to race as the elephant in the room that everyone scrupulously avoids:

> Race has powerful material, political, and economic currency in our society. Rather than dismiss race, we ought to be honest about it and spend time reflecting on it through critical discussion, instead of sweeping it under the carpet and hope that this will settle everything. Racial categories such as "black," "white," and "brown," etc., no matter how imperfect, are not the problem in themselves. The reality is that these categories organize our society. Rather than deny them, we must challenge the interpretations attached to them.

Divergent opinions fuel a range of responses. Some believe that race is real and must be taken into account in explaining social reality, despite people's reluctance to broach the topic (Dei, 2007). Others believe that race should never enter into public discourse, given its unsavoury reputation and potential for mischief-making, so that any continued use inflames more than it enlightens (Hier & Bolaria, 2007). Races do not exist, in other words, only perceptions of group-based differences that may be real in their consequences. Still others see race as a biologically based social construction of political significance in shaping identities and predicting success (Harding, 2002). Race remains a potent social and political category around which individuals and groups formulate identities or organize their resistance within those historical contexts that denied or excluded (Goldberg & Solomos, 2002) them. Admittedly, in contrast to the racial logic that prevailed in the past, race is no longer essential to how people define ourselves in relation to others (Hsu, 2009). Nevertheless, as Omi and Winant (1994, p. 5) once said in acknowledging the salience of race as an identity marker, to be without a racial identity in a racialized society runs the risk of having no identity at all.

This chapter focuses on the politics of race in defining who is who and who gets what in a Canada that allegedly disavows its salience and significance. The chapter is predicated on a simple yet counterintuitive premise about the relations of race to racism. Contrary to popular logic, *race as concept is not the cause of racism; on the contrary, racism produces a rationale for the existence of the race concept.* It is not human differences (race) that make racisms; more to the point, it is racism that legitimizes the relevance of race by signifying (or constructing) human differences, with the intent or effect of marginalizing those labelled as racially inferior (Stanley, 2011). In other words, *racism preceded race, not the other way around,* and it is this interpretation that points to the centrality of racialization in current narratives about race and racism. The chapter begins by acknowledging how the race concept reflects, reinforces, and advances the persistence and proliferation of racisms and how they work in Canada. It continues by pointing out how race constitutes a social construct with controlling functions that reflect specific material and historical conditions. This is followed by examining the politics of race in terms of origins, persistence, transformation, impact, and implications. Race is shown to achieve social significance not because of its biological foundation but by the social meanings ascribed to it (Guess, 2006). The chapter also deconstructs those coded concepts and subtextual discourses by which people continue to attribute social significance to race in everyday life, despite laws and norms that discourage its use to differentiate, deny, or exclude (Li, 2007). The chapter concludes by demonstrating the relevance of race as an organizing principle, a hierarchical system, a predictor of failure or success, and a marker of identity. Particular attention is devoted to reconceptualizing the race concept along the lines of racialization, with special emphasis on how white privilege is constructed, preserved, and enforced in a supposedly colour-blind yet white superiority society.

The Power of an Illusion: Racializing the Colonies

The race concept originated with the onset of European exploration, conquest, and settlement. Contributing factors included the expansion of the cross-Atlantic slave trade, the plunder of indigenous peoples' lands, a range of ideologies from Social Darwinism to eugenics, the appearance of human and biological sciences (with their focus on comparative anatomy), and international competition for valued resources (Fleras, 2012; Brace, 2005). Europeans manipulated the concept of race as one way of domesticating human diversity (Wallis & Fleras, 2008). Racial doctrines originated to condone the negative treatment of those non-Western populations perceived as irrelevant, inferior, or dangerous. Under the sway of these dogmas, Europeans embarked on civilizing crusades that masked intentions for exploiting inhabitants, with a corresponding disregard for their human rights. The imperatives of an expanding capitalist system reflected a need for new foreign markets, investment opportunities, cheap labour, and accessible resources. In addition, European imperialist expansion intensified an obsession with accumulating foreign territories for nationalistic, decorative, or strategic reasons. Admittedly, the race concept did not necessarily originate to justify European control or the domination of others (Coates, 2008). Nor did race thinking give rise to racism; on the contrary, the reverse is more accurate. It is not human differences (race) that foster racisms, but racism that legitimizes the construction of race typologies by classifying human differences into discrete categories (Stanley, 2011). These racialized classifications, when sanctioned by human and biological sciences, made group differences appear more comprehensive, more entrenched, and more scientifically valid (Stocking, 1968; Stepan, 1982).

This predatory approach, known as colonialism, exposed a paradox (Fleras, 2012). First, how could the so-called civilized and Christian nations rationalize and justify the blatant exploitation of others? Second, how could colonialist exploitation be sustained without contradicting the image of Europeans as a sophisticated and enlightened people with a moral duty to civilize and convert? Answers to these uncomfortable questions inspired an ideology that condoned the mistreatment of others as natural, normal, and necessary. The contradiction between Christian ideals and exploitative practices was masked and mediated by the racist conviction that lower-ranked races would benefit from servitude and close supervision (Lerner, 1997). This racist ideology not only rationalized the sorting of populations along racial lines; it also set the tone for asserting absolute European supremacy at the expense of those most vulnerable. Racial doctrines arose to "soften" the impact of imperialist encounters throughout Central and South America, the Caribbean, Africa, Australia, and New Zealand. Dismissing overseas races as subhuman enabled Europeans to exploit supposedly "inferior stocks" with impunity, while oppressing them without remorse or guilt, often under the banner of the white man's burden. A belief that these racial differences were ingrained as fixed and immutable also absolved Europeans of responsibility for improving the plight of the unenlightened. Consciences salved, Europeans could do whatever was necessary to conquer or colonize.

In short, the race concept emerged as an nineteenth-century convention to label, describe, and classify large groups of people by reference to immutable traits such as the colour of the skin. Doctrines of racial superiority began to appear once racial types were assigned a fixed moral value—that is, prescribed by nature as superior or inferior and backed by the unquestioned authority of science. These hierarchies were intrinsically racist in employing the authority of science to confirm the superiority of whites over others (Stepan, 1982). Their impact was devastating especially when the harnessing of military prowess and technological advances imposed a controlling effect on indigenous and tribal populations. The justification of inequality under the race doctrines facilitated the commodification of races as objects for exploitation or control, as targets of pity or contempt, and as victims of progress. The most egregious of these doctrines included Social Darwinism, the notions of a "struggle for survival" and "survival of the fittest" on a global scale; eugenics, the idea that the social, mental, and behavioural qualities of the human "race" could be improved by selective manipulation of its hereditary essence and scientific racism, the premise that racial capacities between populations could be measured and evaluated by statistical means, most notably the IQ test (Fleras, 2012).

Colonizing Aboriginality: The Racism of Colonialism

References to race must go beyond simply seeing it as a discursive construct or explanatory variable. Race reflects, reinforce, and advances the discourse of white supremacy as a racialized system of global domination over the last five hundred years, in the process reinforcing how both local and national articulations of race and racism must be linked to larger transnational projects such as colonialism, globalization, and capitalism (Dua et al., 2005). According to Mills (1997), race is the quintessential racism project to rationalize and legitimate the displacement of indigenous peoples and exploited minorities. Race and racism are crucial to modernity since race is constitutive of the modern state (akin to the importance of religion in the medieval era). Racial classification and exclusion justify the existence of the racialized state, which in turn takes a leading role in enforcing racial exclusion and/or assimilation (Goldberg, 1993; Valls, 2007). To be sure, Mills writes, a cabal of whites did not conspire to make a historical pact (contract) to dominate the world. Nonetheless, whites in position of power have embarked on a mission to maintain and expand their power and privilege through the exploitation of the global South. Canada's Aboriginal peoples proved no exception to invasiveness of colonization.

The settlement and domestication of Canada was predicated on the colonial narrative of racial supremacy and white superiority. Canadian national identity was constructed around the racialization of Aboriginal peoples to facilitate their removal from the nation-building project, forcibly if necessary, or, alternatively, by assimilation and cultural extinction (Thobani, 2007). The largely white supremacist project framed the Aboriginal peoples as racialized others whose inferiority justified the dispossession of land and the destruction of culture (Wallis, Sunseri, & Galabuzi, 2010). Not surprisingly, five hundred years of violent (neo)colonial contact have plunged Canada's Aboriginal peoples into a state of disarray and despair (Adams, 1999; Maaka & Fleras, 2005). Few would dare deny the centrality of race and racism in shaping the colonial encounter that "primitivized" Aboriginal peoples-state/government relations (Wallis, Sunseri, & Galabuzi, 2010; Cannon & Sunseri, 2011; Thobani, 2007; but see Hokowhitu, 2012). Many have documented the scope of racist government policies and the (mis)administration of "Indian" Affairs by state bureaucracy in marginalizing Aboriginal peoples (Frideres & Gadacz, 2012). Little more can be gleaned by rehashing the negative consequences of even well-intentioned actions by those more interested in careerism and empire-building than in advancing Aboriginal well-being (Ponting & Gibbins, 1980; Shkilnyk, 1985). What more can be added to the sorry legacy of official Aboriginal policy that advanced "national interests" at the expense of Aboriginal identity and empowerment? Aboriginal activist Harold Cardinal captured a sense of outrage in his book *The Unjust Society* (1969) when pointing out a history of indifference, ignorance, and bigotry that has long trampled Aboriginal peoples' rights.

The colonizers sought to subordinate and eliminate Aboriginal peoples through a process of assimilation into "civilization," resulting in the "taming" and "caging" of the indigenes that proved every bit as restraining as physical constraints (Churchill, 2002). In some cases, racist government policies deliberately destroyed the viability of Aboriginal communities in the relentless quest to divest them of their land, culture, and tribal authority. In other cases, the demise of Aboriginal peoples came about through unobtrusive yet equally powerful assimilationist measures such as education and missionization. The absorption of aboriginality into Canada was reflected in the damaging consequences of possibly well-intentioned but ultimately destructive government policies and programs such as reserve relocation or the residential school system.

Aboriginal relations with Canada have long been mediated by progressive-sounding policy initiatives, yet marred by duplicity, racism, and expediency. The Aboriginal affairs policy may have evolved through a series of overlapping stages, but has never wavered from its central mission—namely, to solve the "Indian problem" by ensuring there are "no more Indians" through absorption into the system. In keeping with the colonialist spirit of the times but inconsistent with earlier commitments to Aboriginal peoples as "nations within," the federal government approached them as hapless wards of the state with limited civil rights although fully entitled to federal custodial care (this trust relationship was subsequently transformed into a fiduciary responsibility) (Weaver, 1984). The theme of assimilation defined a framework for solving the "Indian problem." In the pithy phrasing of Sir John A. Macdonald in espousing a "no more Indians" national policy: "The great aim of our civilization has been to do away with the tribal system and assimilate the Indian people in all respects with the inhabitants of the Dominion, as speedily as they are fit for the change" (cited in Miller, 1989).

Government integrity left much to be desired in light of racist and evolutionary philosophies that disparaged Aboriginal peoples as inferior impediments to progress (Weaver, 1984). The concept of guardianship reinforced the stereotype of Aboriginal peoples as childlike and unfit to look after themselves except under the stern but watchful eye of Crown-appointed guardians (Ponting & Gibbins, 1980). Aboriginal languages, cultures, and identity were ruthlessly suppressed, while communities were locked into patterns of dependency and despondency that aborted any local development. Perceptions of them as a barbaric race simplified the task of divesting the original occupants of their land and resources. This racialization persists into the present in the form of the paternalistic and archaic Indian Act of 1876, which remains Canada's only legislative framework designed for a racialized minority.

INSIGHT

The Indian Act: Racializing Aboriginal Peoples, Legislating Racist Governance

Our objective is to continue until there is not a single Indian in Canada that has not been absorbed into the body politic, and there is no Indian question, and no Indian department.
—Duncan Campbell Scott, deputy superintendent of Indian Affairs, 1920, cited in Greg Horn, "A Policy Gone Wrong"

Of particular relevance in hastening the goal of "no more Indians" was the Indian Act. Passage of the Act in 1876 may have sought to protect and civilize Aboriginal peoples. Nevertheless, the Act had an eviscerating impact—rather than empowering effect—in racializing Aboriginal realities. It did so by consolidating a government's preoccupation with land management consistent with the 1867 Constitution Act, which conferred federal authority over (1) "Indians and lands reserved for Indians"; (2) First Nations membership and local government; and (3) control over any initiatives leading to their eventual enfranchisement (assimilation). Despite numerous changes, the 1876 framework has remained fundamentally intact as a blueprint for exercising federal jurisdiction over Status Indians. Both Aboriginal leaders and political authorities have long criticized its paternalism and limitations as a framework for micromanaging their needs and mismanaging relations. But, however reviled, the Act offers protections, entitlements, and powers for Status Indians, in effect fostering a perverse appeal for retention, at least until the formulation of a new post-colonial governance framework (Hurley, 2009).

The Indian Act was an essentially racist instrument of containment and control in the colonization of Aboriginal peoples. The Act secured the basic legal status and entitlements of Aboriginal peoples; defined who came under its provisions (who could legally claim Indian status); what benefits Status Indians could expect under the government's fiduciary obligations; who could qualify for disenfranchisement; what to do with reserve lands and trust funds; and how local communities were to be governed in terms of government and money management (Hurley, 2009). Traditional leadership was stripped of its authority as a legitimate political voice (Dickason, 1992), while local governance took the form of elected band councils, many of which were perceived as little more than federal proxies with rubber-stamping powers of administration rather than self-rule (Webber, 1994). Even economic opportunities were curtailed. Under the Indian Act, Aboriginal peoples could not possess direct title to land or private property. They were also denied access to revenue from the sale or lease of band property. Punitive restrictions not only foreclosed Aboriginal property improvements, but also forestalled the accumulation of development capital for investment or growth (Aboriginal land held in Crown trust could not be mortgaged or used as collateral because it was immune to legal seizure). In that land was held in trust, approval from the federal government was mandatory for any development.

The imposition of the Indian Act devolved sweeping state powers to chiefs and band councils to micromanage every aspect of reserve life. The minister of Indian Affairs ultimately exercised authority in micromanaging every aspect of reserve life. Yet the Act empowered the chiefs and band councils with powers to make unilateral decisions over allocation of reserve land and housing without much accountability to members of the community. A contradictory state of affairs is the result: The federal government can manage band affairs by overturning decisions of the council and chief, while the latter have powers that can be exercised without input from and accountability to the community (Imai, 2007). Not surprisingly, the relational status of Aboriginal peoples under the Act fluctuated wildly—at times protected, at times ignored, and at times actively oppressed—but never fully embraced as equal members of Canadian society (Abele, 2004). To the extent that the Indian Act continues to divide and rule nearly a 150 years after its inception, the words of Donna Isaac of Listuguj, Quebec (1997), are sharply resonant: "The *Indian Act* system of government imposed on us so long ago has created such divided communities. We are immobilized by internal political strife. Half of the community often gets ahead at the expense of the other half. Hurt leads to contempt, division brews, and co-operation becomes impossible as hatred grows."

Residential Schools: Racism as Genocide

From the mid-nineteenth century onward, the Crown engaged in a variety of measures to assert control over Canada's Aboriginal peoples (Truth and Reconciliation Commission of Canada, 2012). The Indian Act of 1876 was ultimately such an instrument of control. The Act codified a series of laws and regulations that embraced the notions of European cultural and moral superiority not only to justify the domination and dispossession, but also to aggressively civilize Aboriginal peoples and absorb them into a dominant white culture. Much of the colonialism under the Indian Act was embedded in institutions such as the residential school system (Monture, 2010, p. 25). The mandatory placement of Aboriginal children in off-reserve residential schools fed into these racist assumptions of white superiority and Aboriginal inferiority. The government insisted on removing Aboriginal children from their parents by putting them in educational institutions under the control of religious orders. The rationale for the residential school system was captured in Davin (1879), which promulgated the adage that "how a twig is bent, the tree will grow." Federal officials believed in the need to capture the entire child—adults were dismissed as beyond hope (Davin, 1879)—through segregrated facilities and thorough immersion in Western ways. Day schools didn't work, according to the Davin Report (1879, p. 1) because "the influence of the wigwam was stronger than the influence of the school." Over time, the adoption of English, Christianity, and Canadian customs would be transmitted to their children, resulting in the eventual disappearance of aboriginality. But the residential school system had a more basic motive than simple education: The removal of children from home and parents was aimed at their forced assimilation into Canadian society through the creation of a distinct underclass of labourers, farmers, and farmers' wives (Rotman, 1996). This program sought to destroy Aboriginal language and culture, while supplanting Aboriginal spirituality with Christianity in the hopes of "killing the Indian in the child" (Royal Commission on Aboriginal Peoples, 1996). Sadly, this exercise in Anglo-conformity ended up nearly killing both.

For many Aboriginal peoples, the violence, mismanagement, and perversion of the residential school system is the defining moment in a five-hundred-year history of oppression and obligatory assimilation (Paul, 2012; Rolfsen, 2008; Castellano, Archibald, & Degagne, 2008). The federal government and Canada's major churches formalized the residential school system for remaking Aboriginal children by taking the "Indian" out of the "child," according to Indian Affairs Deputy Superintendent Duncan Campbell Scott, in effect resolving the so-called "Indian" problem once and for all. The residential school system proved to be a thinly disguised instrument of coercive assimilation that proved genocidal in its consequences, partly because of its commitment to (1) remove and isolate children from their homes and communities; (2) eradicate all aspects of Aboriginal culture on the assumption they were inferior or dangerous; and (3) disrupt its transmission from one generation to the next (Fontaine & Farber, 2013; Indigenous Foundation, 2012).

Borrowed from the United States, where industrial schools formed the principal feature of President Grant's "aggressive civilization" policy of 1869

(Davin, 1879), residential schools (or industrial schools, as they were called initially in Canada because of their emphasis on manual and agricultural skills acquisition—namely, domestic service for the girls, carpentry and tinsmithing for the boys—were founded and operated by Protestant and Roman Catholic missionaries, but funded primarily by the federal government under the Department of Indian Affairs. These schools were established in every province and territory except Prince Edward Island, Nova Scotia, and Newfoundland, with the vast majority concentrated in the Prairie provinces. From two residential schools at the time of Confederation, the number of schools expanded to eighty by 1931: forty-four Roman Catholic schools, twenty-one Anglican, thirteen United Church, and two Presbyterian (Miller, 1996). By the time the system wound down in the mid-1990s, a stocktaking revealed the following: A total of seventy Roman Catholic schools with 68,250 students (or 65 percent of the total residential school population), followed by Anglican with thirty-seven schools and 23,100 students (22 percent), United with fourteen schools and 10,500 students (10 percent), Presbyterian with four schools with 1,050 students (1 percent), and seven government-run schools with 2,100 students (2 percent). About 100,000 Aboriginal children entered the system before closures during the 1970s, although four residential schools operated until 1996, albeit under Aboriginal jurisdiction (Miller, 1996). According to the Interim Report of the Truth and Reconciliation Commission of Canada (2012), about 80,000 survivors are still alive at present, with many continuing to suffer from the consequences of abusive behaviour or institutional neglect.

This experiment in forced assimilation through indoctrination proved destructive. Many of the schools were poorly built and maintained, living conditions were deplorable, nutrition portions barely met subsistence levels, and the crowding and sanitary conditions transformed them into incubators of disease. Many children succumbed to tuberculosis, along with other contagious diseases. A report in 1907 of fifteen schools found that 24 percent of the 1,537 children in the survey had died while in the care of the school, prompting the magazine *Saturday Night* to claim: "Even war seldom shows as large a percentage of fatalities as does the education system we have imposed upon our Indian wards" (quoted in Milloy, 1999, p. 91). Or, as Duncan Campbell Scott ruefully noted, "50 percent of the children who passed through these schools did not live to benefit from the education which they have received therein" (cited in Rolfsen, 2008). Other reports, including the Royal Commission on Aboriginal Peoples (1996), concluded that disciplinary terror by way of physical or sexual abuse was the norm in some schools. As one former residential school student told the Manitoba Aboriginal Justice Inquiry:

> My father, who attended Alberni Indian Residential School for four years in the twenties, was physically tortured by his teachers for speaking Tseshalt: they pushed sewing needles through his tongue, a routine punishment for language offenders.... The needle tortures suffered by my father affected all my family. My Dad's attitude became "why teach my children Indian if they are going to be punished for speaking it?" ... I never learned how to speak my own language. I am now, therefore, truly a "dumb Indian." (quoted in Rotman, 1996, p. 57)

Punishment also included beatings and whippings with rods and fists, chaining and shackling children, and solitary confinement. Reports of abuse appeared in anecdotal form by the 1940s, went public during the 1960s and 1970s, but did not incite the public indignation until 1990, when Phil Fontaine, the national chief of the Assembly of First Nations, disclosed his personal experiences. Admittedly, some Aboriginal children benefited even from a school system designed to destroy and assimilate (Indigenous Foundation, 2009). But many suffered horribly in the long run: Children grew up hostile or confused, caught between two worlds, but accepted in neither. Young and impressionable children returned to their families without a sense of self-worth because of verbal and physical abuse that made them feel inferior or confused. Many lost fluency in their own language or a sense of identity with their community ways (Rotman, 1996). Adults often turned to prostitution, sexual and incestuous violence, and drunkenness to cope with the emotional scarring. Worse still, the legacy of residential schools continues to negatively influence relations both across generations and within generations (Mohammed, 2010). As Jennifer Llewellyn (2002) writes:

> The painful legacy of residential schools continues to affect the survivors of residential schools. The effect of the abuses are not however limited to these individuals, but extend to their families, communities, culture, and reach across generational lines. The harms caused by residential schools thus are not limited to the physical and emotional scars from sexual and physical abuse. Rather, fully comprehending the harms of residential schools requires one to understand the relational nature of these harms. The harms of residential schools are at their most fundamental and enduring level harms to the relationships between Aboriginals and non Aboriginals and within the Aboriginal community itself. The harm, and the legacy of the residential schools, is the perpetuation of relationships of oppression and inequality.

This misguided and cruel experiment in racist engineering is unconscionable when judged by contemporary standards of human rights, government accountability, and the politics of Aboriginal claims to self-determining autonomy. Of course, it is easy to judge and condemn actions in hindsight, especially when implemented by people who were genuinely convinced of the moral superiority of Christianity and Western civilization. Many believed that they acted as good Christians by improving the lot of First Nations, even congratulating the government on initiatives as enlightened, given the alternative, namely, eventual extinction because of evolutionary progress unless Aboriginal peoples converted to Christianity and civilization (Indigenous Foundation, 2012). Nor should the complicity of Aboriginal parents be ignored. According to Miller (1996), many insisted on a European-style education for their children, although no one would have condoned the spartan living conditions or extreme punishment, despite an era when corporate punishment was routinely accepted as part of the "spare the rod, spoil the child" mentality. Still, the Royal Commission concluded that the residential school system was an "act of profound cruelty" rooted in racism and indifference and pointed the blame at Canadian society, Christian evangelism, and policies of the churches and government.

The 2008 apology and proposed reparations may prove a useful starting point in acknowledging the injustices in the past that denied recognition of the moral and political stature of Aboriginal peoples as full and complete citizens and human beings. It remains to be seen whether psychologically scarred Natives, broken families, and dysfunctional Aboriginal communities will respond to the balm of compensation packages, counselling centres, and healing programs. Yet danger signals abound. Evidence suggests that Aboriginal peoples and whites tend to frame the apology and reconciliation differently (Denis, 2012). The dominant white frame is individualistic, ahistorical, and final; by contrast, Aboriginial frames tend to be holistic, fluid, and processual. For whites, the apology represents closure; for Aboriginal peoples, it is one step in an ongoing healing process. For whites, it is time to stop dwelling in the past because it has no bearing in the present while complicating any effort to move forward. Such an ahistorical response reflects a Canadian-style polite racism that justifies racial inequality, avoids responsibilities, and defends dominant interests without sounding racist. For Aboriginal peoples, however (to steal a phrase from William Faulkner), the past (history) is not dead, it is not even the past. History is alive and resonates with the present because of racist consequences on both residential school children and their descendants (Fontaine & Farber 2013; Indigenous Foundation, 2009).

Profiling Race: Then and Now

Canadians and Americans are often perceived as poles apart when it comes to race relations. Compared to the United States, where race continues to negatively impact blacks and Latinos (National Urban League, 2009), Canadians generally reject the notion that race mattered or that it should matter (James, 1994, p. 47; Backhouse, 1999). Canada is widely applauded for emphasizing the principles of achievement and merit rather than skin colour as the basis for recognition, reward, and relationships. Canadians also like to revel in the myth of not judging others by the colour of their skin. To the degree that references to race persist, they tend to be muted, often employing circumlocutions such as "visible minorities" to avoid inflaming public passions, and conveyed by proxies such as "ethnicity" for fear of causing an affront (Li, 2003; Fleras, 2008a).

But evidence reinforces the primacy of race politics in Canada. Canada's history was infused by a perception of Canada as a "white man's society," a view reinforced by the Immigration Minister Robert Borden, who declared the Conservative Party stood for a white Canada (cited in Taylor et al., 2007; also Razack, 2002; Thobani, 2007). The ideals of racial purity played a pivotal role in keeping with the notion of Canada as a white nation and white women as "mothers of the race" (Agnew, 2007). Immigration programs rested on racial factors; accordingly, immigrants with darker skins were less desirable than those with lighter skins, and considerable effort was expended to keep them out (Avery, 1995; Satzewich, 2007). Legislators and judges endlessly manipulated classifications of race into rigid signifiers under Canadian law, erected racial hierarchies, justified racial discrimination, denied racial groups the right to vote, and segregated minorities according to race. Constance Backhouse (1999, p. 6) acknowledged how race intersected with class to underscore patterns of privilege and power:

> Racial classifications functioned as the hand servant for many disparate groups as they sought to explain why they were entitled to hold inequitable resources, status, and power over others.... It is equally evident that "racial" ideology was pressed into service as an excuse for the seizure of First Nations lands. "Race" was offered as the definitive explanation for the punitive treatment of Asian immigrants in the late nineteenth century.... Immigrants from southern and eastern Europe, Syria, Armenia, Arabia, India, and the Philippines often found their claim to "whiteness" contested in North America. The discriminatory treatment meted out ... to groups who emigrated to Canada from eastern and southern Europe has also been ideologically fastened to notions of "race."

It is one thing to condemn a racialized past. It is something quite different to acknowledge its persistence and pervasiveness in the present. Race as racism continues to inflict harm and hurt, in large part because where people are socially located in terms of skin colour (proxy for race) will influence how they see themselves, how others see and react to them, and their access to opportunities and outcomes. Racialized minorities bear the brunt of negative treatment, ranging from local snubs to half-hearted service delivery. Participation and decision making are influenced by prevailing stereotypes and racial prejudices, whereas social rewards are allocated on the basis of racial affiliation. Foreign-born racialized minorities tend to earn less than whites even when educational levels are held constant (Pendakur, 2005; Galabuzi, 2006). Minority women and men with professional degrees find it difficult to get jobs consistent with their credentials (Oreopoulos, 2009; Oreopoulos & Decheif, 2012; Roscigno et al., 2007). In a study involving 41,666 interviewees, skin colour (race)—not religion or income—proved to be the single largest barrier in fostering a sense of belonging to Canada. Moreover, the darker the skin, the greater the alienation, namely, young black males (Taylor, 2009). Racialized people of colour continue to be employed as cheap and disposable labour in often menial tasks with many serving as the hewers of wood and drawers of water as part of a racialized division of labour (Galabuzi, 2006; Reitz & Bannerjee, 2007). Even the emergence of race-conscious state policies such as the Employment Equity Act to ameliorate disadvantage have endured criticism as tokenistic or divisive. Clearly, race matters because minority experiences, identities, and opportunities continue to racialized, often against their best interests (Fernando, 2006).

Racialization: "Making Race"

The politics of race have proven virtually indestructible in defining identities, regulating relations, and organizing society. No matter how often discredited or dismissed as intellectually dead, the race concept continues to bounce back as a politically charged marker of differences and discrimination. The concept of race tends to be highly politicized, dynamic, and shifting as well as contradictory and ambiguous, but never far from the thrust and parry of privilege and power (Brace, 2005). In that perceptions of race have proven critical in how reality is defined, organized, and lived by both the dominant and subdominant sectors (James, 2005), the power of an illusion to move mountains cannot be underestimated.

But the concept of race has shifted in recent years (Hier & Bolaria, 2007). Race was once defined as a thing, a tangible object that could be isolated and measured as an objective biological entity. It is now increasingly defined as a process involving the imposition of racially linked meanings by the powerful on those less powerful. Race has evolved from something (a noun) thought to be inherent and genetic to a process (a verb) that is socially constructed and ideologically loaded (Byng, 2012). The language of racialization informs conceptual shift (Markus & Moya, 2010). Racialization may be conceptualized as constructing (making) race—that is, a process of defining, categorizing, and evaluating people and their activities along racial lines (Stanley, 2012). A socially constructed process is involved that (1) designates certain groups (or activities or spaces) as racially different; (2) subjects them to differential treatment by virtue of a tainted association with negative stereotypes; and

(3) disproportionately concentrates racialized minorities in certain domains such as poverty (Hyman, 2009; Galabuzi, 2006). Racialization assigns biological significance to others, so that individuals and groups are racially coded (identified, named, and categorized) along racial lines (Titley & Lentin, 2012; Bleich, 2011; Coates, 2008). Two dimensions prevail: On one side, negative racial significance is conferred on groups of activities on the basis of colour (for example, racializing crime); on the other side, social significance is assigned to certain groups on the basis of perceived racial(ized) physical difference (for example, criminalizing race). To be sure, racialization is not necessarily racism unless the imposition of race-based meanings and assumptions from the vantage point of white superiority is deployed to deny or exclude (Stanley, 2012).

The centrality of racialization as explanatory framework is widely accepted. The concept of race is no longer framed as description derived from physical world out there. It is framed instead as a socially constructed convention that is ideologically loaded within contexts of power (Helleiner, 2012). The significance of this shift from race to racialization cannot be underestimated. Shifting the focus from race as a thing (a biological entity) to race as a process or activity (social meanings assigned to groups of individuals) draws attention away from the physical attributes of minority groups and their presumed inferiority (Guess, 2006). Emphasis instead focuses on the perceptions and motivations of those powerful enough to impose race (racialized) labels that control or restrict (Chan & Mirchandani, 2002). A commitment to race as racialization rejects theories of racism as natural outcome of intergroup contact. Also rejected are references to racisms as a secondary social phenomena whose ideological status perpetuates unequal relations. Instead of simply reducing it to a set of beliefs that affect minority life chances, racism represents the ideological apparatus of a *racialized* social system that generates racially based outcomes. Or, as Bonilla-Silva (1997, pp. 2–3) reminds us, once a society is racialized in term of what is acceptable and who is normal, only then does race emerge as a category of difference and identity.

The implications of this racialization shift are critical in rethinking how race works. Put simply, there is no such thing as race relations in the sense of a "race" of people who stand in a relationship to another "race." Existing instead are relations that have been defined by reference to race—that is, "racialized." To the extent that the race concept has no empirical justification except in the perceptual sense, it is more accurate to speak of relationships that have been "racialized" than race relations per se (Bonilla-Silva, 1997). Furthermore, it is more accurate to say racialized minorities rather than racial minorities, in part to avoid the impression of minorities as a race of persons, in part to acknowledge how minorities are assigned these labels by those with the power to make them stick, in part to reinforce the social constructedness of race concept as a social control device. In reflecting, reinforcing, and advancing relationships of power and politics, reference to race says more about those constructing and imposing the labels than about those who are racialized.

Similarly with respect to racialization and racism. Responses to the question of whether Canada is a racist society may focus on framing Canada as a racialized society, one where (1) socially constructed notions of race matter in terms of shaping peoples lives and life chances; (2) economic and social rewards are allocated along so-called racial lines; (3) norms of desirability and acceptability are defined on racial grounds; and (4) core values reflect and reinforce a Eurocentric whiteness (see also Coates, 2008). Canada originated as a predominantly white man's country in which white was right and might was white. Racialized minorities were assigned a menial and inferior status while their worth was accordingly devalued. A white Canada continues to be defined, organized, and evaluated along racialized lines with respect to what is normal and necessary, acceptable, and desirable. A raft of superficial changes to protocols and incumbents has hardly altered the founding assumptions and foundational principles of Canada's constitutional order that remain anchored along racialized lines in advancing Euro-white interests.

Clearly, then, the relation of racialization to racism is inextricably linked yet analytically complementary. Racism is often defined as a *system* involving a set of practices, norms, and institutional arrangements both reflective of and simultaneously conducive to the creation and maintenance of racialized outcomes in society (powell, 2009). By contrast, racialization refers to a *process*: (1) a process of categorization that inserts people or activities into devalued racial categories based on perceived differences. For example, blacks become racialized in the sense they are signified as sharing essential values and inherent characteristics that generate racial outcomes (Martin-Alcoff, 2007; Coates, 2008); (2) a process in which white society transforms physical differences into hierarchical racial codes in ascending/descending orders of superiority/inferiority; (3) a process by which racial meanings are defined, understood, and attached to particular issues/social problems (Murji & Solomos, 2005); and (4) a process by which people are put into preconceived categories that advantage some and disadvantage others (Paradies, 2005). Inasmuch as the politics of racialization will continue to resonate in a racialized and "white-o-centric" Canada for the foreseeable future, there is little chance of a colour-blind Canada, even if one were attainable or desirable.

Race Matters: From Racial Domination to Racialized Hegemony

The persistence and pervasiveness of race and racisms raises a central question. Will either or both continue to matter in a Canada structured along the principles of white superiority (Wallis & Fleras, 2008)? Or do developments in Canada (and the United States) portend the emergence of a colour-blind ideology and race-neutral (post-racial) society that supersedes the legitimacy of race and racism as explanatory frameworks in defining who gets what and why? Some would argue that we are nearly there (Foster, 2005). For Americans, the election of Barack Obama is proof of an emerging post-racial society wherein race no longer matters in categorizing, treatment, and outcomes (Roberts, 2011; Ikuenobe, 2013; but see Alexander, 2012). Canadians, in turn, point to an official multiculturalism in consolidating Canada's status as a colour-blind society. For others, however, a commitment to colour-blindness resembles the proverbial Trojan horse in concealing racism, invisibilizing minority problems, securing social control, and assuming a de-raced playing field where none exists (Bonilla-Silva, 2002; Feagin, 2006; Doane, 2006). Or, as Thobani, Smith, and Razack (2010, p. ix) point out, despite the significance of race and racism to nation-building, Canada's dominant imagery remains one of an inclusive and multicultural society that has moved beyond the racialized origins and racist actions of the past. But the centrality of race and its intersection with identity markers such as gender and class continues to advance a white/Eurocentric privileged status quo (Joseph et al., 2012; Thobani, 2007). Paradoxically, perhaps, this commitment to colour-blindness and the post-racial may support two opposing agendas (McCardle, 2008): to (1) challenge inequality or (2) challenge those policies that challenge inequality. In short, reference to the racialization of race as a theoretical lens provides insight into a discursive shift, namely, from race as domination to race as hegemony (Winant, 2004).

The appeal of a colour-blind America where neither race nor racism matter has deep historical roots (Goldberg, 2007). Reference to the United States as post-racial was first mooted by the Supreme Court in 1883 and on numerous occasions since then, such as civil rights movement in the 1950s and 1960s in addition to the multicultural movement in the 1990s (Alsultany, 2012) Martin Luther King Jr. once proclaimed a promised land where people would be judged by their actions rather than skin colour. A more updated version dismisses the salience of race in defining who gets what. Race instead is framed primarily about cultural identity and lifestyle choices (Giroux, 2004; see also Gallagher, 2008). Other high-profile supporters of racelessness include William Julius Wilson (1996). Wilson believes the combination of suburbanization and joblessness have elevated class rather than race as the key determinant in shaping the lives of black Americans. Or consider Dinesh D'Souza whose book *The End of Racism* (1995) argued that race/racism were no longer a major barrier to black success. For D'Souza, merit, not racism, was the main culprit in generating inequality or downward social mobility, thus putting the onus back on blacks for constructing a culture of success. Furthermore, factors other than racism must account for socio-economic disparities and social pathologies, given the illegalities of racial discrimination (see also Gallagher, 2008). The conclusion is overwhelming, at least for devotees of a colour-blind ideology: With the end of racism in a post-racial society, it is not society that needs to be less racist in taking steps to remove racist barriers. On the contrary, it is minorities who need to be more responsible, hard-working, and integrative, while those in the anti-racism industry need to scale back their rhetoric in deference to a new reality.

A commitment to the colour-blind and post-racial is striking. A powerful ideology has emerged that not only rationalizes and justifies racial inequalities in society. It also absolves whites (or their proxies, namely, the state or government) of any responsibility for doing something about it (Bonilla-Silva, 2003). A colour-blind society renders race irrelevant in allocating resources; accordingly, there is no justification for race-based equity programs. Nor is there any rationale for taking race into policy-making considerations, even if intended to ameliorate inequality or redress past injustices (Bonilla-Silva, 2003; Doane, 2006). On the contrary, race-based policies for the amelioration of racial inequality (for example, affirmative action or employment equity) are deemed racist, unfair to whites, and violate core values pertaining to the meritocratic principles of a colour-blind society. Disparities reflect the function of perceived cultural inferiorities and lazy work habits, so that minorities have only themselves to blame for their poverty and disempowerment (Goldberg, 2007). Those who challenge the principle of colour-blindness may be themselves accused of racism by virtue of hoisting group difference over shared similarities. Besides, or so the argument goes, minorities have acquired unearned privileges at the expense of whites through affirmative-action initiatives, with the result they have evened the score and cancelled out any racial injustice from the past (hooks, 2013).

But are Canada and the United States on the same post-racial page as advocates contend? Or is it more accurate to say both countries are being reracialized because of social changes (globalization) and ideological shifts (neo-liberalism) that mask and reproduce inequalities behind the balm of post-racial and colour-bland (Winant, 2004; Thobani, Smith, & Razack, 2010)? Is race a thing of the past or will it continue to matter as a predictor of success and failure for the foreseeable future? If the response is no, how does one explain the apparent contradiction between a professed colour-blindness and the persistence of colour-coded inequality (Galabuzi, 2006; also Kochhar, Fry, & Taylor, 2011)? Laws outlawing discrimination at individual and institutional levels have done only so much in removing structural barriers and systemic biases. But references to the racelessness in a post-racial, colour-blind society plays into the hands of a white superiority complex (Simpson, 2008). The moral stakes are high: If whites are advantaged because of skin colour (whiteness), then their dominant status is undeserved and illegitimate. But if whites achieved success on meritocratic grounds, their privileged status is legitimate. In other words, a commitment to a colour-blind playing field preserves the status quo by privileging meritocracy and equal opportunity, while allowing whites to deny race and privilege without really addressing racial injustices (McCardle, 2008). Failure to confront structural racism not only simplifies claims to race-blind society; it also bolsters white privilege, as nicely pointed out by Barlow (2012, p. 18):

> Whites' capacity to deny the existence of racism, while continuing to benefit from racial privileges, was (and is) contingent on the development of structured racism. Once the patterns of racial privilege were built into the "normal" day-to-day operation of interlocking mass institutions, the defense of racism no longer required open claims of white superiority. It became increasingly feasible for whites to defend racial privileges by upholding standards of individual merit, community control, and other allegedly "race-neutral" claims.

A colour-blind racism allows whites to endorse the principle of racial equality without paying the price. Minority failures are pinned on a lack of effort or moral shortcomings rather than on the structural barriers that secure a racialized status quo (Byrd, 2011; Bonilla-Silva, 2003). How else to explain why (1) those who claim to be colour-blind are more likely to engage in predominantly white patterns of social interaction; (2) racialized minorities continue to be denied, excluded, and exploited ostensibly on the basis of skin colour; or (3) whiteness persists as a preferred ideal so that minorities who deviate from these ideals tend to be devalued accordingly (Bonilla-Silva, 2003).

In other words, appearances are deceiving because things are not what they seem to be. The most egregious dimensions of racialized society are no longer tenable in light of Canada's conventions or commitments. But the combination of legal statutes and collective ideals that condemn race and racism are no proof of a post-racial, colour-blind society. Even moves to formally dismantle overt supports for racism cannot dislodge an entrenched structural whiteness and white privilege that hide behind a facade of formal fairness (Doane, 2006; Pitcher, 2009). In theory, formal equality before the law sounds good. In practice, without special treatment to break the cycle of poverty and impoverishment, groups that are disadvantaged because of a late start will continue to fall further behind. Applying similar standards to unequal contexts by treating everyone alike tends to freeze the status quo, alongside a prevailing distribution of power and resources (Lentin, 2008). Or, as Lyndon B. Johnson aptly put it at the commencement address at Howard University on June 4, 1965, when acknowledging how the civil rights movement dismantled legal barriers to individual achievement, but did nothing to remedy the generational impact of white privilege:

> You do not wipe away the scars of centuries by saying, "now you are free to go where you want, do as you desire, and choose the leaders you please." You do not take a man who for years has been hobbled by chains, liberate him, bring him to the starting line of a race, saying, "you are free to compete with all the others," and still justly believe you have been completely fair....

Not surprisingly, the "act" of doing nothing and justifying it on principled grounds is not neutrality. A commitment to the do-nothingness of the post-racial colour-blindness is arguably a thinly veiled racism in defence of a white superiority complex. The following Insight box captures this paradox of formal equality as substantive inequality if context is not taken into account in making evaluations.

INSIGHT

Alphabetism in an Alphabet-Blind Society: A Parable about Racialized Bias
(Adapted from Henry Yu, 2012)

Once upon a time, a professor at the University of Ivory Towers taught a course that included a weekly test to gauge student knowledge of the readings and classroom material. For reasons largely immaterial to this case study, there was an insufficient number of textbooks, which meant some method of allocation had to be devised for divvying up the books. The professor decided to give a book to students based on the alphabetical order of their last (family) name. Textbooks were than issued in order, beginning with students whose family names began with A and continuing until they ran out, ending with last names that started with M.

Several weekly tests into the semester made it abundantly clear: Students who were given a book performed better than those without. Those whose last names began with N to Z protested over what they felt was unfair treatment, claiming an alphabet bias that confers an unfair advantage for some simply because of their last names. Chastened by this criticism of a systemic bias, the professor acknowledged the error of his ways and decided to differently redistribute the textbooks. From then on, the professor explained, students will be evaluated on the grounds of merit rather than on the accidents of a name assigned at birth. The books are then reallocated to the students with the highest grades, and working down the ranking list until the books run out. The professor announces the end of alphabetism since the books are now distributed to those most deserving based on their accomplishments. He proudly proclaims the dawn of a new alphabet-free meritocracy in which underperforming students could no longer blame their failures on a systemically biased system of distribution.

Despite these changes, some students continue to gripe about the unfairness of the arrangement. Those receiving low grades are concerned about the impact of poor scores on their careers. But the professor dismisses these complaints as unfounded. The system is now meritocratic, he argues, because an alphabetism bias no longer prevails in an alphabet-blind society. Furthermore, he counters, any poor results are the student's fault in an alphabet-blind meritocracy that treats everyone fairly and equally. Finally, he urges the complaining students to stop using history as an excuse, to take responsibility for their actions, and to get on with it.

This response does little to allay student concerns. They argue that the new system is fair in theory, and somewhat of an improvement over the alphabet-conscious arrangement. But a system that is theoretically fair, the students claim, has had the perverse effect of reinforcing the unfairness of the past. An alphabet-blind system accentuates past inequities by virtue of ranking students by criteria (grades) received during a period of inequality, while continuing to stack the deck in favour of those who excelled under an inherently biased system. Worst still, by claiming the present is fair and meritocratic, an alphabet-blind system conceals past unfairness yet compromises future prospects.

The moral of the parable? What lessons can be gleaned in terms of how race as racialization works?

1) History matters because legacies of the past continue to impact on the present. The age-old analogy of a foot race is helpful: That is, two runners do not have an equal chance to cross the finish line at the same time if one of the runners is saddled with a ball and chain that is removed only near the end of the race (Bonilla-Silva, 2002).

2) Introduction of fairness or merit as concepts neither creates a just society nor erases an unjust society if the playing field is unequal because of an unjust history or the cumulative impact of white privilege and minority disadvantage. An abstract or formal equality simply freezes the status quo, along with the prevailing distribution of power and privilege.

3) Inequalities and biases tend to systemic and institutional rather than systematic (deliberate) and personal, in large because they are deeply embedded within the opportunity structures of the system.

4) Replace the word "alphabet" with "race" or "colour," "alphabetism" with "racism," and "alphabet-blind" to "race-blind" to provide the reader with insight into how the principle of meritocracy in unequal contexts can prove disabling to those hobbled by the disadvantages of a late start.

Reference to Canada or the United States as colour-blind societies poses a conundrum. Ideally and superficially, this assertion may be the case, but reality suggests otherwise (West, 2012; Alexander, 2012). Canada remains largely colour-coded and deeply divided because race and racism continue to matter in defending white privilege and racialized status quo. For example, a recent report entitled *Spirit Matters* (Sapers, 2013) concluded accordingly. Aboriginal peoples may constitute only about 4 percent of Canada's population, but they comprised 23 percent of the inmates in federal jails, despite repeated pressure from the Supreme Court to pursue culturally specific restorative justice alternatives. As well, the report pointed out how blacks and Aboriginal peoples are five times more likely than their white counterparts to land in an Ontario jail (the figure for young Aboriginal women is ten times). The fact that a similar pattern of disproportional incarceration afflicts indigenous peoples in New Zealand and Australia makes a mockery of references to a colour-blind/post-racial society (Dickson-Gilmore & LaPrairie, 2005). The conclusion is inescapable: Settler societies such as Canada are profoundly racialized and deeply Eurocentric in the founding assumptions and foundational principles that inform their constitutional order. Claims to colour-blindness, notwithstanding, whiteness matters (see next section): White interests and Eurocentric agendas are invariably secured and inevitably advanced, sometimes deliberately, sometimes systemically, but always at the expense of racialized minorities (see Omi & Winant, 1994; Mills, 1997; Goldberg, 2002; Doane, 2006, 2007). In that the norm of racelessness allows racism to continue unchallenged, as Bonilla-Silva (2002) has argued, references to the colour-blind ideology of a post-racial society may well justify supremacist privilege while doing so along seemingly non-racialized lines.

The conclusion is dismaying: Race as a meta-discourse for racialization and racism remains one of the most volatile and divisive issues of this era of political changes and cultural shifts (Altbach et al., 2002). Instead of banishment to the dustbins of history as many expected, predicted, or aspired to, the seemingly antiquated concept of race continues to stalk the collective psyche (Sarich & Miele, 2004).To be sure, race matters not because groups of people are biologically inferior as proclaimed by the bone-headed or bullminded. Rather, it matters because people perceive others to be racially distinct, then rely on these perceptions of difference to discriminate or differentiate—in effect reaffirming W. I. Thomas's prescient notion that "things do not have to be real to be real in their consequences." Race matters by virtue of increasing the probability of something happening, as demonstrated below:

- Race matters in a post-racial, colour-blind society because it is more than simply an error of perception or exercise in rationalization. Rather, as Goldberg (2002) and others note (Thobani, 2007), the race concept proved pivotal in the evolution of the modern nation-state—as

fundamental to national identity and the central core of its societal culture (Pinder, 2010)—resulting in a racial caste-like state well into the middle of the twentieth century, with whites occupying what virtually amounted to a racial dictatorship and racialized apartheid.
- Race matters because post-racial societies remain racialized (Ikuenobe, 2013). That is, societies are known to make a distinction between "us" and "them," assign a devalued division of labour to the "other," and embed this devaluation of the other at the structural and ideological levels. That the founding assumptions and foundational principles of contemporary constitutional orders continue to be racialized along colour-conscious lines points to a singular conclusion. Race will continue to privilege some, while disempowering others (Baber, 2010; Morris & Cowlishaw, 1997).
- Race matters because so-called colour-blind settler societies such as Canada are racialized. A Eurocentric whiteness incorporates Anglo-American values, agendas, and standards as normal and necessary, while others are dismissed as irrelevant or inferior. Notions of race are so deeply implicated in the logic and expressions of racism that the prospects of dismantling a racialized bias are slim.
- Race matters because it reinforces racism. Racism works insidiously well under the dodge of race neutrality and colour-blindness. Paradoxically, however, the reverse may be more true. That is, the pervasiveness of racism in a racialized society is likely to reflect, reinforce, and advance the salience of race in constructing racialized hierarchies (Bonilla-Silva, 1997). As Pepi Leistyna (2004, p. 273) writes in prioritizing racism before race: "It is only in a race conscious society that skin color takes on ... significance." In other words, racism is not necessarily the product of races. Rather, race results from racism, namely, the experiences of those who have been singled out and controlled as racially different in racialized societies (Pitcher, 2009). Similarly, the prioritizing of white privilege can only be exercised in a society racialized along the lines of a white superiority complex.
- Race matters because society remains racialized in ways that systemically privilege some and marginalize others. In a racialized society, minorities may theoretically possess equal rights and equality of opportunity. In reality, they must exercise these rights without the benefit of institutionalized power and advantages of a head start in contexts neither designed with their realities in mind nor constructed to advance their interests. In other words, success is tantamount to swimming upstream since it entails going against the grain of a systemically unlevel playing field.
- Race matters because it plays a positive role as an indicator (or signifier) of identity, community, and history for racialized minorities, even if identifying with racial categories as resistance or justice may elicit yet more racism by reifying race (Goldberg & Solomos, 2002).
- Race matters not because it is real but because people believe it is real, and act accordingly. Race as social location (where one is socially

located in society) is a key factor in shaping how people think and act (and how others interact with them) with regard to identities, experiences, opportunities, and outcomes. It provides and represents a routine way of structuring relations between racialized minorities and the state (Comack, 2011). For example, race not only informs the routines of urban police who perceive racialized minorities and Aboriginal peoples as troublesome constituents. The inner city is also defined as a racialized space so that the simple presence of the racialized other creates suspicion (Canadian Centre for Policy Alternatives, 2009).

- Race matters because it constitutes a moving target that twists and bends across space and over time. The discursive shifts are unmistakable: From race as biological classification to race as social myth; from race as objectively real to the reality of social construction; from race as a thing (a noun) to race as a process (a verb that signifies how social meanings are assigned to physical differences); from race as categories to race as social control; from race as determinative to race as discourse; from race as a personal flaw to society as a racialized structure; from race as attitude to race as constitutional order (Blank et al., 2004; Backhouse, 1999; Guess, 2006; Wallis & Fleras, 2008). In short, instead of treating race as a static object in the world out there, emphasis is on the politics and process of racialization as a socially constructed dynamic of social control.

Grappling with each of these themes demonstrates the inescapable: The politics of race continues to represent one of the most bewildering dilemmas in contemporary society. On one side is the growing belief that Canadians and Americans are beyond race because attitudes have improved to the point where many dismiss its salience in a post-racial society. On the other side, the politics of race are to America as language debates are to Canada, albeit multiplied by a factor of ten (Ibbitson, 2005). As a result, it seems every race-related incident is elevated into a shouting match involving both whites (= racists) and racialized minorities (= second-class citizens) each of whom is automatically prejudged as guilty by association until proven innocent (Wente, 2009). John McWhorter (2009) writes accordingly:

> They're still at it. Aren't we supposed to be over it? Even with a black president. When even the head of the Republican National Committee—of all things—is black, black-white marriages don't even merit a turn of the head (authors note, in the year that Obama was born of mixed race parents, interracial marriages were illegal in nearly one half of the states in the United States), and America's favourite music is hip hop, there are always black people claiming America is all about racism.

In other words, reference to race is neither descriptive nor attitudinal, but deeply political and sharply contested with implications for living together in a social reality constructed along racialized lines (powell, 2009). Under these circumstances, we would do well to remember that perception *is* reality, even when largely unfounded by empirical evidence. Even if race is a fabrication, it is a powerful fiction that impacts profoundly on social reality, in effect reinforcing the sociological axiom that very real consequences can flow from "unreal" phenomena. Nowhere is this more true than in debates over whiteness as privilege in a white-o-centric society.

Whiteness Matters Too: Racialized Privilege in a White Superiority Society

All racism happens because of whiteness.
—*McGill Daily*, November 8, 2012

White privilege is the core pillar of racism.
—E. A. McGibbon and J. B. Etowa, *Anti Racist Health Care Practice*

It is whiteness, not overt racism, that is the dominant problem in the twenty-first century.
—A. Kobayashi, "Now You See Them, How You See Them: Women of Colour"

The white race is a historically constructed social formation. It consists of all those who partake of the privileges of white skin in this society. Its most wretched members share a status higher, in certain respects, than that of the most exalted people excluded from it, in return for which they give their support to a system that degrades them.
—N. Ignatiev and J. Garvey (Eds.), *Credo of Race Traitor*

There is a paradox at play in contemporary race debates. Many believe that race shouldn't matter for two reasons: First, the concept suffers from a lack of empirical validity or biological reality; second, the irrelevance of skin colour (proxy for race) in an ostensibly merit-based and colour-blind society. And yet, in a white-dominated society, race matters. As Henry and Tator (1993) explain, people's skin colour may be the single most important factor in determining their dignity, identity, self-esteem, and opportunities. Or rephrased in slightly more sociological terms, where one is socially located in society with respect to skin colour ("race") will profoundly influence a person's life (experiences), self-image (identity), and life chances (opportunities and outcomes).

Most Canadians will admit that certain minorities are disadvantaged because of skin colour. They may also concede that minority disadvantages do not always reflect individual failure, but may also include restricted opportunity structures as well as colour-coded barriers. But few Canadians are prepared to concede how "whiteness" plays a critical role in privileging some while disprivileging others (Wise, 2005). They are reluctant to acknowledge whiteness as a socially constructed category of race, just as men are often excluded from the category of gender. As a result, whites will see "others" as "races," but view themselves as "raceless," little more than a neutral standard and colourless norm that manages to be everything yet nothing, everywhere yet nowhere. Yet whites are "raced" just as men are "gendered," and failure to acknowledge this reality does a disservice in unpacking the politics of race.

Historically Euro-American societies endorsed and continue to endorse a commitment to the principles and the practices of a white supremacism (hooks, 2013; Itwaru, 2009). Whiteness was perceived as next to godliness—that is, "The apex of white racial ideology was reached when it was assumed that white domination was a God-given right" (Wright, 1945 cited in Forum, 2009, p. 1). Separate but interrelated logics bolstered white supremacy in the United States, including slavery, which anchors capitalism; genocide, which anchors colonialism; and orientalism, which anchors a call to war (A. Smith, 2010). To be sure, Europeans did not automatically become white on disembarking for North American shores. Groups such as Irish or Italians or Jews had to learn and earn this status (Goldstein, 2006). Colonial Canada too was openly and defiantly insistent on its status as white space (Baldwin et al., 2011, pp. 3–4), with whiteness and a white superiority complex as the normal category in the northern imaginary—Canada's immigration minister in 1908 declared "the Conservative Party stands for a white Canada" (cited in Taylor, James, & Saul, 2007, p. 158). As Ian McKay (2008, pp. 350–51) writes:

> Their Canada was in essence a White Settler society, and the nationalism of the majority of its people was a British nationalism. This Canada was ... a grand experiment in "whiteness," an imagined community founded upon the British occupation of the northern section of North America.... To be a true Canadian was to be White, English speaking, and Protestant—with some allowance made for French Canadian Catholics, provided they were deferential to the Empire.... Whiteness in Canada was an expression of confidence in British geo-political might and cultural pre-eminence ... and visualized a future in which the backward and benighted peoples of the world would be redeemed and reordererd through their exposure to their racial and cultural superiors.

Canadians at present would be startled to learn they live in a white space (Gillborn, 2006). Most believe they simply live in a neutral space because whiteness is invisible to them regardless of the domain, from politics to policing, from education to entertainment. However compelling and reassuring, this belief is mistaken. Whiteness is at the core of Canada's identity (Kalman-Lamb, 2011). Yet its status as the unmarked category upon which differences are constructed ensures whiteness conceals its role as an organizing principle in social relations and cultural expressions (Lipsitz, 1995). Every sphere of public life is deeply imbued (racialized) with whiteness as code, imagery, and interaction to the point of normalization and taken for grantedness. For example, the currency design crisis (see "Insight: Too Asian," in Chapter 2) reinforces the perception of whiteness (or non ethnicity) as the norm in Canada (Mahtani, 2012). Or as University of Ottawa law professor Rakhi Ruparelia (2012) writes: "Canada is a society of 'regular,' ethnicity free, white Canadians, and the rest of us—the ethnic 'Canadians'—are guests in our own home, tolerated (sort of), but at perpetual risk of overstaying our welcome."

For Gillborn (2006) this exercise in power and domination goes beyond domain of white privilege, with its tendency to mask the structure and actions of domination that marginalize racialized others (see also Peeples, 2006). Put bluntly, white privilege could not possibly exist outside the context of a white supremacist society. The exercise of white privilege and a white superiority complex is conditional on the existence of white supremacy (not in the sense of white supremacist groups) in the founding assumptions and foundational principles of a racialized constitutional order.[1]

INSIGHT

Canada: White Supremacy or a White Superiority Complex?

References to Canada as a white supremacist society may strike many readers as counterintuitive and needlessly provocative (Foster, 2009). Neither perceptions are intended if employed in a structural sense. A white supremacist society is not about a white apartheid system overrun by neo-Nazi skinheads. Nor does it refer to a caste system in which whites are firmly planted at the top with no possibility of movement up or down the caste ladder. More accurately, it is about acknowledging Canada as structured around the principles and practices of a socially constructed and ideologically loaded society in which:

- founding assumptions and foundational principles embody a commitment to a Euro-white constitutional order

- the society is designed, organized, and controlled by, for, and about whites with the result that racialized minorities may have the same rights and opportunities, but must exercise these rights and achieve success in a system neither designed with them in mind nor constructed to advance their interests

- the society reflects, reinforces, and advances white interests as normal,

> desirable, and acceptable in both overt (systematic) and covert (systemic) ways
>
> - white activities and characteristics are valued as the norm or superior, which is hardly surprising, given the primacy of a white Eurocentrism that interprets reality from a whitestream perspective as natural and normal while other perspectives are dismissed as inferior, irrelevant, or threatening
>
> - the state is complicit in securing preferential access to valued resource such as institutionalized power, privilege and status, and property/wealth
>
> - increasingly (and ironically) white supremacy operates under the guise of a post-racial society (Wise, 2009b), with a corresponding claim to colour-blindness that:
>
>   a) denies the significance of race
>   b) attributes disparities to non-race factors
>   c) dismisses racial discrimination as overstated and not a barrier
>   d) stands in opposition to race-based amelioration (Niemonen, 2007)
>
> Wallis, Sunseri, and Galabuzi (2010) define white supremacy as the process by which whiteness is socially constructed in settler societies to produce and maintain a racial hierarchy that not only defines the contours of a neo-colonial society but also privileges whites at the expense of others.

Metaphor for power? Proxy for privilege? Signifier for supremacy? Code for normalcy? Reference to whiteness as privilege in a white superiority Canada is not intended as a full-bore assault on whites. The editors of *Race Traitor* magazine whose motto, "treason to whiteness is loyalty to humanity," may advocate abolishing the white race (i.e., white privilege). But the focus here is critically self-reflective: first, challenging whites to think of their experience and identities as racialized (Byrne, 2010); second, analyzing whiteness as a power relations, not just a social identity (Kil, 2010; Garner, 2007); third, reflecting on how whiteness operates as a privileged dynamic in a racialized context (Henry & Tator, 2003); and, fourth, acknowledging how white privilege can flourish only within the structural context of a white superiority society (Gilborn, 2006). Three interlinked dimensions of whiteness prevail as part of the consciousness-raising process: (1) as a location of structural advantage that generates a sense of entitlement, creates perks, and elevates social status; (2) as a standpoint (social location) for interpreting reality (white gaze); and (3) as a set of unmarked cultural practices that permeates the entirety of society (Frankenburg, 1993). More specifically, whiteness as:

- a passport to privileges as reflecting a legacy of domination that is taken for granted because it is seemingly non-racialized. The notion of

whiteness is equivalent to owning property, insofar as those who own assets can access this wealth for greater enrichment (but see Trainor, 2008).
- standpoint (or socially location) from which whites understand the world, their position in it, and that of minorities who tend to be defined in deficit terms—that is, a perspective, gaze, or state of mind (mindset) that upholds Eurocentric rules and cultural practices for success as normative and normalizing as well as a largely unmarked and unnamed
- location of structural advantage involving the design and organization of society (including the foundational principles of its constitutional order) for advancing white interests (Evans et al., 2009; also Frankenberg, 1993).
- a structure of domination: Whiteness is more than a series of practices of even privileges; rather, it is intrinsic to the larger social structure and system of domination that rewards those racialized as whites, while marginalizing those defined as non-whites (Nopper, 2003).

In short, whiteness is not employed in the literal sense to convey the biological superiority of a distinct race. Nor is it intended to imply a homogeneous community of similar-minded individuals. Rather, whiteness as a social construction can be conceptualized in multiple ways, namely, as privilege, position, perspective, and practices. For some, whiteness is a term that lacks any inherent meaning except as an empty vessel with which to project mainstream fantasies and minority fears (Hsu, 2009). For others, a culture of whiteness prevails, consisting of rules, priorities, and values that privilege a predominantly Eurocentric way of interpreting reality as normative and normalizing, acceptable and desirable, while other interpretations of reality are dismissed accordingly. Central to critical whiteness studies is a focus on how racialized systems of power and control are constructed, concealed, and normalized so that whites neither see themselves as a race nor their racialized privilege within society (Croll, 2013; Lund & Carr, 2010). Whiteness matters: Just as whiteness as race is rendered invisible, so too are its privileges and benefits (McIntosh, 1988; Satzewich, 2007). What, then, does it mean to be white in Canada (Baldwin et al., 2011, p. 15)?

- Being white means one can purchase a home in any part of town without being "blacklisted" or "red-lined" by the local real estate market.
- Being white allows one to go strolling around shopping malls without the embarrassment of being "blackballed" (e.g., followed, frisked, monitored, or fingerprinted by security staff).
- Being white ensures one a freedom of movement without being pulled over by the police for "driving while black" ("DWB") or "flying while Arab" ("FWA").

- Being white works in my favour in terms of how people perceive my responsibility and skills so that professional success is deemed to have been achieved by merit rather than race or a minority hire.
- Being white simplifies identity construction since whiteness is normal and uncontested, whereas the process of identity construction vis-à-vis the mainstream is a central and ongoing aspect of minority existence, given the need to define their relationship to whiteness (see National Film Board of Canada, 2006).
- Finally, being white allows one to take credit for success without raising suspicion, while blame for failure is yours alone without dragging down the entire community as a representative of your race.
- In other words, being white excuses one from having to feel guilty about, take responsibility for, be judged by, or make excuses for the misdeeds of group members. Or, as a First Australian woman once put it, a white person who commits a crime is blamed as an individual, but the entire Aboriginal community shares the blame for individual indiscretions.

Much of the opprobrium directed at whiteness reflects a paradox. Whiteness is a privilege that is a largely unearned yet tacitly accepted as an advantage in a racialized society that claims to be colour-blind. It represents a process and a phenomena in which whites are advantaged (including a reprieve from most forms of discrimination) simply because their values, experiences, and expectations constitute the default option in society. Stamped into one's skin by an accident of birth (Garner, 2007), whiteness is a kind of "passport" that opens doors and unlocks opportunities, just as identity cards in South Africa once defined privilege by the hue of one's skin colour. Not surprisingly, there is a booming market for skin whiteners in parts of the world where whiteness is equated with beauty, success, and popularity (Fleras, 2011b). The privileging of whiteness is neither openly articulated nor logically deserved, but assumed and universalized as normal and natural, thus transcending scrutiny or criticism. Whiteness is the "natural" way of being human—that is, whites are unaware of their whiteness and privilege in the same way that fish are unaware of their "wetness" because of their immersion in water until, of course, it is too late.

> ## INSIGHT
>
> ### Privileging Able-bodiedness, Disprivileging Disabilities
>
> There aint no white man in this room that will change places with me—and I'm rich. That's how good it is to be white. There's a one legged bus boy in here right now that's going—"I don't want to change. I'm going to ride this white thing out and see where it takes me."
> —Chris Rock, *1999 Bigger and Blacker Quotes*
>
> To understand how white privilege works, Tim Wise (2008) provides an interesting analogy. Take able-bodied people as opposed to individuals with disabilities (reference to left-handedness in a right-handed world works as well). To say that able-bodied people possess advantages (privileges) over people with disabilities who confront numerous obstacles in everyday life is surely beyond debate. Although people with disabilities may overcome these obstacles, that doesn't take away from the fact that these obstacles exist and that the able-bodied have an edge, in part because they have one less thing to worry about from entering a building to crossing a street. Moreover, the fact that some able-bodied people are poor, while some people with disabilities are rich and have power, doesn't alter the rule. People with disabilities may possess the same rights as the able-bodied, but they must exercise these rights in a context neither created to reflect their realities nor constructed to advance their interests. On balance, it pays to be able-bodied—in other words, just as in general it is better to be a member of the dominant white group because of the general advantages (Coates, 2013).[2]
>
> Similarly, as the noted anti-racist scholar Tim Wise (2008) points out, if privilege is associated strictly with money issues, not all whites are economically privileged or able to get everything they want or win every competition. However, if privilege is to include psychological issues, then whites possess race privilege because they have the luxury of not worrying about their "race" as a negative marker in looking for work or housing, whereas even rich black and brown folks may be subject to stereotyping and racial profiling.

The concept of Eurocentrism reinforces how whites perceive the world through a "white gaze" (Henry & Tator, 2003). White ways of looking at the world and human experiences are framed in a manner consistent with their privileged position of power. Attitudes, behaviours, and arrangements that appear normal and ordinary to a white gaze are, in fact, a racialized prism (or lens) through which racist stereotypes and discriminatory actions are sustained and rationalized. But whiteness is as much a matter of interests as of attitudes, of property as of pigment. It also represents a structured advantage that produced unearned gains and rewards for whites while imposing barriers for racialized others (Lipsitz, 2006). Three levels of white gaze (white framing) can be discerned that correspond to some extent with the principles, structures, and practices underpinning a white supremacist society.

- At the most general level of conceptualization, a white framing defines whites as superior in culture and accomplishment, while whiteness comes to symbolize certain values and status positions that signify intellectual, moral, and cultural advancement (Feagin, 2006; Picca & Feagin, 2007; Feagin & Cobas, 2008). Dimensions of a white racialized framing may include (1) a belief in neo-liberal universalism (or rights and commonalities as individuals in a colour-blind society prevail over group differences since differences are only skin-deep); (2) the virtues of a (neo)liberal ideology to justify neutrality of a colour-blind Canada (or America); (3) the centrality of morally autonomous and rights-bearing individuals; (4) the importance of reason and science in advancing both individual and collective progress; (5) distinctive orientations to time and space, including their value and measurement. (In this sense, both a white gaze and white framing are similar to the concept of Eurocentrism, which, too, reflects a tendency to see, interpret, and assess reality from a predominantly white point of view as normal, desirable, and superior.)
- At a deeper conceptual level, whites not only monopolize the levers of state and institutional power (Gilborn, 2006). The prevailing distribution of institutionalized white power and white controlled institutions is seen as unremarkable but as inevitable or deserved. For example, notice how negatively whites react to situations in which racialized minorities are seen as either taking over white spaces (see "Too Asian"? in Gilmour et al., 2012) or depriving whites of their "natural born" entitlements ("I can't get a job [that I'm entitled to] because of preferential minority hires under Employment Equity").
- At the deepest levels (namely, the founding assumptions and foundational principles of the constitutional order) are those stereotypes and prejudices toward racialized minorities that unconsciously reinforce their perceived inferiority, thus accentuating white (especially male) virtues while privileging whiteness as masters of the social universe. White children constantly receive messages that whites/whiteness are superior as the norm and standard while racialized groups aredeffined as deviations and inferior (hooks, 2013).

Herein, then, lies the "genius" of white privilege. Whiteness is *everything yet nothing*: *everything* because whiteness is the normative but unmarked standard by which reality is judged or interpreted without much awareness of the process; *nothing* because many perceive whiteness to be inconsequential in privileging or disprivileging (Garner, 2007). Whiteness shapes people's lives by symbolizing (1) dominance rather than subordination, (2) normativity rather than marginality, and (3) privilege rather than disadvantage. Niemonen (2007) draws attention to other dimensions of whiteness, including:

- a state of being that denies the harm whites have inflicted on minorities
- a position in a hierarchy to which power and privilege are attached and from which they are wielded (racialized social system) (Doane, 2003)
- a standpoint from which others are evaluated
- cultural practices that are perceived as universal and normative yet unnamed
- a form of social capital that accrues benefits yet fails to recognize or admit such advantages

But while whiteness (like power) may be invisible to those who benefit from it, for non-whites it is painfully obvious and blatantly ubiquitous (Applebaum, 2010). Moreover, those without the privilege of whiteness are stigmatized as the "other" and demonized accordingly. Otherness (for example, blackness) represents the antithesis of whiteness in terms of privilege or entitlement—a highly visible stigma (or marked category) that denies, excludes, or exploits. Unlike whites, who rarely experience whiteness, people of colour have little choice except to confront their minority-ness on a daily basis. Those in positions of disadvantage routinely experience the dynamics of being different, of having to defend these differences, and of being disadvantaged by them (Henry & Tator 2003). No aspect of existence, no moment of the day, no contact, no relationship, no response is exempt from the stigma of otherness in a racialized society (Philip, 1996).

To be sure, not everyone views whiteness as an unmarked vehicle of privilege. Whiteness is structured in a way that when racialized minorities intrude on white privilege, whites feel a sense of racial injustice (Priya, 2007). For example, a study by researchers at Tufts University and Harvard concluded that whites now believe they are the primary victims of racism since progress toward equality has transpired at their expense (*New Black Woman*, 2011; also hooks, 2013). Whites may perceive racism as a zero-sum game. Decreases in perceived bias toward blacks are associated with increases in perceived bias toward whites, with the result that anti-white bias is now seen as a bigger social problem than anti-black bias (Norton & Sommers, 2011). They may be uncomfortable with the idea of racialized minorities gaining power since it undermines their belief in white superiority complex. Attacks on a racialized society are viewed as attacks on whiteness, white privilege, and white supremacy, all of which demand reaction to repel these assaults on civilization, the West, democracy, or America (Monteiro, 2003). As well, white supremacist groups have cleverly transformed whiteness into victimhood, in much the same way as some men's movements have depicted males as victims of radical feminism and political correctness. Whiteness is valorized as the hallmark of an endangered or persecuted race, according to supremacists, one under threat and challenge by minorities because of quotas or "reverse discrimination" (see Ferber, 1998; hooks, 2013). Yet these challenges to "whiteness" require a context. True, whites no longer possess the exclusive power and the uncontested privilege of the past. But moving over and making space is not the same as transforming patterns of institutional power or white privilege.

Two final questions remain: First, are whites a race? Technically, no, because there is no such thing as race per se. Yes, because in a world of perceptions where there is no position from nowhere, everybody is perceived to be racially located, whether he or she is aware of it or not. That alone makes it doubly important to decentre whiteness by racializing it *as if* it were a "race" (racialization), if only to paint whites into the picture by recognizing whiteness as a manifestation of the human experience rather than assumed as a universal norm (Jensen, 2010b). Whiteness needs to be racialized/decentred in order to understand the dominant and hegemonic role that it plays in perpetuating exclusion and discrimination (Henry & Tator, 2003). After all, to exclude whiteness as an unmarked race category that stands outside history or convention is to redouble its privilege and hegemony by naturalizing it as normal, inevitable, and superior (Fleras & Spoonley, 1999).

The second question is no less provocative: Is whiteness synonymous with racism as a set of the ideas and practices that inferiorize others through negative and demeaning treatment. To what extent are the *systemically privileged* complicit in perpetuating social injustice? In that whiteness is tied to structures of domination and oppression, does being white make it impossible to be a non-racist (see Applebaum, 2010)?

> *No*, not in the sense that being white automatically makes one a racist. Young adults and new Canadians, for example, may find it unfair to blame them/feel guilty/take responsibility for racist actions in the past. But while the concept of collective responsibility for collective wrongs may be difficult to fathom in a liberal democratic society, there is little question that whites collectively have benefited from the creation of wealth on the backs of racialized minorities (Lipsitz, 2006). Or, as Tim Wise argues (see also hooks, 2013), all people regardless of skin colour but raised in a racialized environment will internalize elements of racist thinking about others and themselves. In addition, the racism in whiteness reflects the Eurocentric tendency to interpret reality from a white point of view (white gaze) as natural and normal, while "othered" viewpoints are dismissed as irrelevant or inferior.

Yes, however, if the largely unearned privileges of whiteness and the benefits of living in a white society are taken for granted rather than acknowledged (Frankenburg, 1993; Mackey, 2002). In a white superiority society designed by, for, and about whiteness, whites derive an advantage or assume a privilege that is built into (inherent) rather than simply the product of individual efforts or ability (Jensen, 2010b). Moreover, whiteness may qualify as racism in that white privilege inheres within the founding assumptions and foundational principles of Canada's constitutional governance in defining who gets what. Whiteness may not intend to dominate and control, but the interplay of white rules and "pale male" agendas may have a controlling effect in perpetuating a racialized status quo in defence of white supremacy. That puts the onus on whites to strategically deploy their whiteness and privilege to challenge racism and racial discrimination.

To sum up, reference to Canada as post-racial and colour-blind is a contradiction in terms. Canada remains racialized and colour-coded because it constitutes a society designed by, for, and about whites to reflect their realities, reinforce their interests, and advance their agendas. A white superiority complex reflects the ideological root of both race and racism as well as the political foundation and constitutional order of all systems of racialized domination (hooks, 2013). Racialized minorities in a white superiority society are victims of discrimination not because of their racial differences, but because of the negative race connotations imposed on them (Rosado, 2013). Similarly, whites are racialized as well, albeit in ways that promote a superiority complex. Not surprisingly, a key component of anti-racism action involves deconstructing/dissecting unearned white supremacist power and privilege (Canadian Council of Churches, 2012). For in the final analysis, the race problem is a white problem encompassing white claims to superiority and supremacy. It is not the convention of race (human differences) that needs to change but systems of exploitation that benefit the racialized majority yet remain largely invisible because of their ubiquity (Rosado, 2013). The challenge lies in de-normalizing whiteness by visibilizing it to create a post-whiteness society (Pinder, 2010). At the core of this de-normalization process is the need to examine the many invisible ways in which white supremacist privilege pervades people's identities, experiences, beliefs and assumptions, and opportunities (Ferber, 2008). Accordingly, the end of racism entails the end of whiteness (Jensen, 2010b). Or, as Ignatiev and Garvey (1996, p. 2) put it in challenging what it means to be white in society (see also Guess, 2006):

The key to solving the social problems of our age is to abolish the white race, which means no more and no less than abolishing the privileges of white skin.... The existence of the white race depends on the willingness of those assigned to it to place their racial interests above class, gender, or any other interests they hold. The defection of enough of its members to make it unreliable as a predictor of behavior will lead to its collapse.

Notes

1. The term "white supremacist society" appears with some frequency in the literature (Rollock & Gillborn, 2011). Like Lorne Foster (2009), I too find the term ambiguous and accusatory (perhaps even needlessly provocative) while failing to convey the structural dynamics of race relations and racism. I prefer the expression "a white superiority society" for two reasons: First, too often a reference to white supremacy conjures up images of neo-Nazi groups with explicitly racist dogmas that demonize minorities while extolling whites. Second, a reference to white superiority complex makes it easier to think of racism as structurally embedded in a racialized society. A white racialized (superiority) society refers to a political, economic, and cultural system in which mainstream whites control power and material resources, notions of white privilege and entitlement are widespread, and relations of dominance and subordination are routinely enacted across a broad range of institutions and everyday encounters (see also Rollock & Gillborn, 2011).
2. Another way to understand the systemic bias of white privilege is to consider what it means to be left-handed in a right-handed world.

CHAPTER 4

DECONSTRUCTING RACISM
PREJUDICE, DISCRIMINATION, POWER

Introduction: The Multi-dimensionality of Racism

Hatred of outgroups is inextricably linked to the human condition. Hate as a catalyst for murder or mayhem is neither unique nor new, despite the more cosmopolitan realities of the twenty-first century. But responses to questions of why people hate are sharply contested. Is it because of our genes? Human nature? Cognitive disorder? A personality malfunction? Cultural values? Situational cues? Is this hatred something intrinsic to the programming of the human species? Or does it reflect a calculated ploy for advancing dominant interests at the expense of others? Even defining the concept of hate and hatred poses a challenge, especially since the words cover an expanding range of human actions, from a mildly negative opinion to a powerful hateful emotion, culminating in a disposition to dehumanize or destroy (Mohr, 2006/2007).

Acts of hate-based hostility have long been perpetuated by one group against another. Ultra-nationalist and religious fundamentalist movements frequently manipulate hate hostility to galvanize support and mobilize people into action out of fear or xenophobia (Davison, 2005/2006). These hostilities remain rooted in negative notions of the "other" as another, including differences related to religion, gender, sexuality, race, and ethnocultures. To be sure, societies such as Canada are increasingly intolerant of such acts or projections, in effect seeking to abolish race-based hate as grounds for exclusion or exploitation (Mohr, 2006/2007). Nevertheless, hostilities toward racialized minorities continue to be expressed in different ways, including prejudging minorities on the basis of stereotypes or ethnocentrism. A survey by the Association for Canadian Studies and Ensemble in March 2013 indicated that 24 percent of Canadians reported victimization by prejudice.

Minorities may be victimized by discriminatory actions that have the intent or the effect of denying, scapegoating, or excluding because of race or ethnicity. They also remain vulnerable to thinly veiled hostilities because of their relative powerlessness within deeply racialized contexts.

In short, racialized minorities are victims of hate hostilities that span the spectrum from attitudes and actions to systems and relations. In some cases, the hostile actions are consciously conveyed, in other cases, they reflect the consequences of actions largely beyond people's awareness or control; and in still other cases, the hostilities are carefully camouflaged behind a thin veneer of civility that conceals or distorts. The totality of these hostilities can be subscribed under the category of racism. But racism does not exist as a monolithic reality. Rather, racisms are a complex and multi-faceted dynamic constructed around different constituents. Each of the constituents or components constitute the building blocks of racisms, namely, prejudice[1] (including ethnocentrism, xenophobia, and stereotypes), discrimination (including harassment), and institutional power. Each contributes to the totality of racism as a compound set of socially constructed beliefs and attitudes as well as (in)actions and consequences that deny or exclude within contexts of power and inequality.

This chapter deconstructs and analyzes the constituents of racism. The concepts of prejudice, including stereotypes, ethnocentrism, and xenophobia (particularly Islamophobia), are analyzed from a social/sociological perspective to reveal their controlling functions. References to discrimination, including harassment, are shown to include both overt/deliberate and covert/unintended patterns. The politics of power—especially institutional power—underscores the racialized underpinnings of both prejudice and discrimination. The relationship between these constituents is also examined, in the process demonstrating that neither prejudice nor discrimination are as critical as the centrality of power in shaping the lives and life chances of racialized minorities. The chapter concludes by demonstrating how the interplay of prejudice, discrimination, and power reflect, reinforce, and advance the racialized inequalities of a racially stratified society. Two ideal typical models of racialized stratification—ethnicity versus racism—offer competing explanatory frameworks for defining who gets what and why.

Prejudice: Prejudging the Other

The concept of prejudice refers to negative, often unconscious, and preconceived notions about others. Prejudice arises because of a normal human tendency to categorize and prejudge people or situations. The processing of information about the world is not inherently racist; after all, everyone makes prejudgments when defining situations. Massive amounts of information are received, then transformed into data, as grounds for navigating our way through life. Our actions often depend on those categories of thought with which to order and organize reality (Cohen, 2011). Dovidio, Gaertner, and Kawakami (2010, p. 315) reinforce this point when they claim that:

> One fundamental process involves human's propensity to categorize objects and people. Categories form an essential basis for human perception, cognition, and functioning: it is a critical process in the way that people actively derive meaning from complex environments.... In this respect, people compromise total accuracy for efficiency when confronted with the often overwhelming complexity of their social world.

Admittedly, these prejudgements may not be easy to discern. Privately held prejudices do not necessarily incite prejudicial behaviour since most individuals are quite adept at compartmentalizing thought and divorcing it from actions (Malla, 2008). Prejudice becomes a problem when people use these prejudgments as a basis for acting in ways that deny or exclude others.

Prejudice may be defined as a set of prejudgments both irrational and unfounded on grounds of existing or compelling evidence. A set of generalized attitudes is embraced that mistakenly encourages people to see and judge others without taking into account individual differences (Holdaway, 1996). Three levels of prejudice can be discerned: cognitive (beliefs), emotional (feelings), and behavioural (actions) (Rosado, 2013). According to psychologist Frances Aboud, prejudice provides a manageable way of organizing the world that addresses people's craving for simplicity, familiarity, order, and control (cited in Abel, 2001). Such ignorance may persist into adulthood. Unlike ignorance, however, prejudice is thought to be inflexible and characterized by a refusal to bend beliefs when presented with contrary evidence. True, the distinction between ignorance and prejudice is rarely clear-cut. Neither prejudice nor ignorance are necessarily synonymous with malicious racism, especially in coping with ambiguity and confusion (for example, Abraham Lincoln fought to abolish slavery, but apparently believed blacks were inferior and beyond the pale of coexistence). Nevertheless, others may interpret this uncertainty or ignorance as prejudice or racism, and react accordingly.

Prejudices consist of a set of preconceived attitudes toward groups arranged in a hierarchical order (Dovidio, Hewson, Glick, & Esses, 2010). But prejudice itself is not a static phenomena. Over time, the dynamics and targets of prejudice evolve. North Americans once despised the Irish as racially inferior and akin to blacks. This race antipathy was subsequently directed at Asians, Jews, and Eastern Europeans. Now Muslims and/or those from the Middle East are at the receiving end of fear, scapegoating, and hostility (Islamophobia). Even within devalued groups, prejudices are not necessarily equally directed or evenly distributed toward all members, with some subsets bearing the brunt of hostilities. Studies indicate that whites express more negative attitudes toward racialized minorities who strongly identify with their culture or religion than to mainstream society (Kaiser & Pratt-Hyatt, 2009). White prejudice tends to be aimed at those minorities who are seen as "uppity," who refuse to know their place, and who reject playing by the rules of the game. As well, prejudice is not restricted to majority or dominant sectors. Minorities too absorb prejudices, which then become the basis of prejudicial action toward others. As Raina Kelley (2009a) of *Newsweek* writes: "Being black doesn't get me a pass on unconscious negative feelings about African Americans or the shame we feel when they become conscious. We see the same cultural indicators as everyone else—back then, hours of riot footage, rap videos, and the OJ trial had created an automatic connection in my mind between African American Los Angelenos and danger."

At times, expressions of prejudice are conscious but politely worded to avoid open offence. At other times, individuals may not be aware of their prejudice except in those split-second situations that expose dormant dislikes. Most of us have implicit biases that can micro-manipulate thinking and behaviour (powell, 2009), especially when making snap decisions about who is hired, who is arrested, and who just "fender-bendered" your car. The Implicit Association Test <www.tolerance.org/supplement/test-yourself-hidden-bias> confirms how most people have hidden and unconscious prejudices toward minorities often at odds with their explicitly articulated egalitarian values (Banaji, 2003; Pager & Quillian, 2005; Sriram & Greenwald, 2009). For example, tests of unconscious stereotyping involving rapid-fire word associations find that nearly 90 percent of whites implicitly associate blackness with negativity, from crime to threats (Feagin, 2006). The distinction between implicit and explicit prejudice is significant (Anderson, 2010; Dovidio, Hewson, Glick, & Esses, 2010). Just as people don't always "speak their minds" from fear of consequences, so too do people not "know their minds" because of self-delusion, culminating in a gap between conscious and unconscious, belief and behaviour. Again, Raina Kelley's (2009b) prescient notion is worth citing:

> I do not think we are a nation of people secretly yearning to scream racial epithets and reinstate Jim Crow. I think we are a nation of people deeply influenced by stereotypes endlessly perpetuated in our culture ... we have automated this stereotyping to the point where it happens not in our conscious mind but in its operating system—working in the back of the brain to help process the reams of information coming at us from every direction.

Reference to prejudice as a kind of "mental residue" should not be discounted as trivial or inconsequential (Caines, 2004). Psychologists and psychiatrists have long asserted the unconscious to be a powerful motivator of actions precisely because it is unobtrusive, relatively stable, not consciously accessible, and difficult to control (Anderson, 2010). Nor does the centrality of the unconscious imply that everyone is a closet racist. Nevertheless, most people are not as colour-blind as they like to think they are (Kelley, 2009b), as conveyed by this passage (Anderson, 2010, pp. 2–3):

> Whites appear, then, to be more supportive of equal rights in principle than of equal rights in practice. When commitment is required to perform specific actions involving their own lives and the status of their own group, they are much less receptive to the idea of equality [this notion of subliminal racism will be discussed in a later chapter].... Bigotry appears to have decreased, but on the other hand, people are not willing to give up their own privileged status. Dominant groups appear increasingly tolerant, but when it comes to sacrificing some of their own comfort or endorsing government assistance for subordinate groups, they are disinclined to favor these remedies.

Different perspectives and explanations account for the origins and persistence of prejudice. Keep in mind that origins are not the same as causes—both root and precipitating—which, in turn, differ from the dynamics of perseverance. Many regard prejudice as a psychological phenomenon with a corresponding set of rigid or authoritarian personality traits (Adorno et al., 1950; Allport, 1954). Others link these prejudgments with a visceral and deep-seated fear of those whose appearances or practices threaten the prevailing status quo. The fact that prejudice may involve a projection of fear or displacement of anxieties upon others is consequential. Such beliefs may say more about the perpetrator than the perpetrated (Dovidio, Hewson, Glick, & Esses, 2010). Still others define prejudice as unmistakably social. Prejudices do not necessarily materialize from deep-seated impulses or expressions of a warped personality. Sociologists are inclined to frame prejudice within a social context involving group interaction for controlling others in the competition for scarce resources. Those in positions of power and authority have a vested interest in fomenting outgroup hostility for purposes of dividing, distracting, or denying. The end result may be discriminatory since the social consequences of prejudices may perpetuate a racialized and unequal system.

Ethnocentrism/Eurocentrism

Ethnocentrism may be defined in two ways. First, it consists of a belief that asserts the superiority of one culture over another. Like prejudice, ethnocentrism is a normal and universal process, reflecting patterns of socialization that focus on in-group loyalty. A belief in cultural superiority is justified by negatively evaluating other cultural practices against one's own standards of right, acceptable, or desirable. Second, ethnocentrism involves the universal tendency to frame (to see and interpret) reality from one's cultural perspective as natural and normal, while dismissing other perspectives as inferior or irrelevant. The notion of ethnocentrism—not in the sense of cultural superiority but as a process for processing information from a fixed point of view—is pivotal in marginalizing minorities by reinforcing mainstream prejudices.

Of course, there is nothing intrinsically wrong with endorsing one's cultural lifestyle as self-evident and preferable. Difficulties arise when these standards become a frame of reference for negatively evaluating others as backward, immoral, or irrational. Further problems appear when these ethnocentric judgments are manipulated to condone the mistreatment of others. In other words, ethnocentrism is a two-edged social phenomenon. Favouritism toward one's group may forge in-group cohesion and morale; it can also foster intergroup tension and outgroup hostility. And when those in positions of power put their ethnocentrism into practice, the results can get ugly.

Related to ethnocentrism is the notion of Eurocentrism. Like ethnocentrism, Eurocentrism may be employed to promote the status of European superiority or, alternatively, as a lens that privileges the normativity of European standards of desirability and acceptability as the basis for assessing the world. As a construct that sanitizes or praises Western societies while patronizing or demonizing the non-West, Eurocentrism constitutes a way of looking at and thinking about the world whose "rightness" applies not only for whites but for people and places everywhere (Shohat & Stam, 1994). Intersecting with the idea of Eurocentrism are questions of whiteness as a racialized identity and white normativity that are critical to the centring of the West (Turney, Law, & Phillips, 2002). To be sure, neither Eurocentrism nor ethnocentrism are synonymous with racism, as Turney, Law, and Phillips argue (see also Shohat & Stam, 1994), but rather an implicit positioning (or discourse), often manifested in ways that can be described as racist.

Stereotypes

Ethnocentrism often generates a raft of stereotypes about outgroup members. Stereotypes are essentially generalizations about others, both unwarranted and unfounded on the basis of available evidence (Dovidio, Hewson, Glick, & Esses, 2010). Some argue that stereotypes represent a by-product of a human cognitive tendency to categorize and simplify (Lee et al., 2009). Others argue that stereotypes emerge when individuals limit their interactions with others, thus relying on first impressions as a basis for information. For example, what many people know about diversity and minorities is rarely gleaned from first-hand experiences. Rather, it is drawn from media messages as the preliminary and often primary point of contact with the world out there (Fleras, 2011c). Predictably, people tend to stereotype outgroups as a uniformly homogeneous and undifferentiated mass rather than being valued as individuals with skills and talents. An essentialized notion is conveyed that slots all individuals into a singular category, then assumes that everyone will act uniformly and behave predictably because of this membership (Essed, 1991). With stereotypes, in other words, a self-fulfilling process comes into play. Those who are stereotyped often live up to them or, more accurately, down to them in the case of underperforming racialized minorities (Steele, 2006).

Still others point to stereotypes as socially constructed patterns of thought control for preserving power and justifying social inequities (see Coates, 2008). Stereotypes do not necessarily represent an error in perception, at least no more so than prejudice constitutes a flaw in erroneously processing information. On the contrary, stereotyping is yet another instrument of social control by vested interests for preserving the prevailing distribution of power and resources, while helping to justify unequal treatment. Think of how the dispossession of Aboriginal peoples' lands was facilitated through their stereotyping as savages, cannibals, and brutes. A pervasive "antiorientalism" in British Columbia fostered hatred against Asian populations, thereby simplifying the task of expelling 22,000 Japanese Canadians from the West Coast in 1942. Hostility toward Arab/Muslim Canadians continues to fester in light of demeaning media stereotypes that portray them as (1) members of a devalued and backward minority, (2) colonized peoples without democratic traditions, and (3) terrorists and religious fanatics hellbent on destruction (Karim, 2002; Goldberg, 2005). However mistaken, this equation is popular: Muslim = Arab = savage = religious fanatic = Islam as violent religion = terrorist = hatred of things Western = destruction (Zahr, 2001).

Like any strategy for simplifying the environment (Dovidio, Hewson, Glick, & Esses, 2010), stereotypes in themselves are harmless. But problems arise when these preconceived mental images justify discriminatory barriers or generate self-fulfilling practices. For example, employers who must make split-second decisions may rely on subconscious stereotypes based on the whiteness (or lack) of last names (white-sounding names are much more likely to receive interviews) when sorting through resumés (Oreopoulos, 2009; Jimenez, 2009). Experiments in the United States found that landlords responded positively to prospective Asian American tenants (perceived as quiet, passive, smart, hard-working, and punctual), but negatively to prospective black and Latino tenants (seen as lazy, prone to violence, and concentrated in low-paying jobs (Feldman & Weseley, 2013). Even model minority stereotypes underestimate the challenges associated with achieving these goals or in trying to be normal. For example, consider the stereotype of strong black women as a celebration of accomplishments under difficult circumstances. This very stereotype can also conceal patterns of suffering, anger, and desperation because of inaccuracies, limitations, and the painful consequences in living up to this image. Black women are subsequently ensnared in a double bind: If they live up to the stereotype, their problems and fears are ignored so that they must fend for themselves. If they admit to weaknesses and vulnerabilities, they are criticized for not living up to the powerful expectations of self-reliance (Newman, 2012).

Not all negative portrayals have an equivalent impact. Context and consequence are critical in shaping different outcomes and responses. Members of a dominant group need not be concerned with negative stereotyping about themselves; after all, as a group, they exercise control over a wide range of representations that flatter or empower. Negative stereotypes might cause discomfort for "pale males"; nevertheless, they as a group possess both the political authority and economic clout to neutralize or deflect. Both institutional power and societal privilege provide a protective buffer, with the result that even a constant barrage of negativity can be absorbed without harm or damage. But for minorities with racialized vulnerabilities, stereotyping is an affliction that cannot be easily deflected or ignored (Elmasry, 1999). Each negative image or unflattering representation expresses, reinforces, and advances their peripheral status as not quite Canadian.

Xenophobia

Xenophobia can be defined as a fear and hatred of the other. Nowhere is this more evident at present than in the widespread fear of and hostility toward Muslims (Taras, 2012). An online poll of 1,522 Canadians commissioned by the Association for Canadian Studies and Canadian Race Relations Foundation demonstrated how 52 percent of the respondents believe Muslims cannot be trusted (70 percent Quebecers versus 43 percent among English Canadians). Nearly as many believe discrimination against Muslims is mainly their fault, while the Internet is fingered as the main conduit for spreading racism in Canada (Boswell, 2012).

Is Islamophobia a form of xenophobic racism (Satzewich, 2011; also Dunn, Kockler, & Salabay, 2007)? Evidence would suggest yes. Since 9/11, Islamophobia has evolved into a triple threat in terms of politics, demographics, and the so-called clash of civilizations (Esposito, 2012). It represents a complex phenomenon amenable to analysis from the perspectives of social anxiety, fear, prejudice, and racism (Ernst, 2013). Islamophobia as cultural racism tends to essentialize, otherize, homogenize, and demonize by conflating all Muslims into a single nation of Islam (Afshar, 2013). It distorts the prism through which Muslims and Islam are viewed, culminating in a fear that leads to hatred, hostility, and discrimination (Lean, 2012; Hennebry & Momani, 2013). Muslim are portrayed as "backward, voiceless, deprived of basic rights, degraded by men, victims of violence, uneducated" (Bangash, 2012; Alsultany, 2012). They are seen as guilty until proven innocent, while Islam is perceived as the cause rather than context for terrorism (Esposito, 2012)—a simple explanation and expediency that exonerates the United States of any wrongdoing in the Middle East. The following stereotypes inform Islam and Muslims (Taras, 2012; also Hennebry & Momani, 2013):

1) Monolithic and static
2) Otherized as culturally incompatible
3) Irrational, primitive, and inferior
4) Aggressive, violent, clash of civilizations—the terrorist within
5) Hijackable ideology to promote political military interests
6) Intolerant of Western criticism
7) Deserving of criticism and discrimination
8) Criminalization of Muslim communities (Commission on British Muslims and Islamaphobia, 1997; Fekete, 2009)

As a result, Islamophobia constitutes a form of racism that reflects (1) discrimination against Muslims across a range of fields; (2) how Muslim women and girls are doubly disadvantaged because of religion and gender; (3) opposition to building of mosques; (4) biased media coverage; and (5) hostility from political parties and extremist groups to gain votes and popularity (ENAR, 2012).

For many, Islamophobia tends to equate Islam and Muslims with extremism (Esposito, 2012). But two distinctions can be discerned. First, the post-9/11 mediascape is dominated by references to good Muslims and bad Muslims, including dangerous Muslim men, imperilled Muslim women, and civilized white Europeans (Razack, 2008, p. 8). Muslims are acceptable and deemed successful if they live in the West and/or abide by the principles and practices of Western society. Second, anti-Muslim and anti-Islam are not necessarily synonymous. Anti-Islam consists of a set of ideas reflecting antipathy to Islam as religion, whereas anti-Muslim racism represents the acting out of these ideas. In other words, Islam is not necessarily the cause of anti-Muslim racism; however, it may provide the rationale (Sivanandan, 2010).

Racial Discrimination: Racism in Action

The word "discrimination" can be employed in different ways. Non-evaluative meanings indicate a capacity to distinguish (e.g., a colour-blind person may not be able to discriminate [distinguish] between blue and green). Evaluative meanings of discrimination can be used positively (a discriminating palate) or negatively (narrow-mindedness). Section 15 of the Canadian Charter of Rights and Freedoms prohibits discrimination on the basis of race, ethnicity, or origins. Yet, the Charter concedes the feasibility of seemingly "discriminatory" measures such as employment equity if employed to assist historically disadvantaged minorities. Distinctions are not discriminatory, the Charter contends, if they have a legitimate goal of levelling the playing field or reversing discrimination. Discrimination is also permissible if demonstrated to be a bona fide occupational requirement. For example, car insurance companies can charge higher premiums (discriminate) for young males under twenty-five years based on driving records for the group as a whole. To be sure, discrimination aimed at an entire group (men) is no longer socially acceptable. It may be tolerated if directed at individuals of particular groups who refuse to comform or comply (Yoshino, 2006). In brief, some forms of discrimination are acceptable—even essential—to the functioning of a complex and democratic society (MacQueen, 1994).

Canada is certainly not immune to patterns of discrimination. The concept of discrimination in terms of what, why, and how has evolved over the course of Canadian social history (Sheppard, 2010):

a) Explicit discriminatory laws and policies prevailed into the late 1940s. Women, especially married women, were not treated as equal citizens under the law but exposed to exclusions and discrimination. Those individuals with physical and mental disabilities endured explicit discrimination premised on eugenics, segregation, or institutionalization. Discrimination against gay men resulted in the criminalization of sexual activity while lesbianism as otherworldly was beyond legal recognition or penalty. Racist exclusions prevailed in immigration, employment, housing, and voting laws, while non-preferred immigrants dealt with a Canada that could best be described as xenophobic, racist, and nativist.

b) A significant shift in thinking about discrimination and inequality emerged shortly after the end of the Second World War. The 1948 Universal Declaration of Human Rights incorporated equality (and anti-discrimination) as one of its foundational principles. Canadian law reform abolished the most egregious patterns of discrimination by eliminating overt forms of state- and government-based discrimination and discrimination within the institution of everyday life based on direct differential treatment. Inception of formal models of equality eventually resulted in the Human Rights act of 1977. The Act set out prohibitions against discrimination in specific contexts (including housing, employment, and social services) and on the basis of unfounded prejudice and stereotypes related to race, religion, and sexual orientation.

c) By the late 1970s and early 1980s, Canadians became increasingly aware of the systems-based nature of discrimination, both pervasive and institutionalized within normal patterns and practices of social exclusion (substantive conceptions of equality). Earlier notions of discrimination as harmful treatment or deliberate exclusion involving negative stereotypes and perpetuated by prejudiced individuals did not necessarily extend to institutions and institutional decision making, which many perceived as fair and rational and based on non-discriminatory factors such as individual merit. But as the promise of formal equality in a post–civic rights era faded, the face of discrimination shifted its focus from something random and discrete to an institutionalized and deeply normative ("systemic") dynamic embedded in a complex interplay of organizational rules, relations, policies, and practices. The consequence of this shift proved transformative. Traditional and formal notions of equality as sameness were replaced by an awareness that institutions had to move over and accommodate needs-based differences. In other words, to paraphrase Colleen Sheppard (2010), the challenge was no longer to get permission to incorporate racialized minorities and women into a white-male-dominated world, but to change the rules that informed conventions to make them more accommodative and responsive to those historically disadvantaged.

Table 4.1, adapted from Sheppard (2010, p. 18), captures the distinction between competing models of discrimination and inequality.

Research reinforces the reality of discrimination in Canada (Reitz & Bannerjee, 2007; McDougall, 2009). Racial discrimination is no longer legal, although informal discriminatory patterns in employment, housing, and social services are still widespread and seemingly perpetuated or tolerated by most whites (Oreopoulos, 2009; Kawakami et al., 2009; Feagin, 2006). According to the Canada's Ethnic Diversity Survey of 2002, nearly 36 percent of racialized minorities indicated they have experienced discrimination because of their race or ethnicity, including 50 percent of blacks and 33 percent of South Asian and Chinese respondents. A Canada–Europe survey study conducted under the launch of the Canada Barometer (Jedwab, 2008) pointed out that 29 percent of Canadians said they experienced discrimination during 2007 (compared to 15 percent of respondents in Europe), with younger Canadians (ages eighteen to twenty-four) more likely to experience it. To be sure, the same study indicated that Canada's commitment to anti-discrimination compares well to other countries, with the third best anti-discrimination framework after Portugal and Sweden (Jedwab, 2008). Nevertheless, there are concerns that newer forms of racism and racial discrimination are inadequately addressed by current strategies (Cassin et al., 2007).

Discrimination may be differently expressed (Dovidio, Hewson, Glick, & Esses, 2010). Expressions include blunt (overt) or oblique (covert), individualized or institutionalized, or deliberate or unintended (with the result that motivation behind the act is less important than its effect on the victim).

Direct forms of discrimination deliberately and openly deny or exclude. By contrast, indirect discrimination arises when the outcomes of rules or procedures that apply equally to everybody have the unintended effect of denying, controlling, or excluding others through no fault of their own. The uncritical application of similar rules to unequal contexts (one-size-fits-all mentality) discriminates by failing to take difference-based disadvantages into account in creating a more level playing field (see also systemic racism). Or put somewhat differently, treating everyone the same may prove discriminatory if the context is not taken into account. For example, consider how the requirement for Canadian experience when it is not a bona fide requirement for a job may well represent a code (seemingly neutral rules that serve as a proxy to disguise prejudice or racism) that penalizes newcomers for not being Canadian enough in terms of communication, interaction, or fitting in (Ontario Human Rights Commission, 2013; Sakamoto et al., 2013). The next Insight follows along this path.

Table 4.1 Rethinking Discrimination: From Direct Impact Model to Adverse Effects Model

Shift from	Shift toward
Discrimination as a largely individual problem reflecting random and discrete incidents	Discrimination as systemic, i.e., deeply and unconsciously embedded within normative values and institutional relations, practices, and policies
Focus on prejudicial attitudes of perpetrators	Focus on the experiential effects on those victimized
Discrimination as differential treatment	Discrimination as similar treatment, i.e., the adverse effects stemming from the differential impact of seemingly neutral rules and rewards
Doing something	Doing nothing
Discrimination framed in terms of distinct and homogeneous social groups	Discrimination reflects overlapping inequalities linked to intersecting identities rather than applied uniformly to whole groups
Individual remedies and treatment	Institutional adjustment

INSIGHT

What's in a Name? Name Discrimination in Canada

It is widely acknowledged that prejudice and discrimination continue to mar immigrant entry into the labour market. But these prejudicial attitudes and discriminatory practices are much more subtle than in the past. Nevertheless, they are real and exert an exclusionary impact. Consider this field experiment by Philip Oreopoulos (2009), a University of Toronto labour economist. Oreopoulos sent out six thousand fictitious CVs for online job vacancies in the Toronto area at a time when the economy was booming. The first set of CVs described a Canadian-born individual with Canadian education and experience, and an English-sounding name. Then he sent out similar CVs to the same vacancies except that the CVs differed slightly: (1) some had a name changed to a more common Chinese, Indian, and Pakistani name; (2) others had a name change and only foreign work experiences and Canadian education; and (3) still others had a name change, foreign work experiences, and foreign education credentials. The numbers of callbacks for interviews were then tabulated by the different types of CVs.

- Interview request rates for English-named applicants with Canadian credentials were three times higher (16 percent versus 5 percent) than resumés with foreign-sounding names and foreign credentials.

- Changing foreign resumés to include only Canadian experience raised callback rates to 11 percent.

- Among resumés with four to six years of Canadian experience regardless of where the degree was obtained had no impact on chances for an interview request.

- Those applicants with English-sounding names received 40 percent more interview requests than those with similar CVs but foreign-sounding names (16 percent versus 11 percent).

In short, names matter in conveying a lot of (mis)information (Feldman & Weseley, 2013; also Awad, 2013). Employer discrimination against foreign-sounding applicants persists even when situated within the context of Canadian credentials and experiences. In a follow-up study that asked recruiters to explain the existence of name discrimination, they responded that employers overwhelmingly treat a name as a code or signal to indicate a lack of prerequisite language or social skills for the job (Oreopoulos & Dechief, 2011). That alone should suggest that any public policy to improve immigrant integration must move beyond a problem-set focused on immigrant characteristics. This focus should be instead on the mindsets of those doing the hiring.

A distinction between covert and overt discrimination is critical. Overt discrimination assumes blatant and insidious forms at both individual or institutional levels. In contrast, covert discrimination is subtle and subversive as well as disguised and coded. It consists of discriminatory treatment that is hidden, difficult to prove, and more obvious to victims than to perpetrators (Feagin, 2006). Racially coded words or euphemistic expressions create a facade of politeness or political correctness, thus masking intentions or obscuring prejudices (Coates, 2008). In paraphrasing Rodney Coates, covert discrimination consists of those subtle and subversive societal practices and norms employed to mask structural arrangements and exclusions that restrict, deny, or distort opportunities for racialized minorities. Discrimination is even more difficult to prove because of the covert biases of a colour-blind society that resists moves toward social equality (rather than challenges social inequality). As Eduardo Bonilla-Silva writes (cited in McCardle, 2008, p. 36):

> During the civil rights movement, the smoking guns for change were such things as signs that read: "No Jews, No Blacks." It was easy to use these as concrete evidence of discrimination.... But with discrimination pushed underground today, and surfacing in far more subtle ways, it's much harder to prove. How does a person of colour effectively argue to a court that he was discriminated against while shopping because clerks followed him around asking, "Can I help you? Can I help you?"

But while covert discrimination has become increasingly salient with the removal of more overt forms, the two have long coexisted, albeit beneath the radar of social awareness. Active (overt) malice and passive (covert) indifference are simply the flip sides of the same coin. Or as Dyson (2004) puts it, if one conceives of racism as a cellphone, the active malice is the ring tone at the highest volume; passive indifference is the ring tone on vibrate. In both cases, the consequences converge by virtue of transmitting a meaningful message.

Discriminations differ in terms of scale and intention (Feagin, 2006). On one side of the *scale* continuum are individual patterns of discrimination directed at others, often but not always reflecting prejudice. On the other side of the continuum are institutional levels of discrimination involving group- or organization-based systems of denial or exclusion. Similarly, drawing attention to *intention* reinforces a distinction between overt (intent to deny or exclude) and covert (unintended harm) discrimination. Four major types of discrimination can be discerned based on these distinctions and dimensions (Feagin, 2006). First, isolated discrimination consists of intentional harmful action taken by an individual of the dominant group but without the support of the dominant group in general. For example, consider a police officer who discriminates/profiles against racialized people despite the service's commitment to equitable policing. Second, small group discrimination involves a similar pattern of isolated discrimination except it involves a larger number of individuals. Take the example of a white supremacist group that discriminates by restricting the rights of racialized minorities. Third, direct institutionalized discrimination involves intentional harm prescribed by the community or organization. Fourth, indirect institutionalized discrimination differs insofar as it consists of dominant group practices that exert a harmful effect without a corresponding intent.

The interplay of these components—namely, differential (direct, both overt and covert) treatment and differential (indirect, both overt and covert) effects—produces a working definition along lines proposed by the United Nations (1966) (also Blank et al., 2004): *Discrimination can be defined as any restrictive act, whether deliberate or not, that has the intent or the effect of adversely affecting (denying or excluding) others on grounds other than merit or ability.*

INSIGHT

Discrimination without Prejudice: Strange Bedfellows?

Is there a relationship between prejudice and discrimination? Is discrimination an act justified by prejudice? Do people act (discriminate) according to their attitudes (prejudice)? Often yes, sometimes no. Prejudice refers to a set of attitudes and beliefs; by contrast, *discrimination* entails a process by which these prejudgments are put into practice. But any causal relationship between the two is problematic. Discrimination can exist without prejudice, especially when negative treatment of racialized minorities is deeply and systemically embedded within the normal functioning of institutions. In other words, institutions can operate on discriminatory grounds even if the individuals themselves are free of prejudice. Conversely, prejudice may flourish without resulting in discrimination. Individuals may be prejudiced, yet compartmentalize these attitudes by refusing to act in a discriminatory manner for fear of losing face or facing retaliation. In brief, prejudice and discrimination are analytically distinct if mutually related concepts that can vary independently under certain conditions.

A study by a white professor Richard LaPiere in 1934 put this prejudice-discrimination link to the test. LaPiere and a young Chinese couple travelled throughout the United States at a time of intense anti-orientalism. The pervasive prejudice toward Asians in general led LaPiere to predict that they would be refused service in hotels, guesthouses, campgrounds, and restaurants. On the contrary, only one establishment out of the 251 frequented by LaPiere refused them service. Several months later, LaPiere sent a letter/survey to each of the establishments they had frequented, asking if they would accept members of the Chinese "race" as guests. Over 90 percent said no, despite having earlier demonstrated hospitality to the Chinese guests, while the others hedged their bets by responding that it depended on the circumstances. Curiously, only one responder provided an unqualified yes (Pager & Quillian, 2005).

Does this "experiment" prove a gap between prejudice (attitudes) and discrimination (actions)? Perhaps, but some caution needs to be taken. First, there is no proof that those who accepted the Chinese as guests were the same individuals who rejected their requests for reservations. Second, did the presence of a white male defuse a potentially discriminatory situation whereas the subsequent letter mentioned only the Chinese couple? With these caveats in mind, a better conclusion might point to the sometimes tenuous relationship between prejudice and discrimination. The presence of situational cues is key. For example, because of its potential to create a scene, direct discrimination even in a racist era may be awkward or embarrassing, while expressing prejudice in a context of relative anonymity makes it easier for people to act out their attitudes. Under the circumstances, Pager and Quillian (2005) argue, it might be better to determine the contextual factors that transform prejudice into discrimination. They also suggest caution in interpreting attitudinal surveys. Surveys of racial attitudes often convey a positive picture (in part because respondents on surveys tend to give socially desirable answers, even if this involves smudging the truth). One thing is clear: The relationship of prejudice to discrimination is complex, situationally adjusted, and subject to multiple interpretations that link popular racist cultures with structural and ideological biases (Dovidio, Hewson, Glick, & Esses, 2010).

Power: Making Racism Sting

There is much to commend in the popular equation: Racism = Prejudice + Discrimination (Fleras, 2012). Racism consists of a complex interplay of ideas and actions, involving a mix of prejudice (stereotyping, xenophobia, and ethnocentrism) with that of discrimination (harassment). Racism also encompasses an ideology with a patterned set of responses that underscores the unequal treatment of minorities through political exclusion, economic exploitation, or social segregation. But the key element in this equation is the addition of power (Dovidio et al., 2010b; Rosado, 2013). Without power, nothing happens. Not just any kind of power, moreover, but power that is institutionalized, i.e., backed by the authority of the state and bolstered by legal arrangements and cultural values. Those with access to institutional power possess the ability to transform human differences into prejudicial attitudes. For example, human differences are not a problem per se; rather, they become a problem in systems where the mainstream presides over racialized minorities, and then justifies the power imbalance by pinning the blame on race (Rosado, 2013). Those in elite positions also possess the power to implement and enforce these patterns of prejudice and discrimination in ways that benefit some, but not others. When combined with power, the interplay of prejudice and discrimination generates racism in its varied manifestation.

Power is a complex and contentious concept that defies simple definition or laundry list of attributes (Olsen, 2011). Many like to think of power as the capacity of A to get B to do something that B would otherwise not do. This predominantly Weberian approach characterizes power as something systematic: (1) possessed by individuals or actors; (2) intentionally and visibly exercised; (3) manifested in open competition or conflicts; and (4) directly observable through interaction (see Prus, 1999). But such a conceptualization is too narrow because it ignores the logic behind systemic power. A neo-Marxist/Foucauldian orientation contends that power (1) is deeply embedded in the founding assumptions and foundational principles of a society's constitutional order; (2) manifests in the structure of social institutions and ideological values; (3) may exert unintended rather than deliberate effects that reflect the normal functioning of the system; (4) infiltrates the minds of the subjects through dominant discourses that divert attention from points of conflict involving discriminatory social structures and unequal social relations (Brunon-Ernst, 2012; Henry & Tator, 2002); and (5) may assume a latent rather than visibly manifested form when setting rules, shaping the parameters of debate, and defining self-serving situations and options (Grabb, 2009). This systemic approach to power reinforces the cliché that power is most powerful when least visible and imprecise, or what Homi K. Bhabha (1998) calls the "tyranny of the transparent" (cited in Pinder, 2013, p. ix).

In short, power is not something that can be measured in either/or terms. Nor should references to power be defined as (1) a "thing" that is possessed by a person or sovereign state; (2) concentrated exclusively in a status or office; (3) reflective of a zero-sum game of winners and losers; (4) coercive in nature; and (5) expressed in negative terms such as "excludes" or "oppresses" or "conceals." Rather, it should be employed in the Foucauldian sense as everywhere and everything—a series of linkages, nodes, and relations dispersed throughout the socio-political body (Foucault, 1991). As Rita Dhamoon (2009) points out, power is best conceptualized as a productive force involving meaning-making, from producing reality to reproducing domains of truth that are subject to change over time and place. In other words, Dhamoon concludes, people exercise power rather than being possessed by it.

References to power can also be conceptualized at varying levels (situational, institutional, systemic) and through different forms (economic, ideological, political) (Olsen, 2011). Situational power refers to the power that actors possess in particular contexts. Institutional power refers to the power of formal rules, official roles, and relationships of authority that often go undetected because of the tacitly assumed and accepted. Systemic power refers to the powers lodged within the structures and values of a capitalistic system, with corresponding control over resources and production (economic power), control over ideas and ideals (ideological power), and control over decision making (political power). Mindful of its extraordinary reach, Sherrow O. Pinder (2013, p. ix) writes, "power is despotic" since it positions marginalized "others" along unequal lines. This assertion raises a perennial question in exploring how racism works: Can minorities be racist?

> ## QUESTION BOX
>
> ### Do Minorities Do Racism?
>
> The relationship between racism and power raises a vexing question. Can minority women and men express racism against the majority sector? Can racialized minorities be racist toward other racialized minorities (see also Satzewich, 2011)? Is it possible for individuals to be racist toward their own racialized kind? Responses will depend on how racism is defined—as biology or power.
>
> Defining racism as biology/race suggests that a racist is anyone who approaches, defines, or treats someone else differently because of his or her perceived race. Thus, minorities can be racist if they exclude or deny whites because of their whiteness. But reference to racism as power points to a different conclusion. However distasteful and uncomplimentary, anti-white statements by racialized minorities may not qualify as racist in the conventional sense. Racialized minorities as a group lack the institutional power to put prejudice into practice in a way that really matters. Only white negative attitudes routinely carry with them the social power inherent in cultural reinforcement and institutionalization of these racial prejudices (Scheurich & Young, 2002). bell hooks (1994) put it cogently when she wrote: "The prejudicial feelings some blacks may express about whites are in no way linked to a system of domination that affords us any power to coercively control the lives and well-being of white folks."
>
> To be sure, minorities are not entirely powerless; after all, power is neither a static resource with one group (whites) monopolizing all the power across all contexts. Nor is it a zero-sum game in which one side always wins, while losses mount on the other side. Racialized minorities do possess individual levels of power; they can also tap into alternative sources of power-making such as boycotts, civil disobedience, and moral suasion. But the power that racialized minority individuals wield in certain contexts lacks the institutional clout to demean, control, or exploit in a meaningful way. In other words, it would appear that conditions of relative powerlessness reduce minority expressions of hate, prejudice, or discrimination to something less than racism.

Racialized Inequality = Prejudice x Discrimination x Power

Canada is a land of paradoxes. From a distance Canada looks like a paragon of virtue in managing racism and racial discrimination. Blatant forms of race-based exclusion are no longer tolerated or condoned. A commitment to the principles of multiculturalism, anti-racism, and inclusion secures a basis for living together with differences in harmony and co-operation. Canada's commitment to engaging diversity and difference is touted as a strength rather than a liability, with vast potential to improve the country's competitive edge in a global economy. Even Aboriginal peoples in Canada are making significant political and economic strides in overcoming the structures and legacy of colonialism, while securing access to land, identity, and political voice as a basis for empowerment (Fleras, 2012).

But a closer inspection suggests a slightly different picture. Canada is plagued by a punishing level of inequality that rewards certain groups yet penalizes others because of race, ethnicity, or aboriginality (Block & Galabuzi, 2011). Racialized minorities do not share equally in the creation or distribution of wealth, power, or social status (Galabuzi, 2006). Rather, they tend to find themselves hierarchically ranked in ascending and descending layers of inequality (i.e., stratified), in the process reinforcing how patterns of social inequality are neither distributed evenly nor randomly allocated, but concentrated among minority groups who cluster in nodes along a racialized *stratification*. Instead of an equitable arrangement, people of colour and newcomers are sorted out unequally along a "mosaic" of raised (dominant) and lowered (subordinate) tiles. Whites tend to perform better in terms of income and education than most racialized minorities (Reitz & Banerjee, 2007; Pendakur & Pendakur, 2011), while the cost of admission into Canada disadvantages newcomers compared to the Canadian-born (Simmons, 2010). A double standard prevails: Those migrants and minorities who excel in Canada may be criticized as "rate busters." Yet those who do poorly in Canada are castigated as "troublesome constituents" or "problem people" in need of costly solutions.

No one disputes the inequalities of racism in the past. Even a cursory inspection of Canada's historical record is an exercise in domination, control, and exploitation (Henry & Tator, 2010; Satzewich & Liodakis, 2013). To be sure, the situation has improved somewhat, thanks to the passage of human rights legislation, over forty years of official multiculturalism, a series of accommodations at institutional levels, and corresponding changes in the ideological climate (Fleras, 2012). But improvements have dislodged only the most egregious forms of exploitation and inequality. Both racialized privilege and systemic biases remain deeply embedded in the founding assumptions and foundational principles that govern Canada's constitutional order. National studies expound what is increasingly obvious: Canadians are not on equal footing when it comes to divvying up the goods (Reitz & Banerjee, 2007). Inequality remains a fact of life for racialized minorities in Canadian society with respect to disparities in power, privilege, and property (Block & Galabuzi, 2011). Canada's labour force may be increasingly diverse; nevertheless, visible (racialized) minorities and newcomers to Canada continue to experience difficulties in securing employment consistent with their educational qualifications or foreign-trained credentials (Public Service Alliance of Canada, 2010). They are perceived as expecting too much, but giving back too little, in the process weakening social cohesion and national identity while making the mainstream feel like strangers in their own land (Amin, 2012). Racialized minorities tend to be excluded from Canada's political corridors at both federal and provincial levels, as well as at local and regional levels, despite some notable exceptions—for example, the election of Canada's first Muslim mayor, in Calgary—which, paradoxically, tend to reinforce the rule. For example, the Greater Toronto Area (GTA) may proclaim "diversity, our strength," but the slogan speaks louder than actions or results. Racialized minorities constitute just 7 percent of all 253 municipal council members across the twenty-five municipalities comprising the GTA. They may account for nearly half of the population of the GTA, but racialized minorities represent only 4.2 percent of the city's corporate senior leadership (Omidvar & Tory, 2012).

The conclusion is inescapable: All the mythmaking at our disposal cannot disguise the fact that Canada remains a racially stratified society wherein racialized differences (racialization) make a difference in defining who gets what and how much (Galabuzi, Casipullai, & Go, 2012). Racism is a deeply embedded and defining characteristic of Canadian history, despite a concerted effort at whitewashing the embarrassment (Walker, 1998; Backhouse, 1999; Thobani, 2007). The end result? Some racialized minorities do well because of or in spite of their race or ethnicity; others suffer and may never recover; and still others do not appear adversely affected one way or the other. This observation raises a number of questions for discussion and debate: What causes racialized inequality? Who is responsible—the victims or the system? Is it because of racism and racial discrimination, a lack of human capital (from education to work experience to language competence), or the play of market forces that squeezes economic opportunities? Is the problem attributable to minority cultures and values that discourage coping and success? Or should the finger be pointed at mainstream structures that, wilfully or unintentionally, compromise minority life chances at considerable cost to themselves and their contribution to Canada (Heath & Cheung, 2007; Yu & Heath, 2007)? Is it appropriate to assume that any disparities in power, privilege, and resources are the result of racism and racial discrimination? Or is racism one of many variables in the causal mix? How often is racism manipulated as a smokescreen to cover people's tracks or as a dodge for confronting reality? Answers to these questions remain at the forefront of vigorous debate, with varied and contradictory responses to the politics of racism in reflecting, reinforcing, and advancing racialized inequality in Canada.

Immigrant inequities and racialized stratification are neither "natural" nor "healthy." On the contrary, the racialization of inequality is highly toxic because of its corrosive effect in fraying the social fabric of society (Wilkinson & Pickett, 2009, 2010). The devaluations and put-downs associated with low social status, dominance hierarchies, and dysfunctional communities can prove dangerously stressful, with devastating impacts, ranging from people's health and life expectancies to the erosion of social trust. The inequitable relationship of racialized minorities and new Canadians to the distribution of valued resources make it abundantly clear: Inequality in Canada is not randomly distributed, but stratified along racial lines (racialized stratification). These racialized disparities are not simply the result of negative mindsets that are amenable to reform. They are deeply embedded within (1) Canada's founding principles and institutional structures; (2) the social systems that trigger inequality; (3) the intergroup dynamics that reinforce patterns of power and privilege; and (4) social fields that distribute life chances in an unequal manner (Scheurkens, 2010). Such a macro-perspective puts the onus on analyzing how racialized inequities are created, expressed, and sustained, as well as challenged and transformed by way of government initiative, institutional reform, and minority assertiveness (see also Fleras, 2012).

Explaining Racialized Disparities

Racialized immigrants are experiencing a marked decline in economic outcomes as corporate Canada continues to fumble the challenge of integrating immigrant talent into the workforce (McDonald et al., 2010; Drummond & Fong, 2010). The much-hyped reference to Canada as a land of opportunity with a skills shortage notwithstanding, thousands of racialized immigrants cannot find work in Canada (McDonald et al., 2010). Immigrant qualifications continue to be dismissed in a risk-aversive corporate Canada, while education degrees and overseas experience are sharply discounted. Of course, it is not just immigrants who suffer because of employment and income gaps. According to the RBC Economics Report (2011), the costs of underutilizing immigrants are prohibitive. If immigrants earned the same amount as the Canadian-born, it is argued, the increase in incomes would amount to $30.7 billion (or 2.1 percent of Canada's GDP), while translating into about 42,000 new jobs.

Is it possible to find explanatory frameworks to account for these disparity gaps? Two theoretical paradigm provide an explanatory framework for racialized inequality with respect to income, unemployment, poverty, and powerlessness. Functionalists tend to blame inequality on ethnicity and individual shortcomings (the ethnicity paradigm); conflict models see the problem as more deeply embedded within institutional and opportunity structures of a fundamentally unequal system (the racism paradigm).

Ethnicity Paradigm—Blaming the Victim

A generation ago, references to racial(ized) stratification were couched within the discursive framework of an ethnicity paradigm (Fleras, 2012). Canadian society was envisaged as an open and competitive marketplace in which individuals competed as equals and were rewarded because of their skills or production. Individual success or failure reflected a person's level of human capital: Those with training, skills, and education succeeded; those without didn't. Ethnic differences were pivotal. On one side, ethnic minorities had to discard the debilitating aspects of their ethnicity that precluded participation. On the other side, those in charge were expected to discard prejudgments that precluded inclusiveness. Inception of a multiculturalism policy in 1971 sought to remove prejudice from the workplace by ensuring people's differences did not get in the way of success or participation. It also sought to depoliticize ethnicity by eliminating its salience as grounds for challenge and change.

According to functionalist perspectives, the failure of minorities to penetrate the market may reflect a lack of expertise or credentials. Efforts to boost their "human capital" would focus on improving minority "skills" consistent with competitive labour force needs. Ethnocultural deficits are no less a deterrent to minority success. As John Porter argued in his landmark book, *The Vertical Mosaic*, ethnicity represents a key variable in predicting the attainment of success in Canada, with non-British and non-French ethnic groups at the bottom of a vertical ranking (see also Helmes-Hayes & Curtis, 1998). Of particular relevance for Porter were those cultural values—from a lack of work ethic to kinship obligations—at odds with upward mobility and occupational performance. Clearly, becoming modern was key. To secure success, ethnic minorities had to abandon their unmodern ethnicity and assimilate by embracing modernist values, even if doing so would risk alienation from a supportive community of like-minded kin (Porter called this dilemma the *ethnic mobility trap*).

The Racism Paradigm: Blaming the System

The concept of inequality underwent a paradigm shift from the 1980s onward. Attainment of formal equality rights failed to increase the equality of outcome that many had anticipated. This was hardly surprising; after all, racialized minorities may have possessed the same rights as all Canadians, but they had to exercise these rights without access to institutionalized powers and the benefit of a head start in contexts that neither reflected nor advanced their interests or experiences. A sharp increase in racialized immigrants from developing countries from the late 1960s onward proved pivotal. A focus on individual attributes, including prejudice and ethnicity as the source of the inequality problem, gave way to an emphasis on discriminatory barriers and racism.

Not surprisingly, multicultural commitments related to ethnicity no longer resonated with the language of relevance. Proposed instead were new equity discourses based on the principle of institutional inclusion, removal of discriminatory barriers at structural levels, and eradication of racism that precluded full and equal participation. References to inequality shifted accordingly from a focus on individuals to structure, from ethnicity to race, from equality of opportunity to equal outcomes, and from a commitment to formal (abstract) equality to substantive equality (equity).

How does a racism paradigm account for these disparities? Institutional structures, local labour market conditions, and protectionism on the part of employers and professional bodies determine lower entry-level earnings as much as prejudicial attitudes and lack of human capital (Reitz & Banerjee, 2007). Foremost among structural factors are the changing composition of immigrants, the attendant racism that accompanies surges in diversity, an inability of employers to evaluate foreign credentials and educational degrees (resulting in a corresponding discounting of these skills), communication problems for non-English and non-French-speaking immigrants, and changes in the labour market because of economic globalization and knowledge-based economies. Increased employment and earnings are often linked with language proficiency in one of Canada's two official languages. Yet many immigrants possess neither French nor English as a first language, even as the federal government is scaling back its English-as-a-second-language (ESL) program (Wayland, 2006). As well, management of unionized workers may find their hands tied in hiring immigrant workers with overseas experience because of collective agreements entrenching seniority rights that insist on filling positions from within the bargaining unit. For example, a regulation (R 274) that forces school boards in Ontario to hire teachers on the basis of seniority to avoid nepotism in hiring is likely to have a negative impact on the employment opportunities of recently graduated racialized minorities, while reducing the diversity of the teaching staff in a multicultural community (Rushowy & Brown, 2013).

A racism paradigm is consistent with the dynamics of a racialization model. The concept of racialization as an explanatory framework denies the existence of a neutral/colour-blind society. Human societies are socially created yet carefully concealed constructions whose founding principles deliberately or inadvertently (systemically) reflect, reinforce, and advance the realities, experiences, and interests of the dominant white sector. The values, ideals, and priorities of those who created or control society are deeply embedded and broadly (hegemonically) enforced. The foundational principles of a society's constitutional order are designed, organized, and operate in ways that promote mainstream priorities often without people's awareness of the systemic bias, mainly by drawing attention to and promoting some aspects of reality as normal and necessary while those of the non-dominant sectors are dismissed as inferior or irrelevant. The result is a racialized society comprising ideas and ideals about what is acceptable or desirable and that promote white-stream interests over those of other racialized groups. Equal rights may remove the legal barriers to individual achievement, but does little to remedy both the cumulative effects of generational gaps and white power structures (Burke, 2012). Or to paraphrase Sandra Lipsitz Bem (1994), in a white-dominated world, minority differences are transformed into minority disadvantages. Clearly, then, a colour-blind society is a contradiction in terms, at least in the foundational sense of the term, since race in a racialized milieu will continue to matter in defining who gets what and why.

Summing Up: Racism as Inequality, Inequality as Racism

The fact that racism and racial discrimination result in poorer outcomes for racialized minorities should come as no surprise. The presence of unequal outcomes should not be dismissed as an unfortunate but superficial expression of episodic bouts of loutishness or ignorance. Nor is white privilege a practice that was grafted on to Canadian society, then rises and falls depending on the social climate and the temperaments of those who hold office. Rather, racialized inequality embodies a predictable and systemic phenomena in white Eurocentric societies whose founding principles and foundational logic are racialized to reflect the realities and experiences of those Euro-whites who created and control the system. As a result, Canadian society is racialized as a white man's country largely because authority and power operate within the logic and laws of a racialized state in dominating racialized minorities through exploitation or exclusion (also Jung, Vargas, & Bonilla-Silva, 2011).

In contrast to the ethnicity paradigm as an explanatory framework is a racism paradigm that emphasizes the bigger picture (Fleras, 2012). According to this paradigm, the problem did not rest with individuals or attitudes per se. Rather, the source of the problem was rooted in the institutional *structures* of society. Inequality and barriers to advancement reflected structural constraints that were largely systemic in advancing "pale male" interests. Applying the metaphor of a competitive footrace with staggered starting blocks made it obvious: Not all contestants were equally positioned to compete in the labour market. The race was rigged because of ascribed characteristics that handicapped some because of skin colour or gender differences, while privileging others for precisely the same reasons. Or to rephrase this differently: Society and the social system may pretend to be value-neutral under the guise of universality and colour-blindness. But the very notion of "an unlevel playing field" puts racialized minorities in a structural bind. On paper, migrants and minorities may possess the same rights and equalities as all Canadians; in reality, they must exercise these rights and equalities in contexts not of their making.

Note

1   Others argue that racism is a specific form of prejudice (Cohen, 2011).

SECTION 2

HOW RACISMS WORK
SECTORS AND EXPRESSIONS

The previous chapters capitalized on three themes: First, racisms in Canada are the elephant in the room that nobody wants to talk about. Second, racisms assume new forms in response to anti-racism interventions, in effect resembling the hydra-headed snake of Greek mythology whose lopped-off heads quickly reappeared (Satzewich, 2011, p. xii). Alternatively, the perception of yet more racism reflects an enhanced sensitivity to minority sensibilities. Third, racisms no longer work the way they once did. Framing racisms as openly discriminatory ignores mounting evidence of racist expressions that are more subtle (interpersonally), structurally located within societal confines (institutional), and so numbingly routine in practice as to escape detection (ideological). With open bigotry now a relic of the past, there is a growing demand for fresh new frameworks that analyze racism along macro-analytic lines without sacrificing those micro-orientations of the situational and everyday.

Consider the possibilities: Racism is neither a uniform concept that reflects a singular experience nor does it encompass a common reality. It is not just a matter of a few bigots with maligned attitudes; it is also institutionalized, structured, and systemic (Bolton & Feagin, 2004). Nor should it be considered a static and unchanging "thing" that is oblivious to wider political contexts, economic changes, and situational realities. Rather, racisms are both historical and contemporary insofar as they change over time, while building on history to exercise powers of domination or control. The resultant proliferation of racisms over time and across space is captured by Rinaldo Walcott and his colleagues in A. Curling and R. McMurty's *Report on the Review of the Roots of Youth Violence* (2008, p. 332):

> Racism takes many forms: from individual insults, stereotypes, and physical violence, to more wide ranging practices that involve systemic practices of deliberate exclusion from the nation's institutions,

to unconscious ways of privileging whites, to disadvantaging racialized people through social and cultural networks, to cultural assumptions and practices which place non white or racialized minorities outside legitimate avenues of power and decision-making.

Not surprisingly, making sense of this conceptual richness is proving a challenge. Questions abound: How does one go about conceptualizing a social phenomenon that spans the spectrum from the personal (micro) to the societal (macro)? Is there a common thread that links patterns of racist thought and racialized behaviour, from the openly spiteful to the covertly but perniciously consequential? Is it possible to theorize a social phenomenon so diverse in its multi-dimensionality that the only commonality is the absence of a common denominator?

The validity and relevance of these questions is beyond doubt. Our ability to live together co-operatively is contingent on conceptualizing the different sectors and diverse expressions of racism in a multicultural Canada. A core question dominates thoughout this section: *How do contemporary racisms work at the individual and interpersonal level, within institutions, and across society at both ideological and structural levels.* The fact that racisms manifest themselves in multiple forms (expressions) and at multiple levels (sectors) creates the basis for a fourfold ideal-typical typology: (1) interpersonal, (2) institutional, (3) ideological, and (4) infrastructural. Each sector is then shown (in the table below) to encompass varying expressions of racisms, including: (1) hate, polite, and subliminal (interpersonal racisms); (2) systematic and systemic (institutional racisms); (3) everyday and normative (ideological); and (4) infrastructural (foundational).

In theory, manifestations of racism in Canada can be slotted into one of these sectors and expressions. In reality, most racist acts rarely fit neatly into one or the other category as much as they overlap and intersect. For example, an act of workplace racism may well embody dimensions of both interpersonal and ideological racism in addition to institutional and infrastructural racisms. Moreover, even individual acts of prejudice or hate are systemic by virtue of being embedded in the broader power relations of a given society, whereas victims of racism and discrimination include both individuals and the harm conveyed to their community at large (Gopalkrishnan & Babacan, 2007). The last chapter in this section on Ivory Tower Racisms captures this multi-sectoral dimension of contemporary racisms at work. Finally, each sectoral expression of racism can be compared and contrasted on the basis of select criteria, namely, source, levels of intent and awareness, style and depth of intensity, scope, and consequences, as demonstrated in the table below. Deconstructing these admittedly ideal-typical sectors and expressions is critical. Doing so demonstrates the complex and multi-dimensional nature of racisms as theory and practice while confirming the complexity and elusiveness of solutions that yield real outcomes.

Table S2.1 Racisms: Sectors and Expressions

Interpersonal	Institutional	Ideological	Infrastructural
hate	systematic	normative	foundational
polite	systemic	everyday	
subliminal			

Table S2.2 Comparing Racism Sectors

Sectors and Expressions of Racism	Sources	Levels of Intent or Awareness	Style or Intensity Levels	Scope or Magnitude	Consequences or Impact
Interpersonal • hate • polite • subliminal	• hatred • dislike • unconscious prejudices	• maximum • intermediate • minimum	• high/explicit • medium/ muted • low/ambivalent	• individual	• direct • indirect • diffuse
Institutional • systematic • systemic	• deliberate • unconscious, inadvertent • normal	• maximum • minimum	• high/explicit • low/ impersonal	• structural	• direct • indirect
Ideological • everyday • normative	• habitual • values, norms	• minimum • maximum/ minimum	• low/ routine • low/high	• cultural	• diffuse • diffuse/ direct
Infrastructural • foundational	• constitutional order	• minimum	• low	• societal	• diffuse

CHAPTER 5

INTERPERSONAL RACISMS

Introduction

Interpersonal racism entails a pattern of dislike that occurs at the level of individuals and relationships (Fleras, 2012). This bias is directed at the "other" because of who he is or what she stands for. On one side are overt racisms, both direct and open; on the other side are more covert expressions that hide behind politeness, political correctness, racially coded subtext, and claims of racial blindness (Coates, 2008). No less covert are those situations where individuals are unaware of their subconsciously hidden bias and hatred. Three expressions of interpersonal racism can be discerned: hate, polite, and subliminal. Hate reflects a direct and intense dislike of others; polite racism is more discreet and indirect as might be expected in a multicultural society where racism is socially taboo; and subliminal racism flourishes at a subconscious level, although expressed by denial, excuses, or rationalizations.

Hate Racism

Hate racism is the kind of racism that most commonly comes to people's minds (Fleras, 2012). It refers to the old-fashioned hatred of the racialized "other" that once prevailed in the past and persists to the present among a handful of the reactionary, undereducated, or defiant. Intrinsic to hate racism is its explicit and highly personalized character. For example, the Anti Defamation League (2012) defines racism as the hatred toward others in the belief they are less than human because their skin colour reveals the true nature of that person. This hate racism is expressed through sharply personal attacks on those perceived as culturally or biologically inferior. Expressions range from the use of derogatory slurs and patterns of avoidance to physical assaults and destruction of property through vandalism.

Even a cursory glance over Canada's historical past exposes a robust legacy of hate racism (Hier & Bolaria, 2007; Cassin et al., 2007). Such a claim may come as a revelation to some readers while others concede how the invention of Canada as multicultural is legitimized on concealing its past. Certain myths are deeply entrenched in our collective memories, especially those that extol Canada's progressive status, the absence of American-style race riots and prolonged slavery, and the entrenchment of multicultural and human rights principles. Close scrutiny suggests otherwise. As a country that proudly and defiantly defined itself as a white man's country, Canada has little to boast of in its treatment of racial, Aboriginal, and ethnic minorities since Confederation (Backhouse, 1999). Chinese, Japanese, Indo-Pakistanis, First Nations, Jews, and blacks have been and continue to be objects of dislike or aversion. Foreigners were routinely imported as a source of cheap menial labour, either to assist in the process of society-building (for example, Chinese for the construction of the railway) or to provide manual skills in labour-starved industries such as the garment trade or resource extraction (Bolaria & Li, 1988).

Once in Canada, many became convenient targets for abuse or exploitation. New Canadians could be fired with impunity, especially during periods of economic stagnation or labour unrest. Then and now, racialized minorities and immigrant Canadians were shunted into marginal employment ghettos with few possibilities for escape or advancement. Nor did anyone take newcomers seriously in making a positive contribution to Canadian society; as a result, their political and civil rights were routinely trampled on without much remorse or redress. Labourers from the Caribbean were shipped to Canada on a temporary basis for seasonal employment, primarily in agricultural fields, to do those precarious (dirty, dull, and dangerous) jobs that Canadians reject at existing wages and work conditions (Hennebry, 2010, 2012). Working conditions proved to be among the worst of any occupation, with many denied fundamental workers' rights because of language barriers, lack of familiarity with the law, and unscrupulous operators. Domestic workers (live-in caregivers) from the Philippines continue to be exploited by some middle-class families who should know better. Finally, Muslim Canadians and those of Middle Eastern origin remain targets of widespread racial profiling in the lingering aftermath of 9/11, which pits the West's so-called secular superiority against the fanaticism of Islamist extremists (Hennebry & Momani, 2013).

Canada and the United States shared much in common because of racism and racial discrimination. Laws and practices were invoked that segregated people of colour, especially blacks, from full and equal participation in Canadian society until the 1950s and 1960s (Walker, 1998). Racist groups such as the Ku Klux Klan also relied on naked violence to cultivate an environment of fear and hatred against minorities throughout the United States and Canada (Barrett, 1987). Of course, hate racism and hate crimes are no stranger to the United States. According to the Southern Poverty Law Centre, the number of hate cells who malign entire groups because of who they are has jumped from 602 in 2000 to 844 in 2006 to 1,007 in 2012. Also worrying is the rapid rise of right-wing anti-immigration groups who resent the presence of undocumented Latino migrants, but just stop short of advocating open hatred. Canada is also a breeding ground for hate crimes. Canada's Criminal Code defines hate crimes as criminal offences that are motivated by open and intense hatred toward an identifiable group because of who they are or what they look like (Dauvergne et al., 2008). The number of hate crimes reported to the police has increased in recent years, although there was a slight decline from 1,482 in 2009 to 1,401 in 2010 (Ha, 2012) to 1,332 in 2011 (Statistics Canada, 2013; Desmond, 2013).[1] Over half (52 percent) of the reported incidents in 2011 were motivated by race and ethnicity, 25 percent attributed to religion, and 18 percent because of sexual orientation. Black Canadians were the most frequently targeted (21 percent) for hate crimes of all types, followed by the Jewish population at 15 percent of all hate crimes. Violent hate crimes (39 percent), such as assaults and uttering threats, were a distant third behind mischief and vandalism (50 percent) as the most reported hate crimes, with gays and blacks as the most common victims. Young adults (60 percent) under the age of twenty-five were most likely to be victims or accused of hate crimes, while 79 percent of hate crimes occurred in major cities.

FYI

Race Statistics: The Perils of Data as Explanation

According to Statistics Canada, in 2011 the Waterloo Region census metropolitan area ranked fourth in Canada for the most hate crimes reported based on population (Peterborough, Ontario, was first, Hamilton second). Of the forty-one hate crimes in the Waterloo Region, twenty-six were race-related, ten based on religion, and five on sexual orientation, down from fifty-five in 2010 and ninety-three in 2009 when Waterloo Region earned the somewhat dubious title of Canada's hate crime capital. The figures for Waterloo Region may conceal more than they reveal. Not only does the lack of nationwide reporting standards skew the numbers reported to the police. Unlike many police services, Waterloo Region possesses a hate-crime unit. Its establishment may well have the effect of either increasing the number reported to the police or, alternatively, decreasing the number of incidents through its deterrence value (Fantoni, 2011).

Comparable data point in the same direction (Cassin et al., 2007; Jedwab, 2008). According to B'nai Brith Canada's League for Human Rights, 1,135 anti-Semitic incidents were reported in 2008, with a 9 percent increase over the previous year and a fourfold increase over the past decade. About one half of the incidents were reported in the final four months, possibly reflecting the combination of a deteriorating economy with the scapegoating of Jews for Israeli military excursions into the Gaza (March 31, 2009, *Canadian Anti Semitic Incidents Rise, Audit Shows*, retrieved from http://jta.org). Two thirds of all anti-Semitic incidents were classified as harassment, about one third as vandalism, and 3 percent involved outright violence. Approximately 50 percent of the incidents took place in Toronto, 25 percent in Montreal. By 2011, the number of anti-Semitic incidents had increased to 1,264 nationwide, including 884 cases of harassment, 348 incidents of vandalism, and thirty-two incidents of violence (Canadian Press, 2012).

White supremacist groups represent the most egregious expressions of far-right hate racism (Perliger, 2012). Ranging in scope from the White Aryan Nation and Western Guard movements to neo-Nazi skinheads in urban areas (Kinsella, 1994; Barkun, 1994), these openly racist groups are committed to an ideology of racial supremacy that asserts the superiority of whites over other races. On the surface, white supremacists may not be explicitly antiminority or even see themselves as racist. They prefer to annoint themselves as white Christians, fusing race and religion into a single nationalist crusade against the forces of evil (Jaret, 1995). Toward that end, they are prepared to transform society along white supremacist lines through converts to their racist cause (Li, 1995). Disaffected youth are an obvious target because of perceived government indifference to their plight in a changing and diverse world. The combination of music, pamphlets, disinformation by telephone hotlines, and the Internet—from chat rooms to web and social networking sites that offer unique ways of spreading hate (Rajagopal, 2006)—concocts an appealing mishmash of neo-Nazi philosophies, KKK folklore, pseudo-Nordic mythology, and anti-government slogans (Kinsella, 1994). Admittedly, there is no way of gauging the number of hard-core supremacists in Canada; nonetheless, even a small number of racist ideologues has the potential to destabilize a society when prejudice is pervasive and the economy splutters.

INSIGHT
Online Racism: Digitalizing Hate

The Internet has become the new battleground in the fight to influence public opinion. While it is still far behind newspapers, magazines, radio, and television in the size of its audiences, the Internet has already captured the imagination of people with a message, including purveyors of hate, racism, and anti-Semites (UN Human Rights Commissioner, 1996, cited in Akdeniz, 2006).

Few saw this coming. In the Internet's initial heyday during the mid- to late 1990s, many predicted that race and racism would disappear from cyberspace. The anonymity of the Internet would allow people to escape from negative racial identities associated with such embodiment. Or, as the famous *New Yorker* cartoon once put it, "On the Internet, nobody knows you're a dog" (Daniels, 2012). Evidence suggests that new and digital media have the potential to challenge conventional frames that racialize. In some cases they do (for example, Aboriginal media). But many rely on and reinforce racial and ethnic stereotypes (cybertypes), thus lapsing into prejudicial bullying patterns when dealing with race and ethnicity (Nakamura, 2002).

The presence and proliferation of digital media technologies debunks this utopian myth of racelessness. The Internet is neither a race-free place nor an inherently democratizing medium (Daniels, 2009a). Race is built into the Internet industry while racism persists online, although played out in new and complex ways unique to the Internet and digital networks of power and privilege (Daniels, 2012; Nakamura & Chow, 2011). The digitally mediated cultural and informational landscape (Nakamura & Chow, 2011) entrenches the cyber-racism of white supremacy as a forum, platform, and communication technology (Rosenthal, 2000) with the result that the new information age is just as racialized as the industrial age, when white supremacists relied on print and the voices of a few leaders to convey and connect (Nakamura, 2002). The conversion to digital media to create membership, sustain loyalty, cultivate collective identity, legitimize credibility, mobilize for action, and foster empowerment (Goodwin, 2012) points to a worrying trend. It debunks those stereotypes that typecast white supremacists as gap-toothed Neanderthals without the neural circuitry to handle the technology. On the contrary, the digitalization of white supremacy is increasingly multivocal and sophisticated and more difficult to challenge (Daniels, 2009a).

Of course, hate racism was a pressing problem long before the emergence and popularization of digital media (Akdeniz, 2006). But the advancement of mobile and digital technologies and platforms provide individuals and groups with a new and potent weapon to produce, support, and easily disseminate racist messages to a wider audience (Daniels, 2012). According to the Simon Wiesenthal Centre, only one racist website existed in 1995, although concerns over digital hate go back to the mid-1980s. By 2005, numbers skyrocketed to nearly five thousand websites for promoting racism and hatred in a variety of languages, including an increase of 25 percent between 2004 and 2005 (Akdeniz, 2006)—ominously indicating how the problem of cyber-racism is deepening rather than atrophying.

And any site that solicits anonymous comments or feedback always runs the risk of eliciting racist diatribes (Jakubowicz, 2012).

Cyber-racism consists of racism on the Internet, including racist websites, images, blogs, videos, and comments on web forums (but not text messages or emails) (Australian Human Rights Commission, 2008). The Internet provides a powerful new technology for communicating white supremacist racist messages: (1) to spread ideas and propaganda (ideology) (white supremacists are known to reposition content on the Internet by twisting ostensibly neutral or positive messages out of context to distort or deceive (Daniels, 2009b); (2) to interact and organize in a more unobtrusive and decentralized manner than in the past; (3) to sell racist paraphanalia from music to games to Nazi memorabilia; and (4) to mobilize individuals and groups into action. Contrary to popular belief, the cyber-racism of white supremacists is not entirely devoted to recruiting individuals to the cause. It also focuses on destabilizing society by challenging the values of racial equality and highlighting racist double standards, while promoting the normalcy and inevitability of a white global supremacy (Daniels, 2009a, pp. 187–88). For example, white supremacists in the United States continue to prey on white insecurities by capitalizing on Obama's status as a black president with a "funny" name who cannot be trusted to safeguard America's white-stream interests (Wise, 2008).

In short, the Internet as platform constitutes a major breeding ground for white supremacism racism (Brown, 2009). The Internet was initially deemed to be a colour-blind and unwalled community that heralded the end of racism. But the dynamics of racism easily moved into the digital age, with the result that racial and class divides are replicated online and reflect what Danah Boyd (2011) calls digital ghettoes. And yet the Internet as medium can be a major player in challenging the racial hatreds of white supremacists. A commitment to the freedom of online expression is crucial in seeking, receiving, and imparting information in the fight against racism (Akdeniz, 2006). Nevertheless, the global, decentralized, and borderless nature of the Internet creates a potentially infinite and unbreakable communications complex. Its broad reach, protection from prosecution, and anonymity are no less pivotal in compromising effective regulation at the national level. In addition, as Akdeniz (2006) explains, there is also the challenge of finding a working balance between controlling racism while protecting freedom of expression. Not surprisingly, the jury is still out on how to deter expressions of racism on the Internet or to enlist the Internet in the anti-racism struggle. The further consolidation of mobile platforms will undoubtedly exert even greater pressure on the politics of race and racism (Daniels, 2012).

Polite Racism, Eh?

Few people at present will tolerate the open expression of racism. Compare this with the past when racism was openly tolerated and socially obligatory. There was no need for politeness or pretence; everything was upfront and openly visible. The passage of constitutional guarantees such as the Canadian Charter of Rights and Freedoms and human rights codes has eroded the legitimacy of hate racism from public discourse. Blatant forms of racism are socially unacceptable, morally repugnant, and legally inadmissible, while less candid expressions of bigotry and stereotyping have increasingly vaulted into place. Overt expressions of racism have shifted from the front stage (public) to the backstage (private), where whites find themselves with other whites. Instead of disappearing in the face of social reprisals and legal sanctions as might have been expected, racism is respectably couched in ways that conceal a dislike of others (Wetherell & Potter, 1993). Politically neutral (and politically correct) language is often employed as a proxy or code to camouflage prejudice and racism. Not unexpectedly, both detection and deterrence are rendered more difficult when racisms are unobtrusive, obliquely couched in the language of political correctness, and politely coded to escape disapproval, as noted in this excerpt:

> Much supposedly new racism is actually old racism—often with modest adaptations to account for societal changes such as formal desegregation or official (if often unenforced) civil rights laws. It is true that most whites today tell survey researchers that they believe in equal opportunity and non discrimination, yet these views operate most often as a rhetorical ethic, one that is only inconsistently and erratically implemented in everyday practice. (Picca & Feagin, 2007, p. x)

Polite racism can be defined as a contrived attempt to disguise a dislike of others through behaviour that outwardly is non-prejudicial in appearance. These politely aversive feelings are not expressed through outright hostility or hate, but often through patterns of avoidance or rejection. Polite racism may consist of the "look" that "otherizes" racialized minorities as different, inferior, and out of place in Canadian society. It also consists of coded or euphemistic language ("those people") to mask inner feelings behind a facade of gentility (Blauner, 1994). This politeness is especially evident when racialized minorities are ignored or turned down for jobs, promotions, or accommodation. For example, when approached by a racialized applicant, an employer may claim a job is filled rather than admit that "no racialized minorities need apply." Another polite way of rejecting undesirable tenants involves the expression "Sorry, the apartment is rented," when the apartment in question is still vacant. Polite racism and closet racists may appear to be a more sophisticated version than open racism. Nevertheless, camouflaging intent behind a smokescreen of platitudes and political correctness does not render the effect on victims any less debilitating as this passage notes: "In some ways I prefer to live in a society where they just say 'You're Black, we don't like you.' Here in Canada, people are hiding behind a mask" (Kolawole Sofowora, cited in the *Toronto Star*, May 2, 1999).

The proliferation of polite racism exposes how thin the veneer of tolerance is, even in a multicultural society that subscribes to the post-racial principles of colour-blindness (Picca & Feagin, 2007). Media whitewashing of racialized minorities can also be seen as a case of polite racism.

CASE STUDY

Media Whitewashing as Polite Racism

Depictions of differences are increasingly acceptable within mainstream media, no more so than in advertising or programming, where the quality and quantity of minority appearances have improved. But this acceptance is conditional: A commitment to Eurocentrism and white superiority may not be openly articulated by media whitewashing. Rather, it is assumed and normalized as the unquestioned norm. Cornell West's reference to a "normative gaze" (or Joe Feagin's "white racial frame") describes how a Eurocentric perspective creates an intellectual lens for framing racialized minorities. In fostering a colour-coded news discourse whose "pale male" gaze is deemed to be pro-white rather than anti-minority (Jiwani, 2006), images of "them" as "those people" are refracted through the prism of whiteness as the unmarked normative and normalizing standard by which others are discredited or discounted. Images of minorities under a racialized gaze are filtered through a white-o-centric point of view, while minority women and men internalize a white way of being looked at (i.e., watch themselves being watched) and act accordingly. Jennifer Kelly (1998, p. 19) writes about the controlling effect of a racialized gaze:

> The importance of the gaze is that it allows a dominant group to control the social spaces and social interactions of all groups. Blacks are made visible and invisible at the same time under the gaze. For example, when black youth are seen it is often with a specific gaze that sees the "troublemaker," "the school skipper" or the "criminal."

In short, racialized minorities are depoliticized under a Eurocentric gaze by transforming (whitewashing) them into people acceptable to the mainstream. The centrality of ratings and advertising revenue puts pressure on whitewashing any potentially controversial representations to reassure mainstream audiences. Whitewashing minorities involves a racialized media gaze that can assume several forms, including the idea of miniaturizing minorities by shrinking their media presence. Whitewashing can also take the form of sanitizing minority appearances by reflecting, reinforcing, and advancing whiteness as the normative standard by which everything is judged. A white-o-centric media gaze ensures the representations of minorities do not discomfort mainstream viewers (see Rockler-Gladen, 2008). Several whitewashing (neutering) strategies are employed to allay (depoliticize) mainstream concerns over uppity minorities:

- Representations of minorities focus on universal experiences rather than experiences unique to that specific group.
- Representations gloss over the politics of minority-ness ranging from exclusion because of racism and racial discrimination or the challenges of faith-based communities in secular societies.

CS
- Representations focus on minorities as unrealistically perfect or laughably quirky.
- Representations of minorities tend toward the desexed by neutering them of a potential threat. Alternatively, certain minorities are portrayed as oversexed, thus increasing their appeal by exoticizing their sexuality.
- Representations about minorities are less about them and more about how others react toward them.

But there is price to pay for whitewashing diversity. The process of taking what is potentially controversial or involves troublesome constituents and airbrushing it into something more palatable for the mainstream says more about the doers than those it is done to. The case study on the television series *Little Mosque on the Prairie* demonstrates the concept of whitewashing as a depoliticizing gaze (Fleras, 2011).

Whitewashing as Depoliticizing: *Little Mosque on the Prairie*

The centrality of a racialized media gaze can be applied to the CBC sitcom hit *Little Mosque on the Prairie*, which premiered in January 2007. Taking its cue from the popular book and television series *Little House on the Prairie*, *Little Mosque* unfolded as a typical sitcom series, but one revolving around a Mosque and Muslim individuals in a small rural Prairie community of Mercy, Saskatchewan (Google Wikipedia has more details about the series). The show consists of stock characters with overly exaggerated qualities, while plot lines and gags revolve around tensions and misunderstandings between Muslims and their dealings with a host of friendly and not-so-friendly townsfolk (Mohammed, 2007). With its tagline "Small town Canada with a little Muslim twist," the show does not depart from conventional sitcoms in deriving its humour from the quirky fish-out-of-water interactions of Muslims (including conservatives versus liberals) with non-Muslims.

The series received considerable praise both nationally and internationally, including a number of countries that purchased syndication rights (Anderson, 2007). Critical reaction to the show has varied: Some see it as groundbreaking in a multicultural society where making fun of religion is not socially acceptable. Admittedly, the series is not the first attempt by media to dispel negative stereotypes through comedy, although the show does normalize Muslims by situating Islam as part and parcel of a multicultural Canada rather than framing them as stoic and alien sojourners with allegiances elsewhere (Nicolo, 2007; Sheikh & Farook, 2007). In contrast to conventional negative stereotyping as typically found in newscasts, the series attempts to humanize Muslims in the eyes of Canadians by poking fun at the stereotypes that stifle Muslim image and identity (Sheikh & Farook, 2007). Moreover, it represents the first attempt by Muslims to use television to reflect upon Muslim communities with respect to the type of image they are portraying and projecting (Mohammed, 2007).

Others are more critical of its popularity and success. They claim the show perpetuates stereotypes and sweeps aside real issues by playing Muslims for laughs (some critics suggest the cartoonishness of characters and plot lines to ramp up the laughs are increasing). Others remind us that sitcoms understandably inflate reality and exaggerate differences for their comedic intent (Sheikh & Farook, 2007). Still, others accuse the series of lacking originality since it mirrors other "hokey British shows" (according to Canadian TV writer John Doyle, *The Guardian*, January 15, 2007)—namely, TV series such as *Ballykissangel* or *Doc Martin*, which too are set in rural communities with a cast of eccentrics, including bumbling buffoons and the impossibly righteous. Nevertheless, its derivativeness aside, the series has broken a media taboo by presenting Muslims outside of the newsroom as personalities or characters with a rightful claim to Canada (Sheikh & Farook, 2007).

Regardless of its critical stance, there is no denying the centrality of a racialized bias that whitewashes (depoliticizes) the series, the storylines, and its characters. The fact that the CBC hired a consultant to flag issues that could offend audiences (Mason, 2007) reinforces this line of argument.

- First, there is a focus on universal experiences rather than a Muslim experience. The show tells universal stories about the foibles and follies of individuals with diverse backgrounds in sustained contact (Anderson, 2007). One of the executive producers, Mary Darling, said, "One thing that attracted us was the universal nature of the idea. I mean anyone in any religious congregation would recognize the kinds of people who are our characters. I mean, people are people. We are one human family, really" (cited in Mohammed, 2007).

- Second, the series depoliticizes the tensions and potential conflicts associated with Islam in a nominally secular Canada. According to its creator, Zarqa Nawaz, in subscribing to the view that humour fosters intergroup understanding, the series provides "an unabashedly comedic look at a small Muslim community living side by side with the residents of a little prairie town" (*The Guardian*, January 15, 2007). By playing Muslims and their encounters with non-Muslims for laughs, potentially awkward situations in the post-9/11 era are channelled into harmless venues.

- Third, the politics of religion are largely defused. For example, critics like Tariq Fatah suggest that the show sanitizes what really happens in the mosques, where preachers may extol political messages. To the extent that the series explores religious-based storylines, politically tinged issues as headscarves or prayer rugs are included as much for their laughs as their politics or, alternatively, collapsed into universal sitcom themes such as family and friends.

- Fourth, the series does provide some insight into Muslim experiences and Islamic faith, including their difficulties in finding a meaningful place within a white Canada. But the focus is primarily on eliciting townsfolk's reactions to the presence of the eccentric other. That Muslims and Islam are little more than comedic fodder for driving plot lines or accentuating character development, the laugh track constitutes an exercise in depoliticizing a potentially disruptive viewing experience.

- Critics attribute the attraction of the series to a portrayal of Muslims as never before seen on TV—that is, as regular people with everyday problems who do not take themselves too seriously (Anderson, 2007). It is interesting to note that America's Learning Channel aired an eight-part series in November 2011 entitled All American Muslim, which also depicted five Muslim families in Dearborn, Michigan, to be just like any other American family (Lopez, 2011). However progressive, moves to dispel misconceptions by normalizing Muslim experiences is tantamount to whitewashing.

Clearly, then, what some see as a strength, others see as a weakness. Playing Muslims for laughs may well defuse anti-Muslim stereotypes and Islamophobic fears. But repackaging Muslims and Islam into something palatable for mainstream consumption and overseas sales manages to sanitize what in reality may be an awkward post-9/11 situation. Playing them for laughs also glosses over those who take their Islam seriously, from the devout to the insurgent, who manipulate religion for ulterior purposes (Lopez, 2011). Such an approach is surely an improvement over the framing of Muslim and Islam as evil and untrustworthy. But any kind of whitewashing comes with a cost that cannot be dismissed.

Subliminal Racism: "Accidental Racists"?

Subliminal racism involves a sub/un/consious individual bias (Tuch & Hughes, 2011). These below-the-conscious biases are internalized through informal socialization, deeply embedded within the subconscious, that surface by accident or in unguarded moments, and reflect a gap between what people say (values they profess to endorse) and what they do (values they prefer to practise). In that subliminal refers to "below the threshold of awareness," subliminal racists are unaware of these deeply buried prejudices and biases. These so-called "closet racists" (Gorski, 2004) appear incapable of escaping those biasing blinkers that foster a dislike of others since the unconscious part of their minds influence behaviour without much awareness. However much subliminal racists may want to comply with their non-prejudicial ideals, as Anderson (2010, p. 9) writes, they cannot escape prevailing stereotypes, resulting in an internal conflict often expressed in ambiguous situations that allow for various interpretations. Not surprisingly, this unconscious dislike is justified on principled grounds instead of crude reductionism, often in contexts of ambiguity where one can deny or exclude on non-racial grounds. With subliminal racism, individuals may publicly endorse a commitment to the principle of equality; nevertheless, they invoke excuses or rationalizations to oppose measures for remedying the problem of inequality (Augoustinos & Reynolds 2001; also Henry & Tator, 2007). Subliminal racists engage in aversive actions such as non-verbal behaviour (from facial expressions to body language) that expose subconscious biases, albeit only if the context is safe, the situation is sufficiently ambiguous, and prejudicial expressions are socially tolerated (Weisbuch et al., 2009; Dovidio, 2009).

A subliminal racism is found among that class of people who openly abhor prejudicial attitudes or discriminatory treatment of minorities. They consciously and knowingly profess that everybody is equal and deserving, yet subconsciously judge and treat some groups negatively by blaming them for undeserved gains or creating social problems (Cassin et al., 2007). Those individuals who profess egalitarian attitudes but refuse to act on this commitment to bring about equality may be acting in a subliminally racist manner. For, in the final analysis, the impact of doing nothing to bring about progressive change in a racialized society is not neutrality; it is a tacit acceptance of an unequal status quo. This refusal to act upon injustices and inequality is justified on principled grounds, thereby protecting a person from accusations of prejudicial attitudes. This passage from Gaertner and Dovidio (1986, p. 3; also Dovidio, Gaertner, & Kawakami, 2010) captures the notion of subliminal racism as negative feelings toward others that lead to avoidance but are justified on different grounds (note: the authors use the term "aversive" racism):

> In contrast to "old-fashioned" racism, which is blatant, aversive [= subliminal] racism represents a subtle, often unintentional form of bias that characterizes many well intentioned white Americans who possess strong egalitarian values and who believe they are non prejudiced. Aversive racists also possess negative racial feelings and beliefs (which develop through normal cognitive biases and socialization) of which they are unaware of or which they try to dissociate from their nonprejudiced self image. Because aversive racists consciously endorse egalitarian values, they will not discriminate directly and openly in ways that can be attributed to racism: however, because of their negative feelings they will discriminate, often unintentionally, *when their indecisiveness or criticism can be justified on the basis of some factor other than race (e.g., criticizing the concept of preferential hiring because it undermines the merit principle of a liberal democracy)* [emphasis mine]. Thus aversive racists may regularly engage in acts of discrimination that sabotage good intentions while they maintain a nonprejudiced self image.

In short, subliminal racism consists of an unconscious expression of negative attitudes by those who consciously uphold egalitarian beliefs. When held accountable for this discrepancy, they justify the disconnect or avoidance of others by upholding principled reasons rather than admit ambivalence or dislike.

What is distinctive about subliminal racism? Rather than being directly expressed (hate) or indirectly expressed (polite), subliminal racism cloaks its unconscious dislike of others behind principled grounds. A general principle is invoked to deny the legitimacy of specific instances (e.g., yes to the principle of workplace diversity, but no to any special measures to achieve this goal on grounds that doing so violates Canada's merit principle or principles of a colour-blind Canada). This reluctance is coded in terms that politely skirt the issue by justifying criticism or inaction on lofty grounds that appeal to a higher sense of fair play, equality, and justice. Subliminal racists may resent racially targeted equity programs because of a perception that playing by the rules deprives them of benefits that are allocated instead to rule-bending racialized minorities (powell, 2009). To be sure, criticism of either government minority policies or racialized minority actions is not necessarily racism per se, and it would be unfair to uniformly tarnish critics for taking issue on principled grounds. Nevertheless, others may perceive motives as suspect, while the unintended consequences of such criticism may have the effect of reinforcing unequal relations.

Several examples of subliminal racism are readily available. Jewish people have long been targets of hate in the belief that they possess too much economic wealth or political power (Anti Defamation League, 2012). But a new strain of anti-Semitism is increasingly directed not at Jews per se or their wealth, given the social unacceptability of such blatant dislike, but involves criticism of Israel's policy toward Palestinians. The new anti-Semitism isn't about destroying Jews. It is about the elites criticizing the state of Israel and its conflation with Zionism for violating Palestian human rights (Chesler, 2003). The acceptable face of anti-Semitism challenges Israel's right to exist as equal members of the family of nations, contests its right to defend borders against enemies, and castigates it for its human rights record while conveniently ignoring human rights abuses in neighbouring countries (Cotler, 2007). For example, Jews have been accused of child abuse by infringing on the rights of male infants through the ritual of circumcision (Sacks, 2012). According to Irwin Cotler (2007), no one is suggesting that Israel is above the law or beyond criticism or unaccountable for human rights violations. But in the interest of fairness, he argues, Israel should be held to the same standards as surrounding Middle East countries. Otherwise, such unduly harsh criticism of Israel on principled grounds may reflect a subliminal dislike of Jews (Weinfeld, 2005; Endelman, 2005; Bunzl, 2005).

There are other examples: Canadians generally are sympathetic toward refugees in distress, but less enamoured with those who are seen as breaking the rules. So-called bogus refugee claimants are not condemned in blunt racist terminology; rather, their landed entry into Canada is criticized on procedural grounds like "jumping the queue." Employment equity initiatives may be endorsed in principle but rejected in practice as unfair to the majority in a so-called colour-blind society. Individuals may support a commitment to inclusiveness as a matter of principle, yet disapprove of its implementation because it violates the principle of meritocracy. In short, subliminal racists are conflicted by competing beliefs: On one side is a commitment to the principle of racial and ethnic equality through government intervention if necessary; on the other is a belief in a colour-blind society that no longer requires special policies and programs for enhancing equality, especially since individuals are primarily responsible for their own problems (Eitzen & Sage, 2010; also Brezina & Winder, 2003). Support for the principle of equality for minorities may be offset by a deep-seated resentment at the thought of doing something that costs or inconveniences. Even doing nothing about "closing the gaps" is justified on principled grounds that special treatment in a post-racial and colour-blind society smacks of "reverse discrimination" or "race-based privileges." The discrepancy between what people say and believe versus what they really mean to say or actually do puts subliminal racism in a category of its own.

INSIGHT
White Racial(ized) Framing: Subliminal Racism in Action

Symbolic interactionists have long argued that people don't just act. Rather, they engage in meaningful interaction. According to symbolic interactionism, individuals define a situation and act upon this definition by linking their meaningful actions with those of others to create patterns of human behaviour. People's definition of situation includes a host of -isms as meaning systems. For example, androcentrism entails seeing the world from a male point of view as natural and normal, together with the belief that everyone is seeing it this way (or would if they could), while other perspectives are dismissed accordingly. Or consider Eurocentrism, namely, the tendency to interpret the world from a white (Anglo-European) perspective as natural and normal with respect to what is desirable and acceptable, in the process rejecting other experiences and viewpoints as less worthy of attention or respect.

Critical to defining a situation is the use of frames. Framing theory acknowledges that a lot is going on in the world at a given point in time, so that each individual must block off—or frame—what is important or relevant while discarding (or ignoring) what isn't useful in defining a particular situation. The analogy of picture framing is useful. When framing a picture, a mat is used to highlight what you think is essential to the picture, while concealing the less important. Similarly, the news media engage in framing by blocking out what is thought to be unnewsworthy, then foregrounding what is newsworthy in ways that bolster appeal to audiences, advertisers, and company values. Individuals normally partake of this selectivity process by framing reality to reflect what they think is acceptable or desirable, by the needs of the situation, or according to values and norms in society. Over time these framed experiences of reality become so routine and deeply embedded that people are generally unaware of their role in shaping action or evaluation.

In short, framing can thus be defined as a process for organizing information in a way that draws attention to some aspects of reality, not to others, in hopes of advancing a preferred reading or understanding consistent with explicit priorities or hidden agendas (Fleras, 2011c). The processing of information is filtered through different lens, including androcentric filters (seeing reality from a male perspective) or Eurocentric filters (seeing reality from a Western point of view. A relatively new concept is the notion of "white racial frames" (or perhaps more accurately, white racialized framing) as a way of seeing how largely unconscious assumptions and beliefs underpin and inform thoughts and actions (Henry & Tator, 2002). For Feagin (2006), a white racial framing constitutes a process and a concept:

1) As a process, a white racialized framing represents a racialized prism (or lens) through which most whites not only see and interpret the world out there (especially those involving racialized situations or encounters), but also rationalize and sustain racist stereotypes and discriminatory actions (Feagin & Elias, 2013; see also McCrae, 2007). In this sense, a white racial framing is similar to the concept of Eurocentrism, which, too, reflects a tendency to see, interpret, and assess reality from a predominantly white perspective as normal, desirable, and superior. Three levels prevail:

- At the most general level of conceptualization, a white racial framing defines whites as superior in culture and accomplishment; conversely, racialized minorities are dismissed as inferior or irrelevant. Whiteness comes to symbolize certain values and status positions while signifying intellectual, moral, and cultural superiority.

- At a deeper conceptual level, whites tend to see the prevailing distribution of institutionalized white power and white-controlled institutions as unremarkable but as inevitable or deserved.

- At the deepest levels are stereotypes and prejudices toward racialized minorities that unconsciously reinforce their perceived inferiority, thus accentuating white (especially male) virtues while privileging whiteness as master of the social universe.

2) As a concept, a white racial framing reflects a generic meaning system endorsed by most whites and assimilated minorities (Feagin, 2006; Picca & Feagin, 2007). This framing of the world consists of deeply held categories of racialized knowledge that routinely and unconsciously influence human behaviour or provide an explanatory framework. This framing is so taken for granted that the white racial frame is rarely questioned or contested by whites. In other words, white racial frames go beyond simple cognition or categorization; instead they involve a

> set of deep, subconscious images, tacitly assumed interpretations, and emotional convictions about race and race relations. Other dimensions of a white racialized framing may include: (a) a belief in (neo)liberal universalism (or peoples' rights and commonalities as individuals in a colour-blind society prevail over group differences since differences are only skin-deep); (b) the virtues of an ideology to justify a colour-blind Canada (or America) as aspiration and description; (c) the centrality of morally autonomous and rights-bearing individuals; (d) the importance of reason and science in advancing both individual and collective progress; (e) distinctive orientations to time and space, including their value and measurement. These white racial frames are routinely, if subliminally, invoked as a dodge or smokescreen, ranging from a rationale to justify patterns of racialized inequality to establishing patterns of interaction with racialized others (Feagin & Cobas, 2008).

How to explain the subliminality of this love-hate relationship toward minorities? Cynics might argue that Canadians are hypocrites whose deep-wired racism is candy-coated by a slurry of platitudinous pieties. After all, coded opposition to official multiculturalism or criticism of Canada's immigration program is rendered more acceptable than brazen expressions of intolerance or hatred (Li, 2007). But subliminal racism is not identical to polite racism. Subliminal racism may well reflect unconscious prejudices that people are genuinely unaware of—or what Paul Gorski (2004) calls closet racism—but surface in unguarded moments of crisis or stress. Or subliminal racism originates when people invoke a higher principle to criticize minorities for doing something that is seen as un-Canadian or inconvenient/costly. Or, alternatively, it entails doing nothing and justifying this inaction on principled grounds when something needs to be done to improve a racialized situation. In both cases, a subliminal racism tolerates a dislike of others behind a folksy veneer of respectability by invoking references to Canadian values as justification (Agnew, 2009).

A subliminal (or aversive) racism consists of people who openly sympathize with victims, support the principle of equality and egalitarianism, and regard themselves as non-prejudiced (Pearson et al., 2009). With subliminality, individuals who possess negative, albeit unconscious, prejudices may unwittingly act in code to maintain their self-image as non-prejudiced and colour-blind. But a certain selectivity prevails in defining a situation. People are unlikely to act inappropriately in situations with strong social norms wherein discrimination would be obvious to others (Pearson et al., 2009). As Henkel, Dovidio, and Gaernter (2006, pp. 103–4) put it:

Because aversive racists consciously recognize and endorse egalitarian values and because they truly aspire to be non prejudiced, they will *not* discriminate in situations with strong social norms [of right and wrong] when discrimination would be obvious to others and to themselves....

Feelings of unease among aversive racist will eventually be expressed, albeit in subtle, indirect, and rationalizable ways. For instance, discrimination will occur in situations in which the normative structure is weak, when the guidelines for appropriate behavior are vague, and when the basis for judgement is ambiguous or confusing. In addition discrimination will occur when an aversive racist can justify or rationalize a negative response or a failure to respond favourably on the basis of some factor other than race.

Note

1. Other surveys indicate a different pattern. According to Statistics Canada's *General Social Survey* (GSS) (2004) based on self-reported victimization survey, a total of 260,000 incidents of hate crime were reported in 2004 or 3 percent of all incidents. Discrepancy between police data and Statistics Canada may reflect the latter's greater threshold for subjectivity in calculating hate crimes, unlike police interpretations, which must adhere to stricter protocals (Dauvergne et al., 2008).

CHAPTER 6

INSTITUTIONAL RACISMS

Introduction: Institutionalizing Racism

Reference to institutional racisms shifts the focus of analysis. An emphasis on individual attitudes and interpersonal relations gives way to those institutional designs, dynamics, and outcomes that secure both white privilege and a racialized status quo. Institutional racism is not about individual actions but about organizational values and practices that create disproportionate outcomes for racialized minorities both in the workplace and the community at large (Better, 2007). Nor is it necessarily the result of racist attitudes on the part of individuals who, in fact, may oppose racism, yet must work within the framework of institutional rules and imperatives (Desmond & Emirbayer, 2009). Analysis begins with the assumption that institutions are neither neutral sites nor passively devoid of agendas or consequences. Rather, institutions are socially constructed conventions both racialized and ideologically loaded. They consist of beliefs and practices that reflect monocultural assumptions about what is acceptable and desirable that systemically benefit or empower some at the expense of others (Agocs & Jain, 2010; Pilkington, 2012). Predictably, racialized minorities find themselves disadvantaged within institutional contexts, not necessarily because of open discriminatory barriers, but because mainstream institutions were neither designed to reflect their realities or experiences nor constructed to advance their interests or agendas.

The concept of institutional racism refers to both overt and covert processes by which organizational practices and standard operating procedures adversely penalize minority women and men through rules, procedures, rewards, and practices that have the intent (systematic) or effect (systemic) of excluding or exploiting (Scheurich & Young, 1997). Institutional racism resides in those organizational policies, culture, and operations that reflect, reinforce, and advance differential access, treatment, and outcomes pertaining to goods, services, and opportunities (Weiner, 2012). It also entails the collective failure of an institution to create a workforce that is representative at all levels; a working climate that reflects, respects, and responds to workplace diversity; and a delivery of services that are both accessible and available as well as culturally appropriate. In some cases, this (dis)advantaging bias is deliberate (systematic racism); in other cases it is systemic—that is, deeply embedded within the foundational rules of institutional systems and expressed in the normal functioning of agencies, governing bodies, and legal systems (Feagin & Elias, 2013; Bruce-Jones, 2010). According to the Ontario Human Rights Commission (2005b), for example, institutional racisms in the workplace may include actions perceived as seemingly routine by the mainstream but which negatively impact racialized workers such as:

- Exclusion from formal and informal networks
- Denial of opportunities for advancement or training that was offered to others
- Excessive monitoring
- Disproportionate blame for an incident
- Assignment to less desirable jobs
- Treating normal disagreements as confrontational or insubordinate
- Characterizing normal communication as rude or aggressive
- Penalizing someone for not getting along with others who themselves exhibit prejudice and discrimination

In other cases, institutionalized discrimination and privilege can be sustained even if there is no deliberate intent to deny or exclude (systemic racism) (Chesler et al., 2005). Bias against racialized minorities may persist because discrimination is so deeply entrenched within institutions (institutionalized) that it becomes the automatic response even without conscious awareness or explicit intent (Mistry & Latoo, 2009, p. 20). Inother words, institutions serve as a site where race and racism are constructed and maintained yet simultaneously obscured and normalized (Joseph et al., 2012). To put these assertions to the test, this chapter explores the intertwining of systematic and systemic racism as they apply to mainstream media. For as bell hooks (2013, p. 12) writes, mainstream media are the foremost instrument in reflecting, reinforcing, and creating the covert racism of a white supremacist society.

Systematic Racism

Systematic racism speaks to a racism that directly and deliberately prevents minorities from full and equal institutional involvement. An institutional racism appears when discriminatory practices are legally sanctioned by the institution (or the state). This exclusion or exploitation of others is expressed

Institutional Racisms 147

by employees who act on behalf and with the approval of the organization (from private institutions to state agencies) (Milloy, 2001).

Systematic institutional racism flourished in societies that endorsed racial segregation. The regime of apartheid in South Africa was a classic example, as was the pre-civil-rights United States. Canada was also tarnished by institutionally racist practices that defiantly and deliberately denied or excluded. Institutions at present can no longer openly discriminate against minorities, lest they attract negative publicity, face legal action, or incite consumer resistance. Nevertheless, systematic institutional racism continues to exist through discriminatory actions endorsed by the corporate culture. Or corporations may deliberately manipulate rules or procedures to deny or exclude racialized minorities perceived as bad for business. The fact that corporations continue to dodge billion-dollar lawsuits for mistreatment of minority workers reinforces the age-old adage "the more things change, the more they stay the same." The following Debate Forum raises the thorny question of whether mainstream media are institutionally racist in portraying racialized minorities.

Debate Forum: Are Mainstream Media Institutionally Racist?

There is nothing natural or normal or inevitable about mainstream media as institutions. Mainstream media are social constructions whose conventionality is carefully concealed so that outputs appear natural or normal and uncontested, while advancing the values, beliefs, and norms of those who construct, own, or control them (Fleras, 2011c). They constitute a racialized institution in that they reflect (embody) and reinforce a dominant culture's perspective with regard to what is normal, acceptable, and desirable about race relations (Littlefield, 2008). Media are powerful in setting the agenda that relate to public discourses about mainstream-minority relations, including:

- providing information about who we are as a society
- reinforcing common values and norms, but at the expense of obscuring hierarchies in society
- articulating information about what happens when people break laws or violate norms, values, and the threat this poses to society
- conveying ways of seeing the world and how people see (or should see) racialized minorities, their relationship to society, and how they should behave (Jiwani, n.d.)

These agenda-setting dynamics raise a provocative question: Are the media racist (Foster, 2009)? Debate over a racist media elicits a variety of responses. For some, the media are racist because of their institutional tendency to deny or denigrate racialized minorities. The singling out of race in negatively defining minority experiences, identities, and outcomes is perceived as racist. Others agree that the media are racist, but for fundamentally different reasons. Media in the past ignored racialized minorities because they fell outside the preferred advertising demographic. But the industry is under pressure to "move over and make space" because of government regulation, minority assertiveness, and commercial imperatives. Yet a commitment to media inclusiveness may be criticized as racist by conferring special treatment on minorities to avoid charges of racism (reverse racism), in the process betraying a commitment to accuracy and impartiality (McGowan, 2001). Still others seem to take an intermediate position—that is, the media are racist at times, although much depends on how racism is defined and applied to media; nevertheless, such a blanket accusation is unfair because of media outputs that are progressive and inclusive (Hier, 2007). How does the debate play out? Are the media racist?

Yes. Most media scholars endorse the view that the media are racist (Jiwani, 2006; Karim, 2002; Mahtani et al., 2008; Henry & Tator, 2009). Historically, (mis)treatment of minority women and men tended to overrepresent them in areas that don't count (crime or entertainment), to under-represent them in areas that do count (political and economic success), and to misrepresent them for the count in the domains in between (Fleras & Kunz, 2001; Fleras, 2011c; also Newman, 2012). This unflattering assessment applied to all mainstream media processes, including newscasting, advertising, filmmaking, and TV programming. Although racism in the media is widely acknowledged, its expression is neither immediately visible nor explicitly expressed as was once the case. The monocultural bias that misrepresented or marginalized is rarely intentional since newsworkers generally do what they can under difficult constraints and organizational conventions (Abel, 1997). Rather, racism is the result of institutional constraints, widely internalized news values and routines, and ignorance of diversities and difference. Nevertheless, racism and racist discourses within media are pervasive and systemic. For example, news media portrayal of diversities and difference may be construed as racist because of the choices that journalists inadvertently but routinely make in articulating and sustaining a racist discourse. A critical discourse analysis to deconstruct ideological messages and negative image demonstrates how language racializes or stigmatizes (otherizes) minorities (Henry & Tator, 2002). This racialization is not conveyed in an openly racist way but through news values and journalist activities within a cultural ideological space that normalizes and naturalizes the primacy of Euro-Canadian belief and norms. In short, the mainstream news media are racist because content is selected and presented to their preferred audience base in ways that normalize prevailing patterns of a white superiority complex.

No. A few media scholars prefer to deny the existence of media racism. For the no side, racism is framed as something that happened in the past, is manipulated by the unscrupulous as an excuse or smokescreen, and reflects pathologies within the minority community (Cohen, 1999). Some critics have taken this one step further by arguing that the media themselves are sites of reverse racism. In a controversial book, William McGowan (2001) argues that political correctness has corrupted American journalism by whitewashing (or colouring) the news. For McGowan, journalists are afraid to write anything negative, judgmental, or critical about minorities or government diversity programs for fear of being labelled as racists, sexists, or homophobes. A pro-diversity newsroom culture that tends to view difference through the lens of cultural relativism also encourages positive minority coverage by (1) ignoring negative stories, (2) putting a positive spin on the negative, or (3) scrutinizing white motives behind those minority stereotypes that undermine community self-esteem. As a result of this kowtowing to minorities, notions of newsworthiness may be considered beyond debate or scrutiny or coverage if deemed to be too critical of minorities or unsympathetic to conventional diversity agendas. Those who transgress this politically correct orthodoxy are subjected to hostility or ostracism. In other words, according to McGowan, what prevails is a kind of reverse racism, one in which minority differences are positively framed, accorded special treatment, or conveniently ignored in contexts of bad news.

Sometimes. Most media scholars acknowledge the existence of news media racism (Mahtani et al., 2008). Others prefer a somewhat less extreme stance by arguing that the problem lies in focusing exclusively on the negative or sensational, in the process often ignoring positive coverage of achievements and developments that contributes to multicultural harmony in Canada (Hier, 2007; Fleras, 2011c). Reality is socially constructed through the media, which paves the way for dominant values to be articulated to the public. As a result, news media are both a reflection and a deflection of reality with respect to what is included and excluded (Pollak & Kubrin, 2007). But it does a disservice to automatically label mainstream media as racist because critics tend to ignore positive coverage of race relations, even if motivated by a business model rather than out of a sense of injustice. As well, positive coverage of diversities and difference can be uncovered with digital media, including Internet sources, alternative mainstream media like the NFB, and of course ethnic and Aboriginal media (Hier, 2007). Access to non-mainstream media secures access to coverage that reflects a more nuanced and complex reading of race relations in Canada, in effect suggesting that media racism is not nearly as pervasive as widely perceived.

It depends. Accusing the news media of racism depends on how racism is defined. There is no question that the media are no longer as blatantly racist in openly condoning white supremacy or minority inferiority. Yet more subtle expressions have proven to be as punishing as their overt cousins. For example, the news media may be accused of subliminal racism because of coded messages. Even if this kind of reading-between-the-lines racism tends to reflect a high level of subjectivity, its impact is unmistakable. But if racism is defined along structural instead of attitudinal lines, another picture appears. Media appear to be institutionally racialized: That is, ideas and ideals about what is normal and desirable with respect to race are so deeply ingrained within the founding assumptions and foundational principles (including the design, operation, and outcomes) of the media's constitutional order that a Eurocentric and racialized perspective defines what is acceptable or necessary, regardless of intent or awareness. In other words, a racist media does not necessarily arise from intentionally biased coverage. Rather, racism in the media reflects a level of coverage that is inadvertently (systemically) biasing because of a relentless one-sidedness that (1) frames minorities as troublesome constituents who are problems or who create problems; (2) interprets the world from a Eurocentric perspective as normal and desirable; and (3) promotes a pretend pluralism (superficial diversity) over those deep differences that demand to be taken into account when necessary. To be sure, no one is suggesting that the news media should sugarcoat all negative stories about minorities as problem people. But if the problem frame is the only kind of story that is conveyed by mainstream media, the cumulative effect is racist in consequences rather than by intent.

Systemic Racism

There is another type of institutional racism that is impersonal and unconscious, without much awareness of its presence or consequences except, of course, by the victimized (Fleras, 2012). Systemic racism is predicated on the premise that institutional rules and procedures can be racist in design, by practice, or in their effects, even if the actors are themselves free of prejudicial discrimination. At the heart of systemic racism is a business-as-usual mindset, with its commitment to treat everyone the same, even if applying equal standards to unequal contexts intensifies disparities. With systemic racism, institutional rules, expectations, and rewards may appear to be universally applicable and ostensibly colour-blind. Paradoxically, however, this one-size-fits-all standardization (aka neutrality) imposes a discriminatory impact on those whose differences are disadvantaging for reasons beyond their control. In other words, treating everyone the same when people's need-based differences must be taken into account may well have the unintended effect of inadvertently excluding those with different experiences, realities, and aspirations.

Systemic racism can be defined accordingly: It is a bias so deeply embedded within an institutional structure that the logical consequences of applying rules evenly and equally to unequal contexts exert an exclusionary effect on racialized others through no fault of their own. Neither intent nor awareness matter with systemic racism. Context and the consequences are critical since seemingly neutral policies and programs may exert an adverse effect. Institutional rules, priorities, and practices may not be inherently racist or deliberately discriminatory. Nor do institutional actors go out of their way to exclude or deprive minorities. But once entrenched (racialized) within institutions, racism no longer requires intent to deny or demean. Rather, the bias is perpetuated by seemingly benign practices and programs (ERASE Racism, 2005). Those institutional rules that are ostensibly universal may have a discriminatory effect, given the inherent (systemic) disadvantages of a system designed and organized by, for, and about the powerful and privileged to reflect and reinforce their experiences and interests as natural, normal, and superior. In short, unlike other forms of racism that are seen as departures from the norm, systemic racism is inseparable from normal institutional functions, processes, and outcomes. Finally, systemic bias may arise because of the logical consequences of well-intentioned policies based on making faulty assumptions, ignoring cultural differences, or dismissing context (Shkilnyk, 1985).

How do mainstream institutions exert a systemic bias against minority women and men? For years, a number of occupations, such as the police, firefighters, and mass transit drivers, imposed minimum weight, height, and educational requirements for job applicants. In retrospect, while not openly racist, these criteria proved systemically discriminatory because they favoured males over females and white applicants over people of colour. Nor was any deliberate attempt made to exclude anyone; after all, equal standards were uniformly applied. Valid reasons may have existed to justify these restrictions;[1] nevertheless, the imposition of these qualifications inflicted a set of unfair entry restrictions, regardless of intent or rationale. But these criteria have had a controlling effect of excluding racialized minorities who, as a group, lacked the criteria for entry or success *through no fault of their own*.

Or consider the systemic bias experienced by migrant agricultural workers from Mexico and the Caribbean who qualify under Canada's Seasonal Agricultural Workers Program. Like all Canadian workers, migrant workers must pay premiums under the Employment Insurance Act. However, unlike Canadian workers, migrant workers must leave Canada upon completion of their authorized work terms, thus making it impossible to qualify for benefits. Put bluntly, migrant workers cannot claim unemployment benefits or sick leave benefits because the Act stipulates that a claimant must be physically in Canada and available for work to receive benefits. In other words, the established rules of the Employment Insurance Act—when evenly and equally applied—have the effect of excluding migrant workers from benefit entitlements for reasons beyond their control. A similar line of reasoning applies to the systemic bias inherent in applying the principle of mandatory minimum sentences under the federal government's crime-fighting agenda. Critics argue that a disproportionate number of black males are charged under mandatory sentencing not because they commit more crime, but because of more intense police surveillance and anti-black racism in the criminal justice system (Makin, 2013). Other examples of systemic racism may include the following: an insistence on Canadian-only experience as a proxy to exclude the entry of new Canadians in search of work (Sakamoto et al., 2013); the devaluation of minority experiences and credentials as a precondition for professional employment; unnecessarily high educational standards for entry into certain occupations; entry exams that do not take a candidate's cultural or racial background into account; and excessively demanding qualifications that discourage membership in professional bodies.

INSIGHT

Framing Racialized Minorities in the News Media: Systematic Bias or Systemically Biasing?

Historically, media (mis)treatment of minority women and men fell into four representational frames, namely, minorities as *invisible, stereotyped, problem people, and depoliticized/whitewashed* (Fleras & Kunz, 2001). This unflattering assessment applied to all mainstream media processes, including newscasting, advertising, filmmaking, and TV programming. Of particular concern is the persistence of news media frames that problematize visibility while normalizing invisibility (Fleras, 2011c). Three key issues must be addressed to see how institutional racisms work in mainstream media:

1) How do mainstream news media frame (portray) minority women and men?

2) Is there an institutional bias in the framing of minorities?

3) Is the bias intentional (systematic) or does it reflect the unintentional consequences of doing news business?

The concept of framing draws on the assumption that media representations of reality are neither natural nor normal. Rather, they constitute socially constructed conventions whose constructedness is carefully concealed to make it appear unproblematic. Framing can be defined as a process of organizing information into packages (frames) through tone, emphasis, and selection (what is in, who is out, who matters, whose voices) that draws attention to some aspects of reality as desirable and acceptable, while dismissing other aspects as inferior, irrelevant, or threatening, all in the hopes of encouraging a preferred reading (interpretation) consistent with media and vested interests yet conveyed as if this reading was unproblematic (natural, normal, unbiased) rather than constructed and ideological (Entman, 1993; Fleras, 2011c). Media frames of events or people tend to bolster interpretations that favour those in power, in large part by promoting a particular problem definition, diagnosis (or causal interpretation), judgment or moral evaluation, and solution (Entman, 1993). Not surprisingly, the politics of framing are inextricably linked to patterns of thought control (propaganda or hegemony), systemically biasing in their consequences rather than their intent (Jiwani, 2010).

Frame No. 1: Invisibility

Numerous studies have confirmed what many regard as obvious. Canada's multicultural diversity is poorly reflected in news media processes and outcomes. Racialized (or visible) minorities are reduced to an invisible status through their under-representation in programming, staffing, and decision making. Admittedly, it would be inaccurate to say that the news media ignore minorities. A "shallows and rapids" treatment reflects a more accurate appraisal—that is, under normal circumstances minorities are ignored or rendered irrelevant by the mainstream press (shallows). Otherwise, coverage is guided by the context of crisis or calamity, involving natural catastrophes, civil wars, and colourful insurgents (rapids). When the crisis subsides, media interest wanes.

Frame No. 2: Problem People
Racialized minority women and men are frequently depicted as troublesome constituents who "are problems," "have problems," or "create problems" (Fleras, 2011c; Nairn et al., 2012). As "problem people" they are taken to task by the media for making demands at odds with national unity, identity, or prosperity. People of colour, both foreign and Canadian-born, are targets of negative coverage, with its focus on costs, threats, and inconveniences. Media reporting of refugees usually refers to illegal entries and the associated costs of processing and integrating them into Canada. Canada's refugee determination system is repeatedly criticized for the entry of those who pose a security threat. Immigrants are routinely cast as potential troublemakers who allegedly steal jobs from Canadians, cheat on the welfare system, take advantage of educational opportunities, lack commitment to Canada, engage in illegal activities such as drugs or smuggling, imperil Canada's unity and identity by refusing to abandon their culture, and undermine its security by spawning homegrown terrorists (Karim, 2006; Hennebry & Momani, 2013).

That newsworthy conflicts and problems occur in minority communities is not the issue at hand. The problem resides in the absence of balanced coverage that often distorts public perceptions of minority experiences and aspirations. This distortion may not be deliberately engineered. Rather, the flamboyant and sensational are accorded disproportionate coverage to satisfy the audience's interests and to sell copy, without much regard for their impact on the lives of those who are sensationalized. To be sure, the news media would be equally irresponsible if they ignored negative news about minorities or sugarcoated news items with a positive spin. But if the problem frame is the only kind of story that is conveyed by mainstream media, then the total picture is racist, albeit in consequences (systemic) rather than by intent. To the extent that coverage of minorities as troublesome constituents is relentlessly one sided in its negativity, no one should discount news media coverage of minorities as akin to a kind of soft propaganda (Fleras, 2008b).

Frame No. 3: Stereotyping
Racialized minorities have long complained of stereotyping by mainstream media. People of colour were historically portrayed in a manner that dovetailed with prevailing prejudices and racist culture. They continue to be stereotyped as dangerous, irrelevant, or inferior, albeit in more indirect ways. Of particular note is the stereotyping of race to crime (Henry & Tator 2002). A fixation with highly visible crimes tends to focus on the poor, often youth

and those of colour, in effect reinforcing racial stereotypes by conflating negativity with distortion. Yet media coverage of street crime is paradoxical—that is, the least frequent forms of crime (violent crime) may be exaggerated, while the most common (white-collar or property crime) tends to be downplayed (Surrette, 1998/2004). An obsession with the sordid and sensational produces coverage that disdains the normative and routine by exaggerating the exception. Behaviour at the extremes comes to define the norm, in part by labelling an entire community for the actions of a few, thus amplifying anxieties over criminalized types whom many see as out of control and in need of more control (Hirst & Patchin, 2005). The end result is a double standard: White criminal behaviour is excused as an aberrant act of an individual; by contrast, black crime remains a "group crime" or "cultural trait" for which the entire community must take responsibility (Wortley, 2003).

Admittedly, media stereotyping is intrinsic to the operational dynamic of an industry that must simplify information by tapping into a collective portfolio of popular and unconscious images. In the same way people depend on stereotyping to simplify those aspects of everyday reality with which they have little direct contact (Dovidio, Hewson, Glick, & Esses, 2010), so too do news media rely on stereotypes for codifying reality and processing information. Limitations in time and space prevent complex interpretations of reality across the spectrum of human emotion, conflict, or contradiction. Violent crime is framed as endemic to individuals and attitudes in certain racialized communities, but largely disconnected from the structures of society (including patterns of discrimination, disadvantage, and inequality). The contextual (social and economic) basis of crime is often ignored by news media that gloss over minority experiences, thus reinforcing a blame-the-victim mentality. But relying on the language of sensationalism to narrate a story can easily distort the parameters of the debate, influence public opinion on social issues, and popularize assumptions about what is normal, desirable, or acceptable.

Frame No. 4: Whitewashing/Depoliticizing/Exoticizing/Othering
The concept of whitewashing reflects different levels of meaning. It can be used in the sense of rendering minorities invisible, in the process removing the presence of minorities from a society's collective consciousness (Tehranian, 2009; Forbis, 2013). Or in the sense of casting white actors as racialized minorities or Aboriginal peoples on the assumption that minority casts are unlikely to generate the same level of mass acceptance as white actors or whitewashed (airbrushed and sanitized) minority actors (Alvarez, 2008). Lastly, whitewashing can be employed to convey a process of depoliticizing differences. Depictions of differences may be increasingly acceptable within mainstream media, but this acceptance comes with strings attached. News

media tend to depoliticize minorities by sanitizing (whitewashing) those differences that are threatening or problematic, in the process rendering them palatable for mainstream palettes. For example, racialized minorities are depoliticized along unthreatening lines—from athlete to entertainer—or in depolitized/exoticized activities such as multicultural festivals. Representations of minorities may also veer toward the desexed thus neutering them of a potential threat, or, alternatively as oversexed, thus increasing their appeal by exoticising their sexuality.

Refusing to take differences seriously reinforces charges of mainstream news media as diversity-aversive. Coverage continues to be distorted by the ethnocentric assumption that migrants/minorities are like "us" or want to be like "us" or must be like "us" if they hope to prosper. Or diversity is marginalized by an unquestioned commitment to liberal universalism in acknowledging how people's commonalities as freewheeling and morally autonomous individuals should prevail for purposes of recognition and redistribution over membership in racially different groups. Difficulties arise, however, when differences really do make a difference in shaping experiences, identities, and opportunities. True, the news media can easily address surface diversity when framed as a cultural tile in Canada's multicultural mosaic. But the news media lack the ideological resourcefulness for addressing the complexities and challenges of deep differences. Yet failure to take differences seriously exacts a controlling effect. Refracting deep diversities through a monocultural lens and imposing a singular and standardized (one-size-fits-all) lens on complex and diverse realities are controlling by virtue of conflating equality with sameness. In that a pretend pluralism endorsed by mainstream media neither takes differences seriously (except as a problem to be solved) nor takes difference into account (except as a source of conflict and confrontation), this one-sidedness amounts to a whitewashing that depoliticizes as it diminishes.

News Media Racism as Systemically Biasing

Many media scholars agree that mainstream media constitute sites of exclusion that, arguably, are biased (Henry & Tator 2002; Mahtani et al., 2008; Jiwani, 2009; Fleras 2011c). Media misrepresentation of differences tend to "normalize invisibility," while "problematizing visibility" by framing minorities and migrants as (1) invisible, (2) stereotyped, (3) problem people, and (4) whitewashed (or depoliticized) (Fleras & Kunz, 2001). In some cases, this bias deliberately excludes, problematizes, or racializes minorities (systematic bias); in other cases, it would appear to be largely impersonal, is deeply embedded within media foundational structures, reflects unintended consequences rather than deliberate attempts to deny or defame, and is indistinguishable from the normal functioning of the news media (systemic bias).

Although a deliberate (systematic) bias in news media framing continues to exist, a systemic bias prevails as well, both impersonal and unintentional, yet no less invidious or invasive. Unlike its systematic counterpart with its deliberate slant and explicit agenda (Soroka & Maioni, 2006), systemic bias involves the unpremeditated consequences of seemingly neutral news media rules that can prove discriminatory when evenly and equally applied. Policy programs and institutional actions may prove systemically biasing if informed by well-intentioned yet ultimately flawed assumptions about what is normal, preferred, or acceptable. The defining feature of systemic bias as a discrimination without prejudice is its perceived normalcy. A "business as usual" framework prevails that unwittingly denies or excludes by applying uniform standards to unequal contexts, thereby freezing an unequal status quo. With a systemic bias, the controlling actors and institutional routines may themselves be free of bias because of their commitment to the seemingly progressive principle of treating everyone the same. In short, systemic bias differs from its systematic counterparts at critical junctures: one is impersonal, the other is deliberate; consequences prevail over intent; routine over random; normal rather than deviant; and structural rather than attitudinal.

How, then, are the news media systemically biasing? News media engage in systemic bias because of a media-centric inclination toward one-sided and one-size-fits-all coverage that is pro-white, conflict-driven, decontextualized, and difference-aversive. A pro-white Eurocentrism is conveyed not in the blatant sense of openly white supremacy. Rather, whiteness is privileged as superior and the normative standard that evaluates, normalizes, and criticizes. An ethno/Euro/centrism reflects an unconscious tendency to interpret reality from a mainstream point of view as natural or superior, while assuming that others do so as well (or want to). So too does a media-centric bias reflect an institutional tendency to privilege its way of framing reality as normal, necessary, and inevitable. For instance, newsworthiness embraces a media-centred bias toward the abnormal over the normal, the negative over the positive, the deviant over the normative, conflict over co-operation, the sensational over substance, and the episodic over the thematic. Furthermore, coverage that is systemically biasing arises when assigning priority to (1) blaming the victim over blaming the system; (2) personalities over structure or context; (3) conflict over consensus or co-operation; (4) a racialized status quo over citizenship and justice; and (5) the episodic and human interest stories over the thematic and contextual.

A similar line of reasoning applies news media coverage of racialized minorities. A news media bias reflects systemically biasing coverage because of a one-sidedness that (1) frames minorities as troublesome constituents who are problems or who create problems; (2) interprets the world from a Eurocentric perspective as normal and desirable; (3) demonizes or vilifes a whole group for the actions of a few while dismissing the acts of whites as the aberration of individuals; (4) routinely associating racialized groups with negative actions or cultures that are incompatible with the mainstream; (5) silences minorities when white authorities speak for them (reinforcing perceptions of minorities as passive, ignorant, and lacking skills while bolstering the concept of the media as white space); and (6) promotes a pretend pluralism (superficial diversity) over those deep differences that demand to be taken seriously (see also Harker, 2012). More specifically, systemically biasing coverage reflects the following racialized frames (see also Harker 2012):

- In that news media tend to focus on conflict as newsworthy or to frame issues around a conflict narrative while glossing over the positives, thus advancing institutional interests rather than the public good, the news media are systemically biasing.
- In that all newscasting defines consensus, order, and social stability as the norm while framing protest, rapid social change, and chaos as deviant and newsworthy, the mainstream media are systemically biasing.
- In that whiteness is routinely privileged as the tacitly assumed norm by which others are judged, the news media are systemically biasing.
- In that minorities are invariably stereotyped as problem people who have problems or who create problems that are at odds with Canada's national interests, the whiff of systemic bias is all too real.
- In that context is rarely included in stories about minorities, in the process reinforcing a blaming the individual frame, the resulting stereotyping is systemically biasing.
- In that the media excel in hiding the hegemonic ideals of white supremacy by naturalizing racial differences and social inequalities so that differential treatment of people is conveyed as normal and acceptable, the effect is systemically biasing (Hall, 2000; Mistry, 2013).

To sum up, are the media racist, thus generating systematic bias? Or are they racialized as white spaces, with the result that their coverage of minorities is systemically biasing? It is argued that racism in the news media does not necessarily originate from intentionally biased coverage. It is doubtful that media decision makers would go out of their way to deliberately misrepresent minorities, given the potential for nasty repercussions, ranging from loss of corporate revenue to derailed career plans. More accurately, news media coverage of minorities is systemically biasing because of how newsworthiness is defined. Yes, news media as a medium of the negative ("the only good news is bad news") negatively frames mainstream realities. Yet there is a world of difference in consequences from negatively framing minorities who neither possess the institutional power to deflect this negativity nor the positive representations to offset the negativity. In other words, as discourses in defence of dominant Eurocentric ideology, the news media don't go out of their way to deny, distort, or exclude. Nevertheless, biases qualify as systemic and controlling when media outcomes reflect the logical yet negative effects of applying seemingly neutral rules evenly and equally to everyone regardless of context or consequences.

Note

1. There is always the danger of overuse. According to Margaret Wente (2010), the popularity of systemic racism is the absence of evidence of proof of its existence. Just a simple reference to its existence is enough to close debate, and anybody who denies its existence is either in denial or too scared to speak out.

CHAPTER 7

IDEOLOGICAL RACISMS

Introduction

Ideological racism constitutes that level of racism pertaining to the social and cultural dimensions of society. Ideological racism points to the prevalence and pervasiveness of cultural values and communication patterns that quietly but cumulatively advance dominant interests at the expense of those perceived as irrelevant and inferior. A distinction between the normative and everyday components of ideological racism is useful. Everyday racism consists of unconscious speech habits and routine everyday actions/interactions that have the cumulative effect of denying and excluding racialized minorities. Normative (or cultural)[1] racism reflects a largely unconscious bias arising from prevailing cultural values that bolster the realities, experiences, and expections of the dominant sector, while disadvantaging or disparaging those perceived as physically different or culturally inferior. With ideological racism (as with institutional racism), individuals are framed as the repositories or carriers of both everyday and normative racisms rather than the source or cause (Bonilla-Silva, 1997).

Everyday Racism: Talk Is Not Cheap

Contemporary racisms are rarely directly expressed. Preferred instead are more socially acceptable practices that achieve the same effect without attracting negative attention (Jonas, 2006). Everyday racism consists of those ordinary racist practices that infiltrate the daily routines of what is societally accepted as normal and normative (Essed, 1991, 2002). Rather than ideologically fuelled rampages, everyday acts of racism occur on the spur of the moment, triggered by a perceived insult, a grievance, a minor conflict attributable to the incivilities of everyday social life (Iganski, 2010). Admittedly, the term "everyday" may be misleading: For many it conjures up notions of the mundane, routine, and ordinary. But the stable, recurrent, and seemingly unchanging forms of the everyday are anything but ordinary or insignificant (Velayutham, 2009; Johnson & Enomoto, 2007). Or, as Howard Winant (2004) puts it, contemporary racism constitutes an exercise in hegemony reflecting the routine practices that create or reinforce hierarchical structures and white privilege. The impact and implications are expressed in several ways: First, acts of everyday racism become normalized through integration into normal routines and interactions (from name-calling to racist jokes to avoidance of close contact) in ways that reinforce unequal power relations. Second, to victims, such routine experiences are deeply distressing and humiliating, resulting in diminished self-esteem and withdrawal from participation in society (Essed, 1991; Velayutham, 2009). Third, failure to address everyday attitudes and behaviour that are frequently not acknowledged or that go unchallenged may well explain the persistence of racisms despite a plethora of racism laws against racial discrimination (Bhavnani, Mirza, & Meetoo, 2005). In short, the symbols, structures, and interactions associated with everyday life reproduce an atmosphere and sensibility that communicate a dislike toward racialized others, while functioning to reinforce notions of white superiority and privilege (Douglas, 2008).

The role of language in perpetuating everyday racism is widely recognized (Essed, 1991; Wetherell & Potter, 1993; Blauner, 1994). This acknowledgement is not necessarily shared by the general public. Too often people see language as equivalent to a postal system, namely, a relatively neutral system of conveyance between sender and receiver for the transmission of messages independently created through a process called thinking. Nothing could be further from the truth: Language (or the way we speak) is intimately bound up with people's experiences of the world, together with efforts to convey that experience to others. It is neither neutral nor value-free but a socially constructed convention that embodies and expresses the beliefs, values, and norms of its creators and conveyors. Rather than a passive or mechanical transmitter of information, languages are loaded with values and preferences promoting some aspects of reality as normal and acceptable while drawing attention away from other aspects as inconsequential or incompatible. The words of a language are not untainted or innocent; on the contrary, they have a connotational dimension by virtue of conveying negative images beyond what is intended. Insofar as ideas and ideals are trapped inside language—in effect influencing patterns of thought and behaviour without our awareness (i.e., hegemony)—the two-edged nature of language is unmistakable. Yes, language can be used to enlighten and inform; yet it can be employed to control, conceal, evade, direct, or dictate.

Language can be readily manipulated to express intolerance. It possesses the potency to socially construct reality by highlighting differences, increasing distance, and sanctioning "otherness" (Ngugi, 2013). It may be used to degrade or ridicule minorities, as Robert Moore (1992, p. 1) demonstrates in his oft-quoted article on racism in the English language, by way of obvious bigotry, colour symbolism (black = bad), loaded terms (Indian massacres), and seemingly neutral phrases that perversely are infused with hidden anxieties ("waves" of immigrants):

> Some may blackly (angrily) accuse me of trying to blacken (defame) the English language, to give it a black eye (mark of shame) by writing such black words (hostile) ... by accusing me of being black-hearted (malevolent), of having a black outlook (pessimistic; dismal) on life, of being a blackguard (scoundrel) which would certainly be a black mark (detrimental fact) against me.

To be sure, the racism implicit in words and metaphors may not be intentional or deliberate. Nor will the occasional use of derogatory words explode into full-blown racism. But however inaccurate the notion that language determines our reality, there is much of value in saying it provides a powerful frame of reference for defining what is desirable and acceptable, normal and important. Language, in short, represents an ideal vehicle for expressing intolerance by highlighting differences or sanctioning inequality through invisible yet real boundaries (Henry & Tator, 2002). And as the Insight box below explains, those who want to change the way we think begin by changing how we speak and the words we use on the linguistic assumption (from the Sapir-Whorf hypothesis to political correctness) that our pattern of speech influences how we think, and vice versa. The concept of political correctness is also based on the principle that words often influence our thoughts and actions. The next Insight box demonstrates how and why.

INSIGHT

Language as Everyday Racism: Racializing "Visible Minority"

Canadians were either shocked or furious to find themselves under UN criticism for something that caught most people off guard (Fleras, 2008a; Kinsella, 2007; Edwards, 2007). In a world swamped with flagrant human rights abuses—from genocide to gendered genital mutilation—the very thought of a UN body accusing Canada for its mislabelling of minorities amounted to what many saw as little more than a case of the proverbial kettle calling the pot black (Fleras, 2008a).

The seventieth session of the Committee on the Elimination of Racial Discrimination (CERD) had concluded that Canada should *"reflect further"* (emphasis added) on the implications of the term "visible minorities" in line with Article 1, paragraph 1, of the International Convention for the Elimination of All Forms of Racial Discrimination. According to CERD, reference to visible minorities as defined by Canada's Employment Equity Act (1995) was problematic not because of malevolent intent, but because of the unintended consequences of unconscious (subliminal) racist assumptions. The core of the criticism was twofold (Fleras, 2008a): First, by *problematizing visibility*, reference to visible minorities was thought to normalize whiteness as the normative standard at the expense of "ab-normalizing" racial minorities, hence the nomenclature was deemed subliminally biasing in light of its racial connotations (see Woolley, 2013). Second, by *normalizing invisibility* under a singular expression, specific minority experiences and identities were glossed over, in effect perpetuating the very exclusion under challenge. Reference to visible minority could be construed as amplifying inequality by systemically reinforcing "any distinction, exclusion, restriction, or preference based on race, colour, descent, or national and ethnic origin."

Reaction to CERD's concerns over the use, implications, and appropriateness of the term "visible minority" generated lively debate (Kinsella, 2007). To be sure, a careful reading of the report did not warrant this outrage, although having the UN publicly express concern is tantamount to hanging out one's dirty laundry for the world to see (Go, 2007). Moreover, the CERD stopped short of equating "visible minority" with racism or a violation of Canada's international treaty obligations. Nor did it expressly prohibit the use of "visible minority" (Kinsella, 2007). But without a review and reflection, it could not condone use of the term that could be construed as polite racism (coding a dislike in oblique terms), subliminal racism (reflecting unconscious prejudices), everyday racism (the role of language in negatively identifying, naming, and classifying minorities on predominantly physical characteristics), or normative racism (reflecting values that privilege the privileged).

Those who challenged this criticism counter-argued that they were simply observing standard usage from which no politics could be inferred. They contended that the CERD's comments about visible minorities misunderstood Canada's justification for its use: (1) as a descriptive typology with ascriptive intent; (2) as a substitute for existing pejorative putdowns (such as "coloureds" or "non-whites"); (3) to emphasize the structural commonalities shared by "people of colour"; and (4) as a euphemistic shorthand to identify, name, and categorize those routinely victimized by racism and racial discrimination (Li, 1995; Tepper, 1996). Still others acknowledged the lack of viable alternatives. Furthermore, how possible is any "aggregation without aggravation" without establishing a binary distinction between "us" and "them," with a corresponding implication of whiteness (or the mainstream) as the norm? Furthermore, without a nomenclature for identifying and classifying the targeted demographic, how can minority equity policies and anti-racist programs be devised (Mayan & Morse, 2001/2002; Edwards, 2007)?

In light of these supportive statements for retention of the expression "visible minorities," the CERD's criticism appeared oddly out of character, but consistent with criticism elsewhere. That much could be expected of a typology that classified people on the criteria of skin colour, in the process not only prioritizing race in a Canada that self-identifies as colour-blind, but also privileging whiteness as the normative standard by which to judge others. Ambiguities prevail: Reference to "visible minority" was positively linked with moves to improve equitable minority participation. But

> the typology had the unfortunate effect of aggregating all "non-whites" without making a distinction based on need, history, location, and cultural specifics (Pendakur, 2005). As put by Synnott and Howes (1996, p. 146), "[visible minority] homogenizes specificities, ignoring differences in power, status, culture, history, and even visibility ... the ethnic stratification system (both economic and ideological) is far more complex than the simple dichotomy visibility/invisibility would suggest."
>
> In short, the link between "visible minority" and the discredited notion of race as science exemplified a coded racism by virtue of categorizing people on physical grounds. In doing so, the concept of visible tended to paradoxically reinforce those exclusionary mindsets that the very creation of the term was designed to correct.

Everyday racism applies to institutional settings as well. These everyday incidents of racial discrimination and manifestations of racism are rooted in systemic structures; after all, the power to make decisions resides at this level as well as in the allocation of resources and rewards (Vukic et al., 2012) For example, multiple forms of racism are played out in the everyday working lives of nurses (Das Gupta, 2009; Wilmot, 2010; also Mapedzahama et al., 2012; Barbee, 1993). Tania Das Gupta (2009) writes of racist treatment in the day-to-day workplace life of nurses that includes (among others) tokenism, infantilization, denial of promotions, work allocation bias, targeting, scapegoating, excessive monitoring, lack of accommodation, segregration, and subjection to racial abuse. Racism in the nursing workplace crosscuts gender and class discrimination (Das Gupta, 2009), while intersecting with other negative identity markers such as race, gender, class, and ability to complicate the lived realities of racialized nurses. Unconscious biases related to and perceptions of race play a role in medical diagnosis (for example, from paying less attention to patient symptoms to interrupting patients or making patients feel less involved in health decisions, resulting in racially biased treatment and medical harm, despite medical practitioners' beliefs that they harboured no negative attitudes or preferences [see also Terrell, 2012; Hoberman, 2007, 2012]). This racist treatment is often conveyed by white coworkers in conjunction with their managers and patients (Deacon, 2011).

Normative (or Cultural) Racisms

Normative racisms involve the perpetuation of racism through norms, values, standards, and beliefs. Certain ideas and ideals within a dominant culture are widely circulated that explicitly or implicitly assert the superiority of some at the expense of others. Or, alternatively, dominant cultural beliefs and values tend to uphold mainstream patterns as the norm, while other cultural systems are devalued accordingly. There is an ethnocentric tendency to interpret and diminish others through a specific cultural lens at the expense of Canada's commitment to justice, equity, and inclusiveness.

Under a normative racism, reference to culture trumps race as a marker of inferiority or exclusion. Cultural others are not rejected or demonized as racially inferior. They are dismissed instead as culturally irrelevant or incompatible or threatening. In some cases, minorities are explicitly criticized; in other cases, the rejection is muted through coded texts or justified on principled grounds ("everyone should be treated alike"—that is, no special treatment) (Li, 2007). Of particular salience to normative racisms is a commitment to (neo)liberal universalism, with its attendant adherence to the universal humanity of individuals as individuals. Liberal universalism as a foundational ideology claims that our commonalities as morally autonomous individuals are much more important for purposes of recognition or reward than membership in racially different and divisive groups. To be sure, there is much to commend in a commitment to commonality as a basis for living together with differences. Yet unanticipated consequences can prove costly. A corresponding commitment to a pretend pluralism under liberal universalism does an injustice to those racialized minorities and Aboriginal peoples whose differences are deep, do matter, and must be taken seriously. In the final analysis, references to normative racism reinforce the centrality of whiteness as the global standard of acceptability and desirability, as explained in the following Insight box.

INSIGHT

Insight: "Racism Lite": Toward a Paler Shade of White

There is a booming market for skin whiteners in those parts of the world where whiteness is equated with beauty, success, and popularity (McPhate, 2005). Women in India have long been accused of using whiteners and skin bleaches to enhance their lives and life chances. But a growing number of men, both rural and urban, are also succumbing to the same pressure and prejudices that once prompted women to use skin lighteners or bleaches, namely, a belief that a pale complexion will enhance success in life, love, and business (Coulter, 2009). The hope is not entirely unfounded: In an India where arranged marriages remain common, matrimonial ads in newspapers confirm this obsession with whiteness by advertising for fairness or lightness in prospective brides and grooms (Coulter, 2009; Sidner, 2009). Consider how this advertisement for White Beauty by Ponds plays into whiteness as an ideal: A "dusky-skinned" woman loses her boyfriend to a lighter-skinned lady. But with White Beauty to the rescue, she reclaims her boyfriend, and marries happily ever after (Shimo, 2008). Bollywood films are also known to feature plot lines that equate love and happiness with a fair complexion, while darker-skinned comrades are doomed to sadness, disgrace, or failure.

Not surprisingly, this campaign for "unnatural/unreal beauty"—in contrast to Dove's Campaign for so-called Real Beauty—has come under attack (Fleras, 2011c). Critics accuse manufacturers of fairness creams of racism by reinforcing stereotypes in a status-conscious society where dark skin is equated with the lower classes in contrast to the higher strata of the light-skinned such as the Brahmin (priestly) caste (Sidner, 2009). Fairness creams are also accused of promoting colonial standards that link whiteness to class, lifestyle, and beauty (Jordan, 1998). The politics of class should not be disregarded: Many Asian countries look down on dark skin not because of racism but because of class. Predictably, nobody wants to be perceived as poor (and dark-skinned) (Kepnes, 2008), exerting additional pressure on whiteness measures. Regardless of the dimensions at play, these perceptions induce a booming business in a male fairness market, including $70 million in perpetually evolving cosmetic products, including whitening soaps, lightening aftershaves, and fairness wipes, in the process proving that bleaching is money because, as they say in Brazil, money bleaches.

It will be interesting in light of such staggering sums to determine the success of campaigns that encourage Asia-Pacific individuals to reject paler complexions as damaging and demeaning while embracing a quest for a lighter shade of pale (Shimo, 2008). The prognosis looks bleak, especially if North American and European standards are anything to go by. Just as Asians undergo body-altering practices to attain an unnatural ideal, so too do white North Americans and Europeans self-inflict wounds through tanning salons and tanning creams, while subjecting themselves to self-mutilation to siphon off unwanted fat through wrinkle-reducing Botox or liposuction procedures. Perhaps these trends reinforce a possible global truth (Asthana, 2008), namely, a universal longing to be impossibly beautiful by doing what comes unnaturally to achieve the unattainable (Asthana, 2008).

Neo-liberalism as Normative Racism

Race relations in Canada and the United States have undergone tumultuous changes since W. E. B. Du Bois famously predicted the colour line as the quintessential problem of the twentieth century. References to racisms continue to proliferate and diversify because of social, demographic, and political disruptions at national and global levels. Of particular note in rethinking how contemporary racisms work in post-racial and colour-blind societies are the ideological shifts associated with neo-liberal ideologies Neo-liberalism consists of ideals that reify the free market as the solution to social problems, while reassigning blame for economic inequality to private and personal domain (Davis, 2007). It entails a set of ideas and ideals that extol the virtues of individual self-sufficiency through more market (including trade liberalization, free trade agreements, and borderless capital flows and investment) and less government in both the economy and the distribution of a society's resources (Wallis, Sunseri, & Galabuzi, 2010). A neo-liberal belief in the racelessness of a colour-blind society departs from the overtly racialized projections of a colour-conscious past. To be sure, this neo-liberal commitment to colour-blindness should *not* suggest that (1) race or racism have declined in significance; (2) racial conditions, ideologies, and practices have been abolished; or (3) race and racism no longer fuse power with ideology in shaping the distribution of value resources. Rather, the focus is on the eventual demise of race and racism as determinants of life chances. Yet these privatized (neo-liberal) racisms are proving to be every bit as political and politicized as their bigoted and blunt counterparts, in effect demonstrating how racism works in those contexts that disavow the relevance of race and racism.

There is paradox at play in these developments: the illusion of inclusion versus the reality of exclusions. On one side, there is a growing perception that both Canada and the United States are moving to endorse colour-blind ideologies. This claim is based on the perception that race, racism, and racial discrimination no longer resonate as they once did in shaping people's perspectives or prospects. The major features of a colour-blind ideology include a commitment to (1) the principles of neo-liberal universalism; (2) cultural rather than biological explanations to account for minority failures or inferiorities; (3) patterns of inequality as normal and inevitable rather than structurally unjust; and (4) claims that race and racial discrimination are irrelevant in explaining inequalities (Bonilla-Silva, 2002). The following developments are offered as proof in discrediting race as a variable in explaining socio-economic disparities and determining possibilities. Segregation and discrimination are illegal in a Canada that commits to the principles of inclusion, multiculturalism, and human rights; the appointment of racialized minorities across all aspects of public life from politics to popular culture (including rap music, hip-hop clothing, and sports gears); and a spike in the number of black elites in film, sports, music, and fashion magazines. Popular culture through the sharing of social space with racialized minorities (including *Cosby Show* reruns, minority success stories, hip-hop and rap styles, and diversity awareness lessons) has given young people a sense of living in an era of racelessness (Gallagher, 2003, 2008). In short, racialized minorities are striding the corridors of success, popularity, and acceptance in ways that seemingly reinforce the irrelevance of race and racism in determining who gets what. To the extent that race and racism persist and punish in shaping opportunities and outcomes, they represent largely toothless relics from the past or are restricted to isolated hate crimes by dysfunctional misfits (Doane, 2007).

On the other side, there is a fundamentally different spin in explaining what is going on. Far from declining in significance, racism and racial discrimination appear to have consolidated and diversified with the result that race remains a major predictor of success and failure. Legal guarantees of formal equality and access sound better in theory than reality. Blacks in the United States are twice as like as whites to be unemployed; the poverty rate for blacks is twice that of whites—the black household median income ($27,000) is two-thirds of the white household median income ($42,000); black family median household wealth is 10 percent that of whites; blacks comprise nearly 50 percent of the prison population (but only 13 percent of the overall population [Alexander, 2012]); blacks remain residentially segregated across massive swathes of American society. In other words, as Giroux (2004) points out, if race and racism no longer mattered in naming, organizing, and allocating, how does one explain why many American blacks are locked into Third World enclaves in the world's richest and most powerful state?

CASE STUDY

"I Have a Dream": Still a Dream?

It was one of those iconic moments, forever etched in American history. Fifty years ago (August 1963), Martin Luther King Jr. delivered his historic "I have a dream" speech in Washington, DC, outlining his vision of a more equitable America in which people (especially blacks) would be judged by the content of their character rather than the colour of their skin.

But five decades later, research indicates the socio-economic status of blacks remains stuck in the past. A survey by the Pew Research Center (August 22, 2013) finds that 45 percent of Americans believe in substantial progress toward racial equality, yet nearly half (49 percent) say a "lot more" remains to be done. Even these figures are misleading: Black Americans are much more pessimistic (79 percent) than whites (44 percent) about the pace of change toward a color-blind society. Gaps have widened in household income and wealth, while other measures—such as poverty rates, unemployment rates, and homeownership rates—have stagnated. Residential segregation remains as much of a problem as it did in past (in the case of Detroit, 80 percent of its inhabitants are black, although seventy years ago, 90 percent were white) (Cable, 2013). Blacks also believe they are less fairly treated than whites by the criminal justice system: According to the Pew Research Center data (2013), black men are six times more likely than their white counterparts to be jailed in a state or federal prison, an increase from 1960, when the figure was five times the rate. Additional injustices continue to pile up. About 35 percent of all blacks say they were discriminated against or unfairly treated because of their race in the past year, compared to 10 percent of whites (Latino figures stood at 20 percent).

CS To be sure, changes and improvements are unmistakable. A new generation of activists have retrofitted King's dream by shifting the struggle from the pulpit to the statehouse, from sidewalks to Facebook and the Twitterverse, and from a focus on civil rights to one more aligned with human rights or a civil rights 2.0 (Sisson, 2013). Blacks are no longer sitting at the back of bus, drinking out of separate water coolers, being sprayed by fire hoses, and set upon by snarling German shepherds during peaceful protest (Cutaia, 2013). State-sanctioned segregation has been abolished, blatant racism is socially unacceptable, open evasions of federal anti discrimination decrees are rare, and Southern whites no longer go unpunished for crimes against blacks. Mixed-race relationships have evolved from a state of pariahdom to the status of new elites as proof of an emerging post-racial and post-national society (Marche, 2012). A black middle class has emerged owing partly to the growth in good public service jobs (Editorial, *Globe and Mail*, August 31, 2013). On measures such as life expectancy and high school completion, the gaps have narrowed as well.

Yet there is no mistaking the social/political/economic gulf that persists between blacks and whites that has prevailed for a half century. Slavery may have been abolished in the nineteenth century, but its legacy persists in the form of discrimination and segregation that is not legally mandated but prevails in schools, neighbourhoods, and workplaces (Cutaia, 2013). Nor is there any doubt of the enduring chasm between how white and black Americans perceive racism and the legacy of slavery's long-term effects (Editorial, *Globe and Mail*, August 31, 2013). The disconnect between whites and blacks in the aftermath of the Zimmerman trial for shooting and killing an unarmed Trayvon Martin speaks volumes of the perceptual divide over racism. Whites tend to believe that racism (from lynching to cross burnings) no longer exists, is a thing of the past, and isn't a problem anymore—a belief bolstered by a June 25, 2013, Supreme Court ruling to that effect—whereas blacks believe racism continues to be manifest in their daily lives and in their socio-economic status (Alpert, 2013). This passage—in response to Obama's confession that he, too, was mistaken for a thug or servant—captures the essence of everyday racism:

> There are very few African American men in this country who haven't had the experience of being followed when they were shopping in a department store.... There are very few African American men who haven't had the experience of walking across the street and hearing the locks click on the doors of cars.... There are very few African American men who haven't had the experience of getting on an elevator and a woman clutching her purse nervously and holding her breath until she had a chance to get off. (Decoste, 2013)

Clearly a racial rashomon (divide) prevails in which white Americans think Martin Luther King's vision of a post-racial America is much closer to reality than do black Americans (Alpert, 2013). Such a divide does augur well for the future of a country where the nightmare of people's skin colour continues to trump the content of their character. Margaret Kimberley (2012), in the Black Agenda Report, captures it movingly:

> Racism is the still the number one modus operandi by which this country functions. It is a permanent part of the thinking of most white people and results in low rates for anything good like employment and high rates of everything bad like incarceration. The unwillingness to address the question of the persistence of racial animus practiced against black people leads to very dangerous dynamic.

In short, race and racism continue to play a major role in defining options and determining outcomes. If anything, a new justification for white supremacy has evolved that capitalizes on post-racial principles of a colour-blind ideology (Wise, 2008). How is this contradiction rationalized? The old racism—bigoted, crude, and overtly racist—defined racial difference in terms of fixed biological categories organized hierarchically in defence of white racial superiority. By contrast, the new neo-liberal racisms operate under different and often invisible guises while proclaiming race neutrality, asserting culture as the marker of difference, and prioritizing race as a private matter of identity rather than a predictor of inequality or a personal choice that hides systems of privilege and disadvantage (Davis, 2007; Giroux, 2004). Neo-liberal racisms reflect the language of colour-blindness and principles of a post-racial society. According to this line of thinking, the best way of removing racial discrimination is by treating everyone the same (equally) regardless of race (Williams, 2011). Admittedly, an ideology of colour-blindness and principles of a post-racial society does not deny the relevance of race as a matter of identity, lifestyle, or heritage. What is rejected are claims assigning blame to race and racism for the massive inequities and differential opportunities in society.

The consequences are hardly trifling: A neo-liberal ideology of colour-blindness enables whites to disregard the interplay of race/racism in establishing assymetrical patterns of exclusion, power, politics, legal rights, educational success, and economic opportunities. Denying the salience of racialized hierarchies allows a colour-blind ideology to proclaim the arrival of a so-called level playing field, while confirming how white successes reflect their own personal initiative. Minorities, in turn, have only themselves to blame for not taking advantage of opportunities available to anyone in a post-racial society. The end result is a colour-blind racism that plays into the hands of a white-stream society as Monica Williams (2011) explains:

> In a colorblind society, White people, who are unlikely to experience disadvantages due to race, can effectively ignore racism in American life, justify the current social order, and feel more comfortable with

their relatively privileged standing in society. Most minorities, however, who regularly encounter difficulties due to race, experience colorblind ideologies differently. Colorblindness creates a society that denies their negative racial experiences, rejects their cultural heritage, and invalidates their own unique experiences.

Lastly, the elimination of race and racism as a disabling force means an end to government-based programs. Initiatives such as employment equity (or affirmative action in the United States) are no longer required to dismantle the historical legacy and effects of racism. Nor are they need to provide minorities with a hand up. Paradoxically, it is argued, those who insist on the need for pro-race equity and anti-racism programs are themselves guilty of racism by treating others on the basis of race when such a need neither exists nor is justifiable (Berliner & Hull, 1995).

The emergence of neo-liberal racisms is consistent with the principles of a colour-blind/post-racial ideology. The ideological logic behind a colour-blind/post-racial society denies the salience of race and racism in securing patterns of power and exclusion. According to the tenets of a colour-blind ideology, the relevance of racism in shaping people's lives and life chances is disappearing. Race no longer matters in judging and disadvantaging so that minority misfortunes are due entirely to personal choices (McCardle, 2008). References to institutionally embedded racisms are discredited, as are notions of structure as a determinant of life chance. Yes, race and racism may be out there, yet represent neither a meaningful restriction nor a threat to anyone's well-being or chances of success (but see hooks, 2013, and Hughey, 2012). Redirecting blame to individuals for success or failure under neo-liberal racism tends to privatize any racist exclusion. Racism is subsequently defined as little more than an attitude born of personal prejudice and ignorance. But the potential for substantial reform is compromised when off-loading responsibility to individual levels for resolution through private negotiations. The neo-liberal state not only removes itself from any role or responsibility in curbing racism or racial discrimination. It also eschews any commitment to playing the role of the guardian of public interest in constructing a multiracial democracy. Small wonder, then, that the racisms of today often revolve around white resentment toward racialized minorities, including anger over minority demands, dismay over a perceived lack of gratitude for changes and initiatives, criticism of their work ethics, and hostility toward those who insist on playing the race card (Sears, 2011). The end result is nothing less than a covert racism in which the ideology of neo-liberalism bolsters a racialized and colour-coded society.

Note

1 Chapter 12, on multicultural racisms, will address a variation of cultural (or normative racism).

CHAPTER 8

INFRASTRUCTURAL RACISMS

Introduction: The Evidence of Things Not Seen

Racisms are never just about individuals, even if people are the perpetrators and carriers as well as beneficiaries or victims. In addition, racisms are foundationally embedded within the structure, functions, and processes of society (Lentin, 2004). The origins and evolution of complex societies embodied a distinction between groups, while the creation of the modern nation-state depended on securing patterns of inclusion and exclusion between the West and the rest. Racisms both in the past and the present were also inextricably linked with state policy and the political climate engendered by state and government actors. This link made it difficult to disentangle the societal racisms from the role of the state in preserving the prevailing distribution of power, privilege, and wealth. The drawing of connections between racisms and the state also reinforces the importance of framing racism as political rather than pathological, a process facilitated by pulling back the covers of racialized beliefs and practices that are sewn into the fabric of society and strewn about in its day-to-day operations (Lehrman, 2003; Cassin et al., 2007; Lenin & Lentin, 2006). Until people realize the need to analyze racisms within the racialized context of a society's constitutional order—or to uncover "the evidence of things not seen," to borrow a phrase from James Baldwin[1]—the likelihood of addressing social injustices is diminished.

There is yet another expression of racism that is deeply entrenched within the foundations of society. An infrastructural racism is predicated on a singularly important premise: The social and cultural contours of a society's constitutional framework are neither neutral nor value-free. More accurately, the socially constructed and ideological loaded set of constitutional principles and practices are infused with a tacitly assumed set of values and beliefs that advantage some and disadvantage others (see also Scheurich & Young, 1997). Inasmuch as the foundational principles and founding assumptions of a society's constitutional order continue to racialize in ways that quietly advance Eurocentric interests, an infrastructural racism is real and powerful, yet difficult to detect, let alone eradicate. This chapter explores the concept of infrastructural racism on the grounds that its distinctiveness as a societal-based bias makes it worthy of a separate category of analysis.[2] The chapter begins by defining and describing the characteristics of infrastructural racism (Mills, 1997; Goldberg, 2002; Bonilla-Silva, 2003). It then demonstrates how an infrastructural racism is anchored in the foundational principles and founding assumptions of a Eurocentric and racialized constitutional order. To illustrate the dynamics of infrastructural racism, the chapter concludes by problematizing the debate over Canada as a racist society.

Infrastructural Racism in Racialized Societies

Racisms in the form of institutional exclusion and interpersonal slurs remain a substantial barrier to exercising citizenship rights and social justice. Their persistence has prompted descriptions of societies as racialized social systems in which social institutions and status hierarchies are profoundly informed, influenced by, and supported by socially defined race categories, racial ideologies, and racist language (Doane, 2006). Such tenacity cannot be simply attributed to personality disorders or to the consequences of a misguided multiculturalism or excessive immigration. Rather, reference to the appearance and persistence of race and racisms in the design, organization, and operations of modern society (or the state) provides a powerful explanatory framework (Bonilla-Silva, 1997; Vickers, 2002; Goldberg, 2002; Feagin, 2006).

Both race and racisms are undeniably linked to the origins, design, and functioning of the modern society. All complex societies are raced (or racialized) inasmuch as they make a distinction between superior and inferior groups (either racially or culturally defined); assign a corresponding division of power, labour, and resources; and embed these distinctions of inequality and inferiority within the founding assumptions and foundational structures of society. The end result? Just as societies are gendered by virtue of androcentric mindsets and partriarchal structures, so, too, are they racialized insofar as society is infrastructured *by*, *for*, and *about* pale-male interests, experiences, and priorities at the expense of racialized others.

A ideal-typical distinction between racial(ized) state and racist states is advised. The modern state is tantamount to a racial(ized) state because it conceives of itself as racially configured in terms of emergence, formation, and development. The racial state is implicated in the reproduction of local conditions of racist exclusion through their manifestations in justice and law enforcement and politics, legislation, and bureaucracy. A range of strategies is employed to construct uniformity, including tactics involving laws, technologies, or census, whose combined purpose is to assert white paramountcy and control, to categorize hierarchically, or to exclude those outside the state (Goldberg, 2002). In contrast to a racial(ized) state whereby race and nation are mutually constitutive of each other, a racist society explicitly endorses a state ideology to establish a set of laws or initiatives for formalizing separate classes of citizenship and compromising civil rights based on racial criteria. Patterns of government actions (or inactions) are critical in reflecting, reinforcing, and advancing the notion and construction of racist society (Lentin, 2004). Consider the institutionalized racism of South Africa's apartheid regime, which officially came into its own with the 1959 Population Registration Act that classified all South Africans by race, while the 1958 Black Self Government Act established homelands as a patchwork of mini-states in the least viable regions of the country. The Black Homeland Citizenship in 1971 stripped the homeland inhabitants of South African citizenship and corresponding rights (National Planning Commission, 2013).

Historically this racialization of society was upfront, open, and unquestioned. The apartheid regime in South Africa and the colour bar in the United States are the most egregious examples of racialized regimes that institutionalized racial discrimination in both law and practice on behalf of white interests. Arguably, the creation of the state of Israel focused on the goal of establishing "a state of the Jewish people" (a 1985 Constitutional Law passed by Knesset), including patterns of segregation and discrimination pertaining to employment, residency, and law. The end result? The privileging of Jewish citizens over non-Jews, while politically and geographically separating Palestinians from Israel, except economically as a source of accessible labour and captive markets (Ahmed, 2009). The settler societies of Australia and New Zealand were no less racialized in proclaiming themselves as "white men" countries through the establishment of constitutional orders that reflected, reinforced, and advanced Eurocentric interests at others' expense (Fleras & Spoonley, 1999).

Canada, too, originated in an era of colonialism (with its corresponding notions of race, racism, xenophobia, Eurocentrism, best captured by the slogan "White is right, might is right; white might is right; might is a white right." Until the 1950s, racism prevailed as a widely accepted package of ideas and ideals that dismissed the value and legitimacy of diversity, while discrimination based on gender or sexuality (as well as race) was routinely practised into the 1960s. A white Canada advocated Eurocentric practices and whitestream conventions that openly and defiantly permeated all dimensions of society, from individual prejudices to institutional biases (Wallis & Fleras, 2008). Racisms in Canada also originated within the context of capitalism.

The depressing of wages and the splintering of working-class solidarity along racialized lines proved integral in consolidating a capitalist mode of production. Paradoxically, while the open racism of the past may be dead, the principles of a white superiority complex continue to justify the racialized distribution of power and wealth (Jensen, 2009). Constance Backhouse (1999, p. 274) criticizes those commentators who insisted on eliminating race from consideration in the mistaken hope of fostering a more egalitarian Canada:

> But proponents of "race-neutrality" neglect to recognize that our society is not a race-neutral one. It is built upon centuries of racial division and discrimination. The legacy of such bigotry infects all of our institutions, relationships, and legal frameworks. To advocate "colour-blindness" as an ideal for the modern world is to adopt the false mythology of "racelessness" that has plagued the Canadian legal system ... and serve[s] to condone the continuation of white supremacy across Canadian society.

Put bluntly, race and racism are not something incidental to the functioning of the state/society both then and now. They are fundamental in establishing and maintaining a system of domination that espouses the colour-blind principles of a post-racial society, yet tolerates colour-conscious discrimination and racism of a racialized system.

Deconstructing the Infrastructural Principles of Canada's Constitutional Order

According to dictionary sources, infrastructure (from the Latin *infra*, meaning below, beneath, underneath, invisible) can be loosely defined as those deeply embedded and tacitly assumed values, agendas, and priorities that underpin societal foundation and functioning. Just as the basic installations and facilities (from roads to power plants to sewers) contribute to the continuance, operation, and growth of communities, so too does the infrastructure of founding assumptions and foundational principles undergird a society's constitutional order. In the broadest sense of the term, a constitutional order can be defined as a combination of core principles, fundamental rules, and normative understandings that collectively establish a functioning social order for regulating relations among a country's governing institutions and their relationships to citizens (Christiansen & Reh, 2009). Or phrased alternatively, a constitutional order consists of a relatively stable set of first principles that foster decision making and political debate over a sustained period of time.

Admittedly, these first principles are neither fixed nor final; rather, they are fluid, evolving, open to dispute and debates, provide a framework for the expression of ordinary political debates, and are not necessarily predictive of behaviour (Tushnet, 2003). For example, the Canadian Constitution espouses a core commitment to colour-blind equality. Nevertheless, there is ample evidence that Canadians continue to uphold a hierarchy of difference that seemingly endorses the primacy of a white superiority complex—in the same way Canada no longer proclaims itself to be a Christian society, although the legacy of Christianity persists, such as prescribed holidays (Christmas) and days of rest. These foundational principles of a constitutional order may be either explicitly articulated or tacitly assumed. For example, Canada's foundational principles are partly expressed within the Constitution and the Charter of Rights, namely the protection and promotion of individual rights, fundamental freedoms, and guarantees of equality. What are not expressly articulated but inferred from reading between the constitutional lines are those hidden assumptions that embody the rules that give rise to conventions. Consider the principle of universal liberalism, including a commitment to our commonalities as individuals, an emphasis on doing rather than being, and a preference for reason rather than emotion as a way of getting things done. Similarly, notions of progress (movement upward and forward) at individual and societal lines qualify as a foundational, if unstated, principle of Canada's constitutional order.

Clearly, then, neither foundational principles nor the constitutional order are ideologically neutral, despite appearances to the contrary. Both are ideologically loaded with values and beliefs that racialize society and the state along Eurocentric lines of what is good, right, or normal, as well as desirable and acceptable. A mistaken belief in infrastructural neutrality is not inconsequential. Such a commitment not only bolsters the widely accepted claim that Canada is a colour-blind society; worse still, it also conceals how the foundational principles of Canada's constitutional order are racialized to protect and promote "white-o-centric" patterns of power and privilege. It is this deeply embedded notion of Eurocentric foundational principles and a racialized constitutional order that inform the concept of infrastructural racism and parlay it into a racist Canada. The following Debate Forum on infrastructural racism captures the complexity of such a concept.

Debate Forum: Is Canada a Racist Society?

Coming to grips with the nature and magnitude of racism in Canada requires both a deft touch and a tough skin (much of this debate is adapted from Fleras, 2012). Some idea of the complexities in conceptualizing Canadian racisms reflects a core question: Is Canada a racist society? The question itself is interesting in demonstrating how reference to racism has drifted from its original meaning (that of a racist act or prejudiced, ignorant individuals) to racism as a societal phenomena (see D'Souza, 1995). As well, responses to this question demonstrate how a simple yes or no answer cannot possibly capture the nuances plying the politics of racisms. If the response is no, how does one explain the continued prominence of a pale-male status quo in setting political and economic agendas, the prevalence of institutionalized racial discrimination, and the lived experiences of racisms at interpersonal levels? If the response is yes, what exactly constitutes a racist society? Are Canadians racist by default? Is a racist society the same as a society of racists? How many incidents of racism constitute a racist society? Is a non-racist Canada attainable? Answers to these questions are complex and contested, yet pivotal in problematizing (deconstructing) the concept of Canada as a racist society.

Reactions to these questions are conflicted. For some, Canada is an inherently racist society in design and outcomes, with a thin veneer of politically correct tolerance that camouflages a pervasive white superiority complex (Lian & Matthews, 1998). To reinforce this point, a highly respected academic from Queen's University has claimed that "we live in a racist society" (cited in the *Kingston Whig-Standard*, June 13, 2003). The Curling-McMurtry Report (2008) did not mince words in castigating what they saw as escalating levels of racism (at least in Ontario). For others, however, Canada is a fundamentally sound society—the least racist society in the world, according to Raymond Chan, the former minister of state for multiculturalism (Chan, 2004). Notwithstanding a few bad apples to spoil an otherwise unblemished barrel, Canada is perceived as a largely colour-blind society because racism is legally banned and socially unacceptable. Those who disagree with the concept of racelessness in Canada are accused of race baiting by playing the racism card. For still others, perceptions of racism in Canada depend on where one stands in the wider scheme of things. Whites may be inclined to understate racism as a random, personal, and irrational aberration from the normal functioning of society. By contrast, racialized minorities tend to see racism as integral and institutionalized within Canada's structural framework (see Tator & Henry, 2006). Yet others argue that debates over the magnitude of racisms depend on deconstructing the politics of context, criterion, and consequence.

Which interpretation is more correct? Is racism in Canada under control or out of control? Responses are trickier than might appear because of difficulties in operationalizing the concept "racist society." First, what is meant by the word "racist" when applied to Canadian society? Is racism about race, biology, culture, ideology, structure, or power? Is racism about treating people differently because of their differences, or treating everyone the same regardless of their differences? Is a racist someone who openly inflicts harm on minorities, or a person whose apathy and indifference reinforce the marginality of racialized women and men? Is a racist someone who vilifies the other as inferior or irrelevant, or a person who claims to be colour-blind yet uncritically embraces a white normativity as necessary and normal? Are mainstream Canadians racist by definition owing to their exalted status in a racialized society, with a corresponding set of benefits that flow from largely unearned privileges that systemically exclude some, but benefit others (Thobani, 2007)?

Second, how do we measure the concept of "a racist society" (Fleras & Spoonley, 1999)? Racism is not only difficult to define; it is also proving tricky to measure (Satzewich, 2011, Ch. 1; also Samuel & Verma, 2010; Galabuzi, 2010).[3] Is a racist society based on a minimum number of racial incidents per year, or should more attention be directed toward those institutionalized biases that inadvertently perpetuate a racialized social order? For example, critics argue that West Virginia is the most racist state in the United States because 17 percent of its voters in primaries pointed to race as a factor in rejecting Obama. Arkansas was second at 13.7 percent (Wilson, 2008). More recently, both Arizona and Alabama have passed laws that make it a state crime for a foreign-born alien (undocumented migrant) to live or work without registration documents required by federal law. As well, the most racist city in the United States is thought to be Hazleton, Pennsylvania, which passed the Illegal Immigration Relief Act in July 2006. The banning of housing and employment opportunities to undocumented immigrants made it one of the strictest anti-immigration laws in the country (Munoz, 2006). Finally, how about the United Kingdom as a racist society because of its 37,000 racially or religiously aggravated crimes recorded in 2011/2012 (one hundred per day) by the police in England and Wales (Burnett, 2013a, p. 6)?

However valid or debatable, such assessments, too much of what constitutes a so-called racist society, is based on surveys that measure racially related incidents. But surveys and statistical measures have inherent drawbacks; after all, what is concealed may prove more informative than what is revealed (Blank et al., 2004; Fisher, 2013b). Surveys cannot reveal the ratio of reported to unreported acts. Increases in the number of reported acts may not reflect more incidents, but rather a greater public awareness of racism, along with an increased willingness to do something about it by pressing charges or utilizing a hate-crime hotline with a 1-800 number. Statistical measures have additional weaknesses. Pollsters are cautious about drawing sweeping conclusions from a few survey questions on racism. According to Donald Taylor of McGill University, polls are a crude measure of public attitudes because of their tendency to simplify complex problems or conceal actual behaviour patterns. Respondents, in turn, appear reluctant to answer truthfully for fear of blowing their cover.

Third, what constitutes a racist society? Logic suggests that a racist society is one in which the national society-building project is explicitly organized around the deliberate exclusion of "others" from entitlements or citizenship. Under such a racist regime, racism is institutionalized when (1) supported by cultural values; (2) expressed through widely accepted norms; (3) tacitly approved by the state or government; (4) codified into laws that openly discriminate against minorities; and (5) explicitly excludes minorities from equal participation as part of the normal functioning of society (Aguirre & Turner, 1995). Prejudice and discrimination toward others is institutionally entrenched in a racist society, while formal boundaries are drawn to separate the racialized haves from the have-nots. In addition, central authorities do little to avert the outbreak of racist incidents at individual or institutional levels; even less is done to deal with these violations when they occur. According to these criteria, apartheid South Africa would have qualified as a racist society. Under an official apartheid, blacks were exploited as miners or domestics in advancing the economic interests of the white ruling class, while a system of race-based segregation separated whites from blacks through an archipelago of black homelands (National Planning Commission, 2013). It would be easy to lump the United States into the same racist category prior to the mid-1950s, given the pervasiveness of the colour bar that segregated blacks as second-class citizens.

Canada, too, could historically be described as a racist society (Walker, 1998). Racism in a white Canada was openly, proudly, and deeply entrenched at individual, institutional, ideological, and infrastructural levels. Minorities were barred from almost every sector of Canadian life as might be expected of a closed and xenophobic society, while immigration policies were exclusionary and racist (Abella, 2013). The present situation would appear significantly different. Canada possesses a panoply of multicultural and anti-racist initiatives incorporating human rights legislation, criminal codes against racial hatred, and sentencing procedures that more severely punish hate crimes. To put these principles into practice, a $56 million anti-racism action plan was instituted in 2005 in conjunction with the departments of labour, immigration, justice, and multiculturalism (Department of Canadian Heritage, 2005). In other words, the sign of an anti-racist society is one that establishes protocols to deter racial discrimination while dealing with racism when it happens. Of course racism exists in Canada, both at the individual level and institutionally, as well as openly and covertly. But saying that there is racism in Canada and that there are racists is not the same as saying that Canada is a racist society. On these grounds, Canada can no longer be regarded as an explicitly racist society, as was once the case in our not-too-distant past.

Yet it may be a bit premature to canonize Canada as a paragon of saintliness. Canadians may not be racists in the flagrant sense of unfurling swastikas or assaulting racialized minorities. Instead, racism in Canadian society is increasingly covert, embedded in normal institutional operations, and beyond the direct discourse of racial terminology (Li, 2007). The language, values, and institutions that predominate in Canada embody a distinctly racial connotation that makes them exclusionary, synonymous with whiteness, and racist in consequence rather than intent (see also Gilroy, 2004). The society that Canadians inhabit is constructed (both deliberately and inadvertently) to reflect, reinforce, and advance the normalcy and desirability of white experiences, Eurocentric values, and mainstream interests. In doing so, racialized differences are transformed into minority disadvantage (Feagin, 2006). Or to rephrase Sandra Lipsitz Bem (1994), just as female differences are transformed into female disadvantages in a male-centred world, so, too, are minority differences synonymous with disadvantages in a "white-o-centric" world.

Put sharply, Canada may be defined as a racist society because it is designed, organized, and prioritized along racialized lines. That is, racism is infrastructurally embedded in Canada's colonial history; embodied in those institutional rules and practices that normalize "pale-male" privilege; and expressed in the language, laws, and rules of Canadian society. Each of these alone or in combination may have the unwitting effect rather than deliberate intent of perpetuating a racially based (racialized) status quo. Racisms in Canada are informed by the Eurocentricity of founding assumptions and foundational principles that continue to govern Canada's racialized constitutional order (Maaka & Fleras, 2005). For instance, Canada's espousal of liberal universalism (a belief that our commonalities as freewheeling individuals is more important for purposes of recognition or redistribution than what divides us as members of racial groups) constitutes a foundational principle that privileges Eurocentric values and institutions as natural and superior rather than seeing them for what they really are: white standards and mainstream norms that masquerade as universal principles.

To sum up, references to Canada as a racialized and racist society must be taken seriously. For in the final analysis, racism is hegemonic (controlling) not because it is embodied in the attitudes of individuals, but because it is institutionalized in the structures of society. Mainstream values and institutions may inadvertently advantage some because of accidents of birth, while racialized minorities (their identities, experiences, and opportunities/outcomes) are disadvantaged for reasons beyond their control. True, all Canadians, even in a racialized society, possess formal equality rights and constitutional protections to that effect. But racialized Canadians must exercise these rights and strive for success without access to institutional power or the benefit of a head start in contexts neither designed to reflect their realities nor constructed to advance their interests. An infrastructural racism could not be more forcefully exposed.

Notes

1 Title borrowed from Jame Baldwin's book (1985).
2 Infrastructural racism, or societal racism in the language of Scheurich and Young (1997), is similar to institutional racism, but exists on a broader societal scale.
3 A study by World Values Survey and reported in the *Washington Post* (Fisher, 2013a) asked people if they would refuse to live next door to someone of a different race—on the assumption that the less racially tolerant would dislike such neighbours. The study concluded (notwithstanding some problems of measurement and interpretation [Fisher, 2013b]) that 51.4 percent of Jordan's population would refuse such an arrangement, followed by India at 43.5 percent. Britain and English-speaking countries once part of the British Empire (including Canada at 2.9 percent) and the United States (3.8 percent) shared low levels of intolerance, as did Sweden (1.4 percent). European countries were divided: Those in the eastern half were less tolerant than the west of the continent, with France an exception at 22.7 percent.

CHAPTER 9

IVORY TOWER RACISMS
AN INTERSECTORAL ANALYSIS

Introduction: "Above the Fray"?

Many take it as axiomatic that racism and racial discrimination contaminate the domain and dynamics of Canadian institutions (Tator & Henry, 2006; Das Gupta, 2009; Hier, 2007; Fleras, 2009). Social institutions have been criticized for failing to remove structural barriers that preclude full and equal participation, thereby reinforcing a racialized status quo around a prevailing distribution of power and privilege. From media and policing to education and health care, institutions are under pressure to accommodate by creating workplaces that are reflective, respectful, and responsive to racialized minorities, while offering services that are available and accessible as well as appropriate to communities of colour (Fleras, 2012). Much energy and expense have gone into the design and implementation of multicultural initiatives and anti-racist programs, although results have proven uneven as might be expected in contexts largely impervious to change, oblivious to alternatives, or resentful of criticism. As well, institutions are often contested terrains involving the interplay of competing interests, power dynamics, hidden agendas, shifting priorities, calculated trade-offs, and competition for scarce resources (Chesler et al., 2005). To be sure, specific issues have changed as have terms of the debate; nevertheless, the politics of racism remains a volatile and divisive issue at institutional levels (Smith, 2010).

Of those institutions expected to be inclusive, few have experienced as much pressure as primary and secondary education (Lund, 2008). Critics have pounced on educational institutions as sites of racism and discrimination for failing to discard a deeply entrenched monoculturalism, in effect sullying Canada's much ballyhooed reputation as a progressive pacesetter for multicultural coexistence (Dei & Calliste, 2000). For Aboriginal peoples, the legacy of residential schooling and the Eurocentricity of provincial schools both on and off reserve reflected and reinforced patterns of cultural extinguishment that bordered on the genocidal. For immigrant Canadians, all aspects of schooling—from teachers and textbooks to policy and curriculum, from daily routines to decision making at the top—were aligned to facilitate cultural indoctrination and societal assimilation of minority students. Admittedly, the explicit assimilationist model that once informed educational circles is rarely articulated. But the logic of assimilation remains an unspoken if powerful ethos at all schooling levels, not in the openly racist sense of deliberate indoctrination of Anglo-conformity principles, but through the hidden agendas and the systemically biasing consequences of a racialized and monocultural schooling system (Fleras, 2012).

Not all educational sectors are similarly targeted for critiques. The sustained scrutiny experienced by primary and secondary educational institutions is not necessarily duplicated at the post-secondary (tertiary) level. The ivory-white towers rarely receive the same level of criticism as racialized sites of inequality and monoculturalism despite mounting concern that not all is institutionally well because of internal and external pressures (Guo & Jamal, 2007; Henry & Tator, 2009). Many may be puzzled by any interpretation of the ivory towers as racist by default or denial. No less puzzling are the scholarly reactions to these charges, with responses ranging from disavowal to agreement to skepticism:

- For some, the very idea of ivory tower racisms constitutes an oxymoron. Who would expect racism in an institutional system designed around and committed to the principles of reason, progressive change, tolerance and openmindedness, and the pursuit of truth and justice (see Maranto, Redding, & Hess, 2009)? The presence of racism and hateful bigots within the academy would appear inconsistent with popular images of an institution that many believe to be "above the fray" and beyond reproach. To the extent that universities claim to be colour-blind institutions, how could it be otherwise, especially if personnel do not actively engage in open acts of racism, sincerely believe that they as individuals are not racist or supportive of racism, or if they do not see race as a reality for defining or excluding others (powell, 2009; Henry, 2004; Chesler et al., 2005). If racism prevails within the ivory-white towers, optimists argue, a sense of perspective is critical. Pockets of racism reflect the workings of a "few bad apples" rather than logical consequences of a "rotten institutional barrel." To imply otherwise is tantamount to impugning the academy's moral integrity while smearing the character of faculty and administration.
- For others, racism and the academy are inextricably linked (Henry & Tator, 2009; Canadian Federation of Students, 2011; Stockdill & Danico, 2012; Law, Phillips, & Turney, 2004; Blaut, 1992). Historically,

universities routinely discriminated against racialized minorities, such as Jews or African Canadians, through entry restrictions and numerical quotas. And they continue to be racist in consequence, if not necessarily in intent, largely because the universities' operational logic (from ideologies and culture to structures, expectations, and rewards) is raceless, colour-blind, or objective despite claims to the contrary (James, 2009). Racisms in the ivory-white towers reflect and reinforce the normalization of a Eurocentric whiteness that privileges the monoculture of white privilege as the referential norm in defining what is acceptable and desirable (Henry, 2004; Samuel, 2006; Agnew, 2007; Enakshu Dua in MacDonald & Woods, 2008). The weight of whiteness that bears down on a Eurocentric academy reinforces the tendency for outcomes and rewards (from publications to tenure) to be allocated along racial lines (Dei & Calliste, 2000; C. Tator in Drolet, 2009). In other words, ideals are one thing and reality quite another. Just because academics espouse liberal and enlightenment ideals, this ideology will not automatically exist for university personnel of colour.

- For still others, the situation is neither as bleak as critics bemoan nor as benign as supporters boast, neither the pandemic critics imply nor the inconsequential blip dismissed as political correctness gone wild. On the contrary, the ivory-white towers embody a confusing mixture and contradictory interplay of progress and regress, inclusion and exclusion, racism and anti-racism. On one side are inclusiveness measures from multi-racial promotional brochures and multicultural festivals to equity offices and international student associations. On the other side, issues of racism and racial discrimination are *not* always taken seriously by the administration, who appear to more interested in public relations than in social justice. Much also depends on how racism is defined in framing the parameters of how much and what kind. That alone makes it doubly important to conceptualize ivory tower racisms in terms of criteria, context, and consequences.
- For still others, universities are not racist per se. More accurately, they are racialized because of how they are organized and designed in terms of what they do, who they serve, who gets what and why, and what they hope to accomplish. The racialization of universities along systemic lines has proven critical in naturalizing and normalizing a Euro-Canadian normativity as the "way we do things around here." Alternative forms of knowledge and ways of knowing tend to be dismissed as inferior or irrelevant (i.e., lacking scholarly integrity and rigour). This racialized business-as-usual motif may not be racist in intent or awareness; rather, it constitutes racism by consequences (systemic racism) (see also Henry & Tator, 2009).

Who is right? Does the *uni-* in university continue to inform, define, and predominate? Or should the prefix *multi-* replace the *uni-* as a more accurate descriptor? To date, data in support of these assertions and positions remain largely impressionistic or media-hyped, often reflecting an uncritical melange of innuendo, common sense, or political correctness. Allegations of academic racism are often ignored because of indifference or are under-researched because of a reluctance to substantiate charges (Stewart, 2009). Evaluations and proposals appear to be derived from anecdotal evidence, often subject to second-guessing and varying interpretations, in the process making it difficult to apply solutions consistent with the problem definition. The few empirically valid studies to address campus racism are thought to be methodologically flawed or ideologically slanted (Henry, 2004; Henry & Tator, 2009). Reflect for a moment on the ideologies at play when accounting for the university-wide under-representation of racialized and Aboriginal faculty. In one Canadian university, for example, those with ethnoculturally diverse backgrounds constitute nearly half the enrolment but only 11 percent of the faculty, with most employed in engineering and the hard sciences (Henry & Tator, 2007). Are these employment disparities the result of systemic racism and institutionalized racial discrimination (blame the system)? Or should a more comprehensive explanation focus on other factors, ranging from cultural differences to notions of personal agency (blame the victim)?

The politics of ivory tower racisms also complicate any move toward inclusiveness. In coping with a growing identity crisis of confidence ("Who are we and what should we be doing?"), twenty-first-century universities must grapple with competing forces. On one side, student bodies are becoming increasingly diverse and cosmopolitan because of immigrant-fuelled growth and expansion of foreign student enrolment. On the other side, a continuing wall of white arrogance or indifference precludes inclusionary moves, while pre-empting tendencies toward critical self-reflection (Audrey Kobayashi in MacDonald & Woods, 2008). In acknowledging that there is much to do because so little has been done, this chapter explores the *politics of racisms within Canada's ivory-white towers*. The chapter provides an example of how multi-sectoral racisms work in contemporary Canada, why references to racisms continue to proliferate despite Canada's bona fides as being post-racial, and the relevance of changing discourses in talking about racism at an institutional level. The chapter is predicated on the premise that institutions in general, and the academy in particular, are neither neutral nor value-free. Rather, they are socially constructed and ideological loaded with beliefs and values that reflect, reinforce, and advance the realities, experiences, and interests of creators, owners, and controllers. Post-secondary institutions are racialized along monocultural lines, including design, values, and practices that normalize and naturalize a Eurocentric way of seeing and doing. The chapter also contends that racisms in the ivory-white towers are (1) real, multiple, and mutating; (2) pervasive, persistent, and patterned; (3) expressed at interpersonal, institutional, ideological, and infrastructural levels; (4) both overt and covert, systematic and systemic; and (5) inextricably linked with broader political, economic, and social trends. The conclusion makes it abundantly clear: Overt discrimination is not the problem with ivory tower racism; more accurately, it is the widespread denial of the academy as predominantly white work spaces that privilege some while disprivileging others (Henry, 2004; Henry & Tator, 2009; Evans & Feagin, 2012).

A central theme of this chapter focuses on debunking misconceptions about ivory tower racisms, while proposing alternative explanations to account for the proliferation of multi-racisms. Put bluntly, the problem of ivory tower racisms is not what many think it is or how it is manifested. First, ivory tower racisms tend to be institutional rather than personal. A racialized bias prevails that is systemically embedded within the founding assumptions and in the foundational principles of a university's constitutional order, including the racialization of the academy along the monocultural lines of a Eurocentric whiteness as the norm. Second, ivory tower racisms often reflect patterns of omission rather than acts of commission. What is not done in ushering about transformative change may prove just as racist as actively working to reinforce a Eurocentric culture of whiteness (see Henry & Tator, 2007). Finally, how does one account for the culture of whiteness and white privilege against the backdrop of mutating forms of racism within the academy (Smith, 2010; Henry & Tator, 2009; Priya, 2007)? Putting these assertions and assessments to the test involves the following questions that secure the topics and themes for debate:

- Is there a problem with racism on Canadian campuses?
- How does racism work in a post-secondary system designed by, for, and about whites?
- Why do ivory-white racisms persist?
- What has been—or can be—done to address the problem?
- What university-based barriers are likely to hinder solutions?

Here is an important caveat at the outset: Racisms may be a constant across the post-secondary domain; nonetheless, a progressive dimension can be discerned. Yes, an indictment of ivory tower racisms is deserved because of past indiscretions and current omissions. Yet any criticism and assessment should be tempered by a sense of balance, proportion, and optimism. A growing number of students, faculty, and administration are actively engaged in the struggle—from consciousness raising to protests and boycotts—to establish an inclusive academy with which to share space, build meaningful communities, affirm the worthiness of all, reward everybody's contribution, support diverse world views, and encourage full and equal participation. Both students and faculty of colour report having positive experiences (ranging from intellectual stimulation to satisfying interpersonal relations) and rewarding outcomes (see also Spafford et al., 2006; Henry, 2004; Chesler et al., 2005). Still, it is worth mentioning a significant disparity. American universities may have been convulsed by culture wars of the late twentieth century that rattled the Eurocentric canons of the "dead white male" academy. By contrast, no comparable movement emerged in Canada to politicize the curricula or the pedagogy, despite Canada's multicultural bona fides. That observation alone should open the floodgates to a range of doubts, dissensus, and debate.

The Ivory-White Towers: Zones of Eurocentrism, Nodes of Whiteness, Sites of Racism

Not long ago, the ivory-white towers were precisely that: sites of progress, refinement, and purity. But now these very same hallowed halls are enduring criticism as bastions of racism and racial discrimination (Chesler et al., 2005; Henry & Tator, 2009; Stewart, 2009). Charges extend to a wide spectrum of culprits, including: under-representation of racialized faculty; excessive demands on faculty of colour as mentors and (token) representation on university committees; the racialization of faculty in classrooms by white students; the dominance of Eurocentric curricula and pedagogy; the delegitimization of alternative knowledge and ways of knowing as too subjective or too political (or ideological) (Brown & Stega, 2005); undervaluation of topics and research utilized by minority faculty; patterned avoidance by white faculty; a culture of whiteness in fostering a chilly climate that excludes or denies; concerns over equitable hiring, promotion, and tenure; and seemingly progressive administrators who appear more adept at "talking the walk" instead of the reverse.

That racisms are thought to flourish in the ivory-white towers is not necessarily the issue. More to the point, the structure, function, and processes that inform the academy continue to be racialized in ways that invariably produce and reproduce patterns of discriminatory bias, not always as something out of the ordinary, but as integral to the foundational principles and everyday practices of a predominantly Eurocentric academic enterprise. The following points provide a snapshot of those racist hotspots under scrutiny and criticism (Chesler et al., 2005):

- *Curriculum and pedagogy:* In terms of curriculum, content remains overwhelmingly biased toward a Eurocentric whiteness (Henry & Tator, 2009). Modest improvements and some notable exceptions have not appreciably dislodged humanities and social science courses from focusing on developments in the global North while neglecting advances in the so-called developing countries, thus reinforcing a perceived superiority of Western culture as the exclusive preserve of intellectual wisdom and activity (Engler, 2004). The Eurocentric domination of the ivory-white towers not only assumes that Western ways of knowing and knowledge are universal rather than a domain specific to a particular cultural framework. The premises, categories, and terms for intellectual debates and academic research are defined accordingly (Multiversity, 2009). For example, textbooks in Canada (as well as Australia and New Zealand) reposition history from a white perspective, while disregarding the viewpoint of indigenous peoples and racialized minorities (Guo & Jamal, 2007). Textbooks are also accused of stereotyping racialized minorities yet privileging Eurocentricity by prioritizing whites as the reference point, with others as departures from this norm (Canadian Press, 2009). Or consider the problem of pedagogy. As Guo and Jamal observe, a deposit model of pedagogy (in which knowledge selected by the instructor is uncritically deposited into the learner) may perpetuate and legitimize racism through the unintended outcomes of the "hidden curriculum."

- *Student body:* Students of colour indicate they are victims of racism because of discriminatory interaction with other students, faculty members, and administration (Samuel & Burney, 2003; Canadian Federation of Students, 2011). For example, on March 21, 2008, the Canadian Federation of Students (2008) released the final report on the needs of Muslim students, highlighting eleven major concerns, ranging from food facilities and availability of prayer space to Islamophobia and Muslim bashing. For racialized minority students, the learning process can be undermined by faculty member bias, doctrinaire ideologies, and lack of knowledge of the cultural others. They report being stereotyped and stigmatized, resulting in what Claude Steele of Stanford University calls "stereotype threat"—that is, the probability that some racialized students will do poorly academically because of society's lower expectations of their intellectual abilities (in McCarthy, 2009). They are either overlooked for their contributions to the academy or are singled out as spokespeople on behalf of their race and ethnicity, even as their heritage and concerns are Disneyfied or demonized. Patterns of marginalization are further complicated and intensified by the intersection of difference and multiple identities (including race, gender, ethnicity, class, age, sexuality) in contexts that are predominantly white, male, and Eurocentric (Spafford et al., 2006). Such a paradox yields the self-incriminating question of what does it mean to be "visibilized" (to imagine oneself as a problem) in an institutional context where whiteness is the normative and normalizing agenda (Kelly, 1998; Hernandez-Ramdwar, 2009).
- *International students:* Racialized international students encounter additional problems related to their "foreignness." Nearly 10 percent of Canada's university enrolment consists of fee-paying foreign students (many from Asian countries), a pattern that reflects the commodification and commercialization of tertiary education because of increased reliance on private funding (Saltmarsh, 2005; Rhoads & Torres, 2006). But this reliance on international students for coping

with a neo-liberal agenda has done little to accommodate their distinct needs and untapped talents, much less to bring about changes in the curriculum, evaluation procedures, and pedagogical techniques (Fleras, 1996). Instructional strategies and classroom environments that condone competitiveness and individual achievement may prove awkward for those foreign students more familiar with collaborative group work (Guo & Jamal, 2007). As well, often foreign students must bear the brunt of suspicion as conniving opportunists who routinely rely on plagiarism and other forms of academic cheating to get around shortcomings, in effect reflecting and reinforcing racialized notions of ability, deviance, and moral deficit (Saltmarsh, 2005).

- *Faculty:* Faculty of colour confront a melange of racisms-related challenges as they negotiate and navigate their way through those racialized spaces within the academy (Spafford et al., 2006; James, 2009; Gibney, 2013). Racialized and gendered minority faculty are generally under-represented outside the hard sciences, routinely overworked because of additional responsibilities from mentoring students to sitting on endless committees, undermined by being excluded from communication loops, and subject to racist slurs or taunts both inside and outside the classroom. They may see their concerns dismissed or trivialized by white colleagues who define themselves as beyond reproach in racial matters to deserve any criticism (Back, 2004). Their scholarly credentials, status, and authority may be questioned (i.e., not taken seriously) or challenged by students, colleagues, or administrators, especially if they teach or do research in domains that are unconventional, that contest notions of white privilege, or that advance the principle of social justice (West-Olatunji, 2007; Monture, 2009). They may be labelled as biased when teaching courses on the politics of differences, yet criticized as dilettantes when teaching courses outside their field—what James and Shadd (2001) refer to as intellectual racism (Spafford et al., 2006). Publishing careers may be compromised because many are swamped with requests to mentor students of colour as well as to sit on countless committees as the (token) minority voice (Canadian Federation of Students, 2011). In short, the multitude of experiences and barriers that reinforce a sense of otherness, including humiliation, marginality, and exclusion, may expose minority faculty to mental anguish and physical stress, thus negating their full capacity to teach, publish, research, and excel (Chesler et al., 2005).
- *Administration:* The few racialized administrators that make it to the top may confront the same challenges as minority faculty. Being cast as different and treated differently may prove career-inhibiting. Yet a commitment to treating everyone exactly the same way may inadvertently reinforce institutional barriers that deter racialized minorities from the upper echelons of success. In either case, the absence of differences at senior levels is counterproductive. Without the input of minority decision makers whose racialized experiences create a potential for thinking outside the box, a business-as-usual mentality

prevails. Such a narrow mindset not only restricts the circle of creativity, but also reflects the monoculturality of an era when universities were literally finishing schools (or playing grounds) for affluent white males pursuing careers as diplomats or clergy in defence of God, Empire, and the King (or Queen).
- *Board of governors:* These highly influential monitoring/guiding bodies continue to be overwhelmingly white and male, not because this demographic is brighter or more skilled, but because they are better connected as corporate wheeler-dealers, with a known capacity to generate revenue for the university (Engler, 2004). Paradoxically, those in positions of institutional authority are often oblivious to the privileges and powers associated with a normative whiteness as the preferred standard in defining what is necessary and normal, desirable and acceptable (McIntosh, 1988). Not surprisingly, they vary in their willingness and capacity to address inequities, bridge the many gulfs of misunderstanding, and respect the many experiences and realities in the ivory-white towers (Dua, 2009). To the extent that they exist, inclusionary initiatives tend to underestimate the gravity of the problem, especially when dealing with symptoms rather than causes (Dua, 2009). These interventions may also be motivated *not* by minority grievance resolution or a commitment to justice, but by a face-saving preference for damage control (to ensure continued alumni support), public relations (to avoid unflattering publicity), and impression management (running a smooth enterprise) (Chesler et al., 2005).

The conclusion appears inescapable if somewhat uncomfortable. The ivory towers are not "above the fray" as commonly assumed; on the contrary, they are no less susceptible than other institutions to charges of racism. To their (dis)credit, universities appear to have done a better job of denying the existence of racisms by cloaking their most egregious expressions behind the hallowed ivy-covered walls of the ivory-white towers. In reality, however, ivory tower racisms constitute a widespread if somewhat under-theorized aspect of university life, embedded in the culture of academia, reflected in curriculum and pedagogy, and reinforced by practices related to hiring, retention, and promotion (Fleras, 1995; Henry & Tator, 2009). Ivory tower racisms are also expressed in varying ways, from the personal and direct to the systemic (impersonal) and indirect (polite) with varying levels of intensity and intent in between. In light of such complexity and challenge, debates over intervention strategies have proven equally contentious. Proposals for reform range from accommodating diversities to promoting equity, from changing mindsets to revamping institutional structures, from incremental reform to transformation change, and from targeting individuals to zeroing in on structures. It is difficult to avoid the following conclusion: The politics of racisms in the ivory-white towers are unlikely to subside in the foreseeable future since there is virtually no agreement as to (1) whether a problem exists, (2) the nature and scope of the problem, (3) proposed solutions, and (4) anticipated outcomes.

Analyzing Ivory Tower Racisms: A Multi-sectoral Analysis

The ivory-white towers are not impervious to the dynamics of racisms in contemporary institutional contexts. In some case, these racisms are expressed in blunt and personal terms; in other cases, racist expressions tend toward the subtle and polite; in still other cases, they are institutionalized and structured through values and practices that deliberately deny or systemically exclude, and in yet other cases they are so deeply embedded within normal institutional functioning that few are aware of their presence, let alone cognizant of the consequences or prepared to do something about it. These varying manifestations of racisms can be organized along the sectoral lines of interpersonal, institutional, infrastructural, and ideological.

Interpersonal Racism

Studies suggest the presence of a relatively small number of *reported* racial incidents on campus (Fleras, 1996; Dua 2009; but see Samuel & Burney, 2003). Only a small percentage of students acknowledge victimization by racist jokes or discriminatory treatment that attracts police attention. Those incidents that come to official attention often involve students vis-à-vis other students in classrooms, residences, and campus bars (Fleras, 1996). Under-reporting to the campus police is likely, with the exception of hostilities such as those between Jews and Muslims, or racist graffiti or name-calling slurs. Even fewer self-identify as targets of violence. This understated pattern of interpersonal racism should come as no surprise. Neither police reports nor self-victimizations surveys are necessarily accurate because of problems ranging from difficulties in interpretation (incidents involving racially different protagonists are not always about race), to potentially over-reporting incidents because of greater ease for doing so or, alternatively, to under-reporting victimization because of embarrassment or fear of reprisals (Dua, 2009).

Furthermore, overt displays of racism are socially unacceptable and in violation of Canadian law and human rights legislation. Hate racisms with their message of racial superiority are rarely openly articulated. What transpires instead are more subtle put-downs and peccadilloes within private contexts that do not explicitly broadcast individual intentions, yet are justified through reasons that are acceptable within the discourses of the academy (Scheurich & Young, 2002). Expressions of polite or subliminal racism (from innuendo to avoidance to chilly climate) tend to prevail, in large part because most individuals at the academy acquire the social skills to compartmentalize and conceal those dislikes that if expressed may detonate careers.

Institutional Racism
Institutional racism entails those patterns of discrimination embedded within organizational rules, rewards, standard operating procedures, and values that have the intent or effect of denying or mistreating "others" (Scheurich & Young, 2002). The exclusion and/or maltreatment of racialized minorities because of institutionalized discrimination and privilege is sustained across the board (from students to administration and boards) and at all levels (culture, structure, and operation). To be sure, institutional rules and arrangements are not openly discriminatory. Nevertheless, the logical consequences of evenly and equally applying these rules and practices to everyone (one size fits all) may exert an exclusionary (discriminatory) impact on others through no fault of their own. Moreover, even those who benefit from racialized privilege are not acting intentionally to harm others while those penalized rarely merit such negative treatment (Chesler et al., 2005). But an unlevel playing field prevails since racialized minorities must excel in an institutional setting that was neither designed with their experiences and realities in mind nor constructed to advance their priorities or interests.

The prevalence of inclusive policies (including anti-racist and equity programs) within the ivory-white towers is a step forward. But Canadian universities continue to be institutionally (or structurally) racist, in part because of (1) a failure to act upon their promises of inclusiveness (anti-racisms initiatives have a lower priority than fundraising or sports programs); (2) a commitment to Eurocentric whiteness that is systemically biasing; and (3) a reluctance to acknowledge the presence of racism beyond an interpersonal level (Tator in Drolet, 2009; Smith in Drolet, 2009; also Chesler et al., 2005; Kuokkanen, 2009). Intent and awareness are relatively unimportant in analyzing systemic patterns of institutional racism. Significance instead is assigned to those institutionally taken-for-granted criteria for success—from publications and tenure to scaling the administrative ladder—that collectively yet inadvertently provide advantage for some, but not others. Racially minoritized faculty confront systemic barriers that diminish their visibility, voice, and access to power relations by virtue of being valued and evaluated through the normative lens of a Eurocentric whiteness (Spafford et al., 2006). In other words, institutional racism in higher education may operate on discriminatory grounds even if the offending individuals are relatively free of prejudice. Examples include an exclusive reliance on a Eurocentric curriculum as systemic bias by virtue of invalidating or excluding minority realities, experiences, and aspirations, regardless of instructor intent or rationale. Not surprisingly, the consequences of even mundane practices may be systemically racist, especially if difference-based needs are discounted when dispensing recognition and rewards.

Ideological Racism

An ideological racism embraces those ideas and ideals (including assumptions, values, beliefs, and norms) that privilege a monocultural way of thinking, saying, and doing as normalizing and normative. Alternative ways are dismissed as irrelevant, inferior, or a threat (difference as deficit). Ideological racisms within the academy reflect its history and status as a predominantly white project in defence of King, God, and Empire. George J. Sefa Dei and Agnes Calliste (2000, p. 11) hammer home the critical role of educational institutions in reproducing, critiquing, and transforming people's understanding of the world and their place in it:

> Our schools, colleges, and universities continue to be powerful discursive sites through which race knowledge is produced, organized, and regulated. Marginalized bodies are continually silenced and rendered invisible not simply through the failure to take issues of race and social oppressions seriously but through the constant negation of multiple lived experiences and alternative knowledges. Colonial and imperial discourses and practices heavily influence how learners come to know race today. Racialized tropes deployed in the social construction of racialized identities and the representation of marginalized bodies as racial "others" are heavily encoded in prevailing ideologies and maintain the validity of conventional academic knowledge. The academic ideologies have become powerful mechanisms of control as conventional ideas produce material consequences.

An institutional culture of Eurocentric whiteness pervades the entirety of the university enterprise. Components of this culture include the continued dominance of ideas and ideals for defining and achieving success, indifference toward alternative models, and belief in an incompatibility between diversity and excellence (Chesler & Crowfoot, 1997; Henry & Tator, 2009). A reliance on the values of liberal-universalism holds ideological sway when expressed in coded language such as colour-blindness, objectivity, academic freedom, equal opportunity, and merit. Each of these value systems possesses sufficient flexibility in meaning not only to reinforce racialized beliefs and practices, but also to mask the centrality of fundamental structures and cultural inequities behind seemingly liberal precepts (Henry & Tator, 2009). Gouws (2008) writes of the challenges in store, albeit in a different context:

> The even bigger challenge for transformation on these campuses is the institutional cultures that are steeped in an apartheid past, being white and male dominated with invisible rules that may alienate and marginalise groups from other cultures. While blatant racism is an indication of the attitudinal racism based on stereotyping and prejudice, structural racism embedded in institutional cultures is far more serious.

A reluctance to acknowledge these cultural blind spots is costly. It reinforces those patterns of entitlement that operate without much awareness or intent, but with unmistakable impact and import. Such denial also makes it difficult for the academy to explore different traditions of knowledge and knowledge-making (Samodien, 2009).

Infrastructural Racism
Reference to infrastructural racism denotes those racisms that govern the foundational principles of a body's constitutional order. Applied to universities, infrastructural racism embodies a pattern of racism that encompasses the deepest and most primary assumptions about the nature of reality (ontology), ways of knowing reality (epistemology), and disputes over right, wrong, and morality (axiology). Contrary to popular belief, universities are neither value-free nor neutral spaces for advancing the dispassionate production of knowledge and ways of knowing (see next section). More accurately, they are deeply interwoven with the social histories and ideological proclivities of particular groups (keeping in mind that universities once served as "finishing schools" for affluent white males). Universities are racialized in ways that bolster certain ideals and practices as worthy of recognition and reward, while articulating what is normal and necessary as well as acceptable and desirable. The founding assumptions and foundational principles of this Eurocentric constitutional order remain anchored in selective discourse and exclusionary practices, including a commitment to the principles of Enlightenment, colonialism, (post)modernity, and liberalism. Not unexpectedly, those who staunchly embrace Eurocentric traditions (including the epistemological, ontological, and axiological) may be so oblivious to other traditions of knowledge and knowing that they unthinkingly ignore or routinely reject the relevance of alternative epistemes (Smith, 1998; Fleras, 2003).

For example, consider the Eurocentricity that informs the ivory-white curricula. What experts call the canon emerges from particular bodies of knowledge and knowing that, in turn, reflect implicit assumptions about who is authorative, what phenomena are worthy of study, and which methodologies and methods should prevail in constructing knowledge (Green, 2004). But the production and evaluation of a racialized canon embraces the values and views of its producers, resulting in a Eurocentric curriculum perceived as discriminatory in legitimizing and rewarding only a partial range of knowledge and knowing (Green, 2004; Chesler et al., 2005; Henry & Tator, 2009). What passes for knowledge, ways of knowing, and knowledge transfers entails a social scientific discourse that privileges abstract empiricism, conceptual models and logical concepts, and objectified language as explanatory and epistemological frameworks (Smith, 1998). There is a cost associated with this intellectual blindness. A commitment to the virtues of objectivity and detachment not only discounts the lived realities of Aboriginal peoples and racialized minority women and men. This commitment also ensures that racialized and Aboriginal faculty who work within non-conventional (i.e., non-Eurocentric) intellectual domains may be subject to marginalization and inferiorization in defining who gets what, as demonstrated in the Insight Box.

INSIGHT

Aboriginality in the Academy: Sanctioned Ignorance, Systemic Indifference, Scholarly Arrogance

The form that racism takes inside a university is related to the ways in which academic knowledge is structured, as well as to the organizational structures which govern a university. The insulation of disciplines, the culture of the institution which supports disciplines, and the systems of management and governance all work in ways to protect the privileges already in place (Linda Tuhiwai Smith, 1998, p. 133).

Insofar as a culture of Eurocentric whiteness persists, the ivory-white towers come by their name honestly. Universities are known to support and reproduce certain patterns of knowledge and knowing that rarely reflect Aboriginal philosophies and world views, in the process silencing aboriginality and rendering it invisible, while visibilizing the normalizing and normative tyranny of whiteness (Kuokkanen, 2009). In contrast to the more holistic frameworks that Aboriginal students carry into the classroom, what passes for university knowledge and knowledge-making is generally fragmented and compartmentalized into disciplines. A commitment to rationalism (with its premise that truth resides independently of human perception of it, notwithstanding challenges by postmodernists) remains central to the university's intellectual traditions. But such a commitment reflects a narrow and one-dimensional understanding of the world. For example, as Joyce Green (2004) notes, students may study John Locke's ideas on private property and state sovereignty. Yet they are rarely exposed to their impact in advancing capitalist property relations within the colonizing context, in the process investing Locke with too much authority at the expense of indigenous approaches to property and political legitimacy.

Predictably, then, Aboriginal students become the focus of change that pigeonholes them into the academic culture and environment. There appears little appetite for embracing aboriginality as an opportunity to enhance the parameters of learning by capitalizing on Aboriginal peoples' perspective and experiences. Instead, a *difference as deficit* mindset prevails that ignores or minimizes aboriginality as inherently problematic or as hurdles to surmount a race-neutral (colour-blind) perspective that mistakenly dismisses aboriginality as irrelevant in a colour-blind academy; that racism and inclusion are no longer a major problem in a post-racial academy; and that issues of inequality and injustice will disappear if all students are treated the same (Guo & Jamal, 2007). Such a blinkered perspective could only be held by those whose privilege and power blinds them from seeing the barriers of inequality, the relations of dominance, and the systemic discrimination within the academy (see also Monture, 2010).

Operating as if only one legitimate intellectual tradition existed poses a problem. As Kuokkanen (2009) argues, other epistemes are dismissed as irrelevant or inferior. Or they are offered only superficial and token acknowledgement, in the process creating a pattern of avoidance and suppression that propels a racism by consequence (Kovach, 2009). Aboriginal students are expected to park their epistemologies at the entrance to the academy by assuming the trappings of a fundamentally different reality. The establishment of intellectual spaces for Aboriginal students, together with programs from counselling to support/access services, are justified on the grounds that Aboriginal students require special assistance if they want to bridge the cultural/intellectual gulf toward success. What remains under-theorized and unattended to are the barriers, namely, the structures, discourses, practices, expectations, values, and assumptions within the academy that underscore the academy's sanctioned ignorance, systemic indifference, and scholarly arrogance.

This inability or unwillingness to acknowledge alternative epistemes is called an epistemological racism (Scheurich & Young, 1997). An epistemological racism tends to perceive research and scholarly writing from Eurocentric forms of knowledge and ways of knowing as normal, desirable, and superior, while assuming that others are doing so, should do so, or would do so if they could, in the process reinforcing James Banks's (1993, p. 4) insightful notion that "all knowledge reflects the values and interests of its creator." With an epistemological racism, the foundation of all theories reflect, reinforce, and advance Eurocentric values. Alternative forms of knowledge and knowing (espistemologies) are excluded, marginalized, distorted, or discriminated against for being beyond the pale of a conventional Western stream of acceptability (Kuokkanen, 2009, p. 179). Conversely, Aboriginal scholars must become accomplished in epistemologies that arise from a history and context that historically proved hostile to their race or culture yet, paradoxically, are viewed by the dominant sector as free of any specific history and culture (see also Scheurich & Young, 2002). An epistemological racism enables the privileged to occupy positions of universality and objectivity while dismissing other ways of knowing to partial and particular positions by virtue of disassociating itself from any commitment to the "outsider within" (Kuokkanen, 2009; see also Carty, 1991). The intent may not be racist, but the consequences are systemically biased in preserving the Eurocentric foundational principles of the ivory-white towers (Fleras, 2003).

Clearly, then, any fundamental change will come about only when the ivory-white towers acknowledge the monoculturality of the academy's structure and discourse. Time will tell if the ivory-white towers are able or willing to confront their ignorance, arrogance, and indifference in excluding other intellectual traditions, while overhauling its Eurocentric normativity of whiteness. The prognosis is not particularly promising. In that universities were largely imperialistic/colonialistic transplants with a civilizing mission role, their intellectual traditions may be anchored in colonialist (and racist and patriarchal) paradigms that reflect, reinforce, and advance Eurocentricity of the global North. But the interplay of ignorance and arrogance with indifference comes with a cost. A refusal to acknowledge how the foundational principles of its Eurocentric constitutional order continue to

> deny or distort reinforces the academy's reputation as remote (ivory-white) and removed (towers). Without disrupting the hegemony of the university as a site of racialized struggles (see also Bannerji et al., 1991), references to the concept of ivory-white towers will continue to buttress a culture of whiteness, either in the traditional sense of sanctity (purity) or, alternatively, in the more common and current sense of a disconnect from reality (isolation).

Constructing a Multi-versity

The politics of ivory tower racisms are simultaneously complex and multidimensional yet nuanced and subtle. These racisms often go beyond the individual and the incidental (sporadic and random) since they are intrinsic to the very structure, values, and operation of academe. Nor are they simply mental quirks involving conscious acts with an intent to hurt or degrade (Fanon, 1967). Ivory tower racisms tend to be institutionalized in ways that reflect and reinforce the normative functioning of the system. The insights of Frances Henry are apropos: "white privilege and power continues to be reflected in the Eurocentric curricula, traditional pedagogical approaches, hiring, promotion and tenure practices, and opportunities for research ..." (Henry, 2004, Appendix).

Nevertheless, universities continue to react to racisms and racial discrimination as if they were the deviations from the norm of an otherwise healthy enterprise, reflecting individual aberrations, and readily solvable by expelling students, counselling sessions, and sensitivity training (Chesler et al., 2005). The Eurocentric whiteness of the academic towers is rarely problematized as the probable problem source in need of transformational change.

A contradiction is clearly in play. The ivory-white towers are increasingly committed toward the principles of inclusiveness and equity. In theory, they are moving away from a position of denial (There's no problem here.) or resistance (What do these people want?) or tokenism (What more do they want?). Both reactive and proactive measures are now in place: Reactive strategies focus on crisis management through damage control and conflict resolution, while, alternatively, proactive strategies emphasize prevention through problem solving (Fleras, 1996). In reality, however, ideals are one thing; implementation and enforcement may prove something else. Proposed strategies tend toward moderate reforms that neither challenge conventional norms nor disrupt a business-as-usual mandate. But how sufficient are reforms that focus on modifying the conventions that refer to the rules rather than challenging the rules upon which the conventions are based? A commitment to inclusiveness must go beyond simply diversifying the faculty and student body. Attention must also focus on respecting and incorporating what racialized minorities want in the way of changes (James, 2009; Dua,

2009). Racialized stakeholders (from students to faculty and administration) want more than token acceptance at the margins of the ivory-white towers. They are seeking transformative change involving a working balance: equality with equity, academic freedom with minority rights, due process with employment equity, inclusiveness with liberal universalism, and anti-racism with a commitment to multiculturalism.

In speaking truth to power, let's be candid. Racisms in the ivory-white towers are rarely about what is openly done in preserving a culture of Eurocentric whiteness. The sheer invisibility of whiteness as privilege and power ensures a level of obliviousness to the patterns of entitlement that flow from the existing racialized arrangement as the preferred normative standard. However potent these racisms are that deny and exclude, equal importance should be attached to what is not being done to bring about transformative change along the lines of equity and inclusion. Ivory-white racisms are systemic, often entailing acts of omission that (1) gloss over a racialized status quo; (2) are incorporated into the functioning of the institution (organizational structure, operating principles, reward systems, policies and programs, and anticipated outcomes) as normal and necessary; and (3) sustained through ideologies that rationalize the normative and normalizing. This racism by omission reflects a failure to engage those systemic biases that inform the foundational principles of the university's constitutional order. In acknowledging a discriminatory effect that marginalizes racialized minorities through no fault of their own, Rob Blauner (1972, pp. 276–77) concludes accordingly:

> For the liberal professor ... racism connotes conscious acts where there is an intent to hurt or degrade or disadvantage others because of their colour and ethnicity.... He does not consider the all white character of an occupation or institution in itself to be racism. He does not understand the notion of covert racism, that white people maintain a system of racial oppression by acts of omission, indifference, and failure to change the status quo.... From this standpoint, the university is racist because people of color are and have been systematically excluded from full and equal participation and power—as students, professors, administrators, and, particularly, in the historic definition of the character of the institution and its curriculum.

The challenge is clearly before us: Ivory tower racisms are unlikely to be eclipsed unless universities acknowledge that racism and discrimination exist and they matter in negatively impacting on university life in general, and faculty careers in particular (Gibney, 2013). A commitment to inclusiveness must address the wall of white resistance, defensiveness, and resentment that not only blocks cultural differences but also dismisses the normalizing culture of whiteness (Back, 2004; Sharma, 2004). Efforts to challenge a monocultural culture of ivory tower racisms must go beyond programs that simply address the personal and the attitudinal (Dua, 2009; but see Kobayashi, 2009). Even if such initiatives were to succeed in dismantling racial prejudice, shifts in attitudes do not necessarily translate into behavioural change, power transfers, institutional transformations, or public policy initiatives. Paradoxically, by implying the emergence of a colour-blind institution (because of improving attitudes and diminishing incidents of open racism), such initiatives may convey a belief that anti-racist programs are no longer necessary because nothing more needs to be done.

But the persistence and pervasiveness of ivory-white racisms attest to the slogan "the more things change...." Reforms that tweak a business-as-usual format are fine to a point, but they cannot be expected to address the root cause of the problem. Proposed instead are institutionally based solutions that disrupt the monocultural (re)production of knowledge and knowing; that acknowledge the centrality of power relations in allocating rights and resources; that focus on institutional practices from pedagogy to curriculum; that probe the culture of Eurocentric whiteness as normative and normalizing; and that deconstruct those foundational principles that undergird the academy's racialized constitutional order. No less important is a commitment to a "targetted universalism" (powell, 2009). A blanket universality or formal equality is rejected in favour of an inclusiveness that ensures similar treatment as a matter of course (equal treatment), yet acknowledges the special needs of Aboriginal peoples and racialized minorities when necessary (treatment as equals).

Clearly, then, a fundamental mindset shift is required in challenging ivory tower racisms. A multi-sectoral racism predominates within the ivory-white towers that (1) is inadvertently secured by official policies and programs; (2) is incorporated into structures, rewards, and operations as normal and necessary; (3) is expressed through a Eurocentric culture of whiteness and structures of dominance and control; and (4) is sustained through ideologies that rationalize discrimination and prejudice as aberrations in a seemingly fair system (Chesler et al., 2005 A subliminal racism is no less important because of subconscious prejudices that influence people's behaviour without their awareness of the influence. Moreover, whiteness experienced in the academy is gendered as well, inasmuch as maleness and the power and privileges associated with masculinity prevails (Monture, 2009). To be sure, varsity racism is produced and reproduced systemically; nevertheless, it is the cultural attitudes and ideological assumptions endorsed by individuals that perpetuate racism (Kobayashi, 2009). Any analysis of ivory tower racism as problem and solution will depend on incorporating the systemic with the subliminal without losing sight of the cultural and ideological.

No less crucial is an awareness of what hasn't been done to improve the potential for an inclusive academy. Expanding diversity initiatives on campus, curricula, courses, texts, pedagogy, and assessment have done little to challenge ivory towers as white spaces aligned along a Eurocentric line (norms, values, expectations, and traditions) (James, 2009). Audrey Kobayashi (2009, p. 72) writes: "The result is a terrible smugness on most campuses, even claims of zero tolerance for racism, but yet a failure to see that *it is whiteness, not overt racism, that is the dominant problem in the twenty-first century*" (emphasis mine). An institutionalized culture of denial and disavowal is likely to prevail as long as Eurocentric whiteness of the ivory tower cultures remains largely invisible to those power brokers who remain convinced of its neutrality, universalism, openness, fairness, objectivity, racelessness, and colour-blindness—and who resist reckoning with these seemingly neutral yet value-laden maxims (Henry & Tator, 2009; James, 2009). A racism that works by default (omission) could not be more forcibly articulated yet quietly imposed.

SECTION 3

EXPLAINING RACISMS, ERASING RACISMS

Most Canadians would agree (at least in public or in principle) that racism is a social problem. A belief in the problematic nature of racism is justified on several accounts: first, the persistence of racism contravenes core Canadian values pertaining to liberal universalism; second, its existence contradicts a constitutional commitment to equality and inclusiveness; third, racism even in its most subtle forms has negative impacts on victims, including emotional harm, social isolation, and psychological distress; fourth, its pervasiveness robs Canada and Canadians of resources and energies for more productive uses; and fifth, the smear of racism undermines Canada's international reputation, to the detriment of global trade and international investment.

Canadians are in much less agreement over the origins (sources) and causes[1] of racism. Explanatory frameworks vary. For some, references to racism are best couched as predominantly a personal problem originating within the individual (Cohen, 2011). A problem is deemed to be personal when individuals occupy the centre of analysis, assessment, reform, and outcome. Insofar as individuals are responsible for its existence, racism is thought to originate with those who behave in a racially discriminatory manner that invites accusations of racism. In some cases, the personal as the problem is rooted in biogenetic sources; in other cases, it is the result of personality flaws that induce anti-social behaviour; and in yet other cases, situational circumstances shape the outcome. Not surprisingly, an individual-focused explanatory framework concurs with causal models of racism that blame the victim for the problem or the lack of solution.

For others, including many sociologists, the best explanatory frameworks are social. Racism constitutes a social (or more accurately, an anti-social) problem whose causes and cures reside within the broader framework of society. Individualist explanations of racism that blame people or the "other" stand in sharp contrast to those social problem models more inclined to blame the system, including values, institutions, and (infra)structures. A problem such as racism is defined as social (or anti-social) when embodying the following preconditions: (1) it originates within the context of human activity; (2) it is defined by some sector of society as a problem; (3) a negative or harmful impact is exerted on some segment of society; and (4) the problem is perceived as amenable to solution through human intervention, including institutional reform, government policy, collective protest, or behavioural modification. Of course, a system-blaming approach neither denies human agency nor absolves people of responsibility for their actions. But it does recognize the importance of situating personal responsibility within a broader context over which individuals have little control in advancing choice and options.

The social problem literature has made it abundantly clear: How a problem is defined and explained will profoundly influence the proposed solution and the probable outcome (Fleras, 2005). If a problem is defined (or framed) in individualistic terms, then the solution must focus on changing the person's attitudes for maximum results. If, however, the problem is formulated along social lines, solutions will aim at changing the social system or aspects thereof. Solutions may range in scope, from the relatively superficial by reforming discriminatory institutional practices, to those that challenge the founding assumptions and foundational principles that inform the constitutional blueprint of society. But solutions require a word of caution: As the civil rights movement in United States demonstrated, and to paraphrase David Mark (2013, p. 140), however well intentioned, sociological reports or experts have never delivered anyone from social problems such as oppression. The goods can only be delivered by the collective challenge of people with common purposes and solidarity through sustained interaction with authority, elites, and opponents.

A similar line of reasoning can be applied to the social problem of racism. Racism is generally framed as a social problem in need of correctional reform depending on its definition, magnitude, and costs. This section capitalizes on this rationale by exploring the causes and continuities of racism with respect to anti-racism initiatives, including an official multiculturalism. The overall theme of this section is fairly straightforward: How racism is defined as a social problem will determine the appropriate level of anti-racism activity. Chapter 10 begins by examining different ways of explaining racisms with respect to their causes, costs, consequences, and cures. The chapter acknowledges the need for conceptual clarity when analyzing the difference between origins and causes, between causes and continuities, and between root and precipitating causes. Insights into the socio-economic disparities between racialized minorities (both Canadian-born and new Canadians) are analyzed and assessed to determine the role of racism in forging these gaps. Chapter 11 addresses the domain of anti-racisms. It demonstrates how different types of anti-racisms correspond broadly with different explanatory levels of racism as a personal problem, an institutional issue, or societal concern. Complicating the anti-racisms project is a growing awareness that racism is hardly an isolated social phenomenon. On the contrary, it intersects with gender and class to amplify the problem by rendering it more difficult to solve. Chapter 12 looks at Canada's official multiculturalism as a contested site in advancing a more inclusive society through the removal of discriminatory barriers. The chapter argues that, despite good intentions, an official multiculturalism may be interpreted as racist in reinforcing patterns of racism in a racialized Canada. The logic behind an official multiculturalism may also yield a distinctly Canadian form of racism in its own right. Finally, Chapter 13 provides a summary of the key debates and controversies over racisms in Canada's multicultural context. The chapter concludes by demonstrating a need to address those polite fictions of a post-racial society that gloss over the inconvenient truths of racisms in a multicultural Canada.

Note

1 For many, the term "causes" is interchangeable with "origins" or "sources." A distinction is preferred. Origins and sources are employed in the macro sense of human evolutionary development, while reference to causes reflects the micro-notion of the individual or the immediate within a contemporary context. The expression "root causes" differs from precipitating or immediate causes. Finally, neither origins nor causes are necessarily synonymous with the persistence and perpetuation of racisms.

CHAPTER 10

CONTESTING RACISMS
CAUSES, CONTINUITIES, COSTS, AND CONSEQUENCES

Introduction: The Explanatory Challenge

Judging by public opinion surveys, a substantial number of Canadians are disengaged from the realities of racisms. Mainstream Canadians are either ignorant of or misinformed about racisms in Canada with respect to causes, continuities, costs, and consequences. Many appear unwilling to acknowledge the institutional context of racism-related disparities in health, housing, and employment, preferring instead to dismiss discrepancies as personal faults (see also Feagin, 2006). Racism is downplayed or denied because of an abiding commitment to liberal universalism and robust multiculturalism, not to mention a belief in a post-racial, colour-blind Canada, with a corresponding tendency to blame minorities, rather than society, for failures. The prospect of admitting the reality of racisms is profoundly unsettling for a settler society. Such an admission compromises the comforting fictions and cherished beliefs of Canada as a just and fair society that accepts people for what they do and who they are. Furthermore, to acknowledge minority disparities because of racisms would also delegitimize the exalted status of white privilege and superiority in a Canada that commits to the principles of meritocracy, inclusiveness, and liberal universalism. The crisis in legitimacy would be disruptive to say the least.

But the rhetoric of denial cannot mask the realities of racisms. Whether we like it or not, approve or disapprove, racisms in Canada exist, and their existence is characterized by a myriad of sources, forms, expressions, and impacts. Patterns of racism are perpetuated when racialized minorities confront prejudice and discrimination that reinforce prevailing allocations of power, privilege, and resources, economic and educational disadvantage, social and political marginalization, and psychological victimization

(Henry & Tator, 2010; Satzewich & Liodakis, 2013). Originating for various reasons from the biological and psychological to the social and cultural, racisms are manifested in individual behaviours, institutional norms and practices, cultural values, and constitutional priorities. Racisms are expressed in many ways and at different levels, from the interpersonal and ideological to the institutional and infrastructural. They arise because of hate (bigotry at both individual and collective levels), or assertions of racialized superiority, or Eurocentric tendencies to dismiss others, or a racialized constitutional order that systemically rewards or denies. Such an expansive array of racisms poses a fundamental challenge: How to construct an explanatory framework that accounts for the magnitude and multi-dimensionality of racisms as process and practices (see also Satzewich, 2011, Ch. 2).

Complicating the politics of racisms are evolving racialized domains. The old racialized domain bordered on the parochial (see Marable, 2004). Both racisms and anti-racisms were situated primarily within the confines of domestic markets and the political nation-state. But racism has moved beyond the nation-state box. For Marable and others (Giroux, 2004), the politics of a new racialized domain encompasses the dynamics of transnational capitalism (resulting in mass unemployment because of outsourcing), the global policies of state neo-liberalism (with its privileging of market dynamics and individual responsibility at the expense of government intervention and the common good), and the realities of globalization and an integrated market economy. The resultant structural barriers culminate in the emergence of a two-tiered civil society: The "haves" on top and those "have-nots" who are hobbled by the dead weight of unemployment, a discriminatory criminal justice system, residential segregation, and erosion of many services for racialized minorities and immigrants.

The chapter is predicated on the premise that, while a dislike, devaluation, and discrimination of "others" is universal, the more interesting question is why? Is it because of genes, evolutionary trends, information processing, personality flaws, cultural values and difference, or social factors related to structures? Or perhaps all these variables are partly correct, in effect exposing the complexities of explaining human behaviour. The chapter is designed to analyze and explain racisms in terms of their origins and causes, their perseverance across time and space, costs to individuals, and consequences for society. The chapter begins by pointing out that racisms are not without cost or consequences, both to racialized minorities as well as to Canada and mainstream Canadians. Racisms are costly because of their negative consequences, although many Canadians do benefit directly or indirectly by the presence of racial discrimination. No less significant are the different causal explanations (theories) in accounting for racisms. A distinction between root causes and precipitating causes provides a sharper insight into its pervasiveness in society and persistence among individuals. Finally, the chapter acknowledges the importance of distinguishing between the causes of racisms and their continuities (persistence) if there is any hope of reduction or removal. A set of questions provides an organizational framework:

1) What are the origins of racism? Do we look to biology, culture, social structure, or personality for origins?
2) In what ways do the origins of racism as explanation differ from causes?
3) Do causal explanatory frameworks that work for individuals still apply to a more macro-level of expressions, from the institutional to the constitutional?
4) Insofar as root causes differ from precipitating causes, what are the immediate factors that create (precipitate) a racist incident?
5) How do the causes of racism differ from their continuities over time?
6) Why do racisms persevere despite widespread disapproval of them as contrary to the principles of a post-racial society? Is it because of fear, greed, ignorance, or arrogance? Or does persistence reflect societal inertia or public disinterest regardless of its dysfunctional effects on society?
7) Why do they persist in the face of anti-racism initiatives to condemn, curb, and control?

Answers to these admittedly complex questions to causes and continuities are elusive, but there is value in addressing the range of possible responses.

Costs and Consequences

Racism costs all Canadians: A toxic environment exists because of prejudices and discriminatory practices in advancing a white superiority complex (McKenna, 1994; also Feagin & McKenny, 2003). Mixed messages are conveyed that often contradict the ideals of a socially progressive society. Patterns of inequality are perpetuated despite Canada's constitutionally protected codes and oft-asserted ideals of inclusiveness, justice, and equality (see also Feagin, 2006). Racism exacts a heavy cost in terms of success and achievements that are blocked or destroyed, in the process betraying Canada's promise by squandering its potential. Racism not only diminishes the number of people who can contribute to Canada; useless energy is also expended that otherwise could be funnelled into more productive channels. Not surprisingly, racism remains a principal cause of alienation and marginalization due to its isolating and polarizing effect, creating tensions within the social fabric of society while precluding minority identification with the nation-state (Wood & Wortley, 2010; Onyeji, 2013). Furthermore, institutions that cannot capitalize on a diverse workforce because of discriminatory barriers or diversity-aversive climates are destined to lose their competitive edge in the global marketplace. The end result is nothing less than a blot upon Canadian society because of racism's capacity to squander its potential and reputation as progressive and prosperous.

The costs of racism are absorbed unevenly across Canada. Racialized minorities confront a restricted set of economic and social opportunities because of racism, while their self-worth plummets from a constant barrage of negative media messages (Fleras, 2012). Exposure to racism may also contribute to the poor health of minority women and men, ranging from high levels of obesity to mental health problems, with corresponding pressure on Canada's much beleaguered health care system (Maioni, 2003; Picard, 2005; Hannah, 2009; Feagin, 2006). Victims of racism and racial discrimination endure debilitating stress in the immediate aftermath. They also experience a dehumanization that can inflict cumulative physical and psychological damage in the long run (Feagin, 2002). A ripple effect ensues: Not only do individuals endure the hurt or isolation, but everyone who shares that person's racialized identity gets scooped up as a potential target (Onyeji, 2013). They are vulnerable to a shared fear of harassment or assault, resulting in a loss of personal security, which, in turn, intensifies isolation and self-defensiveness. To add insult to injury, racism and racial discrimination intersect with other patterns of exclusion and markers of identity (from gender to class) to amplify the costs of denial, exclusion, or exploitation.

Those whose lives are largely immune to racism may wonder what the fuss is all about. Sure, blatant expressions of racism or racial discrimination are painful, but what is the big deal about ethnic jokes or racial slurs, especially when celebrities like Sacha Baron Cohen and Russell Peters make a living from parodying others (but see Wright, 2007)? In reality, racism inflicts a cost on Canada and all Canadians, including racialized minorities, who experience a diminished sense of belonging, self-esteem, and contribution to Canada (Wood & Wortley, 2010). Or, as one person explained in a Dalhousie University study (Race, Violence, Health Project 2002/2003, p. 11), racism boxes in people:

> Racism determines who you are. You want to be who you are but people won't let you. We suppress ourselves to fit into dominant society.... Race creates a psychological maze of "mixed signals and judgements." Anticipating racism makes it difficult for individuals to act or to know how to respond to many situations. Individuals constantly second guess their responses to what is occurring. They feel pressured to be twice as good as everyone else. As a result, individuals feel depressed, disillusioned, and negative.

According to the RVH Project (Race, Violence, and Health Project, 2002/03, pp. 14–15), established to assess the impact of racism on health and well-being, racism is like a disease that can affect personal, family, and community health (both physically, emotionally, and psychologically) because of race-related stress within the workplace (see also Feagin & McKenny, 2003). Participants in the study confirmed this by acknowledging how racism is complex, ongoing, interrelated with other incidents, and all consuming:

> There is no way to unravel a person's experiences of racism, because there is no beginning or end to these experiences in education, employment, interactions with police and the justice system, and within their lives—these threads are interwoven with each other and throughout a person's life. Because racism is "everywhere, everyday, all the time" research participants told us that it forms a "filter" or it becomes a "smog" through which they view the world. Some said it was like water for fish: simply the element in which life is lived.... It is this continuing Canadian reality—a nightmare for some—that our project set out to explore. (Benjamin et al., 2010, p. 2)

Worse still, experiencing racism at the personal level is self-debilitating since "Always having to prove how smart you are takes it toll" (Black Community Forum, 2002/2003, p. 15). Racism negatively impacts on health by causing negative emotional states such as depression, influencing high-risk coping responses such as substance abuse (Hyman, 2009), or increasing the risk of illness (Nestel, 2012). Even subtle forms of racism and racial discrimination—from being ignored and ridiculed to body language and isolating behaviours—may seem unremarkable. Cumulatively, however, they can exert a powerful impact on a person's mental health (Alvarez & Juang, 2010). Yet there is only so much racism-inflicted pain, negativity, and self-hatred the body and mind can endure before the onset of health problems, self-destruction, or perpetuation of more violence. This excerpt from the RVH Project (Black Community Forum, 2002/2003, p. 15) is apropos:

> Participants identified the physical, emotional, and spiritual costs of being the only Black person in a workplace. When you have to be better to be considered equal, you can never allow yourself to stop measuring yourself against others. When you can't afford to make a mistake, you "can't come to a point of relaxation" and simply take your own competence for granted. The constant questioning erodes your confidence and increases an existing sense of isolation.... Since you are considered representative of your race, any failure is not simply personal. You bring down the whole community with you. When you succeed, unfortunately, you don't raise the community—you raise suspicions about whether you could have actually done the work yourself. Someone else is sought to take the credit.

Origins of Racism

Biological Origins

Biological explanations attribute the origins of racism to a biogenetic hard-wiring from an evolutionary past. With biology, essentially racism is seen as an extension of powerful and immutable instincts for survival purposes. Just as people appear to have an innate preference for aligning themselves with closely related blood kin, with the result that racism represents an ancient and deep-rooted impulse for protecting your "own kind," so, too, are people inclined to dislike or fear others unlike them. That is, it is natural to be comfortable in the company of those like us, whereas anyone different is perceived as inferior or racialized as threatening. A xenophobic fear of outsiders may elicit a fight-or-flight response, in effect making it only natural to recoil from what is racially different (Van den Berghe, 1967). Suppression of these instinctive impulses for disliking others doesn't make dislike (i.e., racism) go away. More accurately, suppressing racism (dislike) drives it underground, only to re-emerge in an often explosive rage (from ethnic cleansing to sectarian violence) when the lid is lifted. This visceral and deep dislike of outgroups (racism) may explain the universality and universal appeal of biological explanations.

Psychological Origins

Psychological explanations of racisms tend to focus on deeply entrenched attitudes and distinctly human ways of processing information. Two popular theories prevailed: First, there is the frustration-aggression thesis. This theory explains racism as a type of relief (or catharsis) that displaces inner aggression by projecting racist hostility toward a scapegoat. According to this largely psychoanalytic line of thinking, people who are frustrated in achieving desired goals will respond by *redirecting* their anger. Rather than aiming their hostility at the real source of frustration, which may be too powerful a target to antagonize, aggression is projected instead at a scapegoat group who is largely incapable of resisting. Of particular note is the tendency toward displacement, i.e., to project personal feelings of inadequacy, rage, or fear onto a scapegoated group. Every society relies on its scapegoats whose presence provides the majority with a catharsis (relief or release) to offset a feeling of inferiority.

Second, there is the authoritarian personality theory of racism (Adorno et al., 1950). Personality has long been employed to explain the causes of racism in terms of why some become racists and others do not (Van de Berghe, 1967). According to the authoritarian personality theory, some people who are born with rigid and controlling outlooks express a racialized dislike of others because of who they are. Highly authoritarian personalities tend to exhibit the following attributes: excessive conformity, blind allegiance, submissiveness to authority, intolerance and antagonism to outgroups, insecurity over change, stereotypical (black-and-white) thinking, and a negative view of human nature. Both theories, but especially the authoritarian personality theory, are widely regarded as oversimplistic. There is mounting skepticism in thinking that fascism, racism, conservativism, and so on can be lumped together as slightly different manifestations of a single dysfunctional personality type (Ray, 1988). Nevertheless, many continue to argue that psychological factors, including irrational fear or sense of victimization, constitute a major cause of racisms. Racisms arise because of ignorance or personal inadequacies, including a low self-esteem and a sense of worthlessness that demonizes others who are different as threatening and undeserving in the competition for status or jobs (Sihera, 2009).

Others frame racism in more neutral terms of information processing. For Dovidio et al. (2010b), the psychological foundations of racism reflect the process of creating social categories. Humans are prone to make sense of the world by categorizing their perception of reality along the following lines, including: (1) a belief that groups are distinguished by race-based characteristics; (2) the racial characteristics of one group are defined as inferior; and (3) social power enables these beliefs to translate into disparate outcomes that advantage some and disadvantage others. This line of reasoning leads to a logical conclusion: Racism is an individualized phenomenon to be addressed accordingly, as Elaine Sihera (2009) writes:

> That is why racism will always be difficult to eradicate because it is not a social act. It's an individual one. The causes of racism begin with the individual and can only be resolved by addressing the actions of individuals. It's individual people who behave in a racist manner which is then enhanced by the group and validated by institutions. That is why institutions often remain racist and discriminatory in approach for a long time unless the individuals within them are encouraged to act otherwise.

Cultural Origins

Reference to racism as a function of biology or psychology rarely resonates with relevance for sociology. With the possible exception of sociobiologists (see van den Berghe, 1967), most sociologists would argue that nobody is biologically programmed to hate in a racist manner. There is no compelling proof to believe that people are genetically hard-wired for hate. Rather than an error of genetics or perception, sociologists contend that people are culturally conditioned to be racist by environments that foster ethnocentrism, hate, and racialized outgroup antipathy. Culture as an explanatory framework has displaced the race concept to categorize different groups of humans, to account for the differences between them, and to explain recurrent patterns of belief and behaviour within each group (Lentin, 2005). In contrast to morally reprehensible categories of race, the concept of culture is seen as creating hierarchies that are deemed more acceptable as explanatory variables since they imply relativism, achievement rather than inherency, personal control over outcomes, and the possibility of improvement and progress.

Cultures serve a root cause of racism in those contexts where the cultural other is dismissed as inferior, irrelevant, or disliked. A deterministic culture (culturalism) can do the same work as a biology or race in denying or excluding (Frederickson, 2002). Or in contexts where dominant cultural values perceive the other as a threat to society, racism is manipulated by the majority to justify the control or elimination of the danger. Culture in this case may be reified or essentialized to the point where it serves as the functional equivalent of race (Frederickson, 2002). The vilification of cultural differences as dangerous or distracting through claims of cultural superiority can prove every bit as exclusionary as biologically based ideologies that openly deny or exclude (Fleras, 2004).

Social Origins

The social causes of racism reflect competitive contexts involving a struggle for valued resources, with the "haves" pitted against the "have-nots" in competing for economic survival and survival of the richest. Those in positions of power and privilege will do whatever is necessary to preserve their status, including manipulating racism to tilt the competition in their favour. Both institutions and foundational principles of society are constructed in such a way that the design, operations, and reward structures are systemically biased toward the dominant group. Rather than asking why people fear those who are different, sociologists are more inclined to ask, "What is it about society that generates such fear of outgroups and ignorance or the 'other'?" To the extent that racisms prevail, individuals are conditioned to be racist as part of a socialization process for socially controlling the status quo. For example, for those who endorse a class struggle as the central competitive dynamic in society, racism represents a bourgeois ideology that rationalizes the exploitation of both colonized peoples and racialized domestic workers (Van den Berghe, 1967). Racist ideologies were and continue to be employed for securing ready access to a cheap and disposable labour supply; to destabilize worker solidarity by undermining any potential show of unity or strength; to justify intrusive devices for controlling troublesome minorities; and to secure controlling functions in support of ruling-class interests (Bolaria & Li, 1988).

Racism, in short, originated as a system of social control within competitive contexts. Then as now, it provides a relatively straightforward but effective technique to explain and justify why people get what they deserve or deserve what they get. As an explanatory framework, racism tends to self-perpetuate itself as a self-fulfilling prophecy. Those racialized as inferior and denied access to resources are destined to do more poorly. The resultant outcome of doing poorly because of denial and domination reinforces their subordinate status, which, in turn, justifies further exclusions.

Structural Origins

With structural explanations, the root causes of racism are not necessarily created to deflect or defuse. Rather, they reflect the inherent structures of racialized society. As discussed earlier, all complex societies make a distinction between in-groups and outgroups; assign a corresponding division of labour and rewards along group lines; devalue those deemed to be inferior or who pose a threat; and incorporate this devaluation into the deep structures of society over time. Not surprisingly, Euro-American societies such as Canada tend to be infra-racialized in terms of design, organization, dynamics, and reward structures. This infrastructural racism is particularly evident in the Eurocentric foundational principles and founding assumptions that continue to govern racialized constitutional orders. In other words, people internalize racism because of their embeddedness in a Eurocentric society structured (i.e., defined, organized, and rewarded) along racialized lines with respect to what is normal, acceptable, and desirable.

For many sociologists, racisms are caused by and continue to persist because of social and structural factors (Bolaria & Li, 1988; Satzewich, 1998; Bonilla-Silva, 2002; Feagin, 2006; Lentin, 2008). Neither a transient phenomenon nor an anomalous and unpredictable feature, racisms in Canada are deeply rooted in its historical and economic development, embedded within the institutional structures of an unequal society, endemic to core Canadian values, and integral to Canada-building. Like race, racism arose not simply to explain differences, but to justify conquest, settlement, land appropriation, and economic domination (Macedo & Gounari, 2006). The profoundly racialized nature of Canada-building into a white man's country must be acknowledged. Canada's prosperity as a white man's country was contingent on a structural and open racism toward those who laid the railways, settled the West, extracted timber and mineral resources, and worked the assembly lines. Its quality of life and economic well-being continue to be supported by racialized minorities, many of whom are employed in precarious—low-paying, temporary, and dangerous—jobs (Bishop, 2005). The following Insight box reinforces the significance of structural origins in explaining racisms in Europe and Canada.

INSIGHT

Structure Matters: White Hot Racisms in Europe, Cool White Racisms in Canada

The persistence of racism, xenophobia, and intolerance constitutes one of the more serious challenges to democratic citizenship and multicultural inclusiveness (UN News Centre, 2006). Contributing to this crisis in co-operative coexistence is the pervasiveness of racist violence, political leaders, and parties that openly advocate racist political platforms, incidents of religious defamation, and the criminalization of immigration and asylum seekers. Questions naturally arise: Is it hip to hate? Is there a growing culture of racial hatred? Is it possible to explain transatlantic differences in patterns and politics of racism? Are differences in racial violence the result of economic forces, national character, history and geography, or social and cultural features? This Insight box argues for the need to go deeper by exploring those structural factors that differentiate expressions of racism between Canada and European countries.

The politics of racial hatred are particularly virulent in Europe, where open incidents of interpersonal hate, criminal victimization (assaults), and open institutional discrimination seem to be the rule rather than the exception (ENAR, 2013; Fekete, 2013b; Iganski, 2011). In recent months, racist incidents have included the following: moves to ban minarets from mosques in Switzerland (albeit its status as a country with a celebrated history of religious tolerance); the building of mosques in Italy; France's threat to criminalize the burqa; the election of far-right anti-immigrant parties to the European Parliament; the expulsion of Roma people from public domains; and the extraordinarily high rate of physical violence directed at minorities in the United Kingdom. (In 2011-12, police recorded 37,000 racially or religiously aggravated crimes in England and Wales, compared to 51,000 in 2010-11 [Burnett, 2012, 2013b]). Nationalisms in southern Europe are mobilized around the idea of guarding the nation from an immigration invasion (anti-foreigner racism or xeno-racism), while protecting the interest of the native-born against those of unwanted immigrants (nativism) (Fekete, 2013a).

No less controversial is the growing sense of unease among Europeans in coming to terms with Islam's growing visibility and its perceived threat to European values (Spiegel Staff, 2009; Caldwell, 2009; ENAR, 2012). Negative and Islamophobic portrayal of Muslims in the media continue to impede their acceptance and integration into society (Van Dijk, 2006), while expressions of anti-Semitism reflect attacks on synagogues and cemeteries, in addition to physical assaults on Jewish people; an intense aversion to Roma; a negative climate of opinion toward migrants, refugees, and asylum seekers; and a spiralling number of hate crimes (Burnett, 2013a; ENAR, 2013). Just imagine a statement by a leading Italian senator and leader of an anti-immigration party who compared the country's first black cabinet minister, Dr. Cecile Kyenge, to an orangutan (Dr. Kyenge has also received several death threats) (D'Emilio, 2013).

To be sure, the situation may not be as dire as conveyed by the reports, surveys, or the mainstream media. An ENAR

(2009) report hinted at signs of improvement, including comprehensive legal frameworks and national action plans consistent with principle and proposals of the EU Commission on Human Rights (Hammarberg, 2009). Both EU-wide polls and passage of anti-discrimination legislation in EU countries suggest a majority commitment to abolish racism, racial discrimination, and xenophobia through criminal law. NGOs such as the European Network Against Racism (ENAR) are actively involved in challenging racism and promoting equality in all European nations. Counter-demonstrations over the presence of neo-Nazi cells, together with vigils in support of racialized victims, point to the prevalence of anti-racism movements across Europe (Eurobarometer, 2008). Moreover, caution needs to be exercised in castigating European racism. Patterns of racism vary across European countries and across generations, thus making it easy to overgeneralize, while reports indicating high hate crime levels compared to Canada may reflect differences in data collection and interpretation.

However impressive on paper, good intentions are not the same as implementation and enforcement. Nor can they disguise the fact that discrimination and racially motivated violence are far more widespread than official statistics suggest, according to an EU-wide survey by the European Union Agency for Fundamental Rights (EU-Midis, 2009). On too many occasions, anti-racism and anti-discrimination rights continue to exist as little more than paper rights rather than practical outcomes. Racialized and religious minorities continue to suffer from racist intolerance, discrimination, and prejudice, and treatment as second-class citizens across all indicators from employment and education, from housing to policing (ENAR, 2009). Moreover, judging by the lack of political will and availability of sanctions, governments appear increasingly reluctant to prevent acts of racial discrimination while focusing even less attention on punishing those who perpetuate these often cowardly yet harmful acts. Or in the words of the Hate Crimes Survey (Human Rights First, 2009) in describing how governments are failing to keep pace with violent hate crime across the region:

Racism, anti Semitism, xenophobia, anti Muslim and anti Roma hatred, religious intolerance, homophobia: the list of biases that fuel these crimes is a long one. Attacks range from lethal assaults, to threats and harassment to vandalism and discretion of religious and community property. The perpetrators are individuals acting alone, or in concert with neighbours, co-workers and fellow students, as well as loosely knit and more organized groups that share ideologies of hatred and act upon them. The violence can ruin lives, or end them. It can terrorize whole communities, driving away vulnerable members or forcing them to stay out of sight. Violent hate crimes especially when official response to it is weak or non existent, also attacks the society at large, undermining the very notions of equalitiy and the equal protection of the law.

Evidence points to Europe as a racist hotspot (see Fisher, 2013a). Overt expression of European racism are forceful and direct, and ostensibly positioned to bluntly remind newcomers that Europe is a white Christian (or nominally secular) society. The end result of this racialized violence and discrimination is a sense of resignation that persists among migrants and racialized minorities, many of whom are either uninformed about anti-discriminatory legislation or express a lack of confidence in the ability of authorities to protect them (EU-Midis, 2009).

By contrast, racism in Canada tends to relatively muted, politely conveyed, and often reflecting the use of coded words to deflect attention away from put-downs that potentially deny, exclude, or anger. To the extent that they exist, explicit forms of racisms (both interpersonal and institutional) are generally of an isolated nature, usually involving slurs rather than violent physical action, and are often met with stern rebuke from both the public and authorities.

How to explain this transatlantic discrepancy: White-hot racisms in Europe versus below-the-radar racisms in Canada? Much can be attributed to structural differences and national discourses as they apply to immigrants and immigration (Fleras, 2012). Canada is, sociologically speaking, an immigration society. It possesses a principled set of rules to regulate the intake of immigrants who, for the most part (and because of Canada's proactive admission program), are liberal, legal, and well equipped in terms of skills and credentials. In addition, an immigration society like Canada endorses immigrants and immigration as a positive contribution to society, expects immigrants to become permanent residents by taking out citizenship, and provides a series of programs such as multiculturalism to facilitate their settlement and integration. Finally, a national vision is promulgated that includes immigrant Canadians as an integral component of national identity and critical to Canada-building. The end result is a widespread perception that immigration and immigrants are a relatively low-risk option when managed and under control (Simmons, 2010).

Compare this inclusiveness framework with the exclusionary dynamics that prevail across European countries. European countries tend to see themselves as "complete" societies (Castles & Miller, 2009; Clarkson, 2012) that no longer require permanent newcomers for society-building purposes. Until recently, EU countries rejected any label as immigration societies with a need for programs to regulate immigrant intake, much less to improve either permanent residency or settlement and integration. To the extent that immigrants took root in the postwar reconstruction of Europe, they tended to be descendants and family members of pre-1974 guest workers (who never left) or asylum seekers who were perceived as illegal, illiberal, and ill-equipped for Europe's high-powered economy. But despite their seemingly lack of fit in a secular (or Christian) and (post)modern society, migrants were rarely expelled, not because of compassion but because of fear of besmirching Europe's international image as tolerant (in reaction to its xenophobic and racist past). Nor were minorities under pressure to discard their social and cultural differences, in part because central authorities assumed they would return "home," in part because of a misguided political correctness that recoiled from saying anything negative about differences for fear of being labelled as racist, in part to protect minority cultures from unfair majority culture pressure (Parvin, 2009). The interplay of historical racism with continued racial discrimination in housing and employment further consolidated a minority drift into inward-looking communities of safety.

Clearly, then, Europe's mistake lay in underestimating the structural barriers and cognitive challenges in shifting from complete societies to an immigration society. The fact that European societies were under pressure to become more immigration-oriented resulted in paradigm ambiguities that intensified anxieties and fostered violent behaviour. Without a national vision to define a status and role for migrants, differences proved to be divisive rather than meshing into integration. Adrienne Clarkson (2012), former governor general of

> Canada, contends that European feelings of national superiority breed racist hostility toward outsiders in their midst:
>
>> Europeans look at citizenship in terms of race and blood. Having fought each other for so long over so little territory, an "us" versus "them" mentality, accompanied by the feeling that their people are superior to others, has been bred into their national sensibilities. The immigration integration issues plaguing European societies today can be understood in the context of this racism, pure and simple.
>
> Worse still, the political elite failed to engage the general public in addressing the crisis. Political elites feigned a consensus by emphasizing a commitment to multiculturalism rather than risk public unrest, a minority backlash, or international censure for intolerance. The logic behind this governance gambit was straightforward enough. Advancing the long-standing principle of consociationism (elite co-operation) and consensus democracy for building a stable and ordered democracy across deeply divided societies, the logic sought to forge a level of co-operation and consensus among the establishment in the hopes that elite leaders (1) could contain any backlash in reaction to Muslim migration; (2) keep a lid on prejudice by praising the virtues of tolerance; and (3) tamping down extremism by caving into minority demands or paying them to keep quiet. In the equally mistaken notion that the passage of time would transform Muslims into more secular Europeans, Europeans elites naively assumed that the divide between Islam and the West was antiquated and prone to dissolution, with the result that a liberal, multicultural, and relativistic Europe would have little difficulty in absorbing new arrivals.
>
> Reality proved to be a wake-up call. Instead of integration and co-operation, Europe was convulsed by terrorist events in London and Madrid, reports of polygamy in Sweden, radicalized mosques in Britain, riots over affronts to the Prophet, murders of prominent Dutch personalities by extremists. Instead of consensus politics, the Swiss referendum on minarets exposed a rift between political elites and popular sentiment. As Christopher Caldwell (2009, p. 11) writes: "In no country in Europe does the bulk of the population aspire to live in a bazaar of world cultures. Yet all European countries are coming to the wrenching realization that they have somehow, without anyone actively choosing it, turned into such bazaars."
>
> Politicizing the reality gap between official discourses versus the subterranean concerns that rarely made it into the public has proven pivotal. In lifting the veil of consensus by political correctness, the politicization has exposed and contested those unspoken assumptions of what was best for European countries (see Caldwell, 2009). Not unexpectedly, what exists instead of a racism-free Europe is a deeply rooted problem unlikely to subside in the near future (Aziz, 2009).

Causes of Racism: Root and Precipitating

The reasons why something originated are not necessarily the same as those that explain its causes or persistence. Causes are not the same as continuities when it comes to racisms. Moreover, not all causes of racisms (or origins) are created equally because of the distinction between root and precipitating causes. Precipitating causes are those immediate triggers that prompt individual behaviour. For example, people may engage in acts of racism because of proximate factors: they stereotype, feign superiority, lack familiarity, internalize negative attitudes, or resent minorities because they demand too much or create too many problems. Racism is justified by references to claims for self-protection, revenge, xenophobia, fear, greed, hatred of others, resentment toward them, and perception of others as a threat. For many, the key precipitating factor is ignorance. Racism is widely perceived as the by-product of ignorance of the unknown because of improper socialization. Improving people's knowledge about or sensitivity to diversity will gradually diminish the spectre of racism.

Sociologists often look for reasons beyond and behind those of an immediate nature. For example, instead of asking why and how stereotyping reinforces racism, a root-cause framework poses the question of why stereotyping exists in the first place. Is it because of biology and heredity? Deep psychology? Cultural values? Self-interest? A sorting-out process in a competitive environment? Structural barriers, including those Eurocentric foundational principles that inform a racialized constitutional order? In other words, reference to precipitating causes prompts a micro-orientation that focuses on immediate triggers. By contrast, a root-cause explanatory framework tends toward a macro-orientation because of its "bigger picture" focus on the underlying context, including society, culture, institutions, and structures) as explanatory variables.

Continuities and Persistence

There is little consensus regarding the origins and causes of racisms. References to continuities and persistence are no less splintered, given the complexities of such a multi-dimensional phenomena. No one should be surprised by the question of why racisms continue to persist at a time when we should know better. The fear and ignorance associated with racism seem strangely inappropriate at a time of growing diversity, more opportunity for intercultural interaction, and available information about minorities and difference. As well, considerable time and effort have gone into eradicating racisms, yet they continue to flourish, albeit in more subtle ways. Needless to say, such contradictions—racism as publicly rejected yet privately popular; racism as socially unacceptable yet pervasively persistent; and racism as reality despite declining significance of the race concept and dwindling number of racists—pose a simple but important question: Why?

Many believe that racism perseveres because of its psychological benefits. Racism has a way of making mainstream members feel good about themselves primarily by bolstering a collective self-image of superiority. This notion of racism as "functional" for white folk is captured by Julian Bond of the NAACP (National Association for the Advancement of Colored People) when referring to the tenacity of white supremacist racism (White, 1999, p. 25):

> It's still white supremacy. It still means so much to those who practice it. It defines who they are. It makes them feel that they are better than others. It ensures them positions in employment and college admissions they otherwise might not have. It still puts a lid on the dreams of black people.

In other words—and to paraphrase Derrick A. Bell of New York University, who writes in the Foreword of the *The Perils of Racial Prophecy*—racism is of such value to so many at different levels that its non-existence is unimaginable. Phrased differently, if racialized minorities didn't exist, whites would have invented them, with a corresponding dislike because of who they are or aren't. Of particular note is the degree to which racism connects all whites in an unspoken alliance. Without hostility toward racialized outgroups, critics argue, intra-white fighting would be endemic and conducive to perpetual anarchy (Mills, 1997). Clearly, then, rather than a departure from the norm, racism *is* the norm that bolsters a system designed to augment a racialized status quo.

In addition, racism persists because it provides a coping mechanism for addressing the globalizing demands of contemporary urban society. A sharply demarcated wedge between "us" and "them" provides a buffer for insulating individuals from the pressures of an impersonal and competitive world. It helps to secure an oasis of tranquility in a world of diversity, uncertainty, and change, in addition to providing a measure of meaning in a meaningless world. The dissolution of the familiar and reassuring not only undermines people's sense of social belonging, including a rootedness in traditional collectivities such as kinship or community. The confluence of uncertainty and change also induces individuals to withdraw into racist shells both familiar and emotionally satisfying. A racist dislike of racialized others fosters a sense of relief, continuity, belonging, importance, and security for coping with societal stress because of intense global competition, radicalized individualism, a disintegrating civil society, increasingly porous territorial borders, erosion of the nation-state as the primary source of legitimacy, and cultural upheavals created by the proliferation of digital and mobile technologies.

As well, racism originated and continues to persist within a capitalist Canada because of its usefulness in advancing class interests (Bolaria & Li, 1988). It also secures a resource for the pursuit of diverse goals in competitive contexts. This approach is firmly grounded in a sociology of group competition and rational choice theory—that is, the drawing power of racism provides a competitive edge in the struggle for scarce and valued resources. Those in positions of power will do anything to preserve privilege in the competition for scarce resources, including sowing the seeds of racism to distract or divide, without drawing unnecessary attention to the contradictions and dysfunctions within the system (Galabuzi, 2006). The social history of Canada clearly demonstrates how opportunistic elites manipulated racism in order to mobilize masses into action against those deemed to be racially inferior.

Finally, there are social psychological factors at play to account for persistence. Racism may persist because of indifference or inactivity. Or there may be a disconnect between what people say and what they are willing to do. For example, Canadians like to think of themselves as intolerant of racism with a corresponding willingness to combat it when necessary. Nonetheless, there is evidence to suggest our principles are precisely that: ideals that do not necessarily stack up, especially in contexts of ambiguity or adversity. The next Insight box looks at the persistence of racism at both surface and subsurface levels. It also demonstrates how situational circumstances can either depress expressions of racism or tolerate them.

◻NSIGHT

If a Racist Tree Falls in the Forest and No One Is Around to Hear It ...? The Rhetoric of Anti-racism versus the Reality of Racism

Contemporary race relations are hijacked by an apparent paradox: Open racism is widely condemned, yet acts of racism still frequently occur (Kawakami et al., 2009; also Yong, 2009). This paradox gives rise to yet another conundrum: If there is so much racism, why are there so few anti-racists? One reason for this paradox rests in the tendency for individuals to misjudge people's behavioural responses to racist acts. Research indicates that people tend to overestimate how they and others would react on witnessing an incident of racism. On one side, people believe they would be very upset by a racist act, yet when observing and experiencing such an event, they expressed little emotional distress. On the other side, people tend to exaggerate the degree to which a racist comment would trigger an anti-racist response. The results of these findings suggest that racism perseveres because people are poor predictors of their commitment to anti-racism. Even those who aspire to tolerance or anti-racism may respond with indifference when confronting an act of racism because of unconscious biases that prevent them from acting on their principles by taking action against other people's racist behaviour (see subliminal racism). Such inaction suggests that social deterrents to racism may be weaker than public rhetoric implies; after all, confronting racist individuals can be costly because doing so may be awkward or embarrassing or harmful.

A study to investigate participants' actual and anticipated responses to anti-black slurs puts the paradox to the test. One hundred twenty non-black participants ("experiencers" and "forecasters") were chosen and exposed to an incident involving (1) no racial slur, (2) moderate racial slur, and (3) extreme racial slur. Upon entering the laboratory, the experimenter introduced the experiencer to two male confederates—one black and one white—who posed as fellow participants. Shortly after the experimenter left the room, the black confederate got up to leave on the pretext of retrieving his cellphone, but gently bumped the white confederate's knee along the way. In the control situation of no slur, the incident passed without comment; in the moderate slur condition, once the black confederate left the room, the white confederate remarked, "Typical—I hate it when black people do that." In the extreme racial slur condition, the white confederate exclaimed, "clumsy n-word" (the article used this term). The black confederate then returned, followed by the experimenter, who asked the experiencers to fill out a survey assessing the current situation. The experimenter then asked each experiencer to select one of the confederates as a partner for a subsequent task. In another room, the participants known as the forecasters were presented with a detailed description of the events that experiencers actually encountered, then asked to predict how they would feel if they were in the experiencer position and to predict which confederate would be chosen as partner for the word task.

The results deviated from expectations. The rhetoric of anti-racism did not match the reality of racism. Forecaster predictions of what would happen bore little resemblance to what the experiencers thought or did. Forecasters, in analyzing the racist comment conditions, were more upset than experiencers, who displayed relatively little distress regardless of the type of comment or no comment. More worrying still, in analyzing the racist comment condition, forecasters rarely selected a white confederate as a task partner, while experiencers *were more likely to pick a white confederate partner—even if he made a racist slur—than if he had said nothing.*

In short, the rhetoric of predictions (forecasters) did not coincide with the reality of reactions (experiencers). What egalitarian-minded people say they *will* do may differ from what they *actually* do because of unconscious negative attitudes that shape reaction to spontaneous incidents. Not surprisingly, forecasters substantially misrepresent the extent to which a racist comment would provoke distress or rejection. To be sure, the seeming indifference of experiencers could be explained in different ways. For example, experiencers may have relied on their early socialization to politely look the other way when confronted by deviant actions, particularly in unfocused or unfamiliar contexts (Dijker, 2009). Or although racism carries a heavy stigma, people are less bothered by it than they might expect, and are loathe to confront racist incidents out of embarrassment, fear, or indifference (Yong, 2009). However true such an assessment, the consequences do not bode well. Racism and discrimination continue to persist in society because of people's failure to do something about it in ways they say they would. They claim to be against racism, yet betray themselves by looking the other way out of politeness, indifference, or cowardice.

To sum up, racism cannot be reduced to individual attitudes born of prejudice and ignorance. It is that, yet much more. Racism as a socio-political project emerged within the context of European colonialism, was embedded with the foundational principle of a white man's Canada, inextricably linked with Canada-building, and continues to be institutionalized within Canada's political and social structures (see Lentin, 2004; Mills, 1997). True, individuals are the immediate source and carriers of racisms at institutional, cultural, and societal levels. But individual racisms neither exist in a social and political vacuum nor do they act outside of a specific context. For sociologists, questions about why and how individuals do racism must transcend psychologically oriented factors such as socialization, fear, arrogance, or ignorance. Racism persists not because it constitutes a set of fallacious beliefs or deep-seated personality flaws. It persists because racism constitutes a system of social control involving relations of power within contexts of racialized inequality (Paolucci, 2006; Macedo & Gounari, 2006; Fleras, 2012). In other words, rather than an anomaly in society and its ideals—namely, a kind of irrational or dysfunctional feature of an otherwise rational and sound system—racism is a true expression of societal ideals.

Not surprisingly, explanations of the origins and persistence of racism continue to miss the mark. Instead of asking "Why does racism exist?" the question should be rephrased: "Why shouldn't racism exist in a racialized society whose benefactors benefit from racialized arrangements that preserve privilege, power, and property?" Rephrasing the question in this way is critical. It not only redefines the concept of solutions, it also confirms that racisms cannot be understood apart from the social, cultural, economic, and political context in which they are embedded, expressed, and nourished. The challenge of erasing racisms under these society-building conditions is suddenly more formidable.

CHAPTER 11

ROOTING OUT RACISMS
ANTI-RACISM INTERVENTIONS

Introduction: Problematizing Anti-racism

Most Canadians are no longer racists in the blatant sense of openly vilifying racialized minorities. Long gone are the days of brazenly demonizing others because of their racial appearance. Such incidents unlikely to return in light of numerous checks and balances, which include an anti-discrimination framework that ranks among the world's best (Jedwab, 2008), would abort any repeat of such an occurrence in Canada. Canada's defiantly anti-racist stance notwithstanding, racism continues to thrive in unobtrusive ways, deliberately or unconsciously, through action or inaction, at both individual and institutional levels. Racisms are rarely projected directly at others, thanks to the chilling effect of today's politically correct climate, where even inadvertent criticism of minorities may be denounced as racist. Rather, racisms flourish through the cumulative impact of demeaning slights that quietly accumulate into a "ton of feathers." The stealthiness of racism puts the onus on Canadians to do something about it because, as conveyed by Tim Wise, an American anti-racism educator:

> Those persons called "white" have a particular obligation to fight racism because it's *ours* [emphasis added], created in its modern form by us, for the purpose of commanding power over resources and opportunities at the expense of people of color. Furthermore all whites ... have to address the internalized beliefs about white supremacy from which we all suffer. No one is unaffected by the daily socialization to which we are all subjected—specifically with regard to the way we are taught to think about persons of color in this society. (Wise, 1999, p. 17)

Most would agree. To do something to someone because of his or her skin colour is racist, and somebody should pay for the transgression. But doing nothing to confront racisms may be no less racist in consequence; after all, fence-sitting (through inactivity or silence) should not imply impartiality. More accurately, such seeming neutrality should be seen for what it really is: a tacit acceptance of a racialized and unequal status quo. The only option in bridging the racialized divide requires an explicit anti-racism stand; otherwise, there is the unmistakable whiff of contributing to the problem rather than advancing a solution.

Herein lie the salience and significance of anti-racism as a solution to the racisms problem. Reference to anti-racism involves a range of counter-hegemonic strategies that directly and openly challenge racism and oppressions based on race, class, gender, and sexuality (Dei & Calliste, 2000). By and large, the sprawling nature of anti-racism as discourse and practices reflects varying definitions of racisms. If racism is primarily framed about attitudes (racism as race) or beliefs (racism as ideology) or values (racism as culture), then individual-based strategies are in order. If racism entails racialized structures (both systemic and systematic), a more institutional approach is required. But wholesale transformations are due if racism refers to those Eurocentric foundational principles and power relations that undergird a society's racialized constitutional order. Anything less than a comprehensive framework creates a level of effectiveness that is tantamount to applying a cotton swab to a hemorrhaging wound. Finally, framing racisms as multidimensional in form, process, and outcome calls forth an inclusive anti-racism program incorporating the individual-institutional-ideological-infrastructural nexus. The words of Goldberg (1990a, p. 345) are relevant:

> Just as a plurality may be required for moral condemnation, so no single mode of resistance to racism will succeed exhaustively. Racism's adaptive resilience entails that we have to respond with sets of pragmatic oppositions appropriate to each form that racism assumes. Institutionally overcoming apartheid must take on forms different from opposition to jury practices or discriminatory employment and housing practices....

In general, then, anti-racism can be defined as a set of strategies and tactics for actively challenging patterns of racism, institutional power, and interlocking systems of social oppression (see also Dei, 1996, 2005a, 2005b; Bonnett, 2000; Dei & Calliste, 2000). It consists of action-oriented strategies of transformative change that challenge (interrogate) the structure and dynamics of power, privilege, and social inequality (Hiranandani, 2012). A commitment to anti-racism reflects a level of direct involvement in combatting those cultural values, personal prejudices, discriminatory behaviours, institutional structures, and colonial practices that perpetuate racism (Dei, 2005a, 2005b) Anti-racism initiatives and programs dispute the legitimacy of those deracialized multicultural discourses that emphasize cultural awareness and attitude change as the basis for group harmony. Endorsed instead are initiatives focusing on those structures, ideologies, and practices that produce privilege and generate disadvantage (McCreary, 2009; Niemonen, 2007). In short, anti-racism liberates not by improving sensitivity and celebration through re-socialization. It emancipates and empowers by actively promoting social equality through challenges, resistance, and change. The range of anti-racism is formidable: on the one hand are those anti-racism initiatives that challenge racism by deconstructing its origins as a social problem, in addition to its patterns, functions, and outcomes. On the other hand, anti-racism consists of physical actions through protest, civil disobedience, and subversion by sabotage. In between are a series of personal tactics that take a stand against everyday racism.

Of course, articulating a strategy is one thing. For example, the Canadian government's anti-racism program, A Canada for All: Canada's Action Plan Against Racism, allocated $56 million over five years (2005–10). In acknowledging the need for initiatives to combat racism and racial discrimination, the program sought to ensure the full participation of all Canadians in society and economy through removal of race-related barriers in the workplace (Citizenship and Immigration, 2010). In a study cited by Cassin et al. (2007), provincial/territorial governments promoted the largest number of anti-racism initiatives, followed by various community organizations, although the federal government was the main funder for many of these education-based initiatives. But government priorities in recent years have shifted away from anti-racism initiatives toward the goal of social cohesion and economic opportunity (Citizenship and Immigration, 2010). Moreover, the implementation of an effective anti-racism program may prove something else, as demonstrated by a host of conflicting issues and contradictory contentions:

- First and foremost, racisms are not some singular phenomena that can be isolated for analysis or removal. On the contrary, racism intersects with sexism, classism, ethnocentrism, and ageism to amplify and complicate the challenge of reform. Hence any anti-racism activism must occur alongside efforts to simultaneously combat sexism, ethnocentrism, classism, and other forms of oppression (Dunn et al., 2007). Racisms not only overlap and intersect with the socio-economic structure and political culture of society, which, in turn, are inextricably linked to globalism and globalization (Sivanandan, 2007). The interplay of racism with classism and sexism are also systemic because as relations of power, they are deeply embedded and normalized within the operations of society (Ng, 1993).

- Second, and paradoxically, anti-racism initiatives are themselves perceived as racist in fostering yet more racism, Anti-racism actions are equated with racism when they engage in a practice called non-performativity, namely, promises that rarely deliver the goods in bringing about anticipated changes, in part because the very act of making a promise may be perceived as performing the action (Ahmed, 2006), in part because the performance is the promise. Recommendations to bring about changes through anti-racism initiatives are rarely implemented or enforced. And when they are, the moves lean toward the modest, such as establishing yet another non-performativity agency like a human rights office (Henry, 2004). Finally, anti-racism initiatives can get locked into outdated or inappropriate categories, with the result that some strategies may work well for certain groups, while others may intensify patterns of prejudice and discrimination.
- Third and related to the second point is Canadians' refusal to take problems seriously because of a sense of smug superiority. As Chapters-Indigo announces with its slogan "the world needs more Canada," Canada is so progressive and Canadians are such an enlightened species that the world would be a better place if everyone was more like "us" (Simpson, 2009). The consequences of this "unsinkable moral superiority" are a belief that (1) the situation is fine in Canada; (2) change is unnecessary—after all, why tamper with success; and (3) the world has nothing to teach us when it comes to doing anti-racism.
- Fourth, what should anti-racisms programs look like? Should the goal of anti-racism be to treat everyone the same regardless of difference (universalism)? For example, Canada's Employment Equity program is based on the assumption that all racialized people are subject to the same discrimination and racism as women, people with disabilities, and Aboriginal peoples (Kymlicka in Jimenez, 2012). Or should it be rethought to take differences into account, insofar as the principles of justice and equality are compromised by treating everyone on a level playing field (particularism) (see Woolley, 2013)? A sensitivity to systemic bias is critical here: If an otherwise neutral program reflects flawed assumptions and power imbalances, the effects and consequences of such programs invariably perpetuate and even exacerbate inequalities (powell, 2009). Finally, the anti-racism struggle has evolved over time. Once it may have challenged the state's denial of widespread and institutionalized racism. Now it is contesting the state's denial of its own complicity in creating racism (Burnett, 2013a).
- Fifth, where does one draw the anti-racism line? Societies such as Canada are layered in contradictions. As societies become more diverse and inclusive, they must grapple with the dual prospect of restricting racist speech and associations to protect diversities, yet preserve core constitutional values related to freedom of speech and association (Bleich & Lambert, 2013). Or as Brian Lee Crowley (2013) points out in his response to the crisis over a proposed Charter of Quebec Values, a relatively neutral state is a priority in a multicultural society if it is to

effectively arbitrate conflicts among different groups while enforcing rules in a reasonably impartial manner. The principle of anti-racism is similarly challenged by the demands of reconciling individual freedoms with collective rights. How, then, to balance these values when confronted by those who use liberal democratic freedoms to justify their racist acts (Bleich, 2011)? Do racists have a right to freely speak in public consistent with the principle of freedom of expression? Or does such a concession run the risk of normalizing repugnant views inconsistent with the realities of a diverse society (Runnymede Trust, 2012)?

This chapter is predicated on the premise that if people knew how racisms worked, they could be reduced through anti-racism intervention. However straightforward, this challenge is complicated by growing awareness that racism is deeply personal and often unconscious (subliminal racism) or that it is institutionalized and systemically embedded in the foundational principles and normal routines of mainstream institutions. The chapter begins by looking at the different levels of anti-racism strategies. References to individual and institutional anti-racism frameworks are shown to reflect diverse problem definitions commensurate with the different sectors of racisms examined in Section 2. An inclusive anti-racism seeks to build on the strengths of both of these frameworks while overcoming limitations in each of these approaches. A comparison of the principles of multicultural education and anti-racist schooling provides additional insights into the logic behind anti-racism. This analysis is followed by demonstrating how anti-racism initiatives are themselves internally conflicted over what to do, why, and how with respect to the principles of universalism or particularism. No more so, it is argued, than in the contested domain of black-focus schools against the backdrop of a broader debate involving the politics of multiculturalism.

Anti-racisms: Different Levels, Varying Strategies

Understanding the nature of racisms is crucial in developing an effective intervention strategy (Bhavnani et al., 2005). Racisms framed as personal require more individual anti-racism strategies; those framed along organizational lines require institutional responses; and those that reflect society at large require macro-solutions. Three anti-racism strategies can be discerned: individual, institutional, and inclusive. The first is concerned with modifying individual attitudes and behaviour through law, education, or interaction; the second with eliminating the systemic roots of organizational racism by removing discriminatory barriers; the third combines both individual and institutional strategies into an inclusive anti-racism package that capitalizes on the strengths of each while neutralizing their weaknesses or omissions (Fleras, 2012).

Individual Anti-racisms

Taken at its most obvious level, racism is normally envisaged as a personal problem of hatred, fear, or ignorance (Fleras, 2012). There is an element of truth to this assertion. Racism is often expressed through the thoughts and actions of individuals who dislike others because of differences or perceived threats. As a result, anti-racism strategies must focus on challenging and changing individual behaviours based on prejudice, ethnocentrism, and stereotyping. Three of the more common personal anti-racism strategies for improvement are *interaction, education,* and *law*.

Contact and Interaction. Learning through contact and interaction represents one technique for individual anti-racism change. Interaction with others is proposed for removing prejudicial barriers arising from ignorance and replacing them with insight and sensitivity. But contact in its own right is not necessarily beneficial. It is doubtful whether racism is reduced by the thousands of tourists who escape to the Caribbean each winter. Improvement is unlikely in contexts where interactional patterns tend to recolonize the gap between the haves and the have-nots. The degree of resentment and contempt escalates over time under these potentially degrading circumstances by virtue of reconstituting the colonialist patterns of servitude and deference.

In short, reducing racism through interaction varies with the quality of interaction. For any positive effect, interaction must be conducted between individuals who are relatively equal in status, who collaborate on a common endeavour in a spirit of trust and respect, whose interaction receives some degree of institutional and societal support, and who derive mutual benefit from co-operation of sufficient frequency and duration to foster a working relationship (Jaret, 1995). Interaction between unequals outside a supportive context simply upholds the status quo by perpetuating stereotypes in a negatively charged environment. Or, to put it bluntly, service-type interactions with the support staff at a Caribbean resort are unlikely to bring about positive changes, but more likely to reinforce stereotypes and patterns of inequality.

Legal Intervention. Recourse to law is sometimes upheld as an effective personal deterrent. Laws exist in Canada that prohibit the expression of racial discrimination against vulnerable minorities. The scope of these laws is broad. Some legal measures consist of protection for identifiable minorities through restrictions on majority behaviour. For example, the Supreme Court of Canada has ruled repeatedly that prohibition of hate literature is a justifiable and reasonable limitation on the freedom of speech. Other measures are aimed at removing discriminatory barriers that preclude minority participation within society. On the assumption that most individuals are law-abiding because of the threat of punishment or social ostracism, passage of anti-racism laws focuses on promoting behaviour in outward compliance with the letter of the law. Passage of these and related laws is not intended to alter people's attitudes or conviction, at least not in the short term. A democratic society such as Canada entitles people to their own private thoughts, however repugnant or anti-social. Over time, however, people may realign their beliefs to match their behaviour in hopes of reducing the dissonance between thought and action.

Education and Training. It is widely assumed that education (or training) can diminish racism. According to this line of thinking, racism arises because of ignorance or irrationality. The cure lies in educating people to realize the errors of their ways. Once aware of their mistakes, people are deemed sufficiently rational to make the appropriate adjustments. This notion of enlightenment through learning has put schools in the vanguard of institutions for challenging racism. Milder versions of multicultural education propose modifying individual attitudes through exposure to diversity. Yet there are difficulties in defending the transformative properties of education in challenging racism. Gloria Yamato (2001) captures the futility of quick-fix solutions to a complex problem that has taken centuries to grow, take root, invade space, and morph into variations:

> Many believe that racism can be dealt with effectively in one hellifying workshop, or one hour long heated discussion.... I've run into folks who really think that we can beat this devil, kick this habit, be healed of this disease in a snap. In a sincere blink of a well-intentioned eye, presto—poof—racism disappears. "I've dealt with my racism ... (envision a laying on of hands) ... Hallelujah! Now I can go to the beach." Well fine, go to the beach.

Harder versions of multicultural education encourage individuals to look inside themselves, to examine their own racism and privileged positions, to see how the dominant sector exercises power over racialized minorities, and to take responsibility for the disempowerment of others (McIntosh, 1988). Admittedly, while most white people can see and sympathize with victims of racism, many are incapable of equating whiteness with advantages. They are equally reluctant to see how their privilege is directly and structurally connected with the disempowerment and exploitation of those at the wrong end of racism (Bishop, 2005). Or, to put it in a slightly different way, the hardest thing to change is the attitude you don't know you have (Mistry & Latoo, 2009, p. 22). With whiteness as the engine that drives racism (Doane, 2007), Yamato (2001, p. 153) provides some hard-hitting advice for white folk in the anti-racism struggle when she writes:

You can educate yourself via research and observation rather than rigidly, arrogantly relying solely on interrogating people of color. Do not expect that people of color should teach you how to behave non-oppressively.... Know that you'll make mistakes and commit yourself to correcting them and continuing on as an ally, no matter what.

Finally, critics argue that too many institutions have responded to issues of inequality by promoting an often tepid "diversity" framework with its focus on culture rather than the political and economic structures (Jensen, 2005, 2010a). Yes, there is much to commend in understanding the richness of cultural differences. Yet a focus on culture-based diversity training runs the risk of glossing over how power differences and structural barriers generate the unequal distribution of valued resources. Deployment of a safe and easy multicultural (diversity) training may address an administrator willingness to comply with mission statements and non-prejudicial practices. But it does little to challenge and change the prevailing (and often illegitimate) distribution and hierarchy of power, privilege, and property. Nevertheless, the benefits of rehabilitating the mindset should never be underestimated, and the next case study provides insight into how education about racism can prove to be life-transforming.

CASE STUDY

Racializing Eye Colour as Anti-racism: The Eye of the Storm

In the wake of Martin Luther King Jr.'s assassination in 1968 and disturbed by the calmly racist comments of her pupils, a third-grade teacher in Riceville, Iowa, conducted a simple but effective exercise within an all-white classroom (ABC News, 1970). Jane Elliot sought to deconstruct the nature of prejudice, bigotry, and discrimination, while conveying Martin Luther King's notion that the content of a person's character should be more important than the colour of a person's skin. Elliot wanted to impress on her students the ease with which people (1) assign a social worth on the basis of seemingly irrelevant characteristics over which they had no control; (2) explain behaviour in terms of a physical attribute; and (3) construct a reward system around a baseless distinction. But instead of simply telling the children that prejudice and discrimination are wrong—after all, we have been told repeatedly that racism is wrong and yet still continue to practise or tolerate it— she wanted her students to find out personally and deeply about the meaning of discrimination, its experience in everyday life, and its impact on those who were the most vulnerable.

The exercise ran as follows. On the first day, Elliot divided her third-grade pupils into two groups on the basis of eye colour (blue versus brown), and rewarded them accordingly. The blue-eyed children (as proxy for whites) were defined as superior to the brown-eyed (a proxy for blacks). They received extra privileges both in class and during recess, while even normal routines were withheld from the brown-eyed, who quickly developed a sense of self-loathing and fear. As Elliot points out, the blue-eyed children relished their new empowerment and enthusiastically played along by sharply enforcing the penalties against the brown-eyed. During recess, children resorted to name-calling on the basis of eye colour. Some children even got into fights when teased about their "brown-eyedness." Within the space of fifteen minutes, Elliot observed, "these marvellous, cooperative, wonderful, thoughtful children turned into nasty, vicious, discriminating little third-graders." More important, the distinction appeared to influence test scores. The blue-eyed children scored much higher than usual in daily quizzes compared to the previous class; conversely, the scores of brown-eyed children plummeted.

The brilliance of Elliot's experiment did not end there. The next day Elliot reversed the exercise by announcing a "mistake": It was the brown-eyed children who were superior to the blue-eyed children. Accordingly, it would be the brown-eyed children with the privileges, while the blue-eyed children would go to the end of the line. This role reversal had the "desired effect." For the brown-eyed children, it was payback time, and they eagerly pounced on the opportunity to punish the blue-eyed children for the previous day's inflictions. The same children who had been oppressed the day before quickly assumed the oppressors' role, and vice versa. Predictably, the brown-eyed children did much better in classroom quizzes; the scores of the blue-eyed children declined accordingly.

What can we learn from this experiment? *First*, when social reality is involved, if people define situations as real, they become real in their consequences. The notion that the world can be arbitrarily racialized into fixed and bounded categories (races—with each possessing an assemblage of physical and biological attributes that determine thought and behaviour—has long been discredited by all but a handful of social scientists. Although the concept of race has no empirical or scientific validity, people continue to act as if it does, with an attendant set of negative consequences (from slavery to genocide) for those who are racialized. Similarly, there is no scientific justification for racializing the world into blue and brown eyes, then claiming that one is superior to another. Nevertheless, the dearth of empirical reality did not preclude the creation of some very real consequences for the children. *Second*, there is the idea of a self-fulfilling prophecy. Blue-eyed children, who were defined as superior, excelled in class quizzes unlike the brown-eyed, who did poorly. The next day, the brown-eyed, who were re-racialized as superior, dramatically improved their scores. The speed with which the students adopted and played out their new social identities is both riveting yet disconcerting (Anderssen, 2013). The conclusion: If people are labelled as inferior, they will act according; conversely, if they are defined as superior, people will act successfully. Applied to the real world where this labelling is routinely and constantly enforced, racialized minorities who are deemed to be inferior will assume patterns of inferiority. *Third*, there is the subliminality of racism. While Elliot had hoped to teach the children a lesson about racism, it was clear that they had already internalized notions of

(1) prejudice and discrimination, (2) the unequal distribution of privilege in society, and (3) how some possessed the power to define what counts as difference, and what differences count. Their ability to quickly adapt to and play the role of "master/slave" is not only a testimony to the power of socialization, it also serves as a warning of the challenges in erasing deeply embedded patterns of prejudice and racism.

The story doesn't end here. According to Elliot, the exercise in racializing eye colour may have proven to be a wake-up call for her students (in a follow-up documentary in 1985, the 1970 class, now adults, acknowledged how profoundly the experiment had changed their lives). But the residents of this predominantly white Christian town of one thousand were often less enchanted. Jane and her students were harassed, even called "nigger lovers," while a family-owned business was boycotted by community dissidents. Jane moved away following the death of her father, and was advised by her mother never to return because of continued town antagonism. Rather than be deterred by this hostility, Jane Elliot went on to conduct these exercises in corporations and university settings. As with her schoolchildren, corporate participants are labelled as inferior or superior on the basis of an arbitrary characteristic, then the temporarily favoured group gets to taunt the the inferior minority, often with equally powerful impact. In 2004 she brought this exercise to Canada by way of a documentary entitled *Indecently Exposed*, which explored the racist attitudes toward Aboriginal peoples. And this hatred of racism persists. In an interview in a 2006 issue of *New Scientists*, Jane Elliot, now seventy-three, continues to crusade against the injustices that classify, rank, and deny or reward people on the basis of arbitrary traits.

Multicultural Education versus Anti-racist Schooling: Competing Solutions?

Debates over multiculturalism versus anti-racism[1] as a solution to the problem of racisms never cease to provoke (Ghosh & Abdi, 2004). On one side are those who believe that racism is primarily an individual problem that can be solved by working with the system to change attitudes through multicultural initiatives. In contrast to this predominantly conservative/liberal approach are more explicit anti-racisms strategies. According to the rationale behind anti-racism, racism is fundamentally structural and systemic, hence any proposed solution must focus on transforming the institutional framework of society by removing discriminatory barriers and power differentials.

To put this debate into perspective, consider the contrasts between multicultural education versus anti-racist schooling. A commitment to multicultural education represents a significant shift from the past when a monoculturalism agenda prevailed, with schooling of children largely inseparable from their absorption as hard-working and God-fearing Christians (Alladin, 1996). This can come as no surprise; after all, Canada (like Australia and New Zealand) originated as a local outpost for British cultural expansion, with a corresponding goal to assimilate both the indigenes and immigrants into the colonial hierarchy of cultural power (Jakubowicz, 2005). But schooling and education are now widely committed to the principles of multicultural inclusiveness, albeit relying on different models. On one side are models of multicultural education, with their emphasis on changing individual mindsets through exposure to cultural differences. On the other are anti-racist models that tend to focus on transforming systems by challenging those behaviours and structures that uphold prevailing patterns of power and privilege.

Multicultural education embraces a philosophy of personal change and attitude modification. It consists of activities and curricula that promote an awareness of diversity in terms of its intrinsic value to minorities or to members of society at large, namely, as a colourful add-on to an otherwise Eurocentric agenda (Zine, 2002). The aim of multicultural education is largely attitudinal—that is, to enhance individual sensitivity by improving knowledge about cultural differences (enrichment) and race relations (enlightenment). However progressive sounding, there is no proof that enriched or enlightened attitudes will prompt behavioural changes, much less rise to the challenge of contesting power, difference, and social inequality. Nor is there any evidence to suggest that a "sari, steel bands, and samosas" approach to multicultural education will address the major challenges in education at present, much less initiate reforms for creating schools where all children are valued and respected, feel a sense of belonging, and have access to education that responds to diverse needs of different students (Ghosh, 2002).

In brief, multicultural education strives to promote sensitivity to cultural differences and improve interaction with those perceived as culturally different. But shortcomings prevail because of what some call a "tourist gaze," or a "culinary approach," or a "mix-and-stir mentality" for understanding and valuing differences within a Eurocentric setting. Little is done to interrogate systems of economic power that marginalize minorities and Aboriginal peoples by inserting minority history months into the calendar, displaying ethnic art on walls, having ethnic performers at school assemblies, and including minority heroes and holidays in the curriculum. Nor does this approach do anything about (1) how differences came to be vested in hierarchies of power, (2) the reproduction of a culture of whiteness and white privilege in the classroom, (3) disrupting the normative whiteness of Canadian settler history, or (4) endowing students with the critical tools to challenge and transform an unequal status quo (McCreary, 2009; also Henry, 2004). Failure to address each of these issues raises an awkward question: To what extent is multiculturalism little more than a case of ruling elites controlling unruly "ethnics" because of its tendency to whitewash those histories of whiteness, violence, and racism that persevere (albeit more quietly) into the present? Rita Dhamoon (2009, p. 8) explains:

> Ultimately, liberal multicultural theories mask various issues of power, including (but not limited to) how histories of racial domination continue to shape difference today, why, how, and by whom liberal values are determined to be superior and how these are resisted and how the state regulates various modalities of difference.

By contrast, anti-racist schooling takes its cue from the principle of anti-racism activism—that is, a commitment to challenge, resist, and transform the system through meaningful involvement. Emphasis is on the identification and removal of racially discriminatory barriers at interpersonal and institutional levels both within schooling and outside of it (see also Weiner, 2012). Anti-racist schooling begins with the assumption that minority underachievement is not necessarily caused by cultural differences. It continues by questioning whether cross-cultural understanding can contribute to uprooting the structural roots of inequality without addressing issues of power and subordination (Kivel, 1996; Zine, 2002). Improving minority status is contingent on removing the behavioural dimensions and structural components of racial inequality both within and outside the education system, along with the power and privileges that sustain racism through institutional policies and protocols. Sweeping changes are paramount, in other words, rather than tinkering with multicultural add-ons. As Dei and Calliste (2000, p. 21) point out in differentiating multiculturalism from anti-racism:

> In other words, multiculturalism works with the notion of our basic humanness and downplays inequities of difference by accentuating shared commonalities. Anti racism, on the other hand, views as suspect the whole nation building enterprise as pursued by the dominant, together with the underlying assumptions of empathy, commonality, and good will. Anti racism shifts the talk away from tolerance of diversity to the pointed notion of difference and power. It sees race and racism as central to how we claim, occupy, and defend spaces. The task of anti racism is to identify, challenge, and change the values, structures, and behaviours that perpetuate systemic racism and other forms of societal oppressions.

Points of difference between multicultural and anti-racist schooling prevail, according to Dei and Calliste, despite the perils of classifying reality into binaries of oppositional thought:

> As a discourse and discursive practice, multiculturalism heralds the mosaic, cherishes diversity and plurality and promotes an image of multiple, thriving, mutually respectful and appreciative ethno cultural communities. The anti racism discourse highlights persistent inequities among communities, following on relations of domination and subordination.... To a multiculturalist the issue is one of lack of recognition of the positive contributions of minorities, which stems

from misunderstandings and miscommunication. An anti racist sees the issue starkly as entrenched inequities and power imbalance. Multiculturalism views the problem as manifest in intolerance and lack of goodwill. Anti racism troubles the manifestation of the problem as bias, discrimination, hatred, exclusion, and violence. Multiculturalism perceives prejudice as a violation of democratic rights. Anti racism perceives prejudice as an integral part of the social order. (Dei & Calliste, 2000, p. 21)

Anti-racist schooling can be defined as a proactive and process-oriented strategy that balances the value of difference with the politics of power sharing (Dei, 2000, 2007). It acknowledges how the Eurocentricity of *white-focus* schooling (a reminder that institutions are neither neutral nor value-free) can prove an alienating experience for minority children because of their exclusion from the curriculum, pedagogy, or administration (Zine, 2002). Promoted instead is a multi-centric education, one that captures multiple ways of knowing while challenging Eurocentricity as the sole source of knowledge and knowing (Dei & Calliste, 2000; Kuokkanen, 2009). Acknowledging the validity and value of all knowledge forms ensures that the historical achievements and realities of all traditions are examined, validated, and respected (Zine, 2002). Several processes are pivotal in advancing an anti-racist schooling: (1) an informed discourse that focuses on race and racism as issues of power and inequality rather than matters of cultural difference or personal prejudice; (2) a deconstruction of existing school practices to uncover the structural roots of monoculturalism and inequality; (3) a decentring of Eurocentric knowledge while incorporating minority perspectives into all aspects of teaching and learning; (4) challenging the status quo by fostering engagement and empowerment through political and social activism (Dei, 1996); and (5) politicizing education and schooling to uncover its foundational assumptions and structural inequalities (Dei, 2011). Table 11.1 provides an ideal-typical comparison of multicultural education and anti-racism schooling as competing strategies of change.

The table makes it abundantly clear: Anti-racist schooling differs from multicultural education, at least for purposes of analysis, if not necessarily in practice. An anti-racist schooling questions the foundational principles of education and schooling by challenging their racialized structures, functions, and processes. It calls into question the constitutional framework of schooling by politicizing the very basis of what passes for knowledge and ways of knowing. The pedagogy becomes political, as Giroux (1999) conceded, when exposing how the production of knowledge with respect to truths and truth-making has historically privileged some and disprivileged others. An anti-racist schooling ensures that both students and teachers are offered the opportunity to see how culture is organized, who is authorized

Table 11.1 Multiculturalism and Anti-racism: Oppositional Strategies of Change

	Multicultural Education	Anti-racist Schooling
Focus	Ethnicity/culture	Race/structure
Objective	Celebrate diversities	Dynamics of difference
Problem	Ethnocentrism/prejudice	Discrimination/racism
Solution	Address symptoms	Root causes
Goals	Changing individuals	Transforming the system
Means	Attitudes	Behaviour
Scope	Individuals	Institutions/culture
Style	Accommodative/reform	Challenge//transform
Outcome	Respecting differences	Promoting equity

to speak about different forms of culture, and which cultures are acceptable and which are unworthy of public esteem. They also come to understand the role of power in advancing the interests of dominant social relations; what needs to be done to challenge a Eurocentric constitutional order; and how these unequal relations can be transformed to create an inclusive Canada. Taken together, the goal of anti-racist schooling intends to delegitimize white privileges by discrediting the system of power relations that continue to deny or exclude.

Institutional Anti-racism

There is room for cautious optimism when discussing the effectiveness of individually tailored anti-racist programs. But are these individualized initiatives of sufficient scope to erase racism? Racism may be expressed in and through individuals (who may be regarded as precipitating causes), yet individuals are merely the conduits of racial antipathy. With individual anti-racism, the symptoms are addressed rather than the causes. Not surprisingly, personal solutions such as training or education are criticized as the equivalent of applying a bandage to a cancerous growth—compassionate and humane to be sure, but ultimately self-defeating in light of the magnitude of the disease.

Proposed instead is an institutional approach. According to this line of thinking, racism can be resolved only by attacking it at its source, namely, within the institutional structures that support a racialized society. Racism is not just about individuals with retrogressive beliefs or dormant prejudices. It is rooted instead in institutional structures that provide justifying ideologies and practices in those contexts where the social order revolves around the placement of minorities in racialized categories (Bonilla-Silva, 1997; Lopes & Thomas, 2006). To ensure fairness, institutional measures must be promoted to compensate for the historical and social disadvantages that prevent racialized minorities from competing on a more level playing field. The implications are clear: Just as the problem of racism must be addressed within the broader dimensions of political domination and economic control, so too must different assumptions and strategies be applied beyond those involving personal initiatives.

Institutional anti-racism activism includes direct action through protest or civil disobedience, boycotts, litigation, or legislation (Jaret, 1995). The politics of activism range in scope from those who want to work within the system, to those who prefer working outside of it, in the process raising the question of whether the house of racisms can be dismantled with conventional tools or must rely on unorthodox instruments. For some, pressure and radical change must be applied from without by challenging the rules upon which conventions are based, otherwise the danger of co-optation is ever present. For others, although racism is deeply embedded within institutional structures and often resistant to change, change from within is possible by using—with apologies to Audre Lord (1984, p. 112)—"the master's tools to dismantle the master's house"—by modifying the conventions that refer to the rules.

The diversification of Canada has made it abundantly clear. Institutions such as schooling and education are under pressure to become more accommodative if they aspire to be inclusive in the integration of migrant and minority children. The introduction of multicultural education as intervention has challenged how schools should relate to difference, while raising questions over the dynamics of formal education in a changing and diverse society. Striving to be inclusive of difference-based needs under multicultural education encompasses a variety of interventions to ensure that differences do not disadvantage minority students. Different styles of multicultural education can be observed, ranging in scope and comprehensiveness from "moderate" to more "radical" interventions, including: *enrichment (exposure to diverse customs), enlightenment (instruction about race and ethnic relations), embracive (improving the culture of the classroom), and empowerment* (Fleras, 2012). Of these, the empowerment models come closest to the principle of an anti-racist schooling model.

Most models of multicultural education concentrate on changing the mindsets of the entire student body. By contrast, an empowerment model is directed primarily at motivating and enhancing the academic outcomes of racialized and Aboriginal students. The minority-focus empowerment model reflects a belief that monocultural school systems are failing minority pupils. Minority students do not see themselves represented in a Eurocentric curriculum that rarely acknowledges their achievements and contributions to society. What minority students require is a customized curriculum that incorporates the values they bring to school for improving successful learning outcomes; a school context that capitalizes on minority strengths and learning styles as a basis for achievement; a platform for minority stories in their own voices; and a repudiation of Eurocentric knowledge as the only legitimate form of understanding (Kuokkanen 2009).

Empowerment models come in different shapes. On one side of the empowerment model is the creation of culturally safe places within the existing school system. On the other side is the creation of separate schools for minority pupils, such as Aboriginal youth or youth at risk (Brown, 2005). A minority-centred school provides an alternative learning environment by catering to students for whom mainstream schools are inappropriate even with thoughtful reforms (Dei, 1996, 2005a). It tends to endorse a child-centred approach to schooling in which the experiences, realities, and backgrounds of students become the focal point of education, as promoted by the Brazilian educator Paolo Freire, resulting in learning within familiar contexts alongside different ways of learning and knowledge. For example, an Africentric or African-focused school arrangement seeks to improve academic and social achievement for students at risk by emphasizing the centrality of black experiences in social history, by utilizing black role models as teachers and black teachers as role models, and by customizing content to appeal to those minority students who are alienated and disengaged from a Eurocentric educational system.

CASE STUDY

Black-Focus Schools: Fighting Racism with Race

The politics of race remains a social paradox. On the one hand, racially based distinctions that formerly stigmatized individuals as inferior or irrelevant now serve as marks of distinction for those marginalized groups who are transforming the stigma of oppression into a mark of pride, identity, or resistance (Lerner, 1997). On the other hand, the so-called race card may be played to foster public fears or to manipulate legal decisions that adversely affect minority women and men (Wallis & Fleras, 2008). On yet another hand, references to race may be used to solve problems on the grounds that if race is the problem, it must be part of the solution. For example, "Black Rage" defence strategies are predicated on the principle that the social context in which racialized minorities find themselves forges a state of mind that may induce criminal behaviour (Harris, 1999).

As many have stated (Dunn et al., 2007), two conceptual approaches to anti-racism prevail. One is universalism. With its focus on commonalities, universal human rights, and equality of treatment regardless of race, a universalistic approach is concerned with eliminating the relevance of race. The other is particularism. Particularism is committed to the fundamental plurality of racialized groups because of history and culture, together with special treatment to ensure collective identity and eradicate group inequality. It endorses the value and retention of racial difference, albeit as an aspect of equality and positive identity whereby racialized individuals and groups retain their distinctiveness within equalized power relations. Clearly, the first approach regards race as a problem that has no place in society; the other approach incorporates race as a tool for solving a racialized problem.

The politics of race as solution is captured in the debate over the validity and legitimacy of minority-focused schools (Gordon & Zinga, 2012). The alarmingly high failure rate of some black students in the Toronto school system is generating controversy, despite evidence that something needs to be done to avert the spiralling decline. According to Kristin Rushowy, the education reporter for the *Toronto Star*, more than one half of all young black males by the age of sixteen had fallen behind and had a strong likelihood of dropping out of school. In a 2006 study, 40 percent of students from the Caribbean catchment area did not complete Grade 12; the figures for students from East Africa and West Africa stood at 32 percent and 26 percent respectively. In that desperate times call for desperate measures, black-focus schools were regarded as a solution to the long-standing problem of black academic disengagement and underperformance in predominantly white-focus educational system. In September 2009, Sheppard Public School in North York inaugurated a pilot program establishing an Afrocentric alternative for students from kindergarten to Grade 8 that reflects, reinforces, and advances black experiences, realities, and aspirations in the curriculum, teaching practices, and school environment. In 2011, trustees voted to open a second Afrocentric alternative school to expedite an elementary-to-secondary pathway for students. (Ontario's first Afrocentric high school program at Scarborough's Winston Churchill Colleagiate Institute opened its doors to students in the fall of 2013 [Ferenc, 2013]).

Debates over the value of Afrocentric-infused education are proving to be polarizing: segregation versus integration, exclusive versus inclusive, anti- versus pro-multiculturalism, self-determination versus separation, empowerment versus marginalization, problem or solution (Dei & Kempf, 2013; Wallace, 2009). More specific questions include:

- Should the education system be divvied up on the basis of race and ethnicity (Walkom, 2008)?
- Are Afrocentric schools an anti-racist solution to the problem of racialized schooling? Or do they constitute a well-intentioned but misguided solution likely to generate yet more racism and racialized outcomes?

Some argue that establishing Afrocentric schools offers the best hope for improving black achievement, while providing black youth with choices to improve marks and morale. After all, if the problem of marginalization and unequal educational outcomes are the result of race, it stands to reason that race-specific programs should be part of the solution. Others reject the idea of black-focus schools because it seemingly condones a divisiveness and segregation at odds with the principles of an inclusive multiculturalism. Opponents fear that public funding of race-based schools may balkanize the school system without adequately preparing black students with skills needed in the outside world. By contrast, supporters insist on the importance of providing black students at risk with options beyond the standardized model of education. Determining the validity of each position is proving a tricky affair, especially since any race-based initiative often elicits controversy and discomfort (or outrage). Table 11.2 provides an overview of the arguments for and against the proposal.

Table 11.2: Contesting Black-Focus Schools

Against	For
Separatist in outcome	Inclusive in logic
Segregationist (blacks only)	Black students already de facto segregated
Slippery slope	Alternative schools already exist
Marginalize	Empower (eliminate issues of competition and belonging) + enhance engagement
Skills (hard/soft) = key to success + provincial standards within an Afrocentric framework	Identity = key to success
Defining rationale = race	Defining rationale = choice
Afrocentrism = problem	Eurocentric curriculum/pedagogy = problem
Reform as solution	Transformation as solution

The "For" side tends to frame the debate as one of choice for black youth at risk. In offering an alternative to a system failing an identifiable group, options are customized for those who have trouble fitting into a one-size-fits-all model system. The logic behind these Afrocentric schools, including more than a hundred in the United States, is predicated on a single platform: A Eurocentic focus of public education (from curriculum to administration) can be a profoundly alienating experience for those in a society pervaded by racism and stereotypes (Zine, 2002). What is required is an Afrocentric environment that not only makes curriculum more relevant and engaging but also secures a sense of engagement "to create a black community of positive adult role models; a kind of urban village that feels like family where children are guided to look past the negative caricatures of blacks in pop culture and see their future as players in the wider world" (Brown, 2007, p. ID3). Finally, proponents would argue that even politicizing the school by framing it as race-based is off the mark. More accurately, as others have noted, the school is defined by a set of principles or philosophies (from issues of equity and social justice to notions of personal and collective responsibility and relations) that should inform all forms of schooling.

The "Against" side prefers to frame the issue as one inconsistent with the integrative ethos of public schools systems, the inclusiveness of Canada's official multiculturalism, and the realities of an increasingly diverse and rapidly changing Canada. The danger of schooling by race is threefold: it risks confusing symptoms with causes; it attributes poor achievement levels to school failures while ignoring root factors beyond the control of curriculum; and it assumes that a stop-gap solution can solve a complex problem (Simpson, 2008; Strauss, 2008). And despite the creation of a special First Nations school by the Toronto School Board thirty years ago, including black-focused schools in the Greater Toronto Area as far back as 1935 (Gordon & Zinga, 2012, p. 4), there are fears of a slippery slope into segregation (Walkom, 2008). The option is to fix the entire school system by making it more inclusive through measures that are reflective of, respectful of, and responsive to "blackness" in Canada—in this case more black teachers, black-focused curriculum (from history to contributions to society), and learning styles.

In short, the debate over black-focus schools provides a litmus test for defining equality in a multicultural society. Does true equality arise from treating everyone the same, regardless of their differences? Or is it based on the principle of treating everyone as equals (differently) in achieving an equality of results precisely because of their differences? Is anti-racism inclusiveness about reforms that modify the existing system? Or is it about creating fundamental change by way of alternative institutions that reflect, reinforce, and advance minority interest, experiences, and outcomes? In that definitive answers to this debate don't exist, the politics over black-focus schools express yet another challenge in forging a living together with differences.

Toward an Inclusive Anti-racism

> *We cannot defeat race prejudice by proving that it's wrong. The reason for this is that race prejudice is only a symptom of a materialistic social fact ... the articulate white man's ideas about his racial superiority are rooted deeply in the social system and can be corrected only by changing the system itself.*
> —Oliver Cromwell Cox, *Caste, Class, and Race*

It is relatively easy to define racism as a personal problem. Common sense dictates that people are the cause of racism. People as individuals must reflect critically upon our degree of complicity in perpetuating racism through daily actions. But it is equally tempting to situate racism within a system of vast and impersonal forces that are largely beyond individual control. Such an approach runs the risk of relieving individuals of any responsibility. Neither of these positions is entirely correct. Individuals may not be the root cause of racism; nevertheless, racism is located within and carried by the person. Conversely, systems and structures may generate root causes; nonetheless, institutions do not exist apart from individuals who interact to create, support, maintain, and transform patterns of racism. Each of us must be held accountable for our actions, yet must take into account the social context in which we find ourselves. As Marx once said in *The Eighteenth Brumaire of Louis Bonaparte*, "Men make their own history, but they do not make it just as they please; they do not make it under circumstances chosen by themselves, but under circumstances directly found, given, and transmitted from the past."

Only an inclusive anti-racism approach can deliver the goods with any hope of success (Fleras, 2012). Inclusive anti-racist strategies acknowledge as source and solution the interplay of social forces and individual experiences. With its embrace of contextuality, connectedness, and simultaneity of unequal relations, an inclusive anti-racism acknowledges the interplay of structure with agency (Dei, 2005a, 2005b). Individual efforts to address racism and racial discrimination are essential, but must be supported by institutional mechanisms to be effective (James, 2007). It also recognizes the interlocking nature of oppression (Bishop, 2005). The interdependence of race, class, and gender as intertwined strands of a wider, more complex, and self-perpetuating system of privilege and power makes it abundantly clear: The purging of racism must be confronted holistically for creating an inclusive society based on the principle of living together with differences. Racialized minorities do not find themselves excluded because of race or class or gender. Rather, each of these inequities intersects with the other to amplify overlapping patterns of exclusion and denial. As well, an inclusive approach accepts the importance of framing anti-racism within a broader context. A commitment to anti-racism at the infrastructural level encourages a discourse that seeks to deconstruct (challenge, resist, and transform) institutional biases and barriers.

Note

1 A distinction between anti-racism education and anti-racist schooling is useful. Anti-racism education is about informing people of the need to challenge racism in society in general, education and schooling in particular. By contrast, anti-racist schooling is about taking direct action to create an education system that strives to be free of racism, racialized structures, and unequal power relations.

CHAPTER 12

OFFICIAL MULTICULTURALISM
ANTI-RACISM OR ANOTHER RACISM?

Introduction: The Paradoxes of Canadian Multiculturalism

Many are perplexed by the paradoxes that unsettle Canada's official multiculturalism (Fleras, 2009; Chazan et al., 2011; Haque, 2012). On one side, multiculturalism is perceived as a misguided idea that, unfortunately, is unfolding according to plan. On the other are those who believe that multiculturalism is a good idea gone bad because of twisted politics and diabolical interests. On yet another side is a belief in the inherent goodness of multiculturalism as an idea whose time is "prime." For some, multiculturalism is excessively radical in advocating transformative change; for others it is too reactionary in promising more than it can deliver; for still others, multiculturalism has proven irrelevant regardless of what it does or doesn't do because of intrinsic flaws; and for others still, there are salvageable strengths to be admired alongside exploitable weaknesses (see also Nagle, 2009). Approaches to accommodating differences are no less conflicted. Any multiculturalism that takes differences too seriously is criticized for compromising commitments to equality, inclusion, and national unity. Conversely, one that doesn't take differences seriously enough is chided for compromising people's identities under the guise of hegemonic universalism. Finally, multiculturalism may claim to be inclusive-driven by ensuring that no one is excluded from full and equal participation on grounds of race or ethnicity. Paradoxically, however, a commitment to inclusiveness through diversity accommodation may have the (un)intended effect of reinforcing a racialized status quo.

No matter how revered or reviled, an official multiculturalism is inescapably prone to paradoxes in securing those inclusionary principles for living together with differences. The ambiguous and largely undefined nature of multiculturalism subjects it to questioning and debate (Chazan et al., 2011). Should multiculturalism be framed as an ally of Western universalism? An excuse for ethnic enclaves? A hegemonic device in which the ruling elites control the unruly ethnics? A Canada-building project? A futile exercise full of sound and fury, signifying nothing? A transformational governance in the making (Sharma, 2011)? A commitment to a state multiculturalism has proven two-edged: Its stature as policy and program may enhance national unity, social cohesion, cultural respect, and sense of belonging. But its status as a blank screen upon which people project their fears (and fantasies) may also foster divisiveness, alienation, and racism, in part because of the unintended consequences that often accompany well-intentioned initiatives (Reitz, 2009). Media are to blame as well for ramping up the confusion. Too often news media accuse multiculturalism of anything that goes wrong in minority communities with the result it bears the brunt of negativity by association or default.

Of those paradoxes that pervade multiculturalism, few have generated as much controversy as the puzzling persistence of racism in a multicultural Canada (Henry & Tator, 2010; Chazan et al., 2011). Why does racism persevere in an ostensibly colour-blind yet culturally sensitive society that supposedly embraces the principles of tolerance, respect, and inclusion (see also Forrest & Dunn, 2007)? How to account for the slew of mutating and proliferating racisms in a multicultural milieu that explicitly espouses an anti-racism plank through removal of discriminatory barriers? What is the role of multiculturalism in sustaining racism in a neo-liberal era (Lentin & Titley, 2011)? How can Canadians embrace multiculturalism as a defining characteristic of an inclusive Canada yet also appear so oblivious and/or indifferent to pervasive patterns of racisms? Responses to these questions pivot around yet another set of queries: *Does an official multiculturalism challenge racisms in Canada (multiculturalism as anti-racism)? Or is it more inclined to reflect and reinforce existing Canadian racism and racialized inequalities (a racist multiculturalism)? Or should it be framed as a form of racism in its own right because of what it doesn't do (multicultural racism)?* Answers to these paradoxes framed as questions are highly varied, with varying responses aligned from left to right along the political spectrum. Those on the right accuse multiculturalism of fostering more racism by encouraging race-based collectivities that restrict individual choices while undermining the goal of national unity (Berliner & Hull, 1995). Those on the left dismiss multiculturalism as little more than a racialized opiate that narcotizes (dulls, distracts, conceals) the masses against the reality of historical and structural inequalities (Thobani, 2010). The fact that an official multiculturalism originated as a political act to achieve political goals in a politically acceptable manner reinforces its hegemonic status as a discourse in defence of dominant ideology (see Chazan et al., 2011). Those in the middle are prone to dither and duck depending on which way the political winds are blowing. But any meaningful assessment must make a critical distinction if there is to be any hope of disentangling the issues. That is, it must distinguish what an official multiculturalism says it is doing (inclusive model) from what it really does (hegemonic model).

Canada's model of official multiculturalism is not what it appears to be. On the surface, the ethos of Canada's multiculturalism is unabashedly inclusionary in fostering the ideals of tolerance toward difference, protecting cultural rights and a culture of rights, reducing prejudice, removing discriminatory barriers, eliminating ethnocentrism/Eurocentrism, enhancing equitable access to services, expanding institutional accommodation, improving creative intergroup encounters, and advancing citizenship (Citizenship and Immigration, 2012; Kymlicka, 2008a, 2008b). Multiculturalism strives to accommodate cultural claims in the public sphere as part of a balancing act that incorporates the goals of universal human rights, formal social equality, and an inclusive citizenship (Nagle, 2009). In reality, however, a fundamentally different picture emerges because of the reality gap between the ideal (what multiculturalism says it does) and the real (what it really does). The foundational logic of an official multiculturalism is hegemonic and controlling. Its primary objective is to depoliticize ethnicity by making Canada safe *from* diversities and difference as well as safe for difference and diversities (May & Sleeter, 2010; Fleras, 2009). The implications are sobering if taking a cue from critical race theorists, who argue that society and institutions are organized by, for, and about a white superiority complex. Multiculturalism represents a racism in its own right by taking differences too seriously or not seriously enough. In fostering the illusion of inclusion, multiculturalism also generates new racisms by cloaking the dynamics of racialized social order behind a slurry of platitudinous bromides (Chazan et al., 2011). Grace-Edward Galabuzi (2011, pp. 74–75) nails it nicely when he writes:

> Canadian multiculturalism policy acknowledged the demands of a more inclusive society and the reality of cultural difference, but did not fully break with the monocultural concept of Canadian society. The contradictions and limits inherent in the policy simply overwhelmed it. The dominant liberal ideology presented it as neutral, equating the experiences of all cultural groups and privileged cultural celebration as a positive expression of difference. Moreover it attempted to solve questions of racial difference within a liberal frame that would also secure capitalist relations. Its impact was to obscure race, class, and gender as key determinants of the marginalization, structural oppression, exploitation, and exclusion faced by racialized people in Canada. The privileging of symbolic celebration of cultural difference, then,

had the effect of displacing claims and contestations of exclusion by subaltern racialized populations.

In other words, the hegemony of multiculturalism reinforces racial hierarchies by ignoring the historical inequities of race and ethnic relations (Srivastava, 2007), while sustaining processes of neo-colonialism related to capital accumulation and exploitation of racialized women and men (Chazan et al., 2011; Galabuzi, 2011). Multiculturalism also serves as an instrument in which white power structures are reconstituted by the Canadian state in a politically palatable manner (Thobani, 2007). That Canada's official multiculturalism is inextricably linked to the politics of racism points to the inescapable. Both racism and multiculturalism are thought to be mutually constitutive of each other in ways that amplify the paradox of a distinctive Canadian racism in a multicultural Canada.

This paradox of multiculturalism as progressively inclusive yet potentially exclusionary reinforces a point of contention. Canada's official multiculturalism suffers from a dearth of critical analysis for distinguishing the *ideal* (what an official multiculturalism says it is doing in combating racism) from the *real* (what it is really doing in perpetuating a racialized and racist Canada) (Wood & Gilbert, 2005). Two lines of argument demonstrate the Janus-faced logic of an official multiculturalism. First, a *multicultural racism*: An official multiculturalism constitutes a form of racism in its own right because of its conflicted approach to diversity. Multiculturalism is racism because it doesn't take diversities and differences seriously enough (a pretend pluralism), thus marginalizing minority identities and interests while mainstreaming those of the privileged and powerful. It also constitutes a form of racism because differences are taken too seriously by (1) essentializing cultures as static, homogeneous, and determining; (2) singling out racialized minorities for preferential treatment based on race; (3) condoning seemingly illiberal practices at the expense of individual rights and core values; and (4) ghettoizing minorities into silos of difference that marginalize and exclude, while compromising Canada's liberal democratic traditions in the process (Mansur, 2011; Pacquet, 2008). Second, a racist *multiculturalism* exists because of its complicity in securing a racialized status quo. A commitment to multiculturalism reflects, reinforces, and advances a racialized Canada by virtue of depoliticizing differences, glossing over prevailing patterns of power and privilege, emphasizing cultural differences over structural barriers, refusing to challenge a systemic bias, and casting minorities as problems of cultural integration (see also Lentin & Titley, 2011; Srivastava, 2007). Its racist roots are also revealed when conservative-leaning critics accuse multiculturalism of privileging collective rights over individual rights to the detriment of both liberal values and notions of national unity, security, and identity.

Clearly, then, this admittedly complex relationship between multiculturalism and racism raises a number of questions in need of answers, including:

- Is there a distinct multicultural racism?
- How is it uniquely expressed?
- How does racism work in a multicultural Canada?
- How do multicultural discourses define issues of race, racism, and anti-racism (CRRF, 2008)?
- Should multiculturalism be framed as an anti-racist solution to Canada's racism problem? Or is it an expression of racism in its own right? Or is it racist in reinforcing rather than challenging racialized distributions of power and wealth?
- What is it about an official multiculturalism in a racialized Canada that redefines how racism works, contributes to the proliferation and perseverance of racism, and generates new ways of talking about racism?

To put these questions to the test, the chapter begins by analyzing official multiculturalism in Canada, continues by theorizing Canadian multicultural models, demonstrates how an official multiculturalism is interpreted as racist because of ambiguities in managing cultural diversities, and concludes by discussing multiculturalism as the quintessential expression of a made-in-Canada racism. This chapter is predicated on the premise that references to multiculturalism provide a conceptual lens for analyzing a key contradiction in Canadian society, namely, racism as simultaneously rejected yet at once reproduced in a post-racial Canada that claims to be both multicultural yet colour-blind (Pitcher, 2009). The chapter makes it abundantly clear: There are consequences to pay when acknowledging Canada's official multiculturalism as "more racism" rather than "anti-racism." The very instrument for improving the prospects for living together differently may perversely end up doing the exact opposite.

Theorizing Canada's Official Multiculturalism: Inclusive versus Hegemonic

Canada's official multiculturalism can be theorized along two lines. An inclusive model is based on theorizing what Canada's multiculturalism openly says it is doing in advancing as progressive multicultural governance. A literal and liberal reading of Canada's official multiculturalism embraces a commitment to the society-building principles of inclusiveness through removal of prejudicial and discriminatory barriers. An inclusive multiculturalism commits to anti-racism as well, at least by intent (principle) if not in consequence (practice). By contrast, there is another narrative (or model) that can be discerned from reading between the lines of what is said or done. A hegemonic model reflects a level of theorizing that focuses on what multiculturalism is really doing in terms of its hidden agenda. This points to the possibility of an official multiculturalism as racist in consequence and a form of racism in its own right.

Inclusive Model: Multiculturalism as Anti-racism

Canada's official multiculturalism upholds the concept of an inclusive multicultural model (Fleras, 2009). An inclusive multiculturalism promotes the feasibility of a Canada of many cultures as a basis for living together with differences as long as certain rules are in place, including: (1) the dominant culture is willing to move over and make space for differences; (2) minorities have a right to identify with the culture of their choice without incurring a penalty when partaking of Canadian society; (3) cultural differences are tolerated and respected provided they are lawful, respect people's rights, and uphold constitutional values; (4) everyone agrees to the principle of agreeing to disagree as a basis for (dis)agreement; and (5) minorities must be treated equally (the same) as a matter of routine, although they may receive treatment as equals (differently) when the situation arises.

The principle of inclusiveness applies an anti-racist spin to Canada's multicultural model. A commitment to ensure that no one is excluded from equal participation regardless of race and ethnicity qualifies as anti-racist, at least in intent if not always in practice or consequences. But an inclusive multiculturalism is prone to ambiguities. According to the universalism implicit in this model, our commonalities as rights-bearing and morally autonomous individuals outweigh any racially based group differences, at least for the purposes of recognition and reward, in effect making ethnicity irrelevant as a mark of distinctiveness or distribution. Yes, everyone is entitled to identical (equal) treatment, regardless of who or why because all individuals are equal before the law. Yet there is a downside to this inclusionary pattern that equates sameness with equality. The application of identical treatment to unequal contexts may well have the unintended effect of freezing an unequal status quo. To overcome the tyranny of sameness (treating unequals equally = inequality), a commitment to equitable treatment (treatment as equals) acknowledges the accommodation of difference-based needs. Even group-customized temporary measures may be introduced under an inclusive multiculturalism, including special provisions for language, education, employment, and health care along ethnic lines. Nevertheless, these concessions are neither institutionalized nor racialized, but intended primarily as a temporary measure for addressing the disadvantaged needs of racialized people.

An official multiculturalism is about creating an inclusive Canada where no one is excluded from democratic citizenship and equal participation because of his or her race or ethnicity. Under an inclusive multiculturalism, ethnicity is no longer employed to hierarchically rank Canadians or to arbitrarily exclude them because they lacked so-called founding nation groups' status (i.e., English and French). With multiculturalism in tow, cultural differences are thus transformed into a discourse about *social justice* by prioritizing a commitment to institutional inclusiveness through the removal of discriminatory barriers. Several conclusions follow: First, Canadian multiculturalism is *not* about celebrating differences but about society-building through removal of prejudicial perceptions and discriminatory barriers. Trudeau himself expressed disappointment in how multiculturalism had abandoned its original inclusive intentions when "twisted to celebrate a newcomer's country of origin and not a celebration of the newcomer becoming part of the Canadian fabric" (cited in Cobb, 2005). Second, Canada's commitment to an inclusive multiculturalism is consistent with anti-racism goals: to ensure that all Canadians are fully participating and equally included regardless of their differences. Consider, for example, how the legitimacy of anti-racism initiatives is predicated on changing mainstream attitudes toward acceptance and inclusion. Third, multiculturalism is about managing diversity to ensure inclusion and integration. It was never intended to be a transformational discourse for redefining what is normal, acceptable, and dominant (Comack, 2011).

In short, Canada's inclusive multiculturalism model operates at two intersecting levels: the micro (individual) and the macro (national). Under a micro-level multiculturalism, everyone has the right to be treated equally (the same) regardless of their differences; as well, everybody also has the right to be treated differently (as equals) when required precisely because of their difference-based needs. The effect of ignoring such differences under the guise of colour-blindness may be unjust and inegalitarian (Ghosh, 2011). A macro-level multiculturalism secures the social climate for a society-building governance. The objective is to create an inclusive (non-exclusionary) Canada without undermining either the interconnectedness of the whole (status quo) or the distinctiveness of the parts (Haque, 2012). Diversities are endorsed, to be sure, albeit only to the extent they are equivalent in status, reflect needs rather than culture per se, subject to similar treatment, stripped of history or context, embrace a liberal universalism belief in the essential commonality of all individuals, and accept Canada's self-proclaimed prerogative for defining what constitutes acceptable differences. In advancing the goals of Canada-building through inclusiveness, Canadian multiculturalism is anti-racist in theory, if not necessarily in reality or practice.

A Hegemonic Model of Multiculturalism: Yet More Racism

The foundational logic of Canada's official multiculturalism is arguably hegemonic (Chazan et al., 2011): Multiculturalism constitutes a managerial strategy devised to depoliticize diversity in securing a dominant culture while advancing a Canada-building project that limits diversity to symbolic rather than political forms (Srivastava, 2007; Mackey, 2002). The disruptiveness of difference is depoliticized by the clever expedient of either institutionalizing (co-opting) differences or privatizing them into the personal. Emphasis is focused on neutering potentially troublesome constituents by channelling their decontextualized cultural fragments into relatively harmless avenues of identity or folklore. The potency of diversity is defused through the homogenizing of diversities around the singular commonality of Canadian-Canadian cultural core (Mackey, 2002), so that everyone is *similarly different* (different in the same way) rather than *differently similar* (different but equal). But the displacement of race as popular discourse and critical analysis under multiculturalism does little to dislodge race as an organizing principle of life and society (Galabuzi, 2011). Diversities and difference are further depoliticized (or neutered) by banishing culturally charged symbols from public places to ensure that differences don't disrupt the status quo (see also Kundnani, 2007a). Failure of multiculturalism to interrogate power relations and promote structural changes prompts George Sefa Dei (2000, p. 304) to write scathingly:

> Canadian multiculturalism promotes values such as accommodation, appreciation, commonality, and good will. But this commitment reflects a flawed assumption, namely, "[W]e start from a relatively level playing field that we have access to similar resources and we have comparable values, aspirations, and concerns. Nothing could be further from the reality of those racialized minorities in our community."

A hegemonic model of official multiculturalism can be construed as racist because of its controlling logic. A commitment to transformative social change is displaced by a focus on absorbing (assimilating) minorities into the framework of a racialized Canada without moving over to make meaningful space. Over forty years of official multiculturalism notwithstanding, Canada and Canadians appear reluctant to disengage from the paramountcy of white superiority as a national norm of Anglo privilege and cultural dominance (Thobani, 2007; also Forrest & Dunn, 2007). Embraced instead is a commitment to construct consensus by depoliticizing diversities, in the process conveying the seemingly counterintuitive idea of multiculturalism as a form of neo-racism (Sharma, 2011, p. 96). Two consequences flow from this "illusion of inclusion"—that is, embracing differences without making a difference. First, official multiculturalism has reinforced the ongoing racialization of Canada by rejecting the legitimacy of deep diversities for recognition or reward. Second, official multiculturalism is essentially a hegemonic exercise that rarely disrupts the Eurocentric foundational principles of a racialized constitutional order. It inadvertently, perhaps, promotes a colour-blind and post-racial mentality that eclipses the significance of race, especially at institutional levels (see also Abrams & Moio, 2009).

The politics of hegemony make it abundantly clear: The central mission of an official multiculturalism is the creation of an inclusive Canada without disrupting the status quo and the corresponding distribution of power and privilege (Fleras, 2009). Far from being a threat to the social order, in other words, Canada's multiculturalism constitutes a discourse in defence of dominant ideology, with policies and initiatives that subordinate minority needs to national interests. Depending on where one stands on the political spectrum, such an assessment is cause for concern or a balm of contentment.

INSIGHT

Multiculturalism and Anti-racism as Governance: Duelling Discourses or Discursive Partners?

However much revered or vilified, Canada's official multiculturalism is subject to paradoxes. A commitment to multiculturalism must grapple with the quintessential paradox of a Canada-building governance, namely, how to make Canada safe "for" diversity, yet safe "from" diversity, while, at the same time, making diversity safe "from" Canada, yet safe "for" Canada (see Schlesinger Jr., 1992; Pearson, 2001). A multicultural Canada may be predisposed to accommodate diversity, yet must do so without abdicating a commitment to national unity, the rule of law, or common values (Cardozo, 2005). The rights of minority groups must be incorporated without disrupting either majority rights or the rights of individuals. Not surprisingly, official multiculturalism is embraced by some as a solution to Canada's diversity challenges; others dismiss it as a problem in search of a solution; and still others see it as both problem and solution, depending on the criteria or context (see also Berman & Paradies, 2008).

There is yet another multicultural paradox. For many, multiculturalism and anti-racism are seen as oppositional governance frameworks (Dei, 2000, 2007; but see Srivastava, 2007, pp. 306–7). For critics, multiculturalism as governance is dismissed as little more than a happy-face celebration of superficial differences. The aim of multiculturalism is largely attitudinal—that is, to enhance sensitivity by improving respect for cultural differences, rather than to address broader questions of structural racism, power relations, social oppression, and marginalization of minorities (Dei, 2011). But minority underachievement is not necessarily caused by cultural differences, critics argue. Nor will cross-cultural understanding contribute to any fundamental change in uprooting the structural roots of inequality (Kivel, 1996). In that cultural solutions cannot solve structural problems, moves toward anti-racism must focus on the behavioural and structural components of racialized inequality, along with the power and privileges that sustain racism through institutional policies and procedures. Predictably, an official multiculturalism is criticized as racism by virtue of its commitment to the foundational principles of Canada's white supremacist constitutional order, while glossing over entrenched inequalities and power imbalances (Dei, 2000).

By contrast, an anti-racism[1] governance involves a commitment to challenge, resist, and transform racially discriminatory barriers through direct action. The contesting of white privilege by eradicating structural barriers to full participation rights (Dei, 1996, 2005a) entails active personal involvement in challenging those cultural values, personal prejudices, discriminatory behaviour, and institutional structures that perpetuate racism. What could be further opposed? Multiculturalism is about attitudes, harmonious coexistence, and culture; anti-racism is about systems and structures, transformational challenges and changes, and substantive equality (McCreary, 2009; Sutherland, 2012). Whereas multiculturalism parlays prejudice reduction into a program of accommodation, anti-racism focuses on challenging the ideologies, values, structures, and practices that (re)produce privilege and disadvantage through those broader social processes and institutional arrangements largely invisible to those who benefit from them (McCreary, 2009).

A sense of perspective is helpful. Supporters tend to see multiculturalism as a glass half full, with benefits overflowing the top; detractors prefer to see it as a glass half empty, with any benefits leaking out the bottom. In that both critics and supporters gloss over its multidimensionality, those who stoutly defend multiculturalism as anti-racism are as ideologically slanted as those who disparage it as racist or as the personification of racism. Multiculturalism may be both racist *and* anti-racist simultaneously, at once both liberating yet marginalizing, unifying yet divisive, inclusive yet exclusive, a distraction yet catalytic, with benefits yet costs. In other words, the divide between multiculturalism and anti-racism may be overstated as demonstrated by the following criticisms and counter-criticisms.

- Multiculturalism may be racist in undermining the basis of Canadian unity and identity. Too literal an interpretation of multiculturalism can generate reified and essentialist group distinctions that foster group stereotyping, negative outgroup sentiments at odds with the attainment of social cohesion and national unity; and the racialization of segregated ethnic communities with separate power bases (see Verkuyten, 2007). Yet Canada's official multiculturalism is inclusive by imposing an anti-racism blueprint for advancing an inclusive Canada. The multiculturalism agenda has long endorsed an inclusiveness commitment through promotion of anti-racism since the 1980s, including a primary focus on race relations and elimination of racism and racial discrimination (Ghosh, 2011), and continues to do so, albeit in a more toned-down version (Fleras, 1993; Citizenship and Immigration, 2012). The current emphasis on sharing, interaction, and participation (including social cohesion and integration) points to an inclusive Canada-building by improving the terms of integration for minorities (Kostash, 2000; McRoberts, 2004). Besides, references to structural changes under an anti-racism framework sound good in theory. In practice, neither power relations nor institutional structures undergo change without human agency. Multiculturalism possesses the potential to liberate people's minds from bigotry and intolerance while promoting dialogue and exchange (Ghosh, 2011) as a precondition for reform at structural levels (Dei, 2011). Put bluntly, *structures don't change, people do*, and a commitment to multiculturalism is crucial in creating a mindset for social activism.

- Multiculturalism may be seen as racist and regressive in racializing, ghettoizing, or stigmatizing minorities. With multiculturalism, critics argue (Bissoondath, 1994), minorities are locked into freeze-dried compartments, labelled as ethnic, and dismissed as not quite Canadian. Yet multiculturalism is not about promoting diversity; it is about addressing disadvantage by removing discrimination and reducing prejudice. Multiculturalism commits to building bridges rather than erecting walls, encourages minority women and men to become involved, construct productive lives, contribute to society, and identify with Canada through their ethnicity (McGauran, 2005). It connotes a process for making the mainstream more inclusive rather than making minorities more multicultural through moves to remove discrimination, nurture civic engagement, foster cross-cultural understanding, and promote responsive institutions (see also Chan, 2004).

Even those critics who dismiss official multiculturalism as little more than politically correct whitewash that papers over the contradictions of capitalist society will concede the unavoidable. Multiculturalism has presided over a radical remaking of Canada, from a transplanted mono-colonial enclave to a cosmopolitan society of many cultures and colours, largely by challenging the once-racist narratives of Canada as a white society. The inception of an official multiculturalism over forty years ago constructed a framework for an inclusiveness that renders explicit forms of racism socially unacceptable. Or, as put by George Sefa Dei (2011, p. 16), one of Canada's foremost anti-racist scholars and activists, in defending multiculturalism as an admittedly soft discourse in the struggle against racism: "As an anti-racist educator, I do see multiculturalism as an allied discourse. We should be careful not to reject it outright and in the process remove a valuable first step towards a more critical anti-racist approach."

The conclusion seems inescapable: Both multiculturalism and/as anti-racism *are complementary* as partners in the discursive struggle to erase racism as governance grounds for living together differently yet equitably.

A Critical Model: An Anti-racist Multiculturalism

Opposed to Canada's "hegemonic" multiculturalism is the concept of critical multiculturalisms (Fleras, 2009). The critical discourses that animate America's multiculturalism subvert as they resist, in the process culminating in what is popularly referred to as the "culture wars." A critical multiculturalism transcends the constraints of official policy initiatives. Nor is it compromised by the demands of political engineering or electoral pandering. A discourse of resistance is advocated instead that challenges Eurocentricity by relativizing the white capitalist patriarchy with its exclusionary designs on the "other" (Giroux, 1999; Eisenstein, 1996). A critical multiculturalism is largely bottoms-up driven: It unsettles the prevailing and racialized distribution of power and privileged by capitalizing on the identity politics of those marginalized from the mainstream. Interrogating the traditional hegemony of the dominant group under a critical multiculturalism proposes a fundamental restructuring of the power relations between and within different cultural communities.

It has been said that Canadians and Americans use the same words, but speak different languages. Nowhere is this pithy aphorism more apropos than in the multiplicity of references that litter the multiculturalism landscape across both countries. Canada's inclusiveness multiculturalism with America's critical multiculturalisms provides a contrastive foil (Fleras, 2009):

- Canada's multiculturalism is ostensibly about managing diversity by depoliticizing difference, whereas critical multiculturalisms are about politicizing difference for managing the mainstream. One is criticized for emphasizing commonality over difference; the other for emphasizing difference at the expense of unity.
- Canadian multiculturalism is directed at modifying the mainstream without straining the social fabric; the other is focused on transforming the monocultural firmament upon which society is grounded. If Canada's multiculturalism involves superimposing multicultural diversities on a monocultural state (see Pinder, 2010), America's critical multiculturalism is more concerned with advancing a multi-diversity (or super-diversity) in conjunction with a multicultural state.
- One is officially political, yet seeks to depoliticize diversity for society-building purposes; the other falls outside the policy domain, but politicizes differences as a catalyst for minority empowerment.
- One seeks to depoliticize the relevance of difference as a basis for entitlement or engagement; the other privileges and politicizes the salience of differences in allocating who gets what.
- One is rivetted around the modernist quest for unity and universality as the basis for multicultural governance; the other embraces a postmodernist zeal for differences in challenging the national mythology upon which the monocultural framework of society is constructed.
- One acknowledges respect for diversity and difference devoid of historical context and power relations (a pretend pluralism), while the other focuses on empowerment through cultural politics as racialized minorities strive to recover, preserve, or promote their deep differences.
- Canada's official multiculturalism transforms cultural differences into a discourse about *social inequality*; critical multiculturalism reformulates social inequalities into a discursive framework that values cultural differences within the public domain.
- Unlike a consensus multiculturalism with its liberal universalist propensity for treating everyone the same for purposes of reward or

recognition, a critical multiculturalism endorses the primacy of differently treating the historically disadvantaged for true equality.
- Canada's consensus multiculturalism strives to make society safe *from* difference, in addition to making Canada safe *for* difference. By contrast, the underlying logic of critical multiculturalism seeks to make differences safe *from* society, while making differences safe *for* society.

The rationale behind a critical multiculturalism is counter-hegemonic and anti-racist. This model is critical of Eurocentric cultural agendas that historically denied or excluded those on the margins. The anti-racist bona fides of a critical multiculturalism embrace a politicized and subversive discourse that uncovers and challenges the structural roots of inequality (Naseem, 2011). By contrast, references to Canada's official multiculturalism embrace a commitment to control through consensus, conformity, and compliance. This hegemonic interpretation yields the possibility of framing an official multiculturalism as racist and as racism.

A Racist Multiculturalism in a Racialized Canada

The logic underlying Canada's official multiculturalism is arguably racist. That is, Canada's state multiculturalism as a political instrument in defence of dominant ideology is designed to uphold a racialized status quo. Its hegemonic status as covert racism is further reinforced by the fact that multiculturalism originated and continues to persist as a political act to achieve political goals in a politically acceptable manner. To be sure, an official multiculturalism does not deliberately promote racism in a Canada that subscribes to multicultural principles. In theory, multiculturalism openly challenges it. Nevertheless, the logical consequences of any multicultural policy that glosses over uncomfortable truths is racist by virtue of (1) distracting from more substantial issues, (2) failing to mount a challenge to racialized inequities, and (3) securing and legitimizing a racialized status quo (Haque, 2010). The fact that an official multiculturalism can simultaneously obscure yet enshrine power relations ups the ante for living together. Such an obfuscation also makes it doubly difficult to erase racisms when relying on those very tools that created the problem in the first place.

A racist multiculturalism persists by virtue of what *it doesn't do* in privileging consensus over challenge, conformity over dissensus, containment over empowerment, control over change, and uniformity over diversity. The whiff of racism is reinforced when conflating inclusiveness with integration for those racialized minorities who seek inclusion without assimilation. The whitewashing of injustice is no less racist. Canada is constructed around concealing its colonial past and neo-colonial present through the intervention of a multiculturalism that distracts as it depoliticizes (Dhamoon, 2009; Thobani, 2007). Even the endorsement of tolerance under multiculturalism is highly depoliticizing by ignoring how the marginalized are constituted and constrained by history, power, and mainstream goodwill. Or, as Baldwin, Cameron, and Kobayashi (2011, p. 8) write in pinpointing this illusion of inclusion, "The marginalized are simply objects to be tolerated, but their marginality never requires explanation." Instead of challenging the concept of a racialized Canada, an official multiculturalism *does the opposite*, thereby sowing the seeds of a racist multiculturalism. Of course no one is accusing an official multiculturalism of going out of its way to be racist. Rather, the logical consequences of state-defined multicultural inclusiveness tend to be racist by default *in not doing something when something needs to be done*.

How does a racist multiculturalism work? Multiculturalism in Canada is primarily a top-down political program for integrating migrants and managing minorities. Balancing the national with the social and the cultural compels a state multiculturalism into *managing* diversity to ensure that people don't act upon their differences to unsettle or destroy (see also Kundnani, 2007b). This hegemonic discourse in defence of dominant ideology endorses those policies and initiatives that subordinate minority needs to the "greater good" or "national interests." The disruptiveness of diversity is dispelled by homogenizing differences around a singular commonality so that everyone is similarly different rather than differently similar (Eisenstein, 1996). The objective is neither to challenge nor to change, but to construct consensus by "defanging" the potency of difference for governance purposes. A preoccupation with depoliticizing differences reduces multiculturalism to little more than a superficial distraction that neither addresses the deep diversities of those who want their differences taken seriously nor contests issues of structural inequality, covert social control, and relations of power that sustain a racialized hierarchy (Haque, 2010; May & Sleeter, 2010).

Not surprisingly, those on the left of the political spectrum are highly critical of a state multiculturalism. A capitalist ruse to divide, confuse, and distract the working classes, "multiculti-schism" ghettoizes minorities into occupational structures and residential arrangements, thereby lubricating the prevailing distribution of power and wealth behind a smokescreen of well-oiled bromides (Bolaria & Li, 1988; Dei, 2000; Bannerji, 2000). Multiculturalism is dismissed as a colossal hoax (an opiate for the masses) foisted on the public by vested interests to ensure minority co-optation through an ideological indoctrination (false consciousness) that masks the racism of white supremacism (Chazan et al., 2011; Hage, 1998). It is also criticized as discourse that displaces and silences anti-racism narratives by advancing a culturalist view of Canada (clash of cultures) at the expense of hierarchy, power, and inequality (Thobani, 2010). Multiculturalism not only represents a polite and euphemistic way of concealing yet reproducing unequal power relations, the framing of differences as equal (the same) compromises moves toward inclusion, equity, and justice when privileging culture over more fundamental categories of social analysis such as class, race, or gender. Its status as a discourse in defence of dominant ideology positions multiculturalism as an instrument for micro-managing communities of colour by framing minorities as problems of cultural integration. The effect is to force minorities to articulate aspirations along largely apolitical culturalist lines that often essentialize cultures as fixed and frozen mosaic tiles (Lentin, 2005; Titley & Lentin, 2012).

Those to the political right are no less disenchanted with what they see as a racist multiculturalism. This racist dimension stems from a multiculturalism that ostensibly prioritizes the racial collective (or tribal) over individual rights and freedoms, in the process eroding both national unity and liberal values (Pacquet, 2008; Mansur, 2011). People are individuals in a liberal society and expect to be treated as such rather than as interchangeable widgets in a social engineering experiment. Multiculturalism is criticized as upholding policies in which race rather than judgment or experience is seen as primary in shaping a person's identity and character (Berliner & Hull, 1995. Such a deterministic view of the world claims that a person's political, social, or cultural viewpoints are racially derived, hence racist (Malik, 2008). Or as the noted critic of multiculturalism, Kenan Malik (2012), writes in equating multiculturalism with racism as two sides of the same coin:

> [Multiculturalism] describes a set of policies, the aim of which is to manage diversity by putting people into ethnic boxes, defining individual needs and rights by virtue of the boxes into which people are put, and using these boxes to shape public policy. It is a case, not for open borders and minds, but for the policing of borders, whether physical, cultural or imaginative.

Even the much-touted mosaic metaphor comes in for criticism as racism in disguise. Canada's multicultural discourses remain rooted in an understanding of ethnicity/culture as primordial (frozen in time) and essentialized (static, homogeneous, and rigid) rather than flexible, dynamic, and relational (Bissoondath, 1994). Too literal an interpretation of multiculturalism can generate reified discourses and essentialist group distinctions that foster group stereotyping and negative outgroup sentiments. Social cohesion and national unity are compromised (see Verkuyten, 2007) when membership in a racialized mosaic locks individuals into hermetically sealed silos isolated from the rest of society.

Perceived as racist under a multicultural rubric is the establishment of race-based governance structures. Justifying a colour-conscious regime of racial preferences, reparations, and lawsuits because of minority grievance or victimhood poses a danger. It generates the potential for divisiveness, while eclipsing individual rights to choice and agency against the backdrop of big government social engineering. The elevating of racialized identity over societal citizenship under a "multi-cul-de-sac" multiculturalism runs the risk of dissolving society into an unstable matrix of races, ethnicities, tribes, and special-interest groups in competition for race-based privileges, exemptions, and entitlement (Kirsanow, 2007). Worse still, Stewart Bell writes in *Cold Terror: How Canada Nurtures and Exports Terrorism around the World* (2004) that the openness of uncritical multiculturalism makes Canada vulnerable to infiltration by those terrorists who hide behind a multicultural smokescreen to plot and destroy (Collacott, 2007). Finally, a racist multiculturalism is thought to endorse an anything goes relativism when it ostensibly tolerates practices incompatible with "the Canadian way," yet it is also charged with hypocrisy in offering the illusion of tolerance while punishing behaviour at odds with core values (Stoffman, 2002, 2007). In short, both the right and the left agree that multiculturalism is racist, although they disagree on how and why, as expressed in the comparison below. Keep in mind that the right tends to emphasize a functionalist model of society (society is good, therefore individuals must change) while the liberal/left endorses a conflict model of society (society is exploitative, therefore it [not individuals] must change).

Table 12.1 Critiquing Multiculturalism as Racist: Right versus Left

Multiculturalism for the Right (conservative)	Multiculturalism for the Left (liberal/radical)
• Too radical • Recipe for disaster	• Too reactionary • Opiate of the masses
• Dismantling Canada and Canadian values	• Reinforcing an unequal status quo • Hegemonic • Assimilation in slow motion
• Undermining national interests	• Promoting vested interests
• Tolerates illiberal values at odds with national values • Fosters extremism as smokescreen + political correctness	• Tolerates superficial differences (pretend pluralism) • Intolerant of deep minority differences
• Racist for focusing on race-based groups at the expense of individualism	• Racism for preserving white privilege by whitewashing the past
• Promoting an essentialist tribalism that undercuts liberal democracy + universalism • Diminishes individualism	• Illusion of inclusion • Promoting tribalism that undercuts progressive forces based on class/intersectional analysis • Diminishes collectivity/common interests
• Induces segregation	• Tactic of co-optation/hegemony

Multicultural Racism: A Made-in-Canada Bias

A racist multiculturalism does more than solidify a racialized Canada. It also paves the way for a distinctive Canadian racism in two ways. First, by not taking differences seriously in an era of identity politics and the politics of recognition. Second, by taking differences too seriously, thus running the risk of essentializing cultures or racializing minorities at the expense of equality, unity, and individualism. The possibility of a multicultural racism may well constitute a distinctive Canadian racism.

A multiculturalism that miniaturizes difference is susceptible to charges of racism. The racism in Canada's official multiculturalism is perpetuated by glossing over people's distinct identities as a basis for recognition, reward, or relationships. The ethnicities of minority women and men *are channelled (depoliticized) instead into cultural pursuits at personal levels or private domains*. Rejecting the relevance of differences except in a symbolic and tokenistic manner reinforces the inherent racism within a state multiculturalism. To be sure, diversities and differences may be tolerated under the pretend pluralism of a liberal-leaning, Eurocentric-focused multiculturalism, but only if everyone is different in the same kind of way, if these differences do not violate the laws of the land or interfere with the rights of others, and if central authorities can control what counts as differences and what differences count. Those diversities that veer outside a liberal universalism framework are discounted or discredited while, paradoxically, paying too much attention to cultural differences may have an equally chilling effect. Or as Kuokkanen (2009, p. 11; also Hage, 1998) writes in acknowledging Meyda Yegenoglu's prescient notion, multiculturalism gives rise to a particular form of racism, not by rejecting the values of other cultures, but by tolerating them in the abstract, thereby maintaining a distance (an aloofness) within the context of an empty universality.

This refusal to take differences seriously gives rise to the seemingly oxymoronic expression "multicultural racism." A multicultural commitment to the pretend pluralism of liberal universalism alongside a difference-blind agenda exerts an exclusionary (racist) effect on those who propose to live together albeit by standing apart, insist on having their differences taken seriously, and want these differences incorporated within the public domain. Any multiculturalism that denies and excludes others because of their cultural diversity reinforces its status as a discourse in defence of dominant ideology. In that an official multiculturalism cannot speak the language of deep diversities and politicized difference, it has proven every bit as racist and controlling as racism 1.0 (Kuokkanen, 2009).

No less a racism is a multiculturalism narrative that takes cultural differences too seriously. A commitment to multiculturalism that privileges the centrality of multicultures runs the risk of institutionalizing culture in the public domain, freezing cultural differences as museum curiosities, and reifying cultural communities as fixed and self-contained rather than fluid and in flux (Pieterse, 2007; Nagle, 2009). Even how Canadians talk about multiculturalism reinforces an essentialized framework, especially when reference to Canada's multicultural mosaic remains an emotionally charged yet potentially misleading metaphor. Yes, each tile is distinct, important, and contributes to the overall aesthetic in which the whole is greater than the sum of the parts. Nevertheless, each paint-by-number tile is firmly locked into place because of a mainstream grouting that defines what differences count, and what counts as difference (Mackey, 2002; Johnston, 1994). Not surprisingly, a mosaic metaphor promulgates a "multi-cul-de-sac-ist" (essentialized) reading of ethnicity and difference as primordial, determinative, and immutable rather than flexible, dynamic, and relational.[2] Membership and participation in this sticky mosaic tends to slot individuals into hermetically sealed silos anchored permanently into place, fixed over time, and resistant to change. Pnina Werbner (2012, p. 198) points out the dangers of fossilizing the concepts of cultural as a basis for multiculturalism:

> Multiculturalism, anthropologists argue, reifies and essentializes cultures as rigid, homogeneous, and unchanging wholes with fixed boundaries. It assumes a fixed connection between culture and territory. Its political correctness glosses over internal social problems within ethnic groups. Current theories within anthropology are based on the idea that cultures are creative and changing, internally contested, and heterogeneous. People in one culture constantly borrow from others. Cultures are therefore inescapably hybrid and permeable. For this reason too, cultures do not have a single unified leadership and any attempt by the state to impose one is false and oppressive. Critically also, diasporas have multiple and intersecting identities, including party political affiliations to the left and right.

Those on the political right are also inclined to equate multiculturalism as racism of taking differences too seriously. Any multicultural-inspired special treatment for racial or cultural minorities is, by definition, a form of racism since individuals are defined and constrained by their race. For example, the Ayn Rand Institute (2002) labels multiculturalism as racism in a new and self-righteous guise. According to the institute, multiculturalism's racism arises from imposing a restrictive group membership whose collectivity stifles the freedom, identity, and personal worth of an individual, while compromising the expression of freedom of speech, due process, and equal protection (Mansur, 2011). Multiculturalism as a racism is thought to essentialize minority cultures by chaining people to their traditions, sublimating their wishes to the will of the collectivity and asserting the primacy of group identity at the expense of citizenship and individualism (Malik,

2012). Multiculturalism is also accused of fostering racism by claiming that all cultures are of equal worth regardless of their detractions or achievements (Pacquet, 2008). Multiculturalism as the bigotry of soft racism creates a politically correct social climate that flinches from criticizing minority wrongdoing on the mistaken assumption that all cultures are worthy of equal respect (Mansur, 2011). Table 12.2 provides an overview of multicultural racism and a racist multiculturalism along a left–right (liberal/radical–conservative) continuum.

To sum up, Canada, for the most part, has deployed multiculturalism in a society-building tool for "managing" difference in securing an inclusive status quo. Canada's official multiculturalism may purport to be anti-racist in principle and commitment. In reality, it tends to be racist through omission rather than commission, by consequence rather than intent, by practice rather than theory. Multiculturalism is accused by the left of burying the inequality of race hierarchies and power relations in a vague celebration of symbolic differences (Phillips & Saharso, 2008). Yet it is also denounced by the right for trumping cultural differences at the expense of national unity, core cultural values, and individual rights. The end result is a quintessentially made-in-Canada racism, not because of what it claims to do (to be anti-racist), but because of what it doesn't do in advancing transformational changes and meaningful inclusion.

The reality gap is resounding. Multiculturalism may embody a morally sound and neutral-sounding discourse that conjures up welcoming and inclusionary images. But multiculturalism as the illusion of inclusion masks and sustains unequal relations in defence of a racialized status quo (Bannerji, 2000; Dua et al., 2005). Canada may be portrayed as a site of many cultures interacting with each other on a level playing field, except that reality is not nearly so accommodating. Ignored in this narrative of simply moving over and making cultural space are issues of power, racism, colonialism, Eurocentrism, and white superiority in defining who gets what (Thobani, 2007; Arat-Kroc 2005). Acknowledging the persistence and proliferation of racisms in Canada in terms of how they work makes it abundantly clear. The goal of a racism-free Canada is proving more complex and elusive than widely hyped or many had hoped.

Table 12.2 Racist Multiculturalism versus Multicultural Racism: Ideological Divides

	Left/Liberal	Right/Conservative
Multicultural racism	• Not taking differences seriously enough (a pretend pluralism)	• Taking differences too seriously (essentializes/ghettoizes/relativizes)
Racist multiculturalism	• Glosses over injustices • Depoliticizes diversities	• Imperils national unity by promoting differences • Compromises individual rights

Notes

1 As Dei (2011, p. 18) points out, the *anti-* in anti-racism is not simply oppositional or confrontational but rather "action-oriented" and transformational.
2 A term employed by Rohantin Mistry in his book *A Fine Balance* is the concept of "multi cul de sac," used to describe a multiculturalism that proves a dead end from which minorities cannot escape to participate in society (Morey, 2004).

CHAPTER 13

SUMMARY AND CONCLUSION
INCONVENIENT TRUTHS/COMFORTING FICTIONS

The possibility that as the world changes, so too does racism, cuts to the core of this book. *Racisms in a Multicultural Canada* has argued that racism is not disappearing despite glibly worded claims that Canada is basking in the balm of a post-racial milieu. On the contrary, racism in Canada was shown to persist and propagate by virtue of assuming different forms and diverse dynamics whose intent or effects continue to deny, exclude, or exploit. The book is formed accordingly: Just as race is not simply a set of categories but a system of control, so also is racism more than a slew of individuals with bad attitudes; it is structural rather than incidental because it is deeply embedded in the structural and systemic at institutional and societal levels. Racism is as much a matter of interests as that of attitudes, of property as of prejudice, of structural advantage as of personal failing, of whiteness as of the "other," of discourse as of discrimination, and of unequal power relations as of bigotry. The multi-dimensionality of racism has proven consequential: Gaps between Canadian ideals and Canada's realities create a theoretical space with which to pose questions over the what, how, where, when, and why of contemporary (or postmodern) racisms. This slippage also complicates the challenge of formulating anti-racism strategies capable of advancing the complex yet slippery nature of living together with differences, equitably and in dignity.

Employing a critical framework that puts politics and power at the centre of analysis, the overriding theme of this book points to a pervasive Canadian paradox: *How to account for the seeming proliferation and persistence of racisms in a Canada that abides by the principle of multiculturalism while being committed to postracial principles.* To address these issues, *Racisms in a Multicultural Canada* does not flinch from asking some unsettling questions about the workings, challenges, and contradictions of postmodern racisms. Five questions (or themes) were raised that secure the content and organization of the book, including:

1) What does racism mean in the twenty-first century?
2) Why is racism perceived to be proliferating?
3) How do postmodern racisms work in a contemporary Canada?
4) In what ways have discourses (how we think and talk) about racism shifted in recent years?
5) How do we account for the persistence of racisms in multicultural Canada?

What is racism? What does racism mean within the context of a so-called post-racial world? There is no agreement among scholars or activists over a definition of racism (even the UN refuses to define racism, preferring instead to use the term "racial discrimination" [Taylor, 2011]). Most Canadians are understandably confused and frustrated about racism—what it is, how it works, how to frame it for discussion purposes, what to do about it and how. Much of the uncertainty arises from an indisputable fact: Racism no longer possesses a foundational meaning rooted in the concept of race, with its corresponding notions of (1) a world divided and ranked into inferior and superior races; (2) race as a determinative of thought and behaviour; and (3) differential treatment of people because of their racial pedigree. Without race to anchor the concept, racism appears to be reconfiguring in ways that elude consensus yet elide conceptualizing, while generating controversy and contradictions. Complicating the uncertainty are the diversities within racism. Many group-specific racisms are known to exist, for example, anti-black racism or anti-Muslim racism, each with its own histories, manifestations, and consequences. Not surprisingly, no definitive definition of racism is possible since it arrives in different forms, is opportunistic and relational to other social processes, and possesses a transformative dynamic that mutates over time and across space (Anthias, 2007). Under the circumstances in a world of many racisms, who can be surprised that the notion of a singular definition has given way to the idea that racism is whatever people want it to mean based on the interplay of context, criteria, and consequences?

Do we live in a world of spiralling, out-of-control racisms? Or is it more accurate to say that racisms appear to be snowballing in number and kind because more actions or inactions are defined as racist in an increasingly inclusive Canada? As widely noted, old-fashioned racism has lost so much of its legitimacy that it borders on a universal disgrace (Steele, 2009). Racism is no longer socially acceptable; therefore, most whites avoid blatant expressions of racism, preferring instead polite proxies that play to public decorum. "Brazen" racism has been replaced by those more subtle forms of racism that once were dismissed or ignored as unproblematic. The racism of slavery and lynching, Jim Crow and segregation, and racial slurs and open discrimination has been superseded by debates over the racialized appropriateness of Halloween costumes, the dearth of racialized minorities in corporate Canada, or the reluctance of professional sports teams to discard disparaging references to Aboriginal peoples as team mascots (such as the Braves or the Redskins) (National Congress of American Indians, 2013). But, as Joel Best (2001) has argued in a somewhat different context, when the big problems of the world are solved, the smaller problems assume a larger and disproportional presence in society, in the process appearing to make a bad situation look even worse. Applied to this book, the less obvious forms of racism—from subliminal to systemic to infrastructural—have always existed, admittedly below the radar of public consciousness. Only now, however, people are more aware of them, how they work, the damage they inflict, and react accordingly. In other words, it is partly a problem of perception that is driving the politics of racism: for some, it is under control; for others, it is out of control.

How do postmodern racisms work in a contemporary Canada? Could racism be reduced if people knew how it really works? Racism once worked in an uncomplicated way that was easy to detect. What passed for racism consisted of openly negative beliefs and one-size-fits-all actions deliberately intended to hurt or hinder those members of a devalued race who were deemed (and doomed) to be inferior or expendable. This kind of racism is now déclassé; after all, Canadians believe they live in a post-racial, colour-blind society that commits to social equality of inclusion by rejecting the legitimacy of race and racism to shape people's lives and life chances. The workings of contemporary postmodern racisms differ from conventional patterns of doing racisms in the following ways: (1) there are cumulative effects of seemingly insignificant slights; (2) postmodern racisms are embedded within the broader structures of a white-dominated society; (3) they are based not on what is done, but what is *not* done when doing something is necessary; (4) they take differences too seriously or not seriously enough depending on the context or, alternatively, they treat people the same when their difference-based disadvantages need customized treatment; (5) they use seemingly neutral language (for example, "those" people are "culturally incompatible") that serve as a proxy to disguise dislike of others; (6) they are differently experienced by diverse racialized minority groups especially at different points in their history; (7) they are defined by consequences of people's actions rather than their intentions; and (8) they are focused on inappropriate cultural differences instead of biological (racial) inferiority. In short, references to how racism worked in the past (i.e., an individual problem reflecting random and discrete incidents) now capitalize on the idea that racisms work: (1) systemically, i.e., they are deeply embedded within normative values and institutional relations, practices, and policies; (2) infrastructurally, i.e., in terms of the founding assumptions and foundational principles of a society's constitutional order; and (3) subliminally, i.e., they are at the level of individual unconsciousness and through denial (Jiwani 2006).

How are evolving discourses reframing the way we think and talk about racism? This book begins with the assumption that there is nothing natural or normal about racism. Racism is a socially constructed convention, continually created and recreated by those in positions of power and authority to advance their interests while controlling those who pose a menace to political rule or capitalist expansion. The deconstructing of racism to acknowledge its evolving and multi-dimensional status points to a new discursive framework: the framing of racism as a *verb* or process instead of a static thing or noun. No less important is the framing of racism as normal and inevitable in contexts of group competition. Racism cannot be seen as something simply tacked on to an otherwise race-neutral and colour-blind society. Society itself is deemed to be an essentially white space with the result that racialized minorities must exercise their rights and achieve success on a tilted playing field—that is, in a society designed neither to reflect their realities nor advance their interests. Mounting awareness of society as foundationally racialized puts racialized minorities in the driver's seat for defining what counts as racism and what racisms count. Racism is increasingly defined as a receiver-dependent phenomenon based on the lived experiences and moral authority of racialized minorities as victims. The relationship between racism and race is also contested. Racism creates a justification for the appearance of the race concept (rather than the more intuitive reverse notion of race creates racism). Accordingly, racialization, not race, is key to understanding contemporary racism (racialization is used in the sense of a process that excludes, marginalizes, inferiorizes, and disadvantages certain groups based on their perceived link to biological (or racial) features [Zaman, 2010]). Finally, racism is less frequently framed as a singular experience rooted in the race concept. Proposed instead is a broader framework that reflects overlapping inequalities linked to intersecting identities of gender, class, age, etc., rather than applied uniformly to whole groups.

How do we account for racisms in multicultural Canada? Is there a distinctive Canadian racism? Accounting for racisms in Canada requires a multi-dimensional approach. Racism (however defined) reflects a product of ignorance, arrogance, hate, fear, or indifference. Its origins are systemically ingrained within the institutional barriers and government policies that (however inadvertently) preclude full and equal participation. Racism is also deeply embedded in those founding assumptions and foundational principles of a society's constitutional order often impervious to detection and analysis. Of particular note in accounting for origins and causes is the controversy over an official multiculturalism. Yes, Canada's official multiculturalism ostensibly strives to be anti-racist, and there is evidence to confirm how its existence has contributed to rendering racism socially unacceptable. Yet this book takes the position that Canada's multicultural commitments inadvertently generate a distinctive Canadian racism. Two lines of argument are deployed: first, an official multiculturalism represents a political construct that serves as a proxy to gloss over Canada's racist treatment of Aboriginal peoples and racialized immigrants; second, an official multiculturalism may involve racism when it takes differences too seriously, leading to essentialist readings of diversity or fears of diversity gone wild by eroding the centre that binds Canada. Multiculturalism can also be interpreted as racism when it doesn't take differences seriously enough to accommodate both deep differences and differences within differences in bringing about equitable outcomes. The implications of both positions may invoke racism by virtue of consequences, not by intent, in the process capturing the contradictions embodied in the title of this book.

Living in a Strange Land: Racism without Racists, Racism without Race

If nothing else, this book makes it clear: Canada is a multicultural society of massive contradictions that pose as inconvenient truths. To study racism is to enter a domain of paradox, perplexity, and provocation because, when it comes to the politics of racism, nothing is what it seems to be in a world where appearances are deceiving. Contradictions snowball in a world of racism seemingly stripped of race or racists: racism is publicly rejected yet privately popular; racism is socially unacceptable yet pervasively persistent; people are in denial over racism, yet there is more racism than ever before; and racism is reality despite the declining significance of race and a dwindling number of racists. Open racism is widely condemned in advancing an inclusive multiculturalism, yet acts of racism still frequently occur and undermine a commitment to a multicultural inclusiveness, an inclusive multiculturalism. No one seems to believe in race anymore or in the existence of racists, but many claim to be victims of racists and racisms. Canada may be perceived as a post-racial society that eschews the legitimacy of the race concept for analyzing society and intergroup relations (Titley & Lentin, 2012). Yet race continues to matter, especially in making assumptions about others on grounds of their presumed inferiority vis-à-vis white superiority. It can do so, not because race is real, but because people act as if it were real to produce racialized outcomes. But repeated references to a post-racial society notwithstanding, there is no such thing as a colour-blind Canada. White settler societies such as Canada constitute historically specific and socially constructed conventions that are ideologically loaded and racialized along the lines of whiteness as privilege, superiority, and supremacy (also Bonilla Silva & Dietrich, 2011). The racism that flows from a racialized yet multicultural Canada prevails—with or without racists or race.

To conclude: Canada is rapidly approaching its 150th birthday as a country. There is much to commend in current government efforts to portray Canadian history as one of heroism, daring, risk, and rugged determination. But these comforting fictions too often conceal the inconvenient truths associated with the racism of genocide and exploitation in the building of Canada. Such obfuscation not only does a disservice to those who suffered the slings of a defiantly white Canada, and continue to suffer from its racist legacy. It also reinforces the assertion that reference to racisms in a multicultural Canada is not an oxymoron, but remains a lived reality for many Canadians.

REFERENCES

ABC News. (1970). *The Eye of the Storm*. Documentary by William Peters.
Abel, A. (2001). P Is for Prejudice. *Saturday Night*, June 23, 30.
Abel, S. (1997). *Shaping the News: Waitangi Day on Television*. Auckland: Auckland University Press.
Abele, F. (2004, April). *Urgent Need, Serious Opportunity: Towards a New Social Model for Canada's Aboriginal Peoples*. CPRN Social Architecture Papers. Research Paper F/39.
Abella, I. (2013, February 26). Never Again May None Be Too Many. *Globe and Mail*.
Abella, I., & Troper, H. (1982). *None Is Too Many*. Toronto: Lester & Orpen Dennys.
Abells, Y. (2009, December 2). Violent Acts Continue to Plague Women Worldwide. *National Post*.
Abrams, L. S., & Moio, J. A. (2009). Critical Race Theory and the Cultural Competence Dilemma in Social Work Education. *Journal of Social Work Education*, 45(2), 245–61.
Abu-Laban, Y., & Gabriel, C. (2002). *Selling Diversity: Immigration, Multiculturalism, Employment Equity, and Globalization*. Peterborough, ON: Broadview Press.
ACLC [African Canadian Legal Clinic]. (2009). *Responding to Anti-Black Hate Crime: A Tool Kit*. Toronto: Author.
Adams, H. (1999). *Tortured People: The Politics of Colonization*. Penticton, BC: Theytus Books.
Adams, M. (2007). *Unlikely Utopia*. Toronto: Penguin.
Adkins, J. (2013). Yale Professor Discusses Modern Racism in University of Pittsburgh Lecture, March 28. Retrieved from http://wesa.fm
Adorno, T. S., et al. (1950). *The Authoritarian Personality*. New York: Harper and Row.
Afshar, H. (2013). The Politics of Fear: What Does It Mean to Those Who Are Otherized and Feared? *Ethnic and Racial Studies*, 36(1), 9–27.
Agnew, V. (Ed.). (2007). *Interrogating Race and Racism*. Toronto: University of Toronto Press.
Agnew, V. (Ed.). (2009). *Racialized Migrant Women in Canada: Essays on Health, Violence, and Equity*. Toronto: University of Toronto Press.

Agocs, C., & Boyd, M. (1993). Ethnicity and Ethnic Inequality. In J. Curtis et al. (Eds.), *Social Inequality in Canada* (2nd ed.) (pp. 330–52). Scarborough, ON: Pearson.

Agocs, C., & Jain, H. (2010). Systemic Racism in Employment in Canada: Diagnosing Systemic Racism in Organizational Culture. *Directions: Publication of the Canadian Race Relations Foundation, 5*(2), 149–58.

Aguiar, L. L. M., Tomic, P., & Trumper, R. (2005). Racism, Hate, and Monoculturalism in a Canadian Hinterland. In C. James (Ed.), *Possibilities and Limitations* (pp. 163–74). Halifax: Fernwood.

Aguirre, A. Jr., & Turner, J. (1995). *American Ethnicity: The Dynamics and Consequences of Discrimination*. New York: McGraw-Hill.

Ahmed, N. M. (2009). Is Zionism Racist? Retrieved from www.mediamonitors.net

Ahmed, S. (2006). The Nonperformativity of Antiracism. *Meridians: Feminisms, Race, and Transnationalism, 7*(1), 104–26.

Akdeniz, Y. (2006, January 16–27). Stocktaking on Efforts to Combat Racism on the Internet. Prepared for the Commission on Human Rights. Sixty-second session, Geneva.

Alexander, M. (2012). *The New Jim Crow: Mass Incarceration in the Age of Colorblindness*. New York: New Press.

Alfred, T. (2005). *Wasase: Indigenous Pathways to Action and Freedom*. Peterborough: Broadview Press.

Al-Krenawi, A., & Graham, J. R. (Eds.). (2003). *Multicultural Social Work in Canada*. Toronto: Oxford University Press.

Alladin, I. (1996). Racism in Schools: Race, Ethnicity, and Schooling in Canada. In I. Alladin (Ed.), *Racism in Canadian Schools* (pp. 4–21). Toronto: Harcourt Brace.

Alleyne, M. D. (Ed.). (2012). *Anti Racism & Multiculturalism: Studies in International Communication*. New Brunswick, NJ: Transaction Publishers.

Allport, G. (1954). *The Nature of Prejudice*. New York: Doubleday and Company.

Alpert, E. (2013, August 24). Racial Equality? Whites Say Yes, Blacks No. *Waterloo Region Record*.

Alsultany, E. (2012). *Arabs and Muslims in the Media: Representations after 9/11*. New York: New York University Press.

Altbach, P. G., Lomotey, K., & Rivers, S. (2002). Race in Higher Education: The Continuing Crisis. In W. A. Smith, P. G. Altbach, & K. Lomotey (Eds.), *The Racial Crisis in American Higher Education* (pp. 23–42). Albany: State University of New York.

Altheide, D. L. (2002). *Creating Fear: News and the Construction of Crisis*. New York: Aldine de Gruyter.

Altheide, D. L. (2003). Notes toward a Politics of Fear. *Journal for Crime, Conflict, and Media, 1*(1), 37–54.

Alvarez, A. (2008, April 10). Model Minority: How Women's Magazines Whitewash Different Ethnicities. *Racialicious*. Originally published in Guanabee.

Alvarez, A., & Juang, L. (2010, April). Ignoring Racism Makes Distress Seem Worse. *Journal of Counseling Psychology, 57*(2), 167–78.

American Psychological Association. (2001). *Psychological Causes and Consequences of Racism, Racial Discrimination, Xenophobia, and Related Intolerances*. Intervention by APA, Durban, South Africa. August 31 to September 7.

Amin, A. (2012). *Land of Strangers*. Boston: Polity.

Amin, N. A., & Dei, G. (2006). *The Poetics of Anti-racism*. Halifax: Fernwood.

Andersen, M. L., & Hill Collins, P. (Eds.). (1998). *Race, Class, and Gender: An Anthology* (3rd ed.). Belmont, CA: Wadsworth.
Anderson, B. (2007, October 3). A Little Mosque Grows. *Al Jazeera, News Americas.* Retrieved from http://english.aljazeera.net
Anderson, K. J. (2007). *Race and the Crisis of Humanism.* New York: Routledge.
Anderson, K. J. (2010). *Benign Bigotry: The Psychology of Subtle Prejudice.* New York: Cambridge University Press.
Anderssen, E. (2013, June 26). The Anti Racism Lesson That's Gone Viral 40 Years Later. *Globe and Mail.*
Anthias, F. (2007). Boundaries of "Race" and Ethnicity and Questions about Cultural Belongings. In N. Gopalkrishnan & H. Babacan (Eds.), *Racisms in the New World Order.* Newcastle Upon Tyne: Cambridge Scholars Press.
Anti Defamation League. (2012, March). *Attitudes Toward Jews in Ten European Countries.* New York: First International Resources LLC.
Applebaum, B. (2010). *Being White, Being Good.* Toronto: Lexington Books.
Arat-Koc, S. (2005). The Disciplinary Boundaries of Canadian Identity after September 11: Civilizational Identity, Multiculturalism, and the Challenge of Anti-Imperialist Feminism. *Social Justice, 32*(4), 32–43.
Assante, M. (2011). *As I Run Toward Africa.* Boulder, CO: Paradigm Publishers.
Association for Canadian Studies and Ensemble. (2013, March 20). *Probing Prejudice: A Groundbreaking Study on Place, Frequency, and Sources.* Montreal: Author.
Asthana, A. (2008). We All Know It's Wrong to Judge by Skin Colour ... So Why Do We All Do It? *The Guardian/The Observer.* Retrieved from www.guardian.co.uk
Athwal, H. (2013, July 11). A Culture of Cultural Racism. *Institute of Race Relations.* London: Institute of Race Relations.
Augostinos, M., & Reynolds, K. J. (Eds.). (2001). *Understanding Prejudice, Racism, and Social Conflict.* Thousand Oaks, CA: Sage.
Australian Human Rights Commission. (2006, November 3–4). *New Racisms, New Anti-racisms. Conference Notes.* Canberra.
Australian Human Rights Commission. (2008). *Cyber Racism.* Retrieved from www.humanrights.gov.au
Avery, D. H. (1995). *Reluctant Hosts: Canada's Response to Immigrant Workers, 1896–1994.* Toronto: McClelland and Stewart.
Awad, G. H. (2013). Does Policy Name Matter? The Effect of Framing on the Evaluations of African American Applicants. *Journal of Applied Social Psychology, 43,* 379–87.
Aylward, C. A. (1999). *Canadian Critical Race Theory: Racism and the Law.* Halifax: Fernwood.
Ayn Rand Institute. (2002, November). *Multiculturalism: The New Racism.* A supplemental issue of the newsmagazine *Impact.*
Aziz, M. (2009). Message from the President. *ENAR. Shadow Report on Racism in Europe.* Brussels.
Baber, Z. (2010). Racism without Races: Reflections on Racialization and Racial Projects. *Sociology Compass, 4*(4), 241–48.
Back, L. (2002). The New Technologies of Racism. In D. T. Goldberg & J. Solomos (Eds.), *Companion to Race and Ethnic Studies* (pp. 365–78). Oxford: Blackwell.
Back, L. (2004). Ivory Towers? The Academy and Racism. In I. Law et al. (Eds.), *Institutional Racism in Higher Education* (pp. 1–6). Sterling, VA: Trentham Books.

Back, L., & Solomos, J. (2000). Introduction: Theorising Race and Racism. In L. Back & J. Solomos (Eds.), *Theories of Race and Racism: A Reader* (pp. 1–28). New York: Routledge.

Backhouse, C. (1999). *Colour-Coded: A Legal History of Racism in Canada, 1900–1950*. Toronto: University of Toronto Press for the Osgoode Society for Canadian Legal History.

Baldwin, A., Cameron, L., & Kobayashi, A. (2011). Introduction. In A. Baldwin, L. Cameron, & A. Kobayashi (Eds.), *Rethinking the Great White North* (pp. 1–17). Vancouver: UBC Press.

Balibar, E., & Wallerstein, I. (1991). *Race, Nation, and Class: Ambiguous Identities*. New York: Verso.

Banaji, M. (2003, January/February). Colour Blind? *This Magazine*.

Bangash, S. A. (2012, February 5). *The Silent Voice of the Minority: Immigrant Women in American Media*. San Francisco: Global Press Institute.

Banks, J. (1993). *An Introduction to Multicultural Education, Theory, and Practice*. New York: Allyn & Bacon.

Bannerji, H. (2000). *The Dark Side of the Nation: Essays on Multiculturalism, Nationalism, and Gender*. Toronto: Canadian Scholars' Press.

Bannerji, H., et al. (1991). *Unsettling Relations: The University as Site of Feminist Struggles*. Toronto: Women's Press.

Banton, M. (2005). Historical and Contemporary Modes of Racialization. In K. Murji & J. Solomos (Eds.), *Racialization*. Oxford: Oxford University Press.

Barbee, E. L. (1993). Racism in U.S. Nursing. *Medical Anthropology Quarterly*, 7(4), 346–62.

Barker, M. (1981). *New Racism*. London: Junction Books.

Barkun, M. (1994). *Religion and the Racist Right: The Origins of the Christian Identity Movement*. Chapel Hill, NC: University of North Carolina Press.

Barlow, A. L. (2012). *Between Fear and Hope: Globalization and Race in the United States*. New York: Rowman & Littlefield Publishers.

Barrett, S. R. (1987). *Is God a Racist? The Right Wing in Canada*. Toronto: University of Toronto Press.

Battiste, M. (2009). Editorial Commentary. Systemic Discrimination Against Aboriginal Peoples. *Directions: Canadian Race Relations Foundation*, 5(1).

Baureiss, G. (1985). Discrimination and Response: The Chinese in Canada. In R. M. Bienvenue & J. E. Goldstein (Eds.), *Ethnicity and Ethnic Relations in Canada* (pp. 241–62). Toronto: Butterworths.

Belanger, Y. (2008). *Aboriginal Self-Government in Canada*. Saskatoon: Purich Publishing.

Bell, D. (2008). *Race, Racism, and American Law* (6th ed.). New York: Aspen Publishers.

Bell, S. (2004). *Cold Terror: How Canada Nurtures and Exports Terrorism Around the World*. Toronto: John Wiley and Sons.

Bem, S. L. (1994, August 17). In a Male-Centered World, Female Differences Are Transformed into Female Disadvantages. *Chronicle of Higher Education*, B1–2.

Benedict, R. (1943). *Race and Racism*. New York: George Routledge and Sons.

Benjamin, A., et al. (2010). *Race and Well Being: The Lives, Hopes, and Activism of African Canadians*. Halifax: Fernwood.

Benson, R. (2005). American Journalism and the Politics of Diversity. *Media, Culture, and Society, 27*(1), 5–20.

Berg, M., & Wendt, S. (Eds.). (2011). *Racism in the Modern World: Historical Perspectives on Cultural Transfers and Adaptation.* New York: Berghahn Books.

Berliner, M. S., & Hull, G. (1995). Diversity and Multiculturalism: The New Racism. *Impact.* Newsletter of the Ayn Rand Institute.

Berman, G., & Paradies, Y. (2008). Racism, Disadvantage, and Multiculturalism: Toward Effective Anti-racist Praxis. *Ethnic and Racial Studies, 33*(2), 214–32.

Bernard, E. (2011). Prologue: The Riddle of Race. *Patterns of Prejudice, 45*(1/2), 4–14.

Berry, J., Kalin, R., & Taylor, T. (1977). *Multiculturalism and Ethnic Attitudes in Canada.* Ottawa: Ministry of Supply and Services.

Best, J. (2001). Social Progress and Social Problems. *Sociological Quarterly, 42*(1), 1–12.

Best, J., & Harris, S. R. (2013). *Making Sense of Social Problems: New Images, New Issues.* Boulder, CO: Lynne Rienner Publishers.

Better, S. (2007). *Institutional Racism* (2nd ed.). Boulder, CO: Rowman and Littlefield.

Bhavnani, R., Mirza, H. S., & Meetoo, V. (2005). *Tackling the Roots of Racism: Lessons for Success.* Bristol: Joseph Rountree Foundation and Polity Press.

Biddiss, M. D. (Ed.). (1979). *Images of Race.* New York: Holmes & Meier.

Biles, J., Tolley, E., & Ibrahim, H. (2005). Does Canada Have a Multicultural Future? *Canadian Diversity, 4*(1), 23–28.

Binder, J., et al. (2009). Does Contact Reduce Prejudice or Does Prejudice Reduce Contact? A Longitudinal Test of the Contact Hypothesis among Majority and Minority Groups in Three European Countries. *Journal of Personality and Social Psychology, 96*(4), 8543–856.

Bishop, A. (2005). *Beyond Token Change: Breaking the Cycle of Oppression in Institutions.* Halifax: Fernwood.

Bissoondath, N. (1994). *Selling Illusions: The Cult of Multiculturalism.* Toronto: Stoddart.

Black Community Forum. (2002/2003). *Racism Makes You Sick—It's a Deadly Disease.* Racism, Violence, and Health Project. Halifax: Dalhousie University.

Blackburn, B. T. (2007). *Racial Stacking in the National Football League—Reality or Relic from the Past* (Unpublished doctoral dissertation). University of Missouri, Kansas City.

Blank, R. M., Dabady, M., & Citro, C. (Eds.). (2004). *Measuring Racial Discrimination.* Washington, DC: National Academies Press.

Blatchford, C. (2009, July 24). It's No Accident That Victims Were All Female. *Globe and Mail.*

Blauner, R. (1972). *Racial Oppression in America.* New York: HarperCollins.

Blauner, R. (1994). Talking Past Each Other: Black and White Languages. In F. L. Pincus & H. J. Ehrlich (Eds.), *Race and Ethnic Conflicts* (pp. 18–28). Boulder, CO: Westview Press.

Blaut, J. (1992). The Theory of Cultural Racism. *Antipode: A Radical Journal of Geography, 23,* 289–99.

Bleich, E. (2011). *The Freedom to Be Racist.* New York: Oxford University Press.

Bleich, E., & Lambert, F. (2013). Why Are Racist Associations Free in Some States and Banned in Others? Evidence from 10 Liberal Democracies. *West European Politics, 36*(1), 122–49.

Block, S., & Galabuzi, G.-E. (2011, March). *Canada's Colour-Coded Labour Market: The Gap for Racialized Workers*. Canadian Centre for Policy Alternatives.

Bobo, L. D. (2004). Inequalities That Endure? Racial Ideology, American Politics, and the Peculiar Role of Social Science. In M. Krysan, A. Lewis, & T. Forman (Eds.), *Changing Terrain of Race and Ethnicity* (pp. 13–41). New York: Russell Sage Foundation.

Bolaria, B. S., & Li, P. (1988). *Racial Oppression in Canada* (2nd ed.). Toronto: Garamond.

Bolton, K., & Feagin, J. (2004). *Black in Blue: African American Police Officers and Racism*. New York: Routledge.

Bonilla-Silva, E. (1997). Rethinking Racism: Toward a Structural Interpretation. *American Sociological Review*, 62(3), 465–80.

Bonilla-Silva, E. (2002). The Linguistics of Color Blind Racism: How to Talk Nasty about Blacks without Sounding "Racist." *Critical Sociology*, 28(1/2), 41–64.

Bonilla-Silva, E. (2003). *Racism without Racists: Color-Blind Racism and the Persistence of Racial Inequality in the United States*. Lanham, MD: Rowman and Littlefield.

Bonilla-Silva, E., & Baiocchi, G. (2008). Anything But Racism: How Sociologists Limit the Significance of Racism. In T. Zuberi & E. Bonilla-Silva (Eds.), *White Logic, White Methods* (pp. 137–52). Lanham, MD: Rowman and Littlefield.

Bonilla-Silva, E., & Dietrich, D. (2011, March). The Sweet Enchantment of Color-Blind Racism in Obamerica. *ANNALS, AAPSS [American Academy of Political and Social Sciences]*, 634, 190–99.

Bonilla-Silva, E., & Zuberi, T. (2008). Toward a Definition of White Logic and White Methods. In T. Zuberi & E. Bonilla-Silva (Eds.), *White Logic, White Methods* (pp. 3–30). Lanham, MD: Rowman and Littlefield.

Bonnett, A. (2000). *Anti-racism*. London: Routledge.

Boswell, R. (2012, March 21). Muslims Not Trusted: Poll. *Montreal Gazette*.

Bouchard, G., & Taylor, C. (2008). *Building the Future: A Time for Reconciliation*. Abridged Report of the Commission for Reasonable Accommodation of Religious and Cultural Minorities. Quebec City: Library and National Archives of Quebec.

Bow, C. M. (2009, July 26). Welcome to the "Club." *New York Times*.

Boyd, D. (2011). White Flight in a Networked Public: How Race and Class Shape American Teen Engagement with Myspace and Facebook. In L. Nakamura & P. Chow-White (Eds.), *Race after the Internet* (pp. 203–22). New York: Routledge.

Boyd, M., & Pikkov, D. (2008). Finding a Place in Stratified Structures: Migrant Women in North America. In N. Piper (Ed.), *New Perspectives on Gender and Migration* (pp. 19–58). New York: Routledge.

Boykoff, J. (2006). Framing Dissent: Mass-Media Coverage of the Global Justice Movement. *New Political Science*, 28(2), 201–28.

Brace, C. L. (2005). *"Race" Is a Four-Letter Word: The Genesis of the Concept*. New York: Oxford University Press.

Braddock II, J.-H., Smith, E., & Dawkins, M. P. (2012). Race and Pathways to Power in the National Football League. *American Behavioral Scientist*, 56(5), 711–27.

Bradley, R. N. (2010, September 8). On Postracial America: (In)Glorious Mongrels. *New Black Magazine*.

Brazile, D. (2012, November 1). *In 2012, Racism's Tenacious Hold on U.S.* Retrieved from www.CNN.com

Brezina, T., & Winder, K. (2003). Economic Disadvantage, Status Generalization, and Negative Racial Stereotyping by White Americans. *Social Psychology Quarterly,* 66, 402–18.

Brooks, D. (2007, June 22). When Preaching Flops. *International Herald Tribune.*

Brown, C. (2005, December 1). Mental Health Bill "Biased Against Black Patients." *The Independent.* Retrieved from www.independent.co.uk

Brown, C. (2009). WWW.HATE.COM: White Supremacist Discourse on the Internet and the Construction of Whiteness Ideology. *Howard Journal of Communication,* 20, 189–208.

Brown, E. (2003). *The Condemnation of Little B.* Boston: Beacon Press.

Brown, L. (2007, November 10). Black Only, But Don't Use the "S" Word. *Toronto Star.*

Brown, L., & Stega, S. (Eds.). (2005). *Research as Resistance: Critical, Indigenous, and Anti-Oppressive Approaches.* Toronto: Canadian Scholars' Press.

Brown, M., et al. (2003). *Whitewashing Race: The Myth of a Colorblind Society.* Berkeley & Los Angeles: University of California Press.

Brown, M. J. (2004). *In Their Own Voices: African-Canadians in the Greater Toronto Area Share Experiences of Police Profiling.* Commissioned by the African-Canadian Community Coalition on Racial Profiling.

Bruce-Jones, E. (2010). *Germany: The Time to Deal with Institutional Racism.* Retrieved from www.enargywebzine.eu

Brunon-Ernst, A. (Ed.). (2012) *Beyond Foucault: New Perspectives on Bentham's Panopticon.* Farnham, UK: Ashgate.

Bullard, R. D., Johnson, G. S., & Torres, A. O. (2004). *Highway Robbery: Transportation Racism and New Routes to Equity.* Boston: South End Press.

Bullock, K. H., & Jafri, G. J. (2000). Media (Mis)Representations: Muslim Women in the Canadian Nation. *Canadian Women Studies,* 20(2), 35–40.

Bunzl, M. (2005). Between Anti-Semitism and Islamophobia: Some Thoughts on the New Europe. *American Ethnologist,* 32(4), 499–508.

Burke, M. (2012). *Racial Ambivalence in Diverse Communities: Whiteness and the Power of Color-Blind Ideologies.* Boulder, CO: Rowman and Littlefield.

Burnett, J. (2010). The Politics of "Hate." *ENAR Webzine.* Retrieved from www.enargywebzine.eu

Burnett, J. (2012). An Overview of Racial Violence and Harassment in the UK So Far in 2012. *Diverse Magazine.* Retrieved from www.diversemag.co.uk

Burnett, J. (2013a). Britain: Racial Violence and the Politics of Hate. *Race & Class,* 54(4), 5–21.

Burnett, J. (2013b). *Racial Violence: Facing Reality.* London: Institute of Race Relations.

Byng, M. D. (2012). You Can't Get There from Here: A Social Process Theory of Racism and Race. *Critical Sociology,* 1–12.

Byrd, W. C. (2011). Conflating Apples and Oranges: Understanding Modern Forms of Racism. *Sociology Compass,* 5(11), 1005–17.

Byrne, B. (2010). *White Lives: The Interplay of "Race," Class, and Gender in Everyday Life.* New York: Routledge.

Cable, D. (2013, July). The Racial Dot Map. Demographic Research Group. Weldon Cooper Center for Public Service, University of Virginia.
Caines, L. (2004, Spring). The Deep Roots of Prejudice. *Research*, 38.
Caldwell, C. (2009). *Reflections on the Revolution in Europe: Immigration, Islam, and the West*. London: Anchor Academic Publishing.
Calliste, A., & Dei, G. (Eds.). (2000). *Anti-racist Feminism: Critical Race and Gender Studies*. Halifax: Fernwood Publishing.
Canadian Centre for Policy Alternatives. (2009, January 15). Racialized Policing. *Fast Facts*. National Office, Ottawa.
Canadian Council of Churches. (2012). Cracking Open White Identity Towards Transformation: Canadian Ecumenical Anti Racism Network Examines White Identity, Power, and Privilege. Toronto.
Canadian Federation of Students. (2008). *The Final Report of the Task Force on the Needs of Muslim Students*. Toronto: Author.
Canadian Federation of Students. (2011). *The Final Report of the Task Force on Campus Racism*. Toronto: Author.
Canadian Islamic Congress. (2002). Anti-Islam in Canadian Media Feeds "Image Distortion Disorder." Retrieved from www.canadianislamiccongress
Canadian Mental Health Association (Ontario). (2002). *Immigrants and Refugees*. Retrieved from www.ontario.cmha.ca
Canadian Press. (2009). Forum Hears Claims of Discrimination at Ont. Campuses. CTV News. Retrieved from http://toronto.ctv.ca
Canadian Press. (2012, August 23). B'Nai Brith Report Says Anti-Semitism Up in Canada. *Globe and Mail*.
Canadian Race Relations Foundation. (2008, April 30–May 2). *What Is Canadian Racism? A National Symposium*, Calgary, AB.
Cannon, M. J., & Sunseri, L. (Eds.). (2011). *Racism, Colonialism, and Indigeneity in Canada*. Toronto: Oxford University Press.
Cardinal, H. (1969). *The Unjust Society*. Edmonton: Hurtig Publishing.
Cardozo, A. (2005, September 15). Multiculturalism vs. Rights. *Toronto Star*.
Carleton University. (2003). *The Concept of Race*. Equity Services. Ottawa.
Carlson, K. B. (2012, November 28). Iran Blasts Canada as "Racist" and "Self Centred" for Moving UN Resolution Condemning Islamic Republic's Abuse. *National Post*.
Carmichael, S., & Hamilton, C. V. (1967). *Black Power: The Politics of Liberation*. New York: Vintage.
Carruthers, A. (2013). National Multiculturalism, Transnational Identities. *Journal of Intercultural Studies*, 34(2), 214–28.
Carty, L. (1991). Black Women in Academia: A Statement from the Periphery. In H. Bannerji et al. (Eds.), *Unsettling Relations* (pp. 13–44). Toronto: Women's Press.
Cashmore, E., & Jennings, J. (Eds.). (2001). *Racism: Essential Readings*. Thousand Oaks, CA: Sage.
Cassin, A. M., Krawchenko, T., & VanderPlaat, M. (2007). *Racism and Discrimination in Canada: Laws, Policies, and Practices*. Atlantic Metropolis Centre. Multiculturalism and Human Rights Research Reports no. 3. Ottawa: Department of Canadian Heritage.
Castellano, M., Archibald, L., & Degagne, M. (Eds.). (2008). *From Truth to Reconciliation: Transforming the Legacy of Residential Schools*. Ottawa: Aboriginal Healing Foundation.

Castles, S., & Miller, M. J. (2009). *The Age of Migration: International Population Movements in the Modern World* (4th ed.). New York: Guilford Press.

Central America Women's Network. (2010*). Intersecting Inequalities: A Review of Feminist Theories and Debates on Violence Against Women and Poverty in Latin America.* London: Author.

Chait, J. (2009). Color Commentator. *The New Republic, 18.*

Chan, R. (2004). A Message from the Minister of State (Multiculturalism). *Annual Report on the Operation of the Canadian Multiculturalism Act.* Ottawa: Citizenship and Immigration.

Chan, W., & Mirchandani, K. (2002). From Race and Crime to Racialization and Criminalization. In W. Chan & K. Mirchandani (Eds.), *Crimes of Colour: Racialization in the Criminal Justice System in Canada.* Peterborough: Broadview Press.

Chandra, C. L., & Airhihenbuwa, C. O. (2010). Critical Race Theory, Race Equity, and Public Health: Toward Anti-Racism Praxis. *American Journal of Public Health, 100*(Suppl. 1), s30–s35.

Chandra, S. (2002). The Revolution of Rising Expectations, Relative Deprivation, and the Urban Racial Disturbances of the 1960s. *Abstracts in Economic History.* Retrieved from http://eh.net

Chazan, M., Helps, L., Stanley, A., & Thakkar, S. (2011). Introduction. In M. Chazan et al. (Eds.), *Home and Native Land: Unsettling Multiculturalism in Canada* (pp. 1–14). Toronto: Between the Lines.

Chesler, M., & Crowfoot, J. (1997). *Racism in Higher Education 11: Challenging Racism and Promoting Multiculturalism in Higher Education Organizations.* Working Paper no. 558. Ann Arbor: Center for Research on Social Organization, University of Michigan.

Chesler, M., Lewis, A. E., & Crowfoot, J. E. (2005). *Challenging Racism in Higher Education: Promoting Justice.* Lanham, MD: Rowman and Littlefield.

Chesler, P. (2003). *The New Anti-Semitism and What We Must Do about It.* New York: Jossey-Bass.

Chesler, P. (2013, February 8). What Jonathan Kay Got Wrong. *National Post.*

Chomsky, N. (2007, May 16). *Manufacturing Consent, Media, and the Web.* Interview with Chomsky by Melissa Ray, *The Lance.* University of Windsor.

Christiansen, T., & Reh, C. (2009). *Constitutionalizing the European Union.* New York: Palgrave Macmillan.

Churchill, W. (2002). *Perversions of Justice: Indigenous Peoples and Angloamerican Law.* San Francisco: City Lights.

Citizenship and Immigration. (2010, December). *Evaluation of Canada's Action Plan Against Racism.* Ottawa: Author.

Citizenship and Immigration. (2012). *Annual Report on the Operation of the Canadian Multiculturalism Act—2011/2012. Promoting Integration.* Ottawa: Ottawa.

Clarkson, A. (2012, June 17). Europe's Racism Problem. *Japan Today.* Retrieved from www.japantoday.com

Closs, W. J. (2003, May 16). Racial Profiling Guidelines Ensure Fairness for All. *Kingston Whig Standard.*

Closs, W. J., & McKenna, P. F. (2006). Profiling a Problem in Canadian Police Leadership: The Kingston Police Data Collection Problem. *Canadian Public Administration, 49*(2), 143–60.

CNN.com/Health. (2001, August 27). *Report: Minorities Lack Proper Mental Health Care.* Retrieved from http://archives.cnn.com

Coates, R. (2008). Covert Racism in the United States and Globally. *Sociology Compass, 2*(1), 208–301.

Coates, T.-N. (2008, May 1). This Is How We Lost to the White Man. *The Atlantic.*

Coates, T.-N. (2013, March 6). The Good, Racist People. Op Ed Guest Columnist. *New York Times.*

Cobb, C. (2005, July 4). Canada's Lost Promise of Multiculturalism. *Ottawa Citizen.*

Cohen, J. (1999). *Racism and Mainstream Media. Fairness and Accuracy in Reporting,* October 1. Retrieved from www.fair.org

Cohen, L. J. (2011, January 24). The Psychology of Prejudice and Racism. *Psychology Today.*

Collacott, M. (2007). Submission to the Consultation Commission on Accommodation Practices Related to Cultural Differences (Bouchard-Taylor Commission). Fraser Institute.

Comack, E. (2011). *Racialized Policing: Aboriginal Encounters with the Police.* Halifax: Fernwood.

Commission on British Muslims and Islamophobia. (1997). *Islamophobia: A Challenge for Us All.* London: Runnymede Trust.

Conference Board of Canada. (2004). *The Voices of Visible Minorities.Speaking Out on Breaking Down Barriers.* Toronto: Author.

Conference Notes. (2006, November 3–4). *New Racisms, New Anti-racisms.* Canberra: Australian Human Rights Commission.

Cooper, A. (2006). *The Hanging of Angelique.* Toronto: HarperCollins.

Cooper, G. (1995, November 7). Mental Health Care "Fails Ethnic Minorities." *The Independent.* Retrieved from www.independent.co.uk

Cose, E. (1997). *Color-Blind: Seeing Beyond Race in a Race-Obsessed World.* New York: HarperCollins.

Cotler, I. (2007). The New Antisemitism: An Assault on Human Rights. In M. Fineberg et al. (Eds.), *Antisemitism: The Generic Hatred* (pp. 15–33). Simon Wiesenthal Center. Portland, OR: Vallentine Mitchell Publishers.

Cottle, S. (Ed.). (2000). *Ethnic Minorities and the Media.* Philadelphia & Buckingham: Open University Press.

Coulter, D. (2009, November 6). Beyond the Pale? Indian Men Adopt Skin-Bleaching Trend. *Globe and Mail.*

Cox, O. C. (1948). *Caste, Class, and Race.* New York: Doubleday.

Coyle, J. (2004, January 24). Racist Officer Almost Beyond Sensitivity Training. *Toronto Star.*

Craemer, T., Shaw, T. C., Edwards, C., & Jefferson, H. (2013). "Race Still Matters, However ...": Implicit Identification with Blacks, Pro-Black Policy Support, and the Obama Candidacy. *Ethnic and Racial Studies, 36*(6), 1047–69.

CRIAW (Canadian Research Institute for Advancement of Women). (2002, July). *Women's Experience of Racism: How Racism and Gender Intersect.* Ottawa: Author.

Croll, P. R. (2013). Explanations for Racial Disadvantage and Racial Advantage: Beliefs About Both Sides of Inequality in America. *Racial and Ethnic Studies, 36*(1), 47–74.

Crompton, N. (2012, April 2). The Persistence of Anti-Asian Racism in Vancouver. Part 1. *The Mainlander.*

Cross, A., & Wallace, K. (2009, October 24). Canadian Minorities Alienated: UN. *National Post.*

Crowley, B. L. (2013, September 14). Quebec Charter Wrong in Execution, Not in Principle. *Ottawa Citzen.*

Cryderman, B., O'Toole, C., & Fleras, A. (Eds.). (1998). *Policing, Race, and Ethnicity: A Guidebook for the Policing Services* (3rd ed.). Toronto: Butterworth.

Curling, A., & McMurtry, R. (2008). *Report on the Review of the Roots of Youth Violence.* Toronto: Ministry of Children and Youth Services.

Cutaia, D. (2013, May 16). Being White Is Awesome, So How Could We Be Racists? *York Daily Record.* Retrieved from http:.www.ydr.com

D'Angelo, R. (2013, March 10). Shopping While Black: Racism in Everyday Life. *New York Times,* Opinion Pages.

Dalal, F. (2011). *Thought Paralysis: The Virtues of Discrimination.* London: Karnac Books.

Dalmage, H. (2004). *The Politics of Multiculturalism: Challenging Racial Thinking.* Albany: State University of New York.

Daniels, J. (2008). White Women Who Don't Get Racism. *RacismReview.* Retrieved from www.racismreview.com

Daniels, J. (2009a). *Cyber Racism: White Supremacy Online and the New Attack on Civil Rights.* Lanham, MD: Rowman and Littlefield.

Daniels, J. (2009b, August 5). Fighting Cyber Racism (Repurposing). *RacismReview.* Retrieved from www.racismreview.com

Daniels, J. (2009c, July 28). More Facebook Racism. *RacismReview.* Retrieved from www.racismreview.com

Daniels, J. (2012, December 10). Race and Racism in the Internet Studies: A Review and Critique. *New Media & Society,* 1–25. Retrieved from http://nms.sagepub.com

Das Gupta, T. (2009). *"Real" Nurses and "Others": Racism in Nursing.* Halifax: Fernwood.

Dauvergne, M., Scrim, K., & Brenna, S. (2008). *Hate Crime in Canada.* Ottawa: Canadian Centre for Justice Statistics.

Davin, N. F. (1879). Report on the Industrial Schools for Indians and Half-Breeds [Davin Report]. For the Minister of the Interior. Ottawa.

Davis, A. (1998, Fall). Masked Racism: Reflections on the Prison Industrial Complex. *Colorlines,* 1–4. Retrieved from www.colorlines.com

Davis, D.-A. (2007). Narrating the Mute: Racializing and Racism in a Neoliberal Moment. *Souls, 9*(4), 346–60.

Davison, J. (2005/2006). The Politics of Hate: Ultranationalist and Fundamentalist Tactics and Goals. *Journal of Hate Studies, 5*(1), 37–51.

Daynes, S., & Lee, O. (2008). *Desire for Race.* New York: Cambridge University Press.

Deacon, M. (2011). How Should Nurses Deal with Patient's Personal Racism? Learning from Practice. *Journal of Psychiatric and Mental Health Nursing, 18*(6), 493–500.

de Benoist, A. (1999, Winter). What Is Racism? *Telos, 114,* 11–48.

Decoste, R. (2013, July 22). Racism Is Front Page News for the Ottawa Sun. *Huffington Post.*

Decoste, R. (2013, February 10). The Whitewashing of Canadian Currency. *Huffington Post.* Retrieved from www.huffingtonpost.com

Dei, G. S. (1996). *Anti-racism Education: Theory and Practice.* Halifax: Fernwood.

Dei, G. S. (2000). Contesting the Future: Anti Racism and Canadian Diversity. In S. Nancoo (Ed.), *21st Century Canadian Diversity* (pp. 295–319). Toronto: Canadian Scholars' Press.

Dei, G. S. (2005a). On Race, Anti-racism, and Education. *Directions, 3*(1), 27–34.

Dei, G. S. (2005b). Foreword. In E. Samuel (Ed.), *Integrative Antiracism.* Toronto: University of Toronto Press.

Dei, G. S. (2007). Speaking Race: Silence, Salience, and the Politics of Anti-racist Scholarship. In S. P. Hier & B. S. Bolaria (Eds.), *Race and Racism in 21st Century Canada: Continuity, Complexity, and Change* (pp. 53–60). Peterborough, ON: Broadview Press.

Dei, G. J. S. (2011, Spring). In Defense of Official Multiculturalism and Recognition of the Necessity of Critical Anti Racism. *Canadian Issues,* 15–19.

Dei, G. S., & Calliste, A. (2000). Mapping the Terrain: Power, Knowledge, and Anti-racism Education. In G. S. Dei et al. (Eds.), *Removing the Margins: The Challenges and Possibilities of Inclusive Schooling* (pp. 11–24). Toronto: Canadian Scholars' Press.

Dei, G. S., & Kempf, A. (2005, October 21). *The Application and Impact of Race-Based Statistics to Effect Systemic Change and Eliminate Institutional Racism.* Paper presented at the Canadian Race Relations Foundation Policy Dialogue, North York, ON.

Dei, G. J. S., & Kempf, A. (2007, November 16). Debunking Myths about African-Centred Schools. *Toronto Star.*

Dei, G. J. S., & Kempf, A. (2013). *New Perspectives on African-Centred Schools in Canada.* Toronto: Canadian Scholars' Press.

D'Emilio, F. (2013, July 16). Italy's Premier Decries Senator's Racist Remark. *Waterloo Region Record.*

Deloitte. (2011, November). *Welcome to Canada. Now What? Unlocking the Potential of Immigrants for Business Growth and Innovation.* Summary of Deloitte's Dialogue on Diversity.

Denis, J. S. (2012). Bridging Understandings: Anishinaabe and White Perspectives on the Residential School and Prospects for Reconciliation. In L. Tepperman & A. Kalyta (Eds.), *Reading Sociology: Canadian Perspectives* (pp. 257–62). Toronto: Oxford University Press.

Department of Canadian Heritage. (2005). *A Canada for All: Canada's Action Plan Against Racism.* Ottawa. Author.

Department of Justice Canada. (1998). *Policy of the Department of Justice on Gender Equality Analysis.* Ottawa: Author.

Desmond, M., & Emirbayer, M. (2009). *Racial Domination, Racial Progress.* New York: McGraw-Hill.

Desmond, P. (2013, July 12). Hate Crimes Drop for Second Year. *Waterloo Region Record.*

Dhamoon, R. (2009). *Identity/Difference Politics: How Difference Is Produced and Why It Matters.* Vancouver: UBC Press.

Diab, R. (2008). *Guantanamo North: Terrorism and the Administration of Justice in Canada.* Halifax: Fernwood.

Diangelo, R. (2012). *What Does It Mean to Be White? Developing White Racial Literacy.* New York: Peter Lang.

Dickason, O. (1992). *Canada's First Nations.* Toronto: McClelland and Stewart.

Dickson-Gilmore, E. J., & LaPrairie, C. (2005). *Will the Circle Be Unbroken? Aboriginal Communities, Restorative Justice.* Toronto: University of Toronto Press.

Dijker, A. (2009). Confronting Racism. *Science, 324,* 590–91.

Doane, A. (Woody). (2006). What Is Racism? Racial Discourse and Racial Politics. *Critical Sociology, 32*(2–3). Retrieved from www.brill.nl

Doane, A. (2007). The Changing Politics of Color-Blind Racism. In *The New Black: Alternative Paradigms and Strategies for the 21st Century. Research in Race and Ethnic Relations, 14,* 159–74.

Doane, W. (2003). Rethinking Whiteness Studies. In W. Doane & E. Bonilla-Silva (Eds.), *White Out: The Continuing Significance of Racism* (pp. 3–20). New York: Routledge.

Dodd, D. (2013, August 3). What Is Racism? Most Canadians in a Muddle. *Vancouver Sun.*

Donaldson, J. (2013, March 1). Remembering Vancouver's First Race Riot. *The Tyee.* Retrieved from http://thetyee.ca.

Douglas, D. D. (2008). Racism in Canada: The Evidence of Things Not Seen. *Ardent Review 1*(4), 41–44.

Dovidio, J. (2009). Racial Bias, Unspoken but Heard. *Science, 326*(5690), 1641–42.

Dovidio, J. F., Gaertner, S., & Kawakami, K. (2010). Racism. In J. F. Dovidio (Ed.), *The Sage Handbook of Prejudice, Stereotyping, and Discrimination.* Thousand Oaks, CA: Sage.

Dovidio, J. F., Hewson, M., Glick, P., & Esses, V. M. (2010). Introduction. In J. F. Dovidio (Ed.), *The Sage Handbook of Prejudice, Stereotyping, and Discrimination.* Thousand Oaks, CA: Sage.

Drolet, D. (2009, March 23). Universities Are Not Facing Up to Race Issues, Say Scholars. *University Affairs.*

Drummond, D., & Fong, F. (2010, March 8). *The Changing Canadian Workplace.* Special Report, TD Economics.

D'Sousa, D. (1995). *The End of Racism.* New York: Free Press.

Dua, E. (2007). Exploring Articulations of "Race" and Gender: Going Beyond Singular Categories. In S. Hier & B. S. Bolaria (Eds.), *Race and Racism in 21st Century Canada* (pp. 175–96). Peterborough, ON: Broadview Press.

Dua, E. (2008). Thinking Through Anti Racism and Indigeneity in Canada. *Ardent Review, 1*(1), 31–35.

Dua, E. (2009). On the Effectiveness of Anti-racist Policies in Canadian Universities: Issues of Implementation of Policies by Senior Administration. In F. Henry & C. Tator (Eds.), *Racism in the Canadian University* (pp. 160–96). Toronto: University of Toronto Press.

Dua, E., Razack, N., & Warner, J. N. (2005). Race, Racism, and Empire: Reflections on Canada. *Social Justice, 32*(4), 1–7.

DuBois, W. E. B. (1940). *Dusk of Dawn: An Essay Toward an Autobiography of a Race Concept.* New York: Harcourt Brace.

Duncan, H. (2005). Multiculturalism: Still a Viable Concept for Integration. *Canadian Diversity, 4*(1), 12–14.

Duncanson, J., Freed, D. A., & Sorrensen, C. (2003, February 26). There's Racism All Over the Place. *Toronto Star*.

Dunn, K., Kockler, N., & Salabay, T. (2007). Contemporary Racism and Islamophobia in Australia. *Ethnicities, 7*(4), 564–89.

Dunn, K., & Nelson, J. K. (2011). Challenging the Public Denial of Racism for a Deeper Multiculturalism. *Journal of Intercultural Studies, 32*(6), 587–602.

Durodoye, B. A. (2003). The Science of Race in Education. *Multicultural Perspectives. 5*(2), 10–16.

Dwyer, C., & Bressey, C. (Eds.). (2008). *New Geographies of Race and Racism*. Burlington, VT: Ashgate Publishing.

Dyson, M. E. (2004). *A Michael Eric Dyson Reader*. New York: Basic Civitas Books.

Editorial. (2004, January 1). Racism in Canada. *Canadian Dimension, 39*(1).

Editorial. (2007, November 7). No Segregated Schools. *Toronto Star*.

Editorial. (2009, July 25). Of Race and the Police. *Toronto Star*.

Editorial. (2013, August 31). The Long Tail of Slavery. *Globe and Mail*.

Edwards, S. (2007). UN Calls Canada Racist for "Visible Minorities" Tag. CanWest News Service. Retrieved from www.canada.com

Eisenkraft, H. (2010, October 12). Racism in the Academy. *University Affairs*.

Eisenstein, Z. (1996). *Hatreds: Racialized and Sexualized Conflicts in the Twenty-first Century*. New York: Routledge.

Eitzen, D. S., & Sage, G. H. (2010). *Solutions to Social Problems: Lessons for State and Local Government*. Boston: Allyn and Bacon.

Elmasry, M. (1999, December 16). Framing Islam. *Kitchener-Waterloo Record* (now *Waterloo Region Record*).

Emerson, M. O., & Smith, C. (2001). *Divided by Faith: Evangelical Religion and the Problem of Race in America*. New York: Oxford University Press.

ENAR (European Network Against Racism). (2009). Racism in Europe. *ENAR Shadow Report 2008*. Retrieved from www.enar-eu.org

ENAR. (2012). *Shadow Report 2011/12 on Racism in Europe: Key Findings on Muslim Communities and Islamophobia*. Retrieved from www.enar-eu.org

ENAR. (2013). *Recycling Hatred: Racism(s) in Europe Today. A Dialogue Between Academics, Equality Experts, and Civil Society Activists*. Retrieved from www.enar-eu.org

Endelman, T. M. (2005). Anti-Semitism in Western Europe Today. In D. Penslar et al. (Eds.), *Contemporary Anti-Semitism* (pp. 64–79). Toronto: University of Toronto Press.

Engler, Y. (2004, February 16). *Racism in Canada*. Retrieved from www.zmag.org/znet/

Entman, R. (1993). Framing: Toward a Clarification of a Fractured Paradigm. *Journal of Communication, 43*(4), 51–58.

ERASE Racism. (2005). What Is Institutional Racism? Retrieved from www.eraseracismny.org

ERCI (European Commission Against Racism and Intolerance). (2009). *Annual Report on ECRI's Activities*. Brussels: Author.

Ernst, C. W. (2013). *Islamophobia in America*. New York: Palgrave Macmillan.

Espenshade, T. J., & Radford, A. W. (2009). *No Longer Separate, Not Quite Equal: Race and Class in Elite College Admission and Campus Life*. Princeton: Princeton University Press.

Esposito, J. L. (2012). Foreword. In N. Lean (Ed.), *The Islamophobia Industry: How the Right Manufactures Fears of Muslims*. London: Pluto Press.

Essed, P. (1991). *Understanding Everyday Racism: An Interdisciplinary Study*. Newbury Park, CA: Sage.

Essed, P. (2002). Everyday Racism. In D. T. Goldberg & J. Solomos (Eds.), *Companion to Race and Ethnic Studies* (pp. 202–16). Malden, MA: Blackwell.

Essed, P. (2013). Entitlement Racism: License to Humiliate. In ENAR, *Recycling Hatreds: Racism(s) in Europe. A Dialogue Between Academics, Equality Experts, and Civil Society Activists*. Brussels.

EU-Midis. (2009). *European Minorities and Discrimination Survey*. Brussels: European Agency for Fundamental Human Rights.

Eurobarometer. (2008). *Survey. Discrimination in the European Union: Perceptions, Experiences, and Attitudes*. Retrieved from http://ec.europa.eu

Evans, L., & Feagin, J. R. (2012). Middle-Class African American Pilots: The Continuing Significance of Race. *American Behavioral Scientist*, 56(5), 650–55.

Evans, M., Hole, R., Berg, L. D., Hutchinson, P., & Sookraj, D. (2009, March 23). Common Insights, Different Methodologies: Toward an Infusion of Indigenous Methodologies, Participatory Action Research, and White Studies in an Urban Aboriginal Research Agenda. *Qualitative Inquiry, 15*. Retrieved from http://qix.sagepub.com

Ewan, E., & Ewan, S. (2006). *Typecasting: On the Arts and Sciences of Human Inequality*. New York: Seven Stories Press.

Fanon, F. (1967). *Black Skin, White Masks*. New York: Grove Press.

Fantoni, B. (2011, June 7). Police-Reported Hate Crimes Rise in Canada: StatsCan. *Postmedia News*.

Fayerman, P. (2009). *Nurses and Racism—Medicine Matters*. Retrieved from http://communities.canada.com

Feagin, J. (2002). *The Continuing Significance of Racism: U.S. Colleges and Universities*. Occasional Paper no. 1. Washington: American Council of Education. Office of Minorities in Higher Education.

Feagin, J. (2006). *Systemic Racism: A Theory of Oppression*. New York: Routledge.

Feagin, J., & Cobas, J. (2008). Latinos/as and White Racial Frame: The Procrustean Bed of Assimilation. *Sociological Inquiry*, 78(1), 39–53.

Feagin, J., & Elias, S. (2013). Rethinking Racial Formation Theory: A Systemic Racism Critique. *Ethnic and Racial Studies*, 36(6), 931–60.

Feagin, J., & McKenny, K. D. (2003). *The Many Costs of Racism*. Lanham, MD: Rowman and Littlefield.

Fekete, L. (2009). *A Suitable Enemy: Racism, Migration, and Islamophobia in Europe*. London: Pluto Press.

Fekete, L. (2013a). Reverse Racism and the Manipulation of White Victimhood. In *ENAR 2013 Recycling Hatred: Racism(s) in Europe Today. A Dialogue Between Academics, Equality Experts, and Civil Society Activists*. Brussels.

Fekete, L. (2013b, July). *From Pillar to Post: Pan European Racism and the Roma*. Briefing Paper no. 7. European Research Paper. London: Institute of Race Relations.

Feldman, M. E., & Weseley, A. J. (2013). Which Name Unlocks the Door? The Effect of Tenant Race/Ethnicity on Landlord Response. *Journal of Applied Social Psychology 43*, 416–25.

Ferber, A. L. (1998). *White Man Falling: Race, Gender, and White Supremacy.* Boston: Rowman & Littlefield.
Ferber, A. L. (2008, October 30). I Am Racist! *Huffington Post.*
Ferenc, L. (2013, March 1). Africentric High School Opens in Fall. *Toronto Star.*
Fernando, S. (2006). *Race and the City: Chinese Canadians and Chinese-American Political Mobilization.* Vancouver: University of British Columbia Press.
Finnegan, M., & Johnson, S. (2011, May 11). *Elite Racism.* New York: Amsterdam News.
Fish, S. (1997, Winter). Boutique Multiculturalism, or Why Liberals Are Incapable of Thinking about Hate Speech. *Critical Inquiry, 23*(2), 378–95.
Fisher, M. (2013a, May 15). A Fascinating Map of the World's Most and Least Racially Intolerant Countries. *Washington Post.*
Fisher, M. (2013b, May 17). Five Insights on the Racial Tolerance and Ethnic Diversity Map from an Ethnic Conflict Professor. *Washington Post.*
Fleras, A. (1993). *Multiculturalism in Canada.* Toronto: Nelson Publishers.
Fleras, A. (1996). Behind the Ivy Walls: Racism/Anti-racism on Campus. In I. Alladin (Ed.), *Racism in Education* (pp. 134–77). Toronto: Harcourt Brace.
Fleras, A. (2003). Researching Together Differently: Bridging the Research Paradigm Gap. *Native Studies Review, 15*(2), 109–21.
Fleras, A. (2004). Racializing Culture/Culturalizing Race: Multicultural Racism in a Multicultural Canada. In C. Nelson (Ed.), *Racism Eh? A Critical, Interdisciplinary Anthology on Race in the Canadian Context* (pp. 321–44). Thornhill, ON: Captus Press.
Fleras, A. (2002). *Engaging Diversity: Multiculturalism in Canada.* Toronto: Nelson.
Fleras, A. (2005). *Social Problems in Canada* (4th ed.). Toronto: Pearson.
Fleras, A. (2008a, April 6). *The Politics of Re/Naming.* Paper commissioned by the Department of Justice and delivered at the Ninth National Metropolis Conference, Halifax, NS.
Fleras, A. (2008b, May 16). Systemic Propaganda. Invited paper for the 20 Years of Propaganda conference, University of Windsor, Windsor, ON.
Fleras, A. (2009). *The Politics of Multiculturalism.* New York: Palgrave Macmillan.
Fleras A. (2011a). From Mosaic to Multiversality: Repriming Multicultural Governance in a Postnational Canada. *Canadian Ethnic Studies, 43*(1/2), 17–39.
Fleras, A. (2011b). Multicultural Governance in a Globalizing World of Transmigration and Multiversality: A Case for a Multiversal Multiculturalism in Canada [Special Issue Ethnicity and Governance]. *Canadian Journal for Social Research, 2*(1), 117–27.
Fleras, A. (2011c). *The Media Gaze.* Vancouver: University of British Columbia Press.
Fleras, A. (2012). *Unequal Relations: Introduction to Race, Ethnic, and Aboriginal Dynamics* (7th ed.). Toronto: Pearson.
Fleras, A., & Kunz, J. L. (2001). *Media and Minorities: Misrepresenting Minorities in a Multicultural Canada.* Toronto: TEP.
Fleras, A., & Spoonley, P. (1999). *Recalling Aotearoa: Indigenous Politics and Ethnic Dynamics in New Zealand.* Auckland: Oxford University Press.
Fong, J. (Ed.). (2010a). Foreword. *Out of the Shadows: Woman Abuse in Ethnic, Immigrant, and Aboriginal Communities.* Toronto: Women's Press.
Fong, J. (2010b). Beyond Cultural Stereotypes: Chinese Canadian Helping Professionals' Perspectives on Woman Abuse within the Chinese-Canadian Community in

Toronto. In J. Fong (Ed.), *Out of the Shadows* (pp. 99–131). Toronto: Women's Press.

Fontaine, P., & Farber, B. (2013, October 13). What Canada Committed Against First Nations Was Genocide: The UN Should Recognize It. *Globe and Mail.*

Forbis, M. (2013, April 22). Hollywood Is White and Why That's Wrong. *St. Andrews Foreign Affairs Review.*

Ford, C., & Airhihenbuwa, C. O. (2010). Critical Race Theory, Race Equity, and Public Health: Toward Antiracism Praxis. *American Journal of Public Health, 100*(1), 30–35.

Ford, R. T. (2009, September 30). *A Primer on Racism.* Retrieved from www.slate.com

Forrest, J., & Dunn, K. (2007). Constructing Racism in Sydney, Australia's Largest EthniCity. *Urban Studies, 44*(4), 699–721.

Forum. (2009). American Religion and "Whiteness." *Religion and American Culture: A Journal of Interpretation, 19*(1), 1–35.

Foster, C. (2005). *Where Race Does Not Matter: The New Spirit of Modernity.* Toronto: Penguin.

Foster, L. (2009). The Role of the "Third Media" in Minority Empowerment. In A. Itwaru (Ed.), *The White Supremacist State* (pp. 263–315). Toronto: Other Eye Publisher.

Foucault, M. (1991). *Discipline and Punish: The Birth of a Prison.* London: Penguin.

Foucault, M. (1998). *The History of Sexuality: The Will to Knowledge.* London: Penguin.

Frankenberg, R. (1993). *White Women Race Matters: The Social Construction of Whiteness.* Minneapolis: University of Minnesota Press.

Fraser, G. (2005, March 16). Racism on the Rise. *Hamilton Spectator.*

Fraser, J. (1988, March). Refugee Riddles, Dark Mirrors, and the National Honour. *Saturday Night,* 7–8.

Fraser, J. (2006, June 24). The Toxic Tower. *Globe and Mail.*

Fredericko, C., & Luks, S. (2005). The Political Psychology of Race. *International Journal of Political Psychology, 26*(6), 661–74.

Frederickson, G. M. (2002). *Racism: A Short History.* Princeton: Princeton University Press.

Free Jr., M. D., & Ruesink, M. (2012). *Race and Justice: Wrongful Convictions of African American Men.* Boulder, CO: Lynne Riener Publishing.

Frideres, J., & Gadacz, R. R. (2012). *Aboriginal Peoples in Canada* (9th ed.). Toronto: Pearson Education Canada.

Fukawa, M. (with Fukawa, S.). (2009). *Spirit of the Nikkei Fleet: BC's Japanese Canadian Fisherman.* Pender Harbour, BC: Harbour Publishing.

Gaertner, S. L., & Dovidio, J. F. (Eds.). (1986). *Prejudice, Discrimination, and Racism.* Orlando, FL: Academic Press.

Galabuzi, G.-E. (2004, January). The Contemporary Struggle Against Racism. *Canadian Dimension,* 1–3.

Galabuzi, G.-E. (2006). *Canada's Economic Apartheid: The Social Exclusion of Racialized Groups in the New Century.* Toronto: Canadian Scholars' Press.

Galabuzi, G.-E. (2010). Measuring Racial Discrimination in Canada: A Call for Context and More Inclusive Approaches. *Canadian Journal for Social Research, 3*(2), 24–44.

Galabuzi, G.-E. (2011). Hegemonies, Continuities, and Discontinuities of Multiculturalism and the Anglo-Franco Conformity Order. In M. Chazan et al. (Eds.), *Home and Native Land: Unsettling Multiculturalism in Canada* (pp. 58–84). Toronto: Between the Lines.

Galabuzi, G.-E., Casipullai, A., & Go, A. (2012, March 20). The Persistence of Racial Inequality in Canada. *Toronto Star*.

Gallagher, C. A. (2003). Color Blind Privilege: The Social and Political Functions of Erasing the Color Line in Post Race America [Special Edition on Privilege]. *RGC Journal, 10*(4).

Gallagher, C. A. (2007). *Rethinking the Color Line: Readings in Race and Ethnicity* (3rd ed.). New York: McGraw-Hill.

Gallagher, C. A. (2008). "The End of Racism" as the New Doxa: New Strategies for Researching Race. In T. Zuberi & E. Bonilla-Silva (Eds.), *White Logic, White Methods* (pp. 163–78). Lanham, MD: Rowman and Littlefield.

Garner, S. (2007). *Whiteness: An Introduction*. New York: Routledge.

Gates Jr., H. L. (1998). The Two Nations of Black America. *Brookings Review, 16*(2), 4–7.

Gault, C. (2009, July 29). Who's the Racist? *National Post*.

Gaventa, J. (2003). *Power After Lukes: A Review of the Literature*. Brighton: Institute of Developmental Studies.

Gay, G. (1997). Educational Equality for Students of Color. In J. Banks & C. Banks (Eds.), *Multicultural Education* (pp. 195–228). Toronto: Allyn and Bacon.

Gershevitch, C., Lamoin, A., & Dawes, C. (2010). Racism in Australia: Is Denial Still Plausible? *Race/Ethnicity: Multidisciplinary Global Context, 3*(2), 229–50.

Ghosh, R. (2011, Spring). The Liberating Potential of Multiculturalism in Canada: Ideals and Realities. *Canadian Issues*, 3–8.

Ghosh, R., & Abdi, A. A. (2004). *Education and the Politics of Difference: Canadian Perspectives*. Toronto: Canadian Scholars' Press.

Gibney, E. (2013, April 11). Report Finds Lingering Racism in British Higher Education. *Inside Higher Education*. Retrieved from www.insidehighered.com

Gilkinson, T., & Sauve, G. (2010, September). Recent Immigrants, Earlier Immigrants, and the Canadian Born: Association with Collective Identities. Citizenship and Immigration Canada.

Gillborn, D. (2006). Rethinking White Supremacy: Who Counts in "White World." *Ethnicities, 6*(3), 318–40.

Gilman, N. (2006, June 11). What Katrina Teaches About the Meaning of Racism. SSRC (Social Science Research Council).

Gilmour, R. J., Bhandar, D., Heer, J., & Ma, M. C. K. (Eds.). (2012). *"Too Asian?" Racism, Privilege, and Post-secondary Education*. Toronto: Between the Lines.

Gilroy, P. (2004). *After Empire: Melancholia or Convivial Culture?* London: Routledge.

Giroux, H. (1999). Rewriting the Discourse of Racial Identity: Towards a Pedagogy and Politics of Whiteness. *Harvard Educational Review, 67*(2), 285–320.

Giroux, H. (2004). *The Terror of Neoliberalism: Authoritarianism and the Eclipse of Democracy*. Boulder, CO: Paradigm Press.

Glazer, N. (1997). *We Are All Multiculturalists Now*. Cambridge, MA: Harvard University Press.

Go, A. (2007, January 19). Time to Heed UN Advice on Racism. *Toronto Star*.

Goddard, J. (2009, February 25). Sizing Up Racism in Canada. Retrieved from www.the Star.com

Goldberg, D. T. (1990a). Racism and Rationality: The Need for a New Critique. *Philosophy of the Social Sciences, 20,* 317–50.

Goldberg, D. T. (Ed.). (1990b). *The Anatomy of Racism.* Minneapolis: University of Minnesota Press.

Goldberg, D. T. (1993). *Racist Culture: Philosophy and the Politics of Meaning.* Oxford: Blackwell.

Goldberg, D. T. (2002). Racial States. In D. T. Goldberg & J. Solomos (Eds.), *Companion to Racial and Ethnic Studies* (pp. 233–58). Malden, MA: Blackwell.

Goldberg, D. T. (2005). Racial Americanization. In K. Murji & J. Solomos (Eds.), *Racialization* (pp. 87–102). Oxford, UK: Oxford University Press.

Goldberg, D. T. (2007). Raceless States. In G. F. Johnson & R. Enomoto (Eds.), *Race, Racialization, and Anti-racism in Canada and Beyond* (pp. 206–32). Toronto: University of Toronto Press.

Goldberg, D. T. (2009). *The Threat of Race: Reflections on Racial Liberalism.* Malden, MA: Wiley-Blackwell.

Goldberg, D. T., & Solomos, J. (Eds.). (2002). *A Companion to Racial and Ethnic Studies.* Malden, MA: Blackwell.

Goldberg, J. (2006, November 15). Racism by Any Other Name. *National Review Online.* Retrieved from www.nationalreview.com

Goldstein, E. L. (2006). *The Price of Whiteness.* Princeton: Princeton University Press.

Goodman, A. H., Moses, Y. T., & Jones, J. L. (2012). *Race: Are We So Different?* Malden MA: Blackwell Publishing.

Goodwin, M. (2012, August 7). We Must Respond to the Far Right's Web Threat. *The Guardian.*

Gopalkrishnan, N., & Babacan, H. (Eds.). (2007). Introduction. In N. Gopalkrishnan & H. Babacan (Eds.), *Racisms in the New World Order: Realities of Cultures, Colours, and Identity.* Newcastle: Cambridge Scholars Publishing.

Gordon, M. K., & Zinga, D. M. (2012, March 26). "Fears of Stigmatisation": Black Canadian Youths' Reactions to the Implementation of a Black-Focused School in Toronto. *Canadian Journal of Educational Administration and Policy* (131).

Gorski, P. (2004). Language of Closet Racism: An Introduction. Race, Racism, and the Law: Speaking Truth to Power. Retrieved from http://academic.udayton.edu

Gouws, A. (2008). From Racism to Valuing Diversity. *University World News.* Special Africa Edition. Issue 0002. Retrieved from www.universityworldnews.com

Grabb, E. (2009). *Theories of Social Inequality.* Toronto: Thomson/Nelson.

Grant, T. (2012, September 19). Food-Bank Use Soars as Newcomers Struggle. *Globe and Mail.*

Grant-Thomas, A., & Powell, J. A. (2006, November–December). Toward a Structural Racism Framework. *Poverty & Race.*

Grassroots Policy Project. (n.d.). *Race, Power, and Policy.* Prepared for National Peoples Action.

Grayson, J. P. (2007). Unequal Treatment and Program Satisfaction Among Students of European and Chinese Origin. *Canadian Journal of Higher Education, 37*(3), 51–85.

Green, J. (2003, March–April). Decolonizing in the Age of Globalization. *Canadian Dimension,* 3–5.

Green, J. (2004, November). Equality Quest: It's Time to Undermine the Institutional and Cultural Foundations That Support Inequality. *Briarpatch Magazine.*

Green, J. (2007). Media and Politics. Forum Panelist Response. *SIPP Briefing Note* (20).

Green, J. (2008, March–April). Aboriginal Rights in a Neo Liberal World. *Canadian Dimension,* 22–25.

Grossberg, L. (2007). Stuart Hall on Race and Racism. In B. Meeks (Ed.), *Culture, Politics, Race, and Diaspora: The Thought of Stuart Hall.* London: Lawrence & Wishart.

Guess, T. J. (2006). The Social Construction of Whiteness: Racism by Intent, Racism by Consequences. *Critical Sociology,* 32(4), 649–62.

Gulam, W. A. (2004). Black and White Paradigms in Higher Education. In I. Law et al. (Eds.), *Institutional Racism in Higher Education* (pp. 7–14). Sterling, VA: Trentham Books.

Gunter, L. (2009, July 29). A Man's Home Is His Castle. *National Post.*

Guo, S., & Jamal, Z. (2007). Nurturing Cultural Diversity in Higher Education: A Critical Review of Select Models. *Canadian Journal of Higher Education,* 37(3), 27–49.

Gwyn, R. (1994, November 26). The First Borderless State. *Toronto Star.*

Gwyn, R. (1996). *Nationalism Without Walls: The Unbearable Lightness of Being Canadian.* Toronto: McClelland and Stewart.

Gwyn, R. (2001, March 21). Old Canada Disappears." *Toronto Star.*

Ha, T. T. (2007, August 15). Quebecker's Insecurities Said to Fuel Backlash Against Minorities. *Globe and Mail.*

Ha, T. T. (2012, April 12). Police-Reported Hate Crimes Down Sharply in 2010, Statscan. *Globe and Mail.*

Hage, G. (1998). *White Nation: Fantasies of White Supremacy in a Multicultural Society.* Sydney, Australia: Pluto Press.

Hall, S. (1978). *Racism and Reaction. Five Views of Multi-Racial Britain: Talks on Race Relations.* Broadcast by the BBC TV. London: Commission for Racial Equality.

Hall, S. (1980). Race, Articulation, and Societies Structured in Dominance. In UNESCO (Ed.), *Sociological Theories: Race and Colonialism.* Paris: UNESCO.

Hall, S. (2000). Racist Ideologies and the Media. In P. Marris & S. Thornham (Eds.), *Media Studies: A Reader* (pp. 271–82). New York: New York University Press.

Halstead, M. (1988). *Education, Justice, and Cultural Diversity: An Examination of the Honeyford Affair, 1984–85.* London: Falmer Press.

Hamilton, G. (2007, December 31). The Herouxville Code. *National Post.*

Hamilton, R. (1996). *Gendering the Vertical Mosaic: Feminist Perspectives on Canadian Society.* Toronto: Copp Clark.

Hamilton Spectator. (2007, April 30). Race Plays Role in Traffic Stops: Study. Originally in Associated Press.

Hammarberg, T. (Council of Europe Commissioner for Human Rights). (2009). *Racism: Europeans Ought to Be More Self-Critical.* Retrieved from www.egovmonitor.com

Hanamoto, D. (1995). *Monitored Peril: Asian Americans and the Politics of Representation.* St. Paul: University of Minnesota Press.

Hannah, D. C. (2009). *Can Racism Lead to Weight Gain?* Retrieved from www.diversityinc.com

Haque, E. (2010). Homegrown, Muslim, and Other: Tolerance, Secularism, and the Limits of Multiculturalism. *Social Identities, 169*(1), 79–101.

Haque, E. (2012). *Multiculturalism within a Bilingual Framework: Language, Race, and Belonging in Canada.* Toronto: University of Toronto Press.

Harding, R. (2006). Historical Representations of Aboriginal People in the Canadian News Media. *Discourse & Society, 17*(2), 205–35.

Harding, S. (2002). Science, Race, Culture, Empire. In D. T. Goldberg & J. Solomos (Eds.), *Companion to Racial and Ethnic Studies* (pp. 217–28). Malden, MA: Blackwell.

Harker, J. (2012, July 22). This Is How Racism Takes Root. *The Guardian.*

Harris, L. (Ed.). (1999). *Racism.* Amherst, NY: Humanity Books.

Harris, P. (2012, October 19). Black Gains Stall under Obama. *Guardian Weekly.*

Health Council of Canada. (2012). *Empathy, Dignity, and Respect: Creating Cultural Safety for Aboriginal People in Urban Health Care.* Toronto: Author.

Heath, A., & Cheung, S. Y. (2007). The Comparative Study of Ethnic Minority Disadvantage. In A. Heath & S. Y. Cheung (Eds.), *Unequal Chances: Ethnic Minorities in Western Labour Markets* (pp. 1–44). New York: Oxford University Press.

Heer, J. (2012). Introduction. In R. J. Gilmour et al. (Eds.), *"Too Asian?" Racism, Privilege, and Post-Secondary Education* (pp. 1–16). Toronto: Between the Lines.

Helleiner, J. (2012). Whiteness and Narratives of a Racialized Canada–U.S. Border at Niagara. *Canadian Journal of Sociology, 37*(2), 109–23.

Helmes-Hayes, R., & Curtis, J. (Eds.). (1998). *The Vertical Mosaic Revisited.* Toronto: University of Toronto Press.

Henkel, K. E., Dovidio, J. F., & Gaertner, S. L. (2006). Institutional Discrimination, Individual Racism, and Hurricane Katrina. *Analysis of Social Issues and Public Policy, 6*(1), 99–124.

Hennebry, J. (2010, Spring). Not Just a Few Bad Apples: Vulnerability, Health, and Temporary Migration in Canada. *Canadian Issues,* 73–77.

Hennebry, J. (2012, February 28). Permanently Temporary? Agricultural Workers and Their Integration in Canada. *IRPP.*

Hennebry, J., & Momani, B. (Eds.). (2013). *Targeted Transnationals: The State, the Media, and Arab Canadians.* Vancouver: UBC Press.

Henry, F. (2004). *Understanding the Experiences of Visible Minority and Aboriginal Faculty Members at Queen's University.* Report submitted to Queen's University.

Henry, F., & Tator, C. (1993, May 28). The Show Boat Controversy. *Toronto Star.*

Henry, F., & Tator, C. (2002). *Discourses of Domination: Racial Bias in the Canadian English-Language Press.* Toronto: University of Toronto Press.

Henry, F., & Tator, C. (2003). *Racial Profiling in Toronto: Discourses of Domination, Mediation, and Opposition.* Final draft submitted to the Canadian Race Relations Foundation.

Henry, F., & Tator, C. (2007, February). Through a Looking Glass: Enduring Racism on the University Campus. *Academic Matters.*

Henry, F., & Tator, C. (Eds.). (2009). *Racism in the Canadian University: Demanding Social Justice, Inclusion, and Equity.* Toronto: University of Toronto Press.

Henry, F., & Tator, C. (2010). *The Colour of Democracy: Racism in Canadian Society* (4th ed.). Toronto: Harcourt Brace/Nelson.

Herman, E. (1995). *The Triumph of the Market.* Cambridge, MA: South End Press.

Hernandez-Ramdwar, C. (2009). Caribbean Students in the Canadian Academy: We've Come a Long Way? In F. Henry & C. Tator (Eds.), *Racism in the Canadian University* (pp. 106–27). Toronto: University of Toronto Press.

Herring, C., Keith, V. M., & Horton, H. D. (Eds.). (2004). *Skin Deep: How Race and Complexion Matter in the "Color-blind" Era*. Chicago: University of Chicago Press.

Herrnstein, R. J., & Murray, C. (1994). *The Bell Curve: Intelligence and Class Structure in American Life*. Glencoe, IL: Free Press.

Hervik, Dr. P. (2013). Racism, Neo Racism. In *ENAR 2013 Recycling Hatred: Racism(s) in Europe Today. A Dialogue Between Academics, Equality Experts, and Civil Society Activists* (pp. 43–50). Brussels.

Hesse, B. (2004). Discourses on Institutional Racism: The Geneology of a Concept. In I. Law et al. (Eds.), *Institutional Racism in Higher Education* (pp. 131–48). Sterling, VA: Trentham Books.

Hier, S. P. (2007). Studying Race and Racism in 21st Century Canada. In S. P. Hier & B. S. Bolaria (Eds.), *Race and Racism in 21st Century Canada* (pp. 19–34). Peterborough, ON: Broadview Press.

Hier, S. P., & Bolaria, B. S. (2007). Preface. In S. P. Hier & B. S. Bolaria (Eds.), *Race and Racism in 21st Century Canada* (pp. 9–11). Peterborough, ON: Broadview Press.

Hier, S., & Greenberg, J. (2002). News Discourses and the Problematization of Chinese Migration to Canada. In F. Henry & C. Tator (Eds.), *Discourses of Domination* (pp. 138–62). Toronto: University of Toronto Press.

Hier, S., & Walby, K. (2006). Competing Analytical Paradigms in the Sociological Study of Racism in Canada. *Canadian Ethnic Studies, 38*(1).

Hiranandani, V. (2012). Diversity Management in the Canadian Workplace: Towards an Antiracism Approach. *Urban Studies Research*, 2012, 1–13.

Hirst, M., & Patchin, R. (2005). *Journalism Ethics*. Victoria, Australia: Oxford University Press.

Hoberman, J. M. (2007). Medical Racism and the Rhetoric of Exculpation: How Do Physicians Think about Race? *New Literary History, 38*(3), 505–25.

Hoberman, J. M. (2012). *Black & Blue: The Origins and Consequences of Medical Racism*. Berkeley: University of California Press.

Hokowhitu, B. (2012). Book Review: Racism, Colonialism, and Indigeneity in Canada: A Reader. *Junctures: The Journal for Thematic Dialogue*, (15).

Holdaway, S. (1996). *The Racialisation of British Policing*. New York: St. Martin's Press.

Holthouse. D. (2009). *2009 The Year in Hate. Southern Poverty Law Centre*. Retrieved from www.splcenter.org

hooks, b. (1984). *Feminist Theory: From Margins to Centre*. Boston: South End Press.

hooks, b. (1995). *Killing Rage*. Boston: South End Press.

hooks, b. (2013). *Writing Beyond Race: Living Theory and Practice*. New York: Routledge.

Horn, G. (2011, October 27). *A Policy Gone Wrong*. Retrieved from www.Kahnawakenews.com

Hsu, H. (2009, January–February). The End of White America? *The Atlantic*.

Huber, J. (2008, January 24). Staff Report Endorses Afrocentric Curriculum. *National Post*.

Hughey, M. W. (2009). The Janus-Face of Whiteness: Toward a Cultural Sociology of White Nationalism and White Antiracism. *Sociology Compass, 3*(6), 920–36.

Hughey, M. W. (2012). *White Bound: Nationalists, Antiracists, and the Shared Meaning of Race*. Stanford, CA: Stanford University Press.

Hum, D., & Simpson, W. (2007). Revisiting Equity and Labour: Immigration, Gender, Minority Status, and Income Differentials in Canada. In S. P. Hier & B. S. Bolaria (Eds.), *Race and Racism in 21st Century Canada* (pp. 89–110). Peterborough, ON: Broadview Press.

Human Rights First. (2009). *The 2008 Hate Crime Survey*. Retrieved from www.humanrightsfirst.org

Hundal, S. (2006). The Soft Racism of Low Expectations. *The Guardian*. Retrieved from www.theguardian.com

Hunt, M. O., & Wilson, G. (2011, March). Introduction. *ANNALS, AAPSS [American Academy of Political and Social Sciences] 634*, 6–13.

Hurley, M. (2009, November 23). *The Indian Act*. Prepared for Parliament of Canada, Ottawa.

Hurst, L. (2003, April 12). A Critical Meaning of Bias. *Toronto Star*.

Huston, P. (1995). Intellectual Racism? *Canadian Medical Association Journal, 153*, 1219.

Hylton, K. (2008). *"Race" and Sport: Critical Race Theory*. New York: Routledge.

Hyman, I. (2009). *Racism as a Determinant of Immigrant Health*. Commissioned and funded by the Strategic Initiatives and Innovations Directorate of the Public Health Agency of Canada.

Ibbitson, J. (2005). *The Polite Revolution: Perfecting the Canadian Dream*. Toronto: McClelland and Stewart.

Iganski, P. (2010). The Banality of Racist Violence. *ENAR Webzine*. Retrieved from www.enargywebzine.eu

Iganski, P. (2011). *Racist Violence in Europe*. Brussels: ENAR [European Network Against Racism].

Ignatieff, M. (2000). *The Rights Revolution*. The 2000 CBC Massey Lectures.

Ignatiev, N. (1997, April 11–13). *The Point Is Not to Interpret Whiteness, But to Abolish It*. Paper presented at the Conference on Making and Unmaking Whiteness, University of California, Berkeley.

Ignatiev, N., & Garvey, J. (1996). *Race Traitor*. New York: Routledge.

Ikuenobe, P. (2013). Conceptualizing and Theorizing about the Idea of a "Post Racial" Era. *Journal for the Theory of Social Behaviour, 43*(1), 1–23.

Imai, S. (2007, July). *The Structure of the Indian Act*. Research Paper for the National Centre for First Nations Governance.

Indigenous Foundations. (2009). *The Residential School System*. University of British Columbia. Retrieved from http://indigenousfoundations.arts.ubc.ca

Inside Higher Ed. (2005, October 27). *Dumb and Dumber*. Retrieved from www.insidehighered.com

Ip, M. (1990). Gender, Racism, and the Politics of Chinese Immigration. In R. Du Plessis & L. Alice (Eds.), *Feminist Thought in Aotearoa/New Zealand*. Auckland: Oxford University Press.

Itwaru, A. (Ed.). (2009). *The White Supremacist State*. Toronto: Other Eye Publishers.

Jacobs, B., & Williams, A. J. (2006). *Missing/Murdered Aboriginal Women in Canada: Applying a Gender Based Analysis Within a Culturally Relevant Paradigm*. Paper presented to the Diversity Conference: Human Rights, Diversity, and Social Justice. Retrieved from http://d06.cgpublisher.com

Jakubowicz, A. (2005). Multiculturalism in Australia: Apogee or Nadir? *Canadian Diversity, 4*(1), 15–18.

Jakubowicz, A. (2012). Cyber Racism. In H. Sykes (Ed.), *More or Less: Democracy and New Media* (pp. 215–23). Sydney: Angus & Robertson.

James, C. (1994). The Paradoxes of Power and Privilege: Race, Gender, and Occupational Position. *Canadian Woman Studies, 14*(2), 47–51.

James, C. (2003). *Seeing Ourselves: Exploring Race, Ethnicity, and Culture.* Toronto: Thompson Educational Publishing.

James, C. (2005). *Race in Play.* Toronto: Canadian Scholars' Press.

James, C. (2007). Toward Anti-racism Policies: Making the Case for Social Justice. Directions. *Publication of the Canadian Race Relations Foundation, 3*(2).

James, C. (2009). "It Will Happen Without Putting in Place Special Measures": Racially Diversifying Universities. In F. Henry & C. Tator (Eds.), *Racism in the Canadian University* (pp. 128–59). Toronto: University of Toronto Press.

James, C., & Shadd, A. (2001). *Talking about Differences: Encounters in Language, Culture, and Identity.* Toronto: Between the Lines.

James, R. (2007, November 7). Don't Let Your Discomfort Derail Change. *Toronto Star.*

Jaret, C. (1995). *Contemporary Racial and Ethnic Relations.* Scarborough, ON: HarperCollins.

Jaworksi, J. (1979). *A Case Study of Canadian Federal Government's Multicultural Policies* (Unpublished M.A. thesis). Carleton University, Ottawa.

Jayasurija, L. (1998, September–October). Old Racism, New Racism. *Australian Quarterly,* 4–5.

Jeanpierre, W. A. (1965). Sartre's Theory of "Anti Racism Racism" in His Study of Negritude. *Massachusetts Review, 6*(4), 870–72.

Jedwab, J. (2008, November 6). *Discrimination in Canada and Europe: Perceptions, Experiences, and Attitudes.* Launch of the Canada Barometer. International Association for the Study of Canada, Montreal.

Jensen, R. (2005). *The Heart of Whiteness: Confronting Race, Racism, and White Privilege.* San Francisco: City Lights.

Jensen, R. (2009). Racism Watch: In South Africa, Apartheid Is Dead, but White Supremacy Lingers on. Retrieved from www.trinicenter.com

Jensen, R. (2010a). Beyond Race, Gender, and Class: Reclaiming the Radical Roots of Social Justice Movements. *Global Dialogue, 12*(2).

Jensen, R. (2010b). Whiteness. In S. M. Caliendo & C. D. McIlwain (Eds.), *The Routledge Companion to Race and Ethnicity* (Ch. 3). New York: Routledge.

Jhally, S., & Lewis, J. (1992). *Enlightened Racism: The Cosby Show, Audiences, and the Myth of the American Dream.* Boulder, CO: Westview Press.

Jimenez, M. (2006, September 9). For Muslims, Guilt by Assocation. *Globe and Mail.*

Jimenez, M. (2009, May 21). Right Resume, Wrong Name. *Globe and Mail.*

Jimenez, M. (2012, August 23). Canada's Ethnic Mix a Success. *Globe and Mail.*

Jiwani, Y. (2001). *Intersecting Inequalities: Immigrant Women of Colour, Violence, and Health Care.* Retrieved from www.harbour.sfu.ca/freda/articles/hlth04.htm

Jiwani, Y. (2002). The Criminalization of "Race," the Racialization of Crime. In W. Chan & W. Mirchandani (Eds.), *Crimes of Colour.* Peterborough: Broadview.

Jiwani, Y. (2005). Walking a Tightrope. *Violence Against Women, 11*(7), 846–75.
Jiwani, Y. (2006). *Discourses of Denial: Mediations of Race, Gender, and Violence.* Vancouver: UBC Press.
Jiwani, Y. (2009). Race(ing) the Nation: Media and Minorities. In L. R. Shade (Ed.). *Mediascapes* (3rd ed.) (pp. 271–86). Toronto: Nelson.
Jiwani, Y. (2010). Erasing Race: The Story of Reena Virk. In M. Rajiva & S. Batacharya (Eds.). *Reena Virk* (pp. 82–121). Toronto: Canadian Scholars' Press.
Jiwani, Y. (n.d.). *Racism and the Media.* Stop Racism and Hate Collective. Retrieved from www.stopracism.ca
Johnson, G. F., & Enomoto, R. (Eds.). (2007). *Race, Racialization, and Anti Racism in Canada and Beyond.* Toronto: University of Toronto Press.
Johnston, P. M. (1994). Examining a State Relationship: "Legitimation" and Te Kohanga Reo. *Te Pua, 3*(2), 22–34.
Jonas, G. (2006, January 20). Anti-Semitism's Presentable Cousin. *National Post.*
Jones, C. P. (2000). Levels of Racism: A Theoretical Framework and a Gardener's Tale. *American Journal of Public Health, 90*(8), 1212–15.
Jonsson, P., & Murphy, C. (2009, August 9). Who Learned What in 2009's Race Debate. *Christian Science Monitor.*
Jordan, M. (1998, April 24). Especially in India/Fair Color as a Cultural Virtue: Creams for Lighter Skin Capture the Asian Market. *New York Times.*
Joseph, J., Darnell, S., & Nakamura, Y. (2012). *Race and Sport in Canada: Intersecting Inequalities.* Toronto: Canadian Scholars' Press.
Jung, M.-K., Vargas, J. H. C., & Bonilla-Silva, E. (2011). *State of White Supremacy: Racism, Governance, and the United States.* Stanford, CA: Stanford University Press.
Kaiser, C. R., & Pratt-Hyatt, J. S. (2009). Distributing Prejudice Unequally: Do Whites Direct Their Prejudice Toward Strongly Identified Minorities? *Journal of Personality and Social Psychology, 96*(2), 432–45.
Kalman-Lamb, N. (2011). "A Portrait of This Country": Whiteness, Indigeneity, Multiculturalism, and the Vancouver Opening Ceremonies. *Topia (Canadian Journal of Cultural Studies), 27,* 5–27.
Kareem, N. (2009a). *Black Harvard Professor's Arrest Continues to Generate Controversy.* Retrieved from http://racerelations.about.com
Kareem, N. (2009b). *Are Bars and Clubs Using Dress Codes to Racially Discriminate?* Retrieved from http://racerelations.about.com
Kareem, N. (2009c). *Atlanta Mayoral Election Shows Racial Divides Remain in Obama's America.* Retrieved from http://racerelations.about.com
Kareem, N. (2009d). *Princess and the Frog Tops Box Office, but Is That Good Enough?* Retrieved from http://racerelations.about.com
Karim, K. H. (2002). *Islamic Peril: Media and Global Violence.* Montreal: Black Rose Books.
Karim, K. H. (2006). American Media's Coverage of Muslims: The Historical Roots of Contemporary Portrayals. In E. Poole & J. E. Richardson (Eds.), *Muslims and the News Media* (pp. 116–27). New York: I. B. Taurus.
Kawakami, K., Dunn, E., Karmali, F., & Dovidio, J. (2009). Mispredicting Affective and Behavioral Responses to Racism. *Science, 323,* 276–78.
Kay, J. (2009, March 3). Anti Semitism, Then and Now. *National Post.*

Kelley, R. (2009a, July 13). The Roots of Racism: What We Don't Know Can Hurt Us. *Newsweek.*

Kelley, R. (2009b, July 24). Another "Racial Incident": Debunking Talking Points about the Gates Arrest. *Newsweek Blog.* Retrieved from http://blog.newsweek.com

Kelly, J. (1998). *Under the Gaze: Learning to Be Black in a White Society.* Halifax: Fernwood.

Kepnes, M. (2008). *White Skin: Why Racism in Asia Isn't Quite What You Think.* Retrieved from www.bravetraveler.com

Khayatt, D. (1994). The Boundaries of Identity at the Intersections of Race, Class, and Gender. *Canadian Woman Studies, 14*(2), 6–13.

Kil, S. H. (2010). Review of *Whiteness: An Introduction* by Steve Garner. *Journal of Ethnic and Migration Studies, 36*(3), 538–39.

Kim, W. (2006, October 31). Racial Discrimination Is Bad for Your Health—Literally. *DiversityInc.* Retrieved from www.diversityinc.com

Kimberley, M. (2012). Freedom Rider: Racism Is the Issue. Black Agenda Report, June 27. Retrieved from www.blackagendareport.com.

King, R. (2011). Obama and Race: An Introduction. *Patterns of Prejudice, 45*(1/2), 1–3.

Kinsella, N. A. (2007, June 8). *Sober Second Thought: The United Nations and the Phrase "Visible Minority": The Implications of the Whorfian Hypothesis for Human Rights.* Paper presented at the Globus Conference, University of Regina.

Kinsella, W. (1994). *Web of Hate: Far Right-Right Network in Canada.* Toronto: HarperCollins.

Kirsanow, P. (2007, October 24). Multicultural Racism. *National Review Online.* Retrieved from www.nationalreview.com

Kitossa, T. (2011). Obama Deception? Empire, "Post-Racism," and Hegemonic White Supremacy in the Campaign and Election of Barack Obama. *Journal of Critical Race Inquiry, 1*(2).

Kivel, P. (1996). *Uprooting Racism: How White People Can Work for Racial Justice.* Oakland, CA: AK Press.

Klein, W. (2009). Out of the Woods. *Westport News.* Retrieved from www.westportnews.com

Kobayashi, A. (2001). *"Race" and Racism in Canada.* Race Relations Training Module prepared for Human Resources Department Canada.

Kobayashi, A. (2003, June 13). Police Need Better Race Training, Expert: Accept Racism Exists, Professor Urges. *Kingston Whig-Standard.*

Kobayashi, A. (2009). Now You See Them, How You See Them: Women of Colour. In F. Henry & C. Tator (Eds.), *Canadian Academia: Racism in the Canadian University* (pp. 60–75). Toronto: University of Toronto Press.

Kobayashi, A., & Johnson, G. F. (2007). Introduction. In G. F. Johnson & R. Enomoto (Eds.), *Race, Racialization, and Anti-racism in Canada and Beyond* (pp. 3–16). Toronto: University of Toronto Press.

Kochhar, R., Fry, R., & Taylor, P. (2011, July 26). Wealth Gaps Rise to Record Highs Between Whites, Blacks, and Hispanics. *Pew Research Center. Social and Demographic Trends.*

Kostash, M. (2000). *The Next Canada: In Search of Our Future Nation.* Toronto: McClelland and Stewart.

Kovach, M. (2009). Being Indigenous in the Academy: Creating Space for Indigenous Scholars. In A. M. Timpson (Ed.), *First Nations, First Thoughts* (pp. 51–76). Vancouver: UBC Press.

Kundnani, A. (2007a). *The End of Tolerance: Racism in 21st Century Britain*. London: Pluto Press.

Kundnani, A. (2007b). Integrationism: The Politics of Anti-Muslim Racism. *Race & Class, 48*(4), 24–44.

Kundnani, A. (2009, June 11). The BNP's Success Reflects the New Racism of Our Political Culture. Institute for Race Relations. Retrieved from www.irr.org.uk

Kunz, J. L., & Fleras, A. (1998). Women of Colour in Mainstream Advertising: Distorted Mirror or Looking Glass? *Atlantis, 13*, 48–73.

Kunz, J. L., et al. (2001). *Unequal Access: A Canadian Profile of Racial Differences in Education, Employment, and Income*. A report prepared for the Canadian Race Relations Foundation by the Canadian Council for Social Development, Ottawa.

Kunz, J., & Sykes, S. (2007). *From Mosaic to Harmony: Multiculturalism Canada in the 21st Century*. Ottawa: Policy Research Institute.

Kuokkanen, R. (2009). *Reshaping the University: Responsibility, Indigenous Epistemes, and the Logic of the Gift*. Vancouver: UBC Press.

Kymlicka, W. (1995, Winter). Misunderstanding Nationalism. *Dissent*, 131–37.

Kymlicka, W. (1998). *Finding Our Way: Rethinking Ethnocultural Relations in Canada*. Toronto: Oxford University Press.

Kymlicka, W. (2001). *Politics in the Vernacular: Nationalism, Multiculturalism, and Citizenship*. Toronto: Oxford University Press.

Kymlicka, W. (2005). The Uncertain Futures of Multiculturalism. *Canadian Diversity, 4*(1), 82–85.

Kymlicka, W. (2007a). *Multicultural Odysseys*. Toronto: Oxford University Press.

Kymlicka, W. (2007b). The Global Diffusion of Multiculturalism. In R. Panossian et al. (Eds.), *Governing Diversity: Ethnicity and Democratic Governance*. Kingston: Queen's University Press.

Kymlicka, W. (2007c). The Canadian Model of Diversity in Comparative Perspective. In S. Tierney (Ed.), *Multiculturalism and the Canadian Constitution* (pp. 61–90). Vancouver: UBC Press.

Kymlicka, W. (2007d). Disentangling the Debate. In J. Stein et al. (Eds.), *Uneasy Partners* (pp. 137–51). Waterloo: Wilfrid Laurier University Press.

Kymlicka, W. (2008a). Reply. *Ethnicities, 8*(2), 277–81.

Kymlicka, W. (2008b, August). *The Current State of Multiculturalism in Canada*. Prepared for Canadian Heritage, Multiculturalism, and Human Rights Branch, Ottawa.

Kymlicka, W., & Bashir, B. (2008). *The Politics of Reconciliation in Multicultural Societies*. Toronto: Oxford University Press.

Kymlicka, W., & Opalski, M. (Eds.). (2001). *Can Liberal Pluralism Be Exported? Western Political Theory and Ethnic Relations in Eastern Europe*. New York: Oxford University Press.

Lacy, M., & Kent, A. O. (Eds.). (2011). *Critical Rhetorics of Race*. New York: New York University Press.

Ladner, K. L. (2009). Reconciling Constitutional Orders. In A. M. Timpson (Ed.), *First Nations, First Thoughts* (pp. 279–300). Vancouver: UBC Press.

Lake, M., & Reynolds, H. (2008). *Drawing the Global Colour Line: White Man's Countries and the International Challenge of Racial Equality*. Cambridge, MA: Cambridge University Press.

Law, I., Phillips, D., & Turney, L. (2004). Introduction. In I. Law et al. (Eds.), *Institutional Racism in Higher Education* (pp. vii–xiii). Sterling, VA: Trentham Books.

Lean, N. (2012). *The Islamophobia Industry: How the Right Manufactures Fears of Muslims*. London: Pluto Press.

Lee, J. (2012, May 4). Asian American Exceptionalism and "Stereotype Promise." *The Society Pages*.

Lee, J.-A., & Lutz, J. (2005). Introduction: Toward a Critical Literacy of Racisms, Anti-racisms, and Racialization. In J. Lee & J. Lutz (Eds.), *Situating "Race" and Racisms in Time, Space, and Theory: Critical Essays for Activists and Scholars* (pp. 3–29). Montreal/Kingston: McGill-Queen's University Press.

Lee, M. J., et al. (2009). Television Viewing and Ethnic Stereotypes: Do College Students Form Stereotypical Perceptions of Ethnic Groups as a Result of Heavy Television Consumption? *Howard Journal of Communications, 20*, 95–110.

Lehrman, S. (2003). *Colorblind Racism*. Retrieved from www.alternet.org

Leistyna, P. (2004). White Ethnic Unconsciousness. In P. Leistyna (Ed.), *Cultural Studies: From Theory to Action*. New York: John Wiley and Sons.

Lentin, A. (2005). Replacing "Race": Historizing the "Culture" in the Multiculturalism. *Patterns of Prejudice, 39*(4), 379–96.

Lentin, A. (2008). *Racism: A Beginner's Guide*. Oxford: Oxford University Press.

Lentin, A. (2012). Post-race, Post Politics: The Paradoxical Rise of Culture after Multiculturalism. *Ethnic and Racial Studies*, 1–19.

Lentin, A., & Lentin, R. (2006). *Race and State*. Newcastlle-Upon-Tyne: Cambridge Scholars Publishing.

Lentin, A., & Titley, G. (2011). *The Crisis of Multiculturalism: Racism in a Neo Liberal Age*. London: Zed Books.

Lentin, R. (2004). *From Racial State to Racist State: Ireland on the Eve of Citizenship Referendum*. Variant issue no. 20. Retrieved from www.variant.randomstate.org

Lerner, G. (1997). *Why History Matters: Life and Thought*. New York: Oxford University Press.

Lester, P. M., & Ross, S. D. (Eds.). (2003). *Images That Injure: Pictorial Stereotypes in the Media*. Westport, CT: Praeger.

Levine, A. (2009, May 11). The Quota. *National Post*.

Levitt, C. (1997, July–August). The Morality of Race in Canada. *Society*, 32–37.

Lewington, J. (2009, May 28). Minorities Missing Out on Top Jobs, Study. *Globe and Mail*.

Lewis, S. (1992). *Racism in Ontario*. Report to the African Canadian Legal Clinic (ACLC). Toronto.

Li, P. S. (1988). *The Chinese in Canada*. Toronto: Oxford University Press.

Li, P. S. (1995). Racial Supremacism under Social Democracy. *Canadian Ethnic Studies, 27*(1), 1–17.

Li, P. S. (2003, March 27–28). *Social Inclusion of Visible Minorities and Newcomers: The Articulation of "Race" and "Racial" Difference in Canadian Society*. Paper presented at the Conference on Social Inclusion, Ottawa, ON.

Li, P. S. (2007). Contradictions of "Racial" Discourse. In V. Agnew (Ed.), *Interrogating Race and Racism* (pp. 37–54). Toronto: University of Toronto Press.

Lian, J. Z., & Matthews, R. D. (1998). Does the Vertical Mosaic Still Exist? Ethnicity and Income in Canada, 1991. *Canadian Review of Sociology and Anthropology,* 35(4), 461–77.

Lin, A. C., & Harris, D. R. (2009). *The Colors of Poverty: Why Racial and Ethnic Disparities Persist.* Policy Brief, National Poverty Center on Poverty and Public Policy. Russell Sage Foundation. Ann Arbor: University of Michigan.

Lippard, C. D. (2011). Racist Nativism in the 21st Century. *Sociology Compass* 5(7), 591–606.

Lipsitz, G. (1995). The Possessive Investment in Whiteness: Racialized Social Democracy and the "White" Problem in American Studies. *American Quarterly, 47*(3), 369–87.

Lipsitz, G. (2006). *The Possessive Investment in Whiteness: How White People Profit from Identity Politics.* Philadelphia: Temple University Press.

Littlefield, M. B. (2008). The Media as a System of Racialization. *American Behavioral Scientists, 51*(5), 675–85.

Llewellyn, J. (2002). *Dealing with the Legacy of Native Residential School Abuse in Canada.* Subsequently published in revised form as The Relationship Between Truth and Reconciliation: Bridging the Gap. In M. Castellano, L. Archibald, & M. Degagne (Eds), *From Truth to Reconciliation: Transforming the Legacy of Residential Schools* (pp. 183–203). Ottawa: Aboriginal Healing Foundation.

Lopes, T., & Thomas, B. (2006). *Dancing on Live Embers: Challenging Racism in Organizations.* Toronto: Between the Lines.

Lopez, C. M. (2011, November 23). All American Muslim: A Little Taqiyya on the Prairie. *Family Security Matters.*

Lund, D. E. (2008). *Fostering Acceptance and Integration of Immigrant Students: Explaining Effective School-Based Approaches in Prairie Schools.* Working Paper no. WP01–08. Edmonton: Prairie Metropolis Centre.

Lund, D. E., & Carr, P. R. (2010). Exposing Privilege and Racism in the Great White North: Tackling Whiteness and Identity Issues in Canadian Education. *Multicultural Perspectives, 12*(4), 229–34.

Lupol, M. (2005). *The Politics of Multiculturalism: A Canadian-Ukrainian Memoir.* Edmonton: Canadian Institute of Ukrainian Studies.

Maaka, R., & Fleras, A. (2005). *The Politics of Indigeneity.* Dunedin, NZ: Otago University Press.

MacDonald, K., & Woods, M. (2008, November 14). Confronting a Culture of Silence. *The Journal* [Queen's University], 1–5.

Macedo, D., & Gounari, P. (2006). Globalization and the Unleashing of New Racism: An Introduction. In D. Macedo & P. Gounari (Eds.), *The Globalization of Racism* (pp. 3–24). Boulder, CO: Paradigm Publishers.

Mackay, E. (2002). *The House of Difference: Cultural Politics and National Identity in Canada.* Toronto: University of Toronto Press.

Macklin, A. (1999). Women as Migrants in National and Global Communities. *Canadian Woman Studies, 19*(3), 24–32.

MacQueen, K. (1994, April 23). "I Am a Canadian. Don't Let Me Screw Up." *Kitchener-Waterloo Record* [now *Waterloo Region Record*].

MacShane, D. (2009). *Globalising Hatred: The New Anti-Semitism.* London: Weidenfeld & Nicolson.

Mahtani, M. (2002). Representing Minorities: Canadian Media and Minority Identities. *Canadian Ethnic Studies, 33*(3), 99–131.

Mahtani, M. (2012, August 21). Don't Bank on Inclusivity. *Globe and Mail.*

Mahtani, M., Henry, F., & Tator, C. (2008). Discourse, Ideology, and Constructions of Racial Inequality. In J. Greenberg & C. D. Elliot (Eds.), *Communication in Question* (pp. 120–30). Toronto: Thomson Nelson.

Maioni, A. (2003). Canadian Health Care. In K. Pryke & W. Soderland (Eds.), *Profiles of Canada* (pp. 307–26). Toronto: Canadian Scholars' Press.

Majic, S. (2010). An Opportunity to Publicize the Private: Public Education Campaigns and Domestic Violence in Ontario. In J. Fong (Ed.), *Out of the Shadows* (pp. 29–57). Toronto: Women's Press.

Makin, K. (2013, February 19). Claims of Racism in Sentencing Face Probe. *Globe and Mail.*

Malakhov, V. (2003). Racism and Migrants. *Eurozine.* Retrieved from www.eurozine.com

Malik, K. (2008). Strange Fruit: Why Both Sides Are Wrong in the Race Debate. *Oneworld.* Retrieved from www.oneworld-publications.com

Malik, K. (2012, May 21). *Conflicting Credos but the Same Vision of the World.* Paper presented at the Criticise This: Rethinking the Question of Difference Seminar, Ulcinj, Montenegro. Retrieved from http://kenanmalik.wordpress.com

Malla, P. (2008, March 24). Are You a Racist? *Globe and Mail.*

Mann, E. (2007, July 13). Transit Racism & the Environmental Movement. *Grist: Environmental News and Commentary.* Retrieved from www.grist.org

Mansur, S. (2011). *Delectable Lie: A Liberal Repudiation of Multiculturalism.* Toronto: Mantua Books.

Mapedzahama, V., Rudge, T., West, S., & Perron, A. (2012). Black Nurse in White Space? Rethinking the In/Visibility of Race Within the Australian Nursing Workplace. *Nursing Inquiry, 19*(2), 153–64.

Marable, M. (2004). *Globalization and Racialization.* ZNet Classics. Retrieved from www.zmag.org

Maracle, B. (1996). One More Whining Indian Tilting at the Windmills. In J. Littleton (Ed.), *Clash of Identities* (pp. 15–20). Toronto: Prentice-Hall.

Maranto, R., Redding, R. E., & Hess, F. M. (Eds.). (2009). *The Politically Correct University: Problems, Scope, and Reforms.* Washington, DC: American Enterprise Institute for Public Policy Research.

Marche, S. (2012, October 18). The Postracial Elite. *Esquire.* Retrieved from www.esquire.com

Mark, D. (2013). European Roma at Crossroads: Politics and Empowerment. In *ENAR 2013 Recycling Hatred: Racism(s) in Europe Today: A Dialogue Between Academics, Equality Experts, and Civil Society Activists* (pp. 135–41). Brussels.

Marks, A. (2009, July 5 and 12). For Blacks, a Hidden Cost of Obama's Win? *The Christian Science Monitor.*

Markus, H. R., & Moya, P. M. (Eds.). (2010). *Race Matters: 21 Essays for the 21st Century.* New York: W. W. Norton.

Martin-Alcoff, L. (2007). *Comparative Race, Comparative Racisms.* Published in PhilPapers. Online Research on Philosophy. Retrieved from www.alcoff.com

Martinot, S. (2003). *The Rule of Racialization: Class, Identity, Governance.* Philadelphia: Temple University Press.

Mason, C. (2007, January 16). Little Mosque Defuses Hate with Humor. *New York Times*.

May, S., & Sleeter, C. (2010). Introduction. In S. May & C. Sleeter (Eds.), *Critical Multiculturalism: Theory and Practice* (pp. 1–18). New York: Routledge.

Mayan, M., & Morse, J. (2001/2002). Analyzing the Concept of "Immigrant" and Naming the Practice of Cultural Competence: Implications for Health Care Policy. PCER11 Funded Research Abstract. Retrieved from http://cc.msnscache.com

Mayer, N., & Michelat, G. (2001). Subjective Racism, Objective Racism: The French Case. *Patterns of Prejudice, 35*(4).

McAndrew, M. (1992). Combatting Racism and Ethnocentrism in Educational Materials: Problems and Actions Taken in Quebec. In Ontario Teachers Federation (Ed.), *Racism and Education: Different Perspectives and Experiences* (pp. 49–60). Ottawa: Canadian Teachers Federation.

McCalla, A., & Satzewich, V. (2002). Settler Capitalism and the Construction of Immigrants and "Indians" as Racialized Others. In W. Chan & K. Mirchandani (Eds.), *Crimes of Colour*. Peterborough, ON: Broadview Press.

McCardle, E. (2008, Winter). Sociologists on the Colorblind Question. *Contexts*, 34–37.

McCarthy, S. (2009, September 9). A Test of Fairness. *USA Today*.

McCrae, N. (2007). Review of *Systemic Racism: A Theory of Oppression*. *Community Development Journal, 42*(1), 134–36.

McCreary, T. (2009, September 1). The Myth of the Multicultural Patchwork. *Briarpatch Magazine*.

McDonald, M. G. (2012). Thinking Through Sport, Analyzing Whiteness. *Journal of Multicultural Discourses, 7*(3), 235–41.

McDonald, T., et al. (Eds.). (2010). *Canadian Immigration: Economic Evidence for a Dynamic Policy Environment*. Queen's Policy Studies Series. Montreal/Kingston, ON: McGill-Queen's University Press.

McDougall, G. (2009, October 23). Statement by the UN Independent Expert on Minority Issues. Office of the High Commissioner for Human Rights.

McGhee, D. (2009). *The End of Multiculturalism: Terrorism, Integration, and Human Rights*. Buckingham, UK: Open University Press.

McGibbon, E. A., & Etowa, J. B. (2009). *Anti Racist Health Care Practice*. Toronto: Canadian Scholars' Press.

McGill, J. (2008). An Institutional Suicide Machine: Discrimination Against Federally Sentenced Aboriginal Women in Canada. *Race/Ethnicity, 2*(1), 89–108.

McGowan, W. (2001). *Coloring the News: How Political Correctness Has Corrupted American Journalism*. New York: Encounter Books.

McIntosh, P. (1988). *White Privilege and Male Privilege: A Personal Account of Coming to See Correspondences Through Work in Women Studies*. Working Paper no. 189. Wellesley, MA: Wellesley College, Centre for Research on Women.

McKay, I. (2008). *Reasoning Otherwise: Leftists and the People's Enlightenment in Canada: 1890–1920*. Toronto: Between the Lines.

McKenna, I. (1994). Canada's Hate Propaganda Laws—A Critique. *British Journal of Canadian Studies, 15*, 42–52.

McKerrow, R. (2011). Foreword. In M. G. Lacy & K. A. Ono (Eds.), *Critical Rhetorics of Race* (pp. 1–20). New York: New York University Press.

McKibbon, E., & Etowa, J. (2009). *Anti-racist Health Care Practices*. Toronto: Canadian Scholars' Press.

McParland, K. (2012, September 28). Like Canadian History? You Must Be a Racist. *National Post*.

McPhate, M. (2005, July 11). Skin Bias Sets Tone for Sales Blitz: Bleaching Creams and Skin-Sloughing Treatment Are Big Business in India. *The Inquirer*. Retrieved from http://articles.philly.com

McRoberts, K. (2004). The Future of the Nation State and Quebec–Canada Relations. In M. Seymour (Ed.), *The Fate of the Nation State*. Montreal/Kingston: McGill-Queen's University Press.

McWhorter, J. (2009, July 25). Where Is America on Race? *New York Magazine* reprinted in the *Toronto Star*.

Memmi, A. (1999). *Racism*. Minneapolis: University of Minnesota Press.

Meyers, M. (2004). Crack Mothers in the News: A Narrative of Paternalistic Racism. *Journal of Communication Inquiry*, 28, 124–36.

Miller, D. (Ed.). (2004). *Tell Me No Lies: Propaganda and Media Distortion in the Attack on Iraq*. London: Pluto Press.

Miller, J. [Jody]. (2008). *Getting Played: African American Girls, Urban Inequality, and Gendered Violence*. New York: New York University Press.

Miller, J. [John]. (1998). *Yesterday's News: Why Canada's Newspapers Are Failing Us*. Halifax: Fernwood.

Miller, J. [John]. (2003). What Newspapers Need to Do. *Innoversity Newsletter*, 2(3). Retrieved from www.innoversity.com/newsletter/

Miller, J. [John]. (2005). *Ipperwash and the Media: A Critical Analysis of How the Story Was Covered*. Paper prepared for the Aboriginal Legal Foundation in Toronto. Retrieved from www.aboriginallegal.ca

Miller, J. [John]. (2006). *Media Coverage of Ipperwash Affair Biased, Untrue*. News and Events, Ryerson University. Retrieved from www.ryerson.ca/news/media

Miller, J. R. (1989). *Skyscrapers Hide the Heavens*. Toronto: University of Toronto Press.

Miller, J. R. (1996). *Shingwauk's Vision: A History of Native Residential Schools*. Toronto: University of Toronto Press.

Milloy, C. (2001, January 10). Racism Still Lurks in US Corporate World. *KW Record*.

Milloy, J. S. (1999). *A National Crime: The Canadian Government and the Residential School System*. Winnipeg: University of Manitoba Press.

Mills, C. W. (1997). *Racial Contract*. Ithaca, NY: Cornell University Press.

Mistry, M., & Latoo, J. (2009). Uncovering the Face of Racism in the Workplace. *British Journal of Medical Practitioners*, 2(2), 20–24.

Mistry, R. (2013). *Can Gramsci's Theory of Hegemony Help Us to Understand the Representation of Ethnic Minorities in Western Television and Cinema?* Retrieved from www.theory.org.uk

Mittell, J. (2010). *Television and American Culture*. New York: Oxford University Press.

Mohammed, N. (2007, July). *Little Mosque on the Prairie*: A Canadian Sitcom Takes a Biting Look at the Life of Muslims in the West. *Egypt Today*. Retrieved from www.egypttoday.com

Mohammed, S. (2010). Historicizing Health Inequities: Healing and Vestiges of Residential Schooling. *Indigenous Policy Journal*, 21(3).

Mohr, J. M. (2006/2007). Hate Studies Through a Constructivist and Critical Pedagogical Approach. *Journal of Hate Studies, 6*(1), 65–81.
Monnat, S. (2004). *Toward a Critical Understanding of Gendered Racism in the U.S. Social Welfare Institution.* Retrieved from www.allacademic.com
Monteiro, A. (2003). Race and the Racialized State: A Du Boisian Interrogation. *Socialism and Democracy, 17*(1), 77–97.
Monture, P. (2009). "Doing Academy Differently": Confronting "Whiteness" in the University. In F. Henry & C. Tator (Eds.), *Racism in the Canadian University* (pp. 76–105). Toronto: University of Toronto Press.
Monture, P. (2010). Race, Gender, and the University: Strategies for Survival. In S. Razack, M. Smith, & S. Thobani (Eds.), *States of Race* (pp. 23–36). Toronto: Between the Lines.
Moor, A. (2010, June 5). A European Anti-Muslim Racism. *Huff Post/World/Canada.*
Moore, D. W. (2012, November 4). *What the AP Poll on Racial Attitudes Really Tell Us, Part 1.* iMedia Ethics. Retrieved from www.imediaethics.org
Moore, R. (1992). *Racism in the English Language.* New York: The Racism and Sexism Resource Center for Educators.
Morey, P. (2004). *Rohinton Mistry.* Manchester, UK: University of Manchester.
Morris, B., & Cowlishaw, G. (Eds.). (1997). *Race Matters: Indigenous Australians and "Our" Society.* Canberra: Aboriginal Studies Press.
Mothers United Against Racism. (2005, May 16). *The Police's Fight Against Incivilities Encourages Racial Profiling and Harassment: Minority Mothers.* Press release.
Muharrar, M. (2005, October). Cited in P. Hylton, *Ethnic Profiling and Gang and Gun Violence. Pride,* 12–18.
Mukherjee, A. (1992). Educational Equity for Racial Minorities and the School: The Role of Community Action. In Ontario Federation of Students, *Racism and Education: Different Perspectives and Experiences* (pp. 73–81). Ottawa: Ontario Federation of Students.
Multiversity. (2009). Retrieved from www.multworld.org/multiversity.html
Munoz, D. (2006, July 28). Editorial: The Most Racist City in America: Hazleton, PA. [San Diego] *La Prensa.*
Murji, K., & Solomos, J. (2005). Introduction. In K. Murji & J. Solomos (Eds.), *Racialization: Studies in Theory and Practice* (pp. 1–28). Oxford, UK: Oxford University Press.
Murphy, R. (2009, August 2). The Real Lesson of Obama's Moment. *Globe and Mail.*
Murray, C., & Herrnstein, R. J. (1994). *The Bell Curve: Intelligence and Class Structure in American Life.* New York: The Free Press.
Murray, T. (2008, March 31). So What If I'm a Racist? *Canada Free Press.*
Mustafa, N. (2007, December 12). Aqsa Parvez's Death Lays Bare Flipside of Immigration. *Toronto Star.*
Nagle, J. (2009). *Multiculturalism's Double Bind: Creating Inclusivity, Cosmopolitanism, and Difference.* Burlington, VT: Ashgate Publishing.
Nairn, R., Barnes, A. M., Borell, B., Rankine, J., Gregory, A., & McCreanor, T. (2012). Maori News Is Bad News. *MAI Journal, 1*(1), 38–49.
Nakamura, L. (2002). *Cybertypes: Race, Ethnicity, and Identity in the Internet.* New York: Routledge.
Nakamura, L., & Chow, P. (2011). *Race After the Internet.* New York: Routledge.

Naseem, M. A. (2011, Spring). Conceptual Perspectives on Multiculturalism and Multicultural Education: A Survey of the Field Canadian Issues. *Canadian Diversity*, 9–14.

National Congress of American Indians. (2013, October 10). *Ending the Legacy of Racism in Sports & the Era of Harmful "Indian" Sports Mascots*. Washington, DC: Author.

National Council of Visible Minorities. (2009, May 4). Special Bulletin. Mental Health Week. Ottawa.

National Council of Welfare. (2011, September 28). *The Dollars and Sense of Solving Poverty*. Retrieved from http://www.ncw.gc.ca

National Film Board. (2006). *Race Is a Four Letter Word*. B. Sabaz, dir. Montreal.

National Planning Commission. (2013). Divisive Effects of Institutional Racism. Retrieved from www.npconline.co.za

National Post. (2008, November 22). A Racist Province Is Hard to Prove. *National Post*.

National Urban League. (2009). Racism's Effects: The Urban League's State of Black America. Retrieved from http://contexts.org

Neier, Dr. A. (2013). Can We Learn from the U.S. Content? On Positive Action. In *ENAR 2013 Recycling Hatred: Racism(s) in Europe Today. A Dialogue Between Academics, Equality Experts, and Civil Society Activists* (pp. 124–31). Retrieved from www.enar-eu.org

Nelson, A. (2006). *Gender in Canada* (3rd ed.). Toronto: Pearson.

Nelson, A., & Fleras, A. (1998). *Social Problems in Canada: Conditions and Consequences* (2nd ed.). Scarborough: Prentice-Hall.

Nestel, S. (2012). *Colour Coded Health Care. The Impact of Race and Racism on Canadians' Health*. Wellesley Institute. Retrieved from www.wellesleyinstitute.com

Neugebauer-Visano, R. (1996). Kids, Cops, and Colour: The Social Organization of Police-Minority Youth Relations. In G. O'Bireck (Ed.), *Not a Kid Anymore*. Scarborough, ON: ITP Nelson.

New Black Woman. (2011, May 24). Study: Whites Believe They Are the Victims of Racism More Often Than Blacks. *New Black Woman*.

New York Times. (2012, March 8). Hate Groups on the Rise in U.S. *New York Times*.

Newman, D. M. (2012). *Identities and Inequalities: Exploring the Intersections of Race, Class, Gender, and Sexuality* (2nd ed.). New York: McGraw-Hill.

Ng, R. (1993). A Woman Out of Control: Deconstructing Sexism and Racism in the University. *Canadian Journal of Education*, *18*(3), 189–202.

Ngugi, M. W. (2013, May 29). Learning the American Language of Racism. *Ebony News & Views*.

Nicolo, A. (2007). TV Review: *Little Mosque on the Prairie*. Blogcritics. Retrieved from http://blogcritics.org

Niemonen, J. (2007). Antiracist Education in Theory and Practice: A Critical Assessment. *American Sociologist*, *38*(2), 159–77.

Nittle, N. K. (2012, September 17). Is Zoe Saldana Too Light to Play Nina Simone? Retrieved from http://racerelations.about.com

Nopper, T. K. (2003, Fall). The White Anti-Racist is an Oxymoron. *Race Traitor*.

Norton, M. I., & Sommers, S. R. (2011). Whites See Racism as a Zero-Sum Game That They Are Now Losing. *Association for Psychological Science*, *6*(3), 215–18.

Nwozu, N. L. (2010). Violence Against Women: Nigerian-Canadian Women's Experiences. In J. Fong (Ed.), *Out of the Shadows* (pp. 243–63). Toronto: Women's Press.

Odartey-Wellington, F. (2011). Erasing Race in the Canadian Media: The Case of Suaad Hagi Mohamud. *Canadian Journal of Communication, 36*(3), 395–414.

Olsen, G. M. (2011). *Power & Inequality: A Comparative Introduction.* Toronto: Oxford University Press.

Omar, A. (2012). Islamic Identity in the Canadian Multicultural Context. *Cultural and Pedagogical Inquiry, 3*(2), 16–29.

Omi, M., & Winant, H. (1994). *Racial Formation in the United States: From the 1960s to the 1990s.* London/New York: Routledge.

Omidvar, R., & Tory, J. (2012, March 20). New Glass Ceiling for Minorities. *Toronto Star.*

Ontario Human Rights Commission. (2003). *Paying the Price: The Human Cost of Racial Profiling.* Toronto: Author.

Ontario Human Rights Commission. (2005a). *Fishing Without Fear: Report on the Inquiry into Assaults on Asian-Canadian Anglers.* Toronto: Author.

Ontario Human Rights Commission. (2005b, June 9). *Policy and Guidelines on Racism and Racial Discrimination.* Toronto: Author.

Ontario Human Rights Commission. (2013). *Policy on Removing the "Canadian Experience" Barrier.* Toronto: Author.

Onyeji, C. (2013, June). Individual and Community Impacts of Racist Crime. *ENAR Webzine.* Retrieved from www.enargywebzine.eu

Orbe, M. P., & Harris, T. M. (2001). *Interracial Communication: Theory into Practice.* Boulder, CO: Westview Press.

Oreopoulos, P. (2009, May). *Why Do Skilled Immigrants Struggle in the Labour Field? A Field Experiment with Six Thousand Resumes.* Working Paper Series no. 09-03. Metropolis British Columbia. Vancouver.

Oreopoulos, P., & Dechief, D. (2011, September). *Why Do Some Employers Prefer to Interview Matthew, But Not Samir?* Working Paper Series 11–13. Metropolis British Columbia. Vancouver.

Ornstein, M. (2006). *Ethno-Racial Groups in Toronto, 1971–2001: A Demographic and Socio-Economic Profile.* Toronto: Institute for Social Research.

Pacquet, G. (2008). *Canada's Deep Diversity: A Governance Challenge.* Ottawa: University of Ottawa Press.

Pager, D., & Quillian, L. (2005). Walking the Talk? What Employers Say versus What They Do. *American Sociological Review, 70,* 355–80.

Paolucci, P. (2006). Race and Racism in Marx's Camera Obscura. *Critical Sociology, 32*(4).

Paradies, Y. (2005). Anti-racism and Indigenous Australians. *Analyses of Social Issues and Public Policy, 5*(1), 1–28.

Park, H. (2011). Being Canada's National Citizen: Difference and the Economics of Multicultural Nationalism. *Social Identities, 17*(5), 643–63.

Parrillo, V. (2011). *Understanding Race and Ethnic Relations* (4th ed.). Toronto: Pearson.

Parvin, P. (2009, April 23). Integration and Identity in an International Context: Problems and Ambiguities in the New Politics of Multiculturalism. *Political Studies Review.* Retrieved from www3.interscience.wiley.com

Pascale, C.-M. (2007). *Making Sense of Race, Class, and Gender: Common Sense, Power, and Privilege in the United States.* New York: Routledge.

Pathak, P. (2008). *The Future of Multicultural Britain.* Edinburgh: Edinburgh University Press.

Patterson, O. (1995, November 6). The Paradoxes of Integration. *New Republic,* 1–6.

Patton Jr., A. (1996). *Physicians, Colonial Racism, and Diaspora in West Africa.* Gainesville: University Press of Florida.

Paul, D. (2012). "We Were Not the Savages": Indian Residential Schools. In L. Samuelson & W. Antony (Eds.), *Power and Resistance: Critical Thinking about Canadian Social Issues* (5th ed.) (pp. 146–66). Halifax: Fernwood.

Pearson, A. R., Dovidio, J. F., & Gaertner, S. L. (2009). The Nature of Contemporary Prejudice: Insights from Aversive Racism. *Social and Personal Psychology Compass, 3,* 1–25.

Pearson, D. (2001). *The Politics of Ethnicity in Settler Societies.* London: Palgrave.

Peeples, J. A. (2006). Review of the New Politics of Race: Globalism, Difference, Justice. *Rhetoric and Public Affairs, 9*(4), 718–20.

Peffley, M., & Hurwitz, J. (2010). *Justice in America: The Separate Realities of Blacks and Whites.* New York: Cambridge University Press.

Pendakur, K. (2005). *Visible Minorities in Canada's Workplaces: A Perspective on the 2017 Projection.* RIIM paper no. 05-11. Vancouver: Metropolis Project.

Pendakur, K., & Pendakur, R. (2004). *Colour My World: Has the Majority-Minority Earnings Gap Changed over Time* Working Paper no. 04-11. Research on immigration and integration in the metropolis. Vancouver: Vancouver Centre of Excellence.

Pendakur, K., & Pendakur, R. (2011, May). *Colour by Numbers: Minority Earnings in Canada 1996–2006.* Metropolis British Columbia. Working Paper Series no. 11-05.

Pendakur, R. (2000). *Immigrants and the Labour Force: Policy, Regulation, and Impact.* Montreal/Kingston: McGill-Queen's University Press.

Penslar, D. J. (2005). Introduction. In D. J. Penslar (Ed.), *Contemporary Antisemitism: Canada and the World.* Toronto: University of Toronto Press.

Perigoe, R. (2006, May). *Muslims and Media.* Paper presented to the Congress of Social Sciences, York University, Toronto, ON.

Perkel, C. (2002, October 30). No Racial Targeting Anywhere in Ontario, Police Chiefs Say. *Toronto Star,* p. A3.

Perliger, A. (2012, November). Challengers from the Sidelines: Understanding America's Violent Far-Right. Published by the Combatting Terrorism Center at West Point. Retrieved from www.ctc.usma.edu

Peter, K. (1978). Multi-cultural Politics, Money, and the Conduct of Canadian Ethnic Studies. *Canadian Ethnic Studies Association Bulletin, 5,* 2–3.

Petitpas-Taylor, G. (2008, August 5). *How We Make Sex Work More Dangerous.* Retrieved from http://timestranscript.canadaeast.com

Petitpas-Taylor, G. (2009). *Incarceration Not the Answer to Mental Health Problems.* Retrieved from www.acswcccf.nb.ca

Pew Research Center. (2013, April 22). *The State of Race in America.* Aspen Institute Symposium.

Pew Research Center. (2013, August 22). *King's Dream Remains an Elusive Goal: Many Americans See Racial Disparities.* Pew Research Social and Demographic Trends.

Philip, M. N. (1996). How White Is Your White? *Borderlines, 37,* 19–24.
Phillips, A., & Saharso, S. (2008). Guest Editorial. The Rights of Women and the Crisis of Multiculturalism. *Ethnicities, 8*(3), 291–301.
Picard, A. (2005, February 12). Health's a Black and White Issue: Colour-Blindness Is Killing Minorities. *Globe and Mail.*
Picca, L. H., & Feagin, J. (2007). *Two-Faced Racism Whites in the Backstage and the Frontstage.* New York: Routledge.
Picot, G., Hou, F. & Coulombe, S. (2007). *Chronic Low Income and Low-Income Dynamics among Recent Immigrants.* Analytical Studies Branch Research Paper Series 2007(294). Statistics Canada.
Pieterse, J. N. (2007). *Ethnicities and Global Multiculture.* Lantham, MD: Rowman and Littlefield Publishers.
Pilkington, A. (2012). *Institutional Racism in the Academy: A Case Study.* Sterling, VA: Trentham Books.
Pinder, S. O. (2010). *The Politics of Race and Ethnicity in the United States.* New York: Palgrave Macmillan.
Pinder, S. O. (2013). Introduction: The Concept and Definition of American Multicultural Studies. In S. O. Pinder (Ed.), *American Multicultural Studies: A Diversity of Race, Ethnicity, Gender, and Sexuality* (pp. ix–xxii). Thousand Oaks, CA: Sage.
Piper, N. (2008). International Migration and Gendered Axes of Stratification: Introduction. In N. Piper (Ed.), *New Perspectives on Gender and Migration* (pp. 1–18). New York: Routledge.
Pitcher, B. (2009). *The Politics of Multiculturalism: Race and Racism in Contemporary Britain.* New York: Palgrave Macmillan.
Pitcher, B. (2012). Racism and Capitalism Redux. *Patterns of Prejudice, 46*(1), 1–15.
Plamondon, B. (2013). *The Truth about Trudeau.* Ottawa: Great River Media Publishers.
Pollak, J., & Kubrin, C. E. (2007). Crime in the News: How Crime, Offenders, and Victims Are Portrayed in the News. *Journal of Criminal Justice and Popular Culture, 14*(1), 59–82.
Ponting, R., & Gibbins, R. (1980). *Out of Irrelevance.* Toronto: Butterworths.
Potok, M. (2009). *Diversity and Its Discontents.* Southern Poverty Law Centre. Retrieved from www.splcenter.org
powell, j. a. (2009). Post-racialism or Targetted Universalism? *Denver University Law Review, 1.*
Powell, R. (2000). Overcoming Cultural Racism: The Promise of Multicultural Education. *Multicultural Perspectives, 2*(3), 8–14.
Powell, T. B. (2003). All Colors Flow into Rainbows and Nooses. *Cultural Critique, 55.*
Prashad, V. (2000). *The Karma of Brown Folk.* Minneapolis: University of Minnesota Press.
Priya, K. (2007, Fall). Beyond Colorblindness and Multiculturalism: Rethinking Anti Racist Pedagogy in the University Classroom. *Radical Teacher, 80.*
Prus, B. (1999). *Beyond the Power Mystique: Power as Intersubjective Accomplishment.* Albany: State University of New York Press.
Public Service Alliance of Canada. (2010, January 29). *March 21: International Day for the Elimination of Racial Discrimination.* Retrieved from http://psacunion.ca
Pulido, L. (2000). Rethinking Environmental Racism: White Racism and Urban Development in Southern California. *Annals of the Association of American Geographers, 90*(1).

Purwar, N. (2004). Fish In or Out of Water: A Theoretical Framework for Race and the Space of Academia. In I. Law et al. (Eds.), *Institutional Racism in Higher Education* (pp. 49–58). Sterling, VA: Trentham Books.

Putnam, R. (2007). E Pluribus Unum: Diversity and Community in the Twenty-first Century. *Scandinavian Political Studies, 30*(2), 137–74.

Pyke, K. (2004, August 14). *Internalized Gendered Racism in Asian American Women's Accounts of Asian and White Masculinities*. Paper presented to the American Sociological Association meetings, San Francisco. Retrieved from www.allacademic.com

Race, Violence, and Health Project Study. (2002). *Caught at the Intersection*. Funded by the Canadian Institute of Health Research and Institute of Gender and Health. Halifax: Dalhousie University.

Rankin, J., & Winsa, P. (2012, March 10). Police Strategy Targets Violent Areas. *Toronto Star*.

Rasmussen, B. (2013). Making Sense of Walt: A Psychoanalytic Understanding of Racism. *Psychoanalytic Social Work, 20*, 50–61.

Ray, J. J. (1988). Why the F Scale Predicts Racism: A Critical Review. *Political Psychology, 9*(4), 671–79.

Razack. S. (2002). *Race, Space, and the Law: Unmapping a White Settler Society*. Toronto: Between the Lines.

Razack, S. (2004). *Dark Threats and White Knights: The Somalia Affair, Peacekeeping, and the New Imperialism*. Toronto: University of Toronto Press.

Razack, S. (2008). *Casting Out: The Eviction of Muslims from Western Law and Politics*. Toronto: University of Toronto Press.

Razack, S., Smith, M., & Thobani, S. (2010). Introduction. In S. Thobani, S. Razack, & M. Smith (Eds.), *States of Race: Critical Race Feminisms for the 21st Century* (pp. 1–22). Toronto: Between the Lines.

RBC Economics. (2011, December). *Immigrant Labour Market Outcomes in Canada: The Benefits of Addressing Wage and Unemployment Gaps. Current Analysis*.

Reitz, J. (2009). Assessing Multiculturalism as a Behavioural Theory. In R. Breton, K. K. Dion, & K. L. Dion (Eds.), *Multiculturalism and Social Cohesion: Potential and Challenges of Diversity* (pp. 1–43). New York: Springer Science+ Business Media.

Reitz, J., & Bannerjee, R. (2007). Racial Inequality, Social Cohesion, and Policy Issues. In K.Banting et al. (Eds.), *Belonging* (pp. 489–546). Montreal: IRPP.

Rendall, S., & Macdonald, I. (2008). *Making Islamophobia Mainstream*. FAIR: Challenging Media Bias and Censorship. Retrieved from www.fair.org

Renzetti, C. (2009). Social Class, Race, and Intimate Partner Violence. *RacismReview*. Retrived from www.racismreview.com

Report of the Commission on Systemic Racism in the Ontario Criminal Justice System. (1995). Toronto: Queen's Printer for Ontario.

Rhoads, R. A., & Torres, C. A. (Eds.). (2006). *The University, State, and Market: The Political Economy of Globalization in the Americas*. Palo Alto, CA: Stanford University Press.

Richeson, J. (2008). The Threat of Appearing Prejudiced and Race-Based Attentional Biases. *Psychological Science, 19*, 98–102.

Ritzer, G. (2007). Racialized Gender. *Blackwell Encyclopedia of Sociology*. New York: Wiley-Blackwell.

Roberts, D. (2011). *Fatal Intervention: How Science, Politics, and Big Business Recreate Race in the Twenty First Century.* New York: New Press.

Rockler-Gladen, N. (2008, April 29). Minority Media Representations: Common Representations of Gays, African Americans, and Other Minorities. *Media Literacy.*

Rodriguez, I. (2009). "Diversity Writing" and the Liberal Discourse on Multiculturalism in Mainstream Papers. *Howard Journal of Communication, 20,* 167–88.

Roediger, D. R. (2008). *How Race Survived U.S. History: From Settlement and Slavery to the Obama Phenomenon.* London: Verso.

Rolfsen, C. (2008, September–October). After the Apology. *This Magazine.*

Rogers, A., & Pilgrim, D. (2010). *A Sociology of Mental Health and Illness* (4th ed.). New York: McGraw-Hill.

Rollack, N., & Gillborn, D. (2011). *Critical Race Theory (CRT).* British Educational Research Association online resource. Retrieved from www.bera.ac.uk

Rosado, C. (2013). *The Undergirding Factor Is POWER. Toward an Understanding of Prejudice and Racism.* Critical Multicultural Pavilion Research Room. Retrieved from www.edchange.org

Rosenthal, D. (2000). *Current Problems and Possible Strategies for Combatting Racism on the Internet.* Prepared for the UN High Commissioner on Human Rights, Geneva.

Roscigno, V., Garcia, J. L., Mong, S., & Byron, R. (2007). Racial Discrimination at Work: Its Occurrence, Dimensions, and Consequences. *Research in Race and Ethnic Relations, 14,* 111–35.

Rotman, L. I. (1996). *Parallel Paths: Fiduciary Doctrine and the Crown–Native Relationship in Canada.* Toronto: University of Toronto Press.

Roy, P. (1989). *A White Man's Province.* Vancouver: UBC Press.

Royal Commission. (1996). *People to People, Nation to Nation: Highlights from the Report on the Royal Commission on Aboriginal Peoples.* Ottawa: Minister of Supply and Services Canada.

Runnymede Trust. (2012, October 24). *The Runneymede Race Debate: Do Racists Have a Right to Be Heard?* Conference notes.

Ruparelia, R. (2012, August 22). The Currency of Racism in Canada. *Toronto Star.*

Rusche, S. E., & Brewster, Z. W. (2008). "Because They Tip for Shit!": The Social Psychology of Everyday Racism in Restaurants. *Sociology Compass, 2*(6), 2008–29.

Rushowy, K. (2007, November 7). Black-focused School Debate Set. *Toronto Star.*

Rushowy, K., & Brown, L. (2013, September 11). Seniority Hiring Rule Challenged. *Toronto Star.*

Rushton, P. (1995). *Race, Evolution, and Behavior: A Life History Perspective.* New Brunswick, NJ: Transaction Publishers.

Sacks, Chief Rabbi L. (2012, July 11). Europe's New Anti-Semitism. *Huffington Post.* Retrieved from www.huffingtonpost.com

Sakamoto, I., Jeyapal, D. Bhuyan, R., Ku, J., Fang, L., Zhang, H., & Genovese, F. (2013, March). *An Overview of Discourses of Skilled Immigrants and "Canadian Experience": An English-Language Print Media Analysis.* CERIS Working Paper no. 98.

Saltmarsh, S. (2005). "White Pages" in the Academy: Plagiarism, Consumption, and Racist Rationalities. *International Journal for Educational Integrity, 1*(1), 1–11.

Sammel, A. (2009). *Turning the Focus from "Other" to Science Education: Exploring the Invisibility of Whiteness.* Springerlink. Retrieved from http://blogs.springer.com

Samodien, L. (2009, May 10). Varsities Still Battling with Racism. *Pretoria News.*
Samuel, E. (2006). *Integrative Anti Racism: South Asians in Canadian Academe.* Toronto: University of Toronto Press.
Samuel, E., & Burney, S. (2003). Racism, eh? Interactions of South Asian Students with Mainstream Faculty in a Predominantly White Canadian University. *The Canadian Journal of Higher Education, 33*(2), 81–114.
Samuel, J., & Verma, R. P. (2010). The Development of Benchmarks and Indicators for Compiling a Report Card on Racism in Canada. *Canadian Journal of Social Research, 3*(2), 3–23.
Sanchez, G., & Romero, M. (2010). Critical Race Theory in the U.S.: Sociology of Immigration. *Sociology Compass, 4*(9), 779–88.
Sapers, H. (2013). *Spirit Matters: Aboriginal People and the Corrections and Conditional Release Act.* Report Office of the Correctional Investigator. Tabled in Parliament.
Sarich, V., & Miele, F. (2004). *Race: The Reality of Human Differences.* Boulder, CO: Westview Press.
Satzewich, V. (Ed.). (1998). *Racism and Social Inequality in Canada: Concepts, Controversies, and Strategies of Resistance.* Toronto: Thompson Educational.
Satzewich, V. (2000). Whiteness Limited: Racialization and the Social Construction of "Peripheral Europeans." *Histoire sociale/Social History, 23,* 271–90.
Satzewich, V. (2004, January–February). Racism in Canada: Change and Continuity. *Canadian Dimensions,* 20.
Satzewich, V. (2007). Whiteness Studies: Race, Diversity, and the New Essentialism. In S. P. Hier & B. S. Bolaria (Eds.), *Race and Racism in 21st Century Canada* (pp. 67–84). Peterborough, ON: Broadview Press.
Satzewich, V. (2010). Measuring Racism: A Case for Verstehen. *Canadian Journal for Social Research, 3*(2), 45–57.
Satzewich, V. (2011). *Racism in Canada.* Toronto: Oxford University Press.
Satzewich, V., & Liadokis, N. (2013). *"Race" and Ethnicity in Canada: A Critical Introduction* (3rd ed.). Toronto: Oxford University Press.
Satzewich, V., & Shaffir, W. (2009). Racism versus Professionalism: Claims and Counter-Claims about Racial Profiling. *Canadian Journal of Criminology and Criminal Justice, 51*(2), 1–12.
Satzewich, V., & Wong, L. (Eds.). (2006). *Transnational Identities and Practices in Canada.* Vancouver: UBC Press.
Saul, J. R. (2008). *A Fair Country: Telling Truths about Canada.* Toronto: Viking.
Scheurich, J. J., & Young, M. D. (1997). Coloring Epistemologies: Are Our Research Epistemologies Racially Biased? *Educational Researcher, 26*(4), 4–16.
Scheurich, J. J., & Young, M. D. (2002). White Racism Among White Faculty. In W. A. Smith, P. G. Altbach, & K. Lomotey (Eds.), *The Racial Crisis in American Higher Education* (pp. 221–39). Albany: State University of New York.
Scheurkens, U. (2010). Introduction. In U. Scheurkens (Ed.), *Globalization and Transformations of Social Inequality.* New York: Routledge.
Schlesinger, A., Jr. (1992). *The Disuniting of America: Reflections on a Multicultural Society.* New York: W. W. Norton.
Schoenfeld, G. (2004). *The Return of Anti-Semitism.* San Francisco: Encounter Books.
Sears, D. O. (2011, April 22). Racial Resentment at Its Root. *New York Times.*

Seymour, R. (2010, April 15). The Changing Face of Racism. *International Socialism,* (126).
Shaheen, J. (2001). *Reel Bad Arabs.* New York: Interlink Publishing Group.
Sharkey, B. (2009, December 24). Four Movies Straddle the Racial Line. *Toronto Star.*
Sharma, N. (2011). Canadian Multiculturalism and Its Nationalisms. In M. Chazan et al. (Eds.), *Home and Native Land: Unsettling Multiculturalism in Canada* (pp. 85–101). Toronto: Between the Lines.
Sharma, S. (2004). Transforming the Curriculum? The Problem with Multiculturalism. In I. Law et al. (Eds.), *Institutional Racism in Higher Education* (pp. 105–18). Sterling, VA: Trentham Books.
Sheikh, A., & Farooq, M. (2007, February 16). Square Peg, Round Hole. *Silhouette.*
Sheppard, C. (2010). *Inclusive Equality: The Relational Dimensions of Systemic Discrimination in Canada.* Montreal/Kingston: McGill-Queen's University Press.
Shimo, A. (2008, November 14). The Quest for a Lighter Shade of Pale. *Maclean's, 121*(46), 150–52.
Shkilnyk, A. (1985). *Poison Stronger Than Love.* New Haven, CT: Yale University Press.
Shohat, E., & Stam, R. (1994). *Unthinking Eurocentrism: Multiculturalism and the Media.* New York: Routledge.
Siddiqui, H. (2000, April 20). An Abysmal Record of Hiring Minorities. *Toronto Star.*
Sidner, S. (2009, September 9). Skin Whitener Advertisements Labeled Racist. CNN.com/asia. Retrieved from www.cnn.com
Sihera, E. (2009). The Real Cause of Racism. *Enzine Articles.* Retrieved from http://enzinearticles.com
Silverberg, C. (2004, October 20). After Stonechild: Rebuilding Trust. *Globe and Mail.*
Simmons, A. (2010). *Immigration and Canada: Global and Transnational Perspectives.* Toronto: Canadian Scholars' Press.
Simpson, J. (2008, January 30). Memo to Toronto School Board: Are You Nuts? *Globe and Mail.*
Simpson, J. (2009, March 7). Yes, We Love Our Country, but the "Best in the World"? Get Real. *Globe and Mail.*
Simpson, J. L. (2008). The Color-Blind Double Bind: Whiteness and the (Im)Possibility of Dialogue. *Communication Theory, 18,* 138–59.
Sinha, S. (2006). Generating Awareness for the Experiences of Women of Colour in Ireland. In R. Lentin & R. McVeigh (Eds.), *After Optimism: Ireland, Racism, and Globalisation.* Belfast: Metro Erieann Publications.
Sisson, C. K. (2013, August 19 and 26). Defending the Dream: New Generation Takes Up Martin Luther King Jr.'s Torch. *Christian Science Monitor,* 6–32.
Sivanandan, A. (2002, November 15–16). *The Contours of Global Racism.* Speech delivered to the conference on Crossing Borders: The Legacy of the Commonwealth Immigration Act of 1962, London Metropolitan University, London, UK.
Sivanandan, A. (2007). Foreword. In A. Sivanandan, *The End of Tolerance.* London: Pluto Press.
Sivanandan, A. (2009). Foreword. In L. Fekete, *A Suitable Enemy.* London: Pluto Press.
Sivanandan, A. (2010, March 15). Fighting Anti-Muslim Racism: An Interview with A. Sivanandan. Institute of Race Relations.

Skuterud, M. (2010). The Visible Minority Earnings Gap Across Generations of Canadians. *Canadian Journal of Economics, 43*(3), 860–81.

Small, S. (2002). Racisms and Racialized Hostility at the Start of the New Millennium. In D. T. Goldberg & J. Solomos (Eds.), *Companion to Racial and Ethnic Studies* (pp. 259–81). Malden, MA: Blackwell.

Smith, A. (2010). Indigeneity, Settler Colonialism, White Supremacy. *Global Dialogue, 12*(2).

Smith, C. C. (Ed.). (2010). *Anti Racism in Education: Missing in Action*. Ottawa: Canadian Centre for Policy Alternatives.

Smith, E. (2004). *Nowhere to Turn? Responding to Partner Violence against Immigrant and Visible Minority Women*. Canadian Council of Social Development. Submitted to the Department of Justice.

Smith, L. T. (1998). *Decolonizing Methodologies: Research and Indigenous Peoples*. London: Zed Books.

Solomos, J., & Back, L. (1996). *Racism and Society*. London: Macmillan.

Solomos, J., & Bulmer, M. (2005). *Researching Race and Racism*. New York: Routledge.

Soroka, S., & Maioni, A. (2006, February 1). Little Signs of Bias in News Coverage. *Toronto Star*.

Southern Poverty Law Center. (2007). *The Year in Hate*. Intelligence Report. Retrieved from www.splcenter.com

Southern Poverty Law Center. (2009, Fall). Colorblindness: The New Racism? *Teaching Tolerance, 36*.

Soutphommasanes, T. (2013). *Don't Go Back to Where You Came from*. Sydney: University of New South Wales Press.

Sowell, T. (2004). *Affirmative Action Around the World: An Empirical Study*. New Haven, CT: Yale University Press.

Spafford, M. M., Nygaard, V. I., Gregor, F., & Boyd, M. A. (2006). Navigating the Different Spaces: Experiences of Inclusion and Isolation among Racially Minoritized Faculty in Canada. *Canadian Journal of Higher Education, 36*(1), 1–27.

Spencer, J. W., Holstein, J., Loseke, D., & Berbier, M. (2007). *Social Problems Theory*. Society for the Study of Social Problems. Retrieved from www.sssp1.org

Spiegel Staff. (2009, December 11). Fears of Eurabia. How Much Allah Can the Old Continent Bear? *Spiegel online*. Retrieved from www.spiegel.de

Spoonley, P. (1993). *Racism and Ethnicity in New Zealand*. Auckland: Oxford University Press.

Spoonley, P. (2005). Multicultural Challenges in a Bicultural New Zealand. *Canadian Diversity, 4*(1), 19–22.

Sriram, N., & Greenwald, A. G. (2009). The Brief Implicit Association Test. *Experimental Psychology, 56*(4), 283–94.

Srivastava, S. (2007). Troubles with "Anti-Racist Multiculturalism": The Challenges of Anti-racist and Feminist Activism. In S. P. Hier & B. S. Bolaria (Eds.), *Race and Racism in 21st Century Canada* (pp. 291–312). Peterborough, ON: Broadview Press.

Staff Writer. (2008). *Minorities Have Trouble Getting Help*. Retrieved from www.healthyplace.com

Stanley, T. J. (2011). *Contesting White Supremacy: School Segregation, Anti-racism, and the Making of Chinese Canadians*. Vancouver: UBC Press.

Stanley, T. J. (2012). Analyzing Racisms in the Workplace. *Canadian Diversity, 9*(1), 53–57.

Stasiulis, D. K. (1999). Feminist Intersectional Theorizing. In P. Li (Ed.), *Race and Ethnic Relations in Canada* (2nd ed.) (pp. 347–97). Toronto: Oxford University Press.

Stasiulis, D. K., & Bakan, A. B. (2005). *Negotiating Citizenship: Migrant Women in Canada and the Global System.* Toronto: University of Toronto Press.

Statistics Canada. (2007, January 20). Study: Low-Income Rates among Immigrants Entering Canada. *The Daily.*

Statistics Canada. (2013, July 11). Police Reported Hate Crimes. *The Daily.*

Steele, S. (2006). *White Guilt.* New York: HarperCollins.

Steele, S. (2009, December 30). *Obama and Our Post-Modern Race Problem.* Retrieved from http://online.wsj.com

Steinhorn, L., & Diggs-Brown, B. (1999). *By the Color of Our Skin: The Illusion of Integration and the Reality of Race.* New York: Dutton.

Stepan, N. (1982). *The Idea of Race in Science: Great Britain, 1800–1960.* London: Macmillan.

Stewart, A. (2009). *You Must Be a Basketball Player: Rethinking Integration in the University.* Halifax: Fernwood Publishing.

Steyn, M. (2006, October 2). Keeping It Real Is Real Stupid. *Maclean's.* 58–59.

Stockdill, B., & Danico, M. Y. (Eds.). (2012). *Transforming the Ivory Tower: Challenging Racism, Sexism, and Homophobia in the Academy.* Honolulu: University of Hawaii Press.

Stocking, G. (1968). *History of Anthropological Theory.* New York: Free Press.

Strauss, G. (2008, January 27). Don't Fight Racism with Racism. *Globe and Mail.*

Strauss, M. (2003, November 1). Antiglobalism's Jewish Problem. *Foreign Policy*, 58–67.

Sue, D. W. (2003). *Overcoming Racism: The Journey to Liberation.* San Francisco: John Wiley and Sons.

Sun Media. (2007, January). *Racial Tolerance Report.* Leger Marketing.

Surrette, R. (1998/2004). *Media, Crime, and Criminal Justice: Images and Realities.* Toronto: Wadsworth.

Sutherland, R. S. (2012). Reductio ad Hitlerium: The New Racism—a Challenge for the Anti-racist Movement? *Context, 3*(2).

Taguieff, P.-A. (2009). *Rethinking Anti Racism.* Published by the Ministere Des Affaires Etrangeres. Retrieved from www.diplomatie.gouv.fr

Tanovich, D. M. (2006). *The Colour of Justice: Policing Race in Canada.* Toronto: Irwin Law.

Taras, R. (2012). *Xenophobia and Islamophobia in Europe.* Edinburgh: Edinburgh University Press.

Task Force. (2009). *The Final Report of the Task Force on Campus Racism.* Ottawa: Canadian Federation of Students.

Tastsoglou, E., & Preston, V. (2006, March 25). Gender, Immigration, and the Labour Market: Where We Are and What We Still Need to Know. *Policy Matters.*

Tastsoglou, E., Ray, B., & Preston, V. (2005, Spring). Gender and Migration Intersections in a Canadian Context. *Canadian Issues*, 91–93.

Tattersall, I., & DeSalle, R. (2011). *Race? Debunking a Scientific Myth.* College Station: Texas A&M University Press.

Tator, C., & Henry, F. (2006). *Racial Profiling in Canada: Challenging the Myth of a Few Bad Apples.* Toronto: University of Toronto Press.

Taylor, L. C. (2009, May 14). The Darker the Skin ... the Less You Fit. *Toronto Star.*

Taylor, L., James, C., & Saul, R. (2007). Who Belongs? Race and Racialization in Canada. In G. F. Johnson & R. Enomoto (Eds.), *Race, Racialization, and Anti-racism in Canada and Beyond* (pp. 151–78). Toronto: University of Toronto Press.

Taylor, P. (2011, September 26). UN Still Struggling to Define Racism Ten Years On. *Global Journal.*

Teelucksingh, C. (Ed.). (2006). *Claiming Space: Racialization in Canadian Cities.* Waterloo, ON: Wilfrid Laurier University Press.

Teelucksingh, C., & Galabuzi, G.-E. (2005). *Working Precariously: The Impact of Race and Immigrant Status on Employment Opportunities and Outcomes in Canada.* Report for the Canadian Race Relations Foundation, Toronto.

Tehranian, J. (2009). *Whitewashed: America's Invisible Middle Eastern Minority.* New York: New York University Press.

Tepper, E. (1996). *Visible Minorities and Bill C-64.* Final Report. Prepared for the Workplace Equity Policy, Labour Program, Department of Human Resources Development Canada.

Terrell, K. (2012, May 9). Doctor's Attitudes about Race Can Affect Your Health. Retrieved from www.bet.com

Thobani, S. (2007). *Exalted Subjects.* Toronto: University of Toronto Press.

Thobani, S. (2010, March 15). Multiculturalism Displaces Anti-racism, Upholds White Supremacy. *Restructure.* Retrieved from http://restructure.wordpress.com

Thobani, S., Smith, M., & Razack, S. (2010). Preface: A Decade of Critical Race Studies. In S. Thobani, S. Razack, & M. Smith (Eds.), *States of Race: Critical Race Feminisms for the 21st Century* (pp. ix–xxi). Toronto: Between the Lines.

Thompson, D. (2008). Is Race Political? *Canadian Journal of Political Science, 41,* 525–47.

Titchkosky, T. (2011). *The Question of Access: Disability, Space, Meaning.* Toronto: University of Toronto Press.

Titley, G., & Lentin, A. (2012, July 13). Racism Is Still Very Much with Us, So Why Don't We Recognise It? *The Guardian.* Retrieved from www.guardian.co.us

Toure. (2012, July 12). Romney Plays the Race Card. *Time Ideas.*

Trainor, J. S. (2008). *Rethinking Racism: Emotion, Persuasion, and Literacy Education in an All-White High School.* Carbondale: Southern Illinois University Press.

Trepagnier, B. (2010). *Silent Racism: How Well-Meaning White People Perpetuate the Racial Divide.* London: Paradigm Publishers.

Trumper, R., & Wong, L. L. (2007). Canada's Guest Workers: Racialized, Gendered, and Flexible. In S. P. Hier & B. S. Bolaria (Eds.), *Race and Racism in 21st Century Canada* (pp. 151–70). Peterborough, ON: Broadview Press.

Truth and Reconciliation Commission of Canada. (2012). *Interim Report.* Winnipeg: Author.

Tuch, S. A., & Hughes, M. (2011). Whites' Racial Policy Attitudes in the Twenty-first Century: The Continuing Significance of Racial Resentment. *ANNALS, AAPSS, 634,* 134–41.

Turney, L., Law, I., & Phillips, D. (2002). *Institutional Racism in Higher Education: Building the Anti Racist University: A Toolkit.* Leeds, UK: University of Leeds.

Turton, A. R., Hattingh, H., Maree, G. A., Roux, D. J., & Classen, M. (Eds). (2007). *Governance as a Trialogue: Government-Society-Science in Transition.* New York: Springer.
Tushnet, M. (2003). *The New Constitutional Order.* Princeton: Princeton University Press.
Tyson, C. A. (1998). A Response to "Coloring Epistemologies." *Educational Researcher,* 27(9), 21–22.
UCLA School of Public Affairs/Critical Race Studies. (n.d.). *What Is Critical Race Theory?* Retreived from http://spacrs.wordpress.com
UN News Centre. (2006, March 7). *Racism and Racial Discrimination on Rise Around the World, UN Expert Warns.* Retrieved from www.un.org
UNESCO World Report. (2009). *Investing in Cultural Diversity and Intercultural Dialogue.* New York: UNESCO.
UNIFEM [UN Development Fund for Women]. (2009). *Violence Against Women Fact Sheet.* Retrieved from www.unifem.org
United Nations. (1966, March 7). *International Convention on the Elimination of All Racial Discrimination.* New York: Author.
United Nations. (2006, November 7). *Rise of Racism, Intolerance Is Serious Threat to Democratic Process, Third Committee Told.* Retrieved from http://presszoom.com
University of Michigan News Service. (2012, October 29). *Attitudes Toward African Americans Have Worsened Since 2008.*
Valdes, F. J., Culp, M., & Harris, A. P. (Eds.). (2002). *Crossroads, Directions, and New Critical Race Theory.* Philadelphia: Temple University Press.
Valls, A. (2007). Review of the Racial State by David Theo Goldberg. *Constellations.* Retrieved from www.politicalreviewnet.com
Van den, Berghe, P. (1967). *Race and Racism: A Comparative Perspective.* New York: John Wiley and Sons.
Van Dijk, T. A. (2006, December 16). *Racism and the European Press.* Presentation for the European Commission Against Racism and Intolerance, Strasbourg.
Vasta, E., & Castles, S. (1996). *The Teeth Are Smiling: The Persistance of Racism in a Multicultural Australia.* Sydney: Allen & Unwin.
Vega, T. (2012, September 23). Debate over Race and Casting. *New York Times.*
Velayutham, S. (2009). Everyday Racism in Singapore. In A. Wise & S. Velayutham (Eds.), *Everyday Multiculturalism* (pp. 259–72). London: Palgrave.
Verkuyten, M. (2007). Social Psychology and Multiculturalism. *Social and Personality Psychology Compass,* 1(1), 280–97.
Vickers, J. M. (2002). *The Politics of Race: Canada, Australia, and the United States.* Kemptville ON: Golden Dog Press.
Vukic, A., Jesty, C., Matthews, V., & Etowa, J. (2012, June 12). *Understanding Race and Racism in Nursing: Insights from Aboriginal Nurses.* ISRN Nursing. Retrieved from www.hindawi.com
Vukov, T. (2003). Imagining Communities Through Immigration Policies. *International Journal of Cultural Studies,* 6(3), 335–53.
Walcott, R. (2011). Disgraceful: Intellectual Dishonesty, White Anxieties, and Multicultural Critique Thirty-Six Years Later. In M. Chazan et al. (Eds.), *Home and Native Land: Unsettling Multiculturalism in Canada* (pp. 15–30). Toronto: Between the Lines.

Walcott, R. (2012). Preface. Thinking Race in Canada: What the Critique of Race and Racism in Sports Brings to Anti-Racism Studies. In J. Joseph, S. Darnell, & Y. Nakamura (Eds.), *Race and Sport in Canada: Intersecting Inequalities* (pp. ix–xviii). Toronto: Canadian Scholars' Press.

Walker, J. W. St. G. (1985). Racial Discrimination in Canada: The Black Experience. *Canadian Historical Association Booklet* no. 41.

Walker, J. W. St. G. (1998). *"Race," Rights, and the Law in the Supreme Court of Canada*. Waterloo, ON: Wilfrid Laurier University Press.

Walkom, T. (2008, February 3). McGuinty Should Veto Black Schools. *Toronto Star.*

Wallace, A. (2009, January–February). The Test. *This Magazine.*

Wallis, M., & Fleras, A. (Eds.). (2008). *The Politics of Race.* Toronto: Oxford University Press.

Wallis, M., & Kwok, S.-M. (Eds.). (2008). *Daily Struggles: The Deepening Racialization and Feminization of Poverty in Canada.* Toronto: Canadian Scholars' Press.

Wallis, M., Sunseri, L., & Galabuzi, G.-E. (2010). Introduction: Tracking Colonial and Contemporary Racialization Patterns. In M. Wallis, L. Sunseri, & G.-E. Galabuzi (Eds.), *Colonialism and Racism in Canada* (pp. 1–12). Toronto: Nelson.

Walton-Roberts, M. (2011). Multiculturalism Already Bounded. In M. Chazan et al. (Eds.), *Home and Native Land: Unsettling Multiculturalism in Canada* (pp. 102–22). Toronto: Between the Lines.

Warburton, R. (2007). Canada's Multiculturalism Policy: A Critical Realist Narrative. In S. P. Hier & B. S. Bolaria (Eds.), *Race and Racism in 21st Century Canada* (pp. 275–90). Peterborough, ON: Broadview Press.

Ward, O. (2012, November 4). Race Could Determine Outcome. *Toronto Star.*

Ward, O. (2013, March 16). Q&A with Angela Davis. *Toronto Star.*

Warry, W. (2007). *Ending Denial: Understanding Aboriginal Issues.* Peterborough: Broadview Press.

Wayland, S. V. (2006). *Unsettled: Legal and Policy Barriers for Newcomers to Canada.* Literature Review. Law Commission of Canada/Community Foundations of Canada.

Weaver, S. (1984). *Making Canadian Indian Policy: The Hidden Agenda.* Toronto: University of Toronto Press.

Webber, J. (1994). *Reimagining Canada.* Montreal/Kingston: McGill-Queen's University Press.

WebMD. (2004, December 7). *How Immigration Affects Mental Health.* Retrieved from www.webmd.com

Weiner, M. F. (2012). Towards a Critical Global Race Theory. *Sociology Compass,* 6(4), 332–50.

Weiner, N. (2012). Introduction: Best Practices for Countering Racism in the Workplace. *Canadian Diversity,* 9(1), 8–11.

Weinfeld, M. (2001). *Like Everyone Else but Different: The Paradoxical Success of Canadian Jews.* Toronto: McClelland and Stewart.

Weinfeld, M. (2005). The Changing Dimensions of Contemporary Canadian Antisemitism. In D. J. Penslar (Ed.), *Contemporary Antisemitism: Canada and the World.* Toronto: University of Toronto Press.

Weisbuch, M., Pauker, K., & Ambady, N. (2009). The Subtle Transmission of Race Bias Via Televised Nonverbal Behavior. *Science, 326*(5690), 1711–14.

Welch, S., & Sigelman, L. (2011). The "Obama Effect" and White Racial Attitudes. *ANNALS, AAPSS, 634,* 207–16.
Wente, M. (2008, January 15). On the Case for Black Schools. *Globe and Mail.*
Wente, M. (2009, July 30). Barack Obama's Teachable Moment. *Globe and Mail.*
Wente, M. (2009, November 19). Breakdown: Canada's Mental Health Crisis: The Immigrant Challenge. *Globe and Mail.*
Wente, M. (2010, March 11). The Scourge of Invisible Racism. *Globe and Mail.*
Wente, M. (2013, July 16). America's Race Curse. *Globe and Mail.*
Werbner, P. (2012). Multiculturalism from Above and Below: Analysing a Political Discourse. A Response to Meer and Modood. *Journal of Intercultural Studies, 33*(2), 197–210.
West, C. (2009). Toward a Socialist Theory of Racism. *Race and Ethnicity.* Retrieved from http://race.eserver.org
West, C. (2012). Foreword. In M. Alexander (Ed.), *The New Jim Crow.* New York: New Press.
West-Olatunji, C. (2007). *Response to the Noose Hanging Incident at Columbia University.* Retrieved from www.amcdaca.org
Weston, M. A. (2003, February 21). *Journalists and Indians: The Clash of Cultures.* Keynote speech at the Symposium on American Indian Issues in the California Press. Retrieved from www.bluecorncomics.com/weston.htm
Wetherell, M., & Potter, J. (1993). *Mapping the Language of Racism: Discourse and the Legitimation of Exploitation.* New York: Columbia University Press.
White, N. J. (1999, April 23). Beyond 2000: Home to the World. *Toronto Star.*
Wigmore, G. (2013, October 21). The Canadian Slave Trade. *National Post.*
Wilkinson, R., & Pickett, K. (2009). *The Spirit Level: Why Equality Is Better for Everyone.* Equality Trust.
Wilkinson, R., & Pickett, K. (2010). Inequality: The Enemy Between Us? Why Inequality Matters. *Kosmos, 9*(1), 5–8.
Williams, M. (2011, December 27). Colorblind Ideology as a Form of Racism. *Psychology Today.*
Willis, K., & Yeoh, B. (Eds.). (2000). *Gender and Migration.* Northampton, MA: Edward Elgar Publishing.
Wilmot, S. (2005). *Taking Responsibility, Taking Direction: White Anti-racism in Canada.* Winnipeg: Arbeiter Ring Publishing.
Wilmot, S. (2010). Book Review of *Real Nurses and Others: Racism in Nursing* by Tania Das Gupta. *Socialist Studies, 6*(1), 184–86.
Wilson II, C. C., Gutierrez, F., & Chao, L. M. (2003). *Racism, Sexism, and the Media: The Rise of Class Communication in Multicultural America* (3rd ed.). Thousand Oaks, CA: Sage.
Wilson, J. K. (2008, May 14). *West Virginia: The Most Racist State in the Democratic Primaries.* Retrieved from www.obamapolitics.com
Wilson, W. J. (1996). A Look at the Truly Disadvantaged. *Online Forum.* Retrieved from www.pbs.org
Winant, H. (1998). Racism Today: Continuity and Change in the Post–Civil Rights Era. *Ethnic and Racial Studies, 21*(4), 89–97.
Winant, H. (2004). *The New Politics of Race: Globalism, Difference, Justice.* Minneapolis: University of Minnesota Press.

Wingfield, A. H. (2009). Racializing the Glass Escalator. *Gender & Society, 23*(1), 5–26.
Winsa, P. (2012, August 11). U.S. Backlash Against Cop Stops. *Toronto Star.*
Wise, A., & Velayutham, S. (Eds.). (2009). *Everyday Multiculturalism.* London: Palgrave.
Wise, T. (1999, July–August). Exploring the Depths of Racist Socialization. *Z Magazine,* 17–18.
Wise, T. (2002, June 24). A Look at the Myth of Reverse Racism. *Race and History.*
Wise, T. (2005). Race to Our Credit: Denial, Privilege, and Life as a Majority. Retrieved from http://academic.udayton.edu.race/
Wise, T. (2008). *Between Barrack and a Hard Place: Racism and White Denial in the Age of Obama.* San Francisco: City Lights Books/Open Media Series.
Wise, T. (2009a). Racism 2.0: Private Clubs and Public Prejudice. *Counterpunch.* Retrieved from www.zmag.org
Wise, T. (2009b, July 27). Racism and Implicit Bias in Cambridge. *Racism Review.* Retrieved from www.racismreview.com.
WFMH. (2008, December 17–19). *Report of an International Experts Forum on Reducing Disparities in Mental Health Services for Racial and Ethnic Minorities.* World Federation Mental Health Centre for Transcultural Mental Health. Retrieved from www.wfmh.org
Wong, D. H. T. (2007). *Escape to Gold Mountain: A Graphic History of the Chinese in Canada.* Vancouver: Arsenal Pulp Press.
Wood, P., & Gilbert, L. (2005). Multiculturalism in Canada: Accidental Discourse, Alternative Vision, Urban Practice. *International Journal of Urban and Regional Research, 29*(3), 679–91.
Wood, P. B., & Wortley, S. (2010, August). *AlieNation: Racism, Injustice, and Other Obstacles to Full Citizenship.* Ceris Paper no. 78. Toronto: Ontario Metropolis Centre.
Woolley, F. (2013, June 10). "Visible Minority": A Misleading Concept That Ought to Be Retired. *Globe and Mail.*
Wortley, S. (2003). Misrepresentations or Reality? The Depiction of Race and Crime in the Canadian Print Media. In B. Schissel & C. Brooks (Eds.), *Critical Criminology* (pp. 87–111). Halifax: Fernwood Publishing.
Wortley, S. (2005). *Bias Free Policing: The Kingston Data Collection Project. Preliminary results.* Toronto: University of Toronto and the Centre for Excellence for Research on Immigration and Settlement.
Wortley, S., & Tanner, J. (2005). Discrimination or "Good" Policing? The Racial Profiling Debate in Canada. In *Canada: Our Diverse Cities* (pp. 197–204).
Wright, P. (2007, January–February). Essay of Borat and Sarah Silverman for Make Benefit of Cultural Learnings about Racism. *This Magazine,* 42–43.
Xiao-Feng, L., & Norcliffe, G. (1996). Closed Windows, Open Doors: Geo-politics and the Post 1949 Mainland Chinese Immigration. *Canadian Geographer, 40*(4), 306–19.
Yamato, G. (2001). Racism: Something About the Subject That Makes It Hard to Name. In M. L. Andersen & P. H. Collins (Eds.), *Race, Class, and Gender: An Anthology* (pp. 150–58). Scarborough, ON: Wadsworth/Nelson.
Yassine, A.-Q. (2001). *Causes of Racism in Britain.* Retrieved from www.immi.se
Yong, E. (2009). *Not Exactly Rocket Science.* Retrieved from http://scienceblogs.com
Yoshino, K. (2006, January 15). The Pressure to Cover. *New York Times Magazine.*

Young, I. (1990). *Justice and the Politics of Difference*. Princeton: Princeton University Press.

Yu, H. (2012). The Parable of the Textbook. In R. J. Gilmour et al. (Eds.), "Too Asian?" Racism, Privilege, and Post-secondary Education (pp. 17–27). Toronto: Between the Lines.

Yu, S., & Heath, A. (2007). Inclusion for All But Aboriginals in Canada. In A. Heath & S. Y. Cheung (Eds.), *Unequal Chances: Ethnic Minorities in Western Labour Markets* (pp. 181–220). New York: Oxford University Press.

Zachariah, M. (2004). Cosmopolitan Multiculturalism: An Exploration. In M. Zachariah (Ed.), *Canadian Multiculturalism: Dreams, Realities, Expectations* (pp. 21–30). Edmonton: Canadian Multicultural Education Foundation.

Zahr, A. G. (2001, March 28). Fashionable Racism. *Michigan Daily*. Retrieved from www.michigandaily.com

Zaman, H. (2010, Fall). Racialization and Marginalization of Immigrants: A New Wave of Xenophobia in Canada. *Labour/Le Travail, 66*, 163–82.

Zine, J. (2002). Inclusive Schooling in a Pluralistic Society. *Education Canada, 42*.

Zong, L. (2007). Recent Mainland Chinese Immigrants and Covert Racism in Canada. In S. P. Hier & B. S. Bolaria (Eds.), *Race and Racism in 21st Century Canada* (pp. 111–30). Peterborough, ON: Broadview Press.

Zuberi, T., & Bonilla-Silva, E. (Eds.). (2008). *White Logic, White Methods: Racism and Methodology*. Lanham, MD: Rowman and Littlefield.

INDEX

Abdi, A., 232
Abel, A., 99
Abele, F., 67
ablebodiedness, 90
aboriginality, 64–71, 194–96
Aboriginal peoples, 5, 64–71, 103. *See also* aboriginality; Indigenous peoples
Aboriginal women, 10, 20–21
Abrams, L.S., 45
Action Plan Against Racism, x
Adams, Michael, 22
Adrienne K., 20–21
African-Americans, 166–69
African-Canadians, 5
Afrocentric. *See* Black-focus schools
Agnew, Vijay, 183
Agocs, Carol, 145
Ahmed, Sara, 226
Akdeniz, Y., 131, 132
Alexander, M., 28, 40, 56, 59, 76
Alfred, Taiaiake, 5
Alladin, Ibrahim, 232
alphabetism, 79–80
Altheide, David, 17
Anderson, K.J., 101
Anthias, Floya, ix, 264
anti-black, 264
anti-Asian, 32–37
anti-Muslim, 264. *See also* Islamophobia
anti-racism intervention, 202–3, 220–21, 223–42; defining, 224; inclusive, 241–42; individual, 228–32; institutional, 232–41; multiculturalism as, 248–55; problematizing, 223–27
anti-racist schooling, 234–36, 242; vs. anti-racism education, 242
anti-semitism, 6, 130, 139
apartheid, 173
Arat-Kroc, S., 261
Arendt, Hannah, 41–42
aversive racism, 138, 142. *See also* subliminal racism
Avery, Donald, 72
Aylward, Carol, 44, 45
Ayn Rand Institute, 260

Babacan, H., 53
Back, Les, 188, 197
Backhouse, Constance, 4, 5, 9, 32, 71, 72, 83, 116, 128, 174
Baldwin, A., 88, 256
Bannerjee, Rupa, 73, 107, 115, 119
Bannerji, H., 7, 256, 261
Barlow, A.L., 78
Battiste, M., 28
Baureiss, G., 32
Belanger, Yale, 5
Bell, Derrick, 219
Bell, Stewart, 258
Benjamin, A., 209
Berg, M., 6
Berliner, M.S., 257
Best, Joel, 14–15, 265

Bhavanani, R., ix, 160, 227
bias, 79–80, 95
Bishop, A., 4, 213, 229, 241
Bissoondath, Neil, 253, 257
Black-focused schooling, 238–41
Blacks. See African-Americans; African-Canadians
Blauner, Rob, 52, 133, 197
Bleich, Eric, 226, 227
Block, Sheila, 6, 115, 116
B'nai Brith Canada, 130
Bolaria, B. Singh, xiv, 4, 14, 33, 43, 56, 61, 128, 212, 213, 219, 256
Bolton, K., 12
Bonilla-Silva, Edwardo, ix, 2, 12, 29, 39, 42, 44, 57, 74, 77, 82, 110, 159, 166, 172, 213, 267
Brace, C. Loring, 63
Burley, S., 187, 190
Burnett, J., 2
Byrd, W.C., 30

Caldwell, Christopher, 217
Calliste, Agnes, 181, 192, 224, 234, 235
Cameron, L., 256
Canada: as racist society?, 176–79; and distinctive racism?, 266–67
Canada-building, 25
Canada's Action Plan Against Racism, 225
Canadian Charter of Rights and Freedoms, 105–6, 132
Canadian Council of Churches, 94
Canadian Federation of Students, 182, 187, 188
Cannon, M., 5
capitalism, 4. See also Marx
Cardozo, Andrew, 251
Carruthers, A., 22
Casipullai, A., 116
Castellano, M., 68
Castles, Stephen, 216
Chan, Wendy, 74
Chapters-Indigo, 226
Charter of Quebec Values, 226
Chazan, M., 22, 243, 244, 245, 246, 249, 256

Chesler, P., 182, 186, 188, 189, 191, 192, 193, 198
Chinese, 32–37, 128
Churchill, Ward, 65
Citizenship and Immigration Canada, 225, 251
Clarkson, Adrienne, 216–17
Coates, R., 12, 56, 63, 74, 75, 90, 127
Collacott, Martin, 258
colonization, 5, 62–71
colour-blind, x, 10, 12, 13, 26, 31, 58–60, 61, 62, 76–79, 81, 94, 121, 169, 170, 182, 183. See also post-racial
colour-blind racism, 78
comforting fictions, 263–68
Committee on the Elimination of Racial Discrimination (CERD), 161–62
constitutional order, 224. See also Eurocentrism; whiteness
contesting racisms, 205–22
Cosby Show, 166
Cotler, Irving, 135
critical multiculturalism, 253–55
critical race theory, 45
Crompton, Rosemary, 35
Crowley, Brian Lee, 226
culture, 52
culture of whiteness, 185, 186, 194
Curling, Alvin, 7, 123, 176
cyber-racism, 131–32

Dalmage, H., 56
Daniels, J., 131
Das Gupta, Tania, 4, 9, 31, 163, 181
Dauvergne, M., 143
Davin Report, 68
Davis, Angela, 45, 50
Dechief, D., 73
Dei, George Sefa, xiii, 18, 47, 56, 61, 182, 183, 224, 225, 234, 235, 238, 239, 241, 250, 251, 252, 253, 256, 262
deconstructing racism, 97–122; by name, 109; definition of, 111; direct vs. non-direct, 108; overt vs. covert, 109–110; vs. prejudice, 118
Denis, J.S., 71
Dhamoon, Rita, 51, 113, 233–34, 255

Dickason, Olive 67
Dickson-Gilmour, E.J., 81
Dietrich, D., 57
Din, M., 20, 21
discrimination, 105–12, 115
Disney, 16
Doane, Ashley, 78, 81, 166, 172, 229
Donaldson, J., 33, 34, 35
Douglas, D.D., 31, 160
Dovidio, J.F., xiii, 28, 99, 100, 102, 103, 107, 112, 138, 142, 154, 211
D'Souza, Dinesh, 76
Du Bois, W.E.B., 165
Dua, Enakshu, 1, 4, 7, 22, 64, 183, 189, 190, 196, 261
Dunn, 239

Edwards, S., 161
Eisenstein, Zillah, 253, 256
Elliot, Jane, 230–32
Employment Equity, 226
ENAR, 214–15
Enomoto, Randy, 160
Essed, Philomena, 103, 159, 160,
Esses, Victoria, 31, 99, 100, 102, 103, 107, 154
ethnicity paradigm, 118
Etowa, J.B., xii, 84
eurocentrism, xii, 42, 44, 101–2, 156, 175, 178, 185, 186, 193, 198, 213, 224, 236, 238, 245, 253. *See also* whiteness
Europe, 214–17
Eye of the Storm, 230–32

Farber, Bernie, 65, 71
Farook, M., 135, 136
Fatah, Tariq, 136
Feagin, Joe, ix, 4, 9, 12, 44, 57, 91, 107, 110, 133, 134, 141, 146, 172, 178, 207, 208, 209, 213
Fekete, Liz, 39, 214
Ferber, A.L., 93, 94
Fernando, S., 57, 73
Fontaine, Phil, 65, 70, 71
Foster, C., 76, 86, 95, 118, 147
Foucault, Michel, 51, 113
framing, 140–43, 152–55, 202
Frederickson, George, 212

Frideres, Jim, 65
Fukawa, M., 5

Gadacz, Rene, 65
Gaertner, Samuel, 138, 142
Galabuzi, Grace-Edward, viii, x, 4, 6, 11, 56, 57, 65, 73, 74, 115 116, 165, 177, 220, 245, 246, 249, 250
Gallagher, C.A., 76, 77
Garvey, J., 94
genocide, 67–70
Ghosh, R., 26, 232, 233, 249, 251, 253
Gibbins, Roger, 65, 66
Gilbert, L., 246
Gilborn, D., 45, 47, 85, 86, 91
Gilman, N., 27, 28, 29
Gilmour, R.J., 34, 35, 91
Giroux, Henry, vii, viii, 1, 76, 206, 253
Goldberg, David Theo, 55, 62, 64, 76, 77, 81, 82, 172–73, 224
Gopalkrishnan, N., 53
Go, Avvy, 116, 162
Gordon, M.K., 239, 241
governance, 25
Grabb, Ed, 113
Green, Joyce, 193, 194
Guess, T.J., 83, 94
Guo, S., 182, 187, 188, 194

Hage, Ghassan, 256, 259
Hall, Stuart, 40, 52
Halloweenism, 19–21
Hannah, D.C., 208
Haque, Eve, 23, 243, 249, 255, 256
Harris, D.R., 57
hate crime, 129
hate racism, 127–32
head tax, 34
Heath, Anthony, 116
Heer, J., 35, 43
hegemony, 76–78, 160, 178, 249–51
Helleiner, J., 74
Hennebry, Jenna, 105, 128, 153
Henry, Frances, x, xv, 4, 6, 7, 84, 87, 90, 92, 113 115, 137, 141, 148, 153, 155, 161, 176, 181, 181–86, 192, 193, 196, 199, 205, 226, 233, 244
Hier, Sean, viii, x, xiv, 4, 7, 9, 14, 56, 61, 128, 148, 149, 181

Hiranandani, V., 224
history of Canadian racism, 127–28
hooks, bell, 52, 77, 91, 92, 93, 146
how racism works, 123
Hull, G., 257
Hum, D., 9
Hurley, M., 67
Hyman, Irene, 79, 209

Ibbitson, John, 83
ideological racisms, 159–70, 192–93; everyday, 159–63; normative, 163–70
Ignatieff, Michael, xi
Ignatiev, Noel, 94
Ikuenobe, P., 76, 82
inclusive multiculturalism, 248–49
inconvenient truths, 263–68
India, 164–65
Indian Act, 66–67
Indigenous Foundation, 70, 71
Indigenous peoples, 5
infrastructural racisms, 171–79, 193–94
institutional racisms, 145–58, 191; systematic, 146–49; systemic, 150–58
interpersonal racisms, 127–43, 190; hate, 127–32; polite, 132–37; subliminal, 137–43
Islamophobia, 40, 99, 104–5
ivory tower racisms, 181–99; challenging, 196–99

Jain, H., 145
Jamal, Z., 182, 187, 188, 194
James, Carl, xv, 71, 73, 183, 188, 196, 199, 242
Jaworsky, John, 23
Jedwab, Jack, 107, 130, 223
Jews, 5, 190. See also anti-Semitism
Jim Crow, 59
Jimenez, Marina, 103, 226
Jiwani, Yasmin, 134, 148, 152, 155
Johnson, K., 20, 21
Johnson, Genevieve, 160
Johnson, Lyndon B., 79
Joseph, J., 146

Kalman-Lamb, Nathan, 79
Karim, Karim H., 103, 148, 153
Kawakami, K., viii, 99, 107, 220

Kelley, Raina, 100
Kelly, Jennifer, 134, 187
Kempf, Arlo, 239
King, Martin Luther, Jr., 167–68, 230
King, R., 56, 57
Kinsella, N., 130, 161, 162
Kitossa, Tamari, 59
Kivel, Paul, 251
Kobayashi, Audrey, xii, 9, 50, 184, 198, 199, 256
Kostash, Myrna, 251
Ku Klux Klan, 5, 128
Kundnani, Arun, viii, 12, 50, 51, 256
Kunz, Jean Lock, 23, 60, 148, 152
Kuokkanen, R., 191, 194, 195, 235, 238, 259
Kymlicka, Will, 4, 22, 226, 245

Lambert, F., 226
language, 160–62
LaPiere, Richard, 111
LaPraire, Carole, 81
Lee, J., 35
Lee, Joanne, ix, 12
lefthandedness, 95
Lentin, Alana, ix, 2, 8, 18, 28, 29, 49, 60, 78, 171, 213, 222, 267, 244, 246, 257
Lentin, R., 171
Levitt, Cyril, 14
Lewis, Stephen, 39
Li, Peter, 2, 4, 32, 33, 35, 44, 50, 62, 72, 128, 130, 142, 162, 178, 212, 213, 219, 256
Lian, J.Z., 176
Lin, A.C., 57
Liodakis, Nikolaos, 4, 115, 206
Lippard, C.D., 11, 28
Lipsitz, G., 93
Little Mosque on the Prairie, 135–37
Llewellyn, Jennifer, 70
Lord, Audre, 237
Lund, Darren, 181
Lupul, Manoly, 4
Lutz, John, ix, 12

Maaka, Roger, 65, 178
Mackey, Eve, 94, 249
Mahtani, Minelle, 86, 148, 149, 155
Malik, Kenan, 257, 260–61

Maioni, A., 156, 208
making race. *See* racialization
Mansur, Salim, 22, 246, 257, 260, 261
Marable, M., 206
Martin, Trayvon, 58
Marx, Karl, xv, 242
Matthews, R.D., 176
May, S., 245
McCalla, A., 55
McCreary, T., viii, 233, 251
McDonald, 117, 183, 184
McDougal, Gaye, xii
McGibbon, E.A., xii, 84
McGowan, William, 148
McIntosh, Peggy, 189
McKay, I., 95
McKenna, I., 207
McMurtry, Roy, 7, 123, 176
McParland, K., 7
McRoberts, Kenneth, 251
media, 17, 134–37, 147–49, 152
Miller, J.R., 66, 69, 71
Miller, M.J., 216
Milloy, C., 147
Milloy, J.S., 69
Mills, Charles, 64, 172, 219, 222
minorities as racist, 114
Mirchandani, K., 74
Mistry, Rohinton, 262
model minority racism, 32–37
Mohammed, S., 135, 136
Moio, J.A., 35
Momani, Bessma, 105, 128, 153
monocultural, 182, 184, 197–98. *See also* whiteness
Monture, Patricia, 67, 188, 195, 198
Moore, R., 161
multicultural education, 232–34, 236, 238–40
multicultural racism, 246, 259–61
multiculturalism, 7, 18, 22–26, 243–62; as anti-racism, 248–49; vs. anti-racism, 251–53; criticism of, 258; inclusive, vii; paradoxes of, 243–47; as racism, 259–61; racist, 255–58; theorizing, 247–55
multiversity, 196–99
Murphy, Rex, 58

Muslims, 135, 137, 187, 190. *See also* Islamophobia

Nagle, John, 243, 245, 260
Nakamura, Lisa, 131
neo-liberalism, 60
neo-liberal racism, 165–66, 169
neo-Nazi, 130–32
neo-racism, ix, 29
Nestel, S., 209
Ng, R., 225
Niemonen, J., 87, 92, 225
Nittle, N.K., 16, 19, 58
Norcliffe, G., 33, 34
normative racism. *See* ideological racism
nursing, 163

Obama, Barack, 55, 57, 58–60, 76, 168
Obama Effect, 58–60
official multiculturalism. *See* multiculturalism
Omar, A., 23
Omi, M., 46, 62, 81
online racism, 131–32
Ontario Human Rights Commission, 146
Onyeji, C., 207, 208
Oreopoulos, Philip, 73, 103, 107, 109

Pacquet, Gilles, 22, 246, 257, 261
Palestine, 139
paradoxes of racism, 14–16
Paul, D., 65
Pearson, A.R., 28, 142
Pearson, David, 251
Pendakur, K., 73, 115, 163
Pendakur, R., 115
Picard, André, 208
Picca, L.H., 133
Pickett, Kate, 117
Pinder, Sherrow, 7, 18, 82, 94, 112, 254
Pitcher, Ben, xiii, 78, 247
Plamondon, B., 23
polite racism, 132–37
Ponting, Rick, 65, 66
Porter, John, 118
post-modern, 2
post-modern racism, 28, 265–66
post-racial, vii, x, 4, 31, 42, 58–50, 76–79, 83, 94, 264. *See also* colour-blind

post-secondary, 181–99
Potter, J., 160
powell, j.a., 226
power, 112–14, 115
prejudice, 97–98, 98–105, 115; as unconscious, 100; vs. discrimination, 111
profiling race, 71–73
Prus, Bob, 113

race, 55–95; attitudes towards, 57–58; and colonization, 62–71; profiling of, 71–74; as racism, 75; in relation to racism, 62; rethinking, 73–75; as social construction, 56, 61, 73; in USA, 57, 58–60
race blind. See colour-blind; post-racial
race card, 6
race mattered, 55–56, 62–64
race matters, 56–57, 61, 76–84
Race, Violence, Health Project, 29, 208–9
racialization, 73–75, 93, 119–20
racialized, 82
racialized Canada, 255. See also Eurocentrism; whiteness
racialized hegemony, 76–78
racialized inequality, 115–21
racialized society, 172–74
racial(ized) states vs. racist states, 172–73
racism: aversive, 138, 142; banality of, 41–42; causes, of, 205–7, 217–18; and colonization, 62–71; comforting fictions, 263–68; constituents of, 97–122; contesting, 205–22; continuity of, 218–22; as culture, 49–50; cyber-racism, 131–32; debating, 10–13; deconstructing, 37–40, 97–122; defining, viii–ix, 38, 47–53; definition of, 264; explaining, 117–19, 201–3; framing, 6–7; as genocide, 67–70; as Halloweenism, 19–21; ideological, 159–70; as ideology, 43, 48–49; inconvenient truths, 263–68; inequality as, 119–21; in Europe, 214–17; infrastructural, 171–79; institutional, 145–58; interpersonal, 127–43; ivory tower, 181–99; and language, 160–62; media, 134–37, 147–49, 152; as multiculturalism, 22–26, 266–67; neo-liberal, 170; online, 131–32; origins of, 210–13; as paradox, 119–20; paradoxes of, 13–21; perceptions of, 14–15, 264–66; politics of, xii, 3–26; postsecondary, 181–99; as power, 51–52; practice of, xiii; problematizing, xiv; as race, 47–48, 75; reaction to, 6–7; reappraising, 1–2, 5–6, 27–53; as resistance, xiii; as social control, 212–13; as social problem, 201–2; as structure, 44–45, 50; structure, 214–17; theorizing, ix, 42–47; theory, xi; vs. racisms, viii; without race, 59, 267; without racists, 3, 4, 267
racism 1.0, 27, 32
racism card, 12, 17–18
racism "lite," 164–65
racism paradox, 118–19
racisms 2.0, 19–21, 28–30, 32, 59
racist multiculturalism, 246, 249–51
racist society, 177–79
Razack, Sherene, 4, 9, 45, 76, 77, 105
reconceptualizing racism, 27–53
Reitz, Jeffrey, 22, 72, 107, 115, 119, 244
residential schools, 67–71
Rock, Chris, 90
Rockler-Gladen, N., 134
Rolfsen, C., 68, 69
Rollack, N., 45, 47, 95
Rosado, C., 112
Roscigno, V., 73
Rotman, L.I., 70
Roy, Patricia, 33, 34
Royal Commission on Aboriginal Peoples (RCAP), 68, 69, 71
Ruparelia, R., 86

Sakamoto, I., 108, 151
Samuel, E., 177, 183, 187, 190
Sapers, Howard, 81
Satzewich, Vic, vii, xii, 2, 4, 6, 10, 12, 28, 33, 55, 72, 114, 115, 123, 177, 206, 213
Scheurich, J.J., 190, 191, 195
Scott, Duncan Campbell, 66, 68, 69
Seasonal Agricultural Program, 151
Sharma, S., 197, 244

Sheikh, A., 135, 136
Sheppard, C., 106–7
Shkilnyk, Anastasia, 150
Shohat, Ella, 102
Simmons, Alan, 211
Simpson, J., 78
Simpson, O.J., 100
Simpson, W., 9
Sivanandan, A., x, 225
slavery, 5, 53, 56, 59, 85
Sleeter, C., 245
Smith, A., 85
Smith, Linda Tuhiwai, 194
Smith, Malinda, 4, 45, 76, 77, 91
social construction, 184
Social Darwinism, 64
Solomos, John, 62, 82
Soroka, S., 156
Spafford, M.M., 187, 188, 191
Spencer, J.W., 1
Spirit Matters, 81
Spoonley, Paul, 93, 173
Srivastava, S., 246, 249, 251
Stam, Robert, 102
Stanley, T.J., ix, 61, 63, 74
Statistics Canada, 129
stereotypes, 102–4
stereotype threat, 187
Steyn, Mark, 17
Stoffman, Daniel, 258
stratification, 115
structure, 214–17
subliminal, 137–43
Sunseri, L., x, 4, 5, 11, 65, 85, 87, 165
Supreme Court of Canada, 228
Sutherland, R.S., 252
Sykes, Stuart, 23
Synnott, A., 163
systematic racism, 146–49
systemic bias, 79–80, 95, 152
systemic racism, 150–58

Taras, R., 104, 105
Tator, Carol, x, xv, 4, 6, 7, 84, 87, 90, 92, 113, 115, 137, 141, 148, 153, 155, 161, 176, 181–86, 191, 192, 193, 199, 205, 244

Tepper, Eliot, 162
Thobani, Sunera, xii, 4, 7, 8, 45, 64, 71, 76, 77, 82, 87, 116, 176, 244, 246, 250, 255, 256, 261
Thomas, W.I., 79–80, 81
Titley, Grant, 8, 28, 29, 49, 60, 244, 246, 257
"too Asian," 35, 36–37, 91
Toronto, 4, 6, 116
Trepagnier, B., 10, 12, 13, 42
Truth and Reconciliation Commission, 69

United States, 57, 76–78, 103, 166–69, 253–55. *See also* Obama Effect
university racism, 181–99

Vancouver, 4, 16, 34
van den Berghe, Pierre, 211, 212
Van Dijk, T., 214
Velayutham, S., 160
Verkuyten, M., 257
Vertical Mosaic, 118
Vickers, Jill, 48, 172
Vukic, A., 163

Walby, K., viii, x
Walcott, Renaldo, 40
Walker, James, 4, 32, 116, 128
Walkom,Thomas, 239, 241
Wallis, Maria, x, 4, 7, 11, 12, 56, 60, 63, 65, 78, 83, 87, 165, 173, 238
Walton-Roberts, Margaret, 22
war against terrorism, 7
Waterloo Region, 129
Weaver, Sally, 66
Weinfeld, Morton, 139
Wendt, S., 6
Wente, Margaret, 58
Werbner, Pnina, 260
West, C., 28, 44
Wetherall, M., 160
white Canada, vii, 5, 72, 75, 82, 85, 173–74, 253
whiteness, xii, 74, 82, 84–95, 164–65, 185, 186, 199, 233. *See also* eurocentrism

white privilege, 78, 87–88
white racial(ized) framing, 134, 140–43
white superiority, 84–95
white supremacy, 86–87, 95, 130–32. *See also* white superiority
whitewashing, 134–37, 154
Wilkinson, Richard, 117
Williams, Monica, 169
Wilmot, S., xii
Wilson, William Julius, 76
Winant, Howard, 8, 15, 46, 62, 77, 81, 160
Winfrey, Oprah, 57, 59
Wise, Tim, 13, 53, 59, 85, 90, 223
Wong, D.H.T., 32, 33, 35
Wood, P., 207, 208, 246

Woods, Tiger, 57, 59
Woolley, F., 226
Wortley, Scot, 207, 208

xenophobia, 104
Xiao-Feng, L., 33, 34

Young, I., 190, 191, 195
Yu, Henry, 79–80, 116

Zachariah, M., 51
Zimmerman, George, 58
Zine, Jasmin, 233, 234, 235, 240
Zinga, Dawn, 239, 241
Zong, L., 6
Zuberi, T., 2